From Pleasure Machines to
Moral Communities

From Pleasure Machines to Moral Communities

An Evolutionary Economics without *Homo economicus*

GEOFFREY M. HODGSON

The University of Chicago Press
Chicago and London

Geoffrey M. Hodgson is research professor at the University of Hertfordshire Business School, England, and the author or coauthor of over a dozen books, including *The Evolution of Institutional Economics* and *Darwin's Conjecture*.

The University of Chicago Press, Chicago 60637
The University of Chicago Press, Ltd., London
© 2013 by The University of Chicago
All rights reserved. Published 2013.
Printed in the United States of America

22 21 20 19 18 17 16 15 14 13   1 2 3 4 5

ISBN-13: 978-0-226-92271-3 (cloth)
ISBN-13: 978-0-226-92273-7 (e-book)
ISBN-10: 0-226-92271-5 (cloth)
ISBN-10: 0-226-92273-1 (e-book)

Library of Congress Cataloging-in-Publication Data

Hodgson, Geoffrey Martin, 1946–
    From pleasure machines to moral communities : an evolutionary economics without homo economicus / Geoffrey M. Hodgson.
        pages cm
    Includes bibliographical references and index.
    ISBN-13: 978-0-226-92271-3 (cloth: alkaline paper)
    ISBN-10: 0-226-92271-5 (cloth: alkaline paper)
    ISBN-13: 978-0-226-92273-7 (e-book)
    ISBN-10: 0-226-92273-1 (e-book)
1. Economics—Moral and ethical aspects.   2. Economic man.   I. Title.
HB72.H655 2013
    330.1—dc23

                                            2012010481

♾ This paper meets the requirements of ANSI/NISO Z39.48-1992 (Permanence of Paper).

To the memory of my mother

CONTENTS

Economic man has dominated economic discourse for more than a century. He is rational and self-interested. On his utility-maximizing persona, economists have erected many theories of economic behavior. His well-ordered preference function is used to explain human cooperation and organizational cohesion, as well as his preoccupation with acquisition and pecuniary incentives. But numerous experiments seem to have shaken key theoretical predictions. The purely self-interested individual has proved elusive. With his one-dimensional objective of utility, economic man has been given too heavy a burden to bear. He has expired under its weight. May he rest in peace.

From the 1940s to the 1980s, most economists would have regarded the criticisms in the preceding paragraph as misguided and stopped reading right there. Selfishness was regarded as a legitimate simplifying abstraction. But this is no longer the unchallenged view among economists. Although controversy remains, the rise of behavioral and experimental economics and other developments have given critical sentiments a renewed legitimacy and vitality.

But I wish to go a bit further. The aim here is not simply to replace economic man with a more rounded rational individual, perhaps with an "other-regarding" utility function that takes into account the utility received by others. This would be inadequate. It is argued here that if utility maximization is broadened from narrow self-interest, then it becomes an almost empty theoretical assumption, and this too can be buried without much loss alongside its former bearer—economic man.

We can make utility functions more complex in a variety of ways, including meta-preferences and multiple selves. But the idea that the problem can be adequately solved at this level is a manifestation of what might be described as "individualism," as defined by the neglected English economist John A. Hobson (1901, p. 67) when he wrote of "the protean fallacy of individualism, which feigns the existence of separate individuals by abstracting and neglecting the social relations which belong to them and make them what they are." Economic man is a pleasure machine, whose preference function appears miraculously, without reference to human evolution, and seemingly detached from his social and natural environment.

Note that Hobson's depiction of individualism says nothing about individual liberty or rights. His complaint is orthogonal to the old debate between political individualism and socialism. It is not about whether individuals should be valued. They should. It is about the failure of all attempts to understand the individual apart from society. We ought to defend human rights, individual autonomy, personal privacy, much individual ownership, and the crucial role of individual incentives (including prosocial motivations). But these are not purely individual matters because they depend also on other institutions. Individualists or not, we must rely on institutions as well. "Individualism"—as Hobson defined it—is an *analytical* impossibility, at least for any social science.

Because economic man is a pleasure machine, concerned only with his own satisfaction, any adequate notion of moral motivation is absent. His sole objective is pleasure. By contrast, real humans are often concerned with "doing the right thing," sometimes even against their own interests, and notwithstanding that their moral code may be flawed. We seek honor and justice, as well as our own prosperity and prestige. We sometimes act out of duty and not mere self-interest. We have moral motivations because we have long evolved as social beings, and we are affected profoundly by our interactions with others. We are brought up to emulate our peers and to accept the rules of our community. "Doing the right thing" in this context is much more than raising our utility or pleasure. It is acting according to some social code of behavior that is understandable to, if not shared by, others. Otherwise it would be indistinguishable from mere personal preference.

Contrary to widespread misinterpretation, by some of his supporters as well as his critics, the ideas of Charles Darwin reveal the limits of self-interested individualism and help us to understand the moral values that are essential to any society and economy. I use Darwinism, along with arguments from philosophy and elsewhere, to attack some of the deficiencies in mainstream economics, particularly its longstanding reliance on individualism and utilitarianism. This book complements *Darwin's Conjecture*, which I coauthored with Thorbjørn Knudsen (Hodgson and Knudsen

2010). Here I extend the evolutionary outlook in the previous joint work to include moral and policy-oriented issues.

The year 1871 saw the publication of two seminal installments of self-interest at the foundation of economics (Jevons 1871; Menger 1871).[1] Ironically, it was also the year when Darwin (1871) published an evolutionary explanation of altruism and cooperation, which took over one hundred years to be confirmed broadly by theoretical and empirical research. A key refutation of self-interest appeared in the same year of two classic statements in its defense.

An evolutionary outlook is not merely an optional extra. Although all attempts by philosophers to identify *the* scientific method have failed, there are at least two vital requirements for theories in the social sciences. The first is a substantial degree of empirical corroboration. The second is the incorporation of a causally plausible account of how mechanisms lead to outcomes (Bunge 1959; Woodward 2003). Such plausibility includes consistency with our understanding of human evolution. Theoretical simplicity and generality, where possible, are also among the virtues, but they should not be pursued at the cost of any of the above. Yet much of mainstream economics, even when it predicts correctly, lacks a causally plausible and informative account of human motivation that is grounded on our understanding of human evolution. Evolution has to be a vital guide, additionally informed by our knowledge of social relations and culture. When we make assumptions about human agents we are required to ask how possibly they could have evolved and have had a survival advantage for our species. Taking account of this point involves a major challenge to much of existing economics and leads to its rebuilding on evolutionary foundations.

One reason for this book was my long-held view that our understanding of social institutions and organizations is inadequate unless we appreciate the moral motivations of individuals within them and how those institutions help to sustain and replicate these moral sentiments. No society or economy can function without moral bonds and rules. Furthermore, the nature of moral sentiments can be reduced to neither individual utility nor mere conformism to norms; they have to be understood in terms of morality in a meaningful sense. Moral claims are more than matters of conve-

---

1. Walras (1874) followed. The neoclassical achievements of 1871–74 were later described as the "marginal revolution." (Myint [1946] is the earliest known use of this term to describe the rise of marginalism in economics.) This term not only conflates quite different 1870s thinkers but also overlooks earlier pioneers of the marginal utility approach and the massive later contribution of Marshall (Ekelund and Hébert 2002).

nience or convention. Morality is a group phenomenon involving delibera-tive, emotionally driven, and inescapable rules. Individuals are profoundly affected by prevailing moral norms in the group to which they relate.

Accepting the importance of morality does not mean denying that individuals are self-interested. We are selfish, to a major extent. In some contexts, people can do evil things. But we are also moral beings, and our ethical feelings and beliefs—well formed or otherwise—play an additional ubiquitous role in our interactions with others, even in the modern acquis-itive world of business and consumerism. Even Mafia gangsters and other criminals generally live by moral codes, albeit highly deficient ones.

Moral motivations have been overlooked in much of heterodox, as well as mainstream, economics. Despite their prominent pronouncements on policy, Marxism, post-Keynesianism, the Austrian school, and much of contemporary evolutionary and institutional economics have largely ne-glected the deeper analysis of morality and often sidestepped the possibil-ity of moral motivation.

An adequate understanding of how institutions function must acknowl-edge moral as well as self-regarding motivations. Moral motivations were emphasized by members of the German historical school and acknowl-edged by original institutionalists such as Thorstein Veblen and John R. Commons. But these institutionalists lacked a developed theory of morality that could be integrated into an analysis of how institutions work. Institu-tionalist successors, such as Clarence Ayres (1918, 1944, 1952) and J. Fagg Foster (1981), wrote much on ethics and values, but their concern was more to establish principles of policy evaluation and less to explain human motivation. Much of the new institutional economics—of Oliver William-son (1975, 1985) and others—has retained a version of self-interested eco-nomic man, albeit with incomplete knowledge and bounded rationality.

There are some exceptional and contrasting genres. John Maynard Keynes (1973, p. 297) insisted in 1938 that economics is a "moral sci-ence . . . it employs introspection and judgment of value." But this un-derdeveloped stance has had only a slight impact on subsequent Keynes-ian economics. The tradition of "social economics" has long emphasized ethical values (Lutz 1990, 1999), but its influence remains marginal. Some feminist economists have broken with utility-maximizing economic man to embrace theories that underline social commitment and caring (Folbre 1995, 2009; J. Nelson 1995; Jochimsen 2003; Nussbaum 2003). Morality has been emphasized by a few prominent unorthodox economists such as Kenneth Boulding (1969) and Amartya Sen (1987a). But it is still generally neglected in this discipline. Economics remains largely an amoral science.

But to understand human agents and their institutions, it is necessary to bring moral motivations back into the picture. Fortunately, there is now a flourishing stream of recent evolutionary studies—spanning several disciplines including anthropology, primatology, philosophy, and economics—that can help to fill the gaps. In embracing Darwinian theory to help deal with this problem, I am also reminded of Veblen's example in bringing Darwinian principles into the social sciences to help understand the origins and function of specific social phenomena. Veblen understood well that our assumptions about human nature had to be consistent with our understanding of human evolution. And he appreciated more than anyone the challenge that this meant for mainstream economics. But we need to go further than Veblen and others to acknowledge the role of morality in sustaining institutions and enhancing social cohesion in any society. Remarkably, on the latter point we can still learn a great deal from the founder of modern economics—Adam Smith. It is no accident that the author of *Moral Sentiments* was also a major influence on Darwin.

Part of an alternative to the morally denuded utilitarianism that has pervaded economics for about 150 years is an ethical discourse buttressed by ongoing evaluations of human need. Morality and need are connected in the analysis of both human motivation and welfare. A moral value found in all cultures is the importance of caring for the perceived needs of others, even if only in one's own group. This motivational trait contributes to group survival (Darwin 1871). Clearly, our caring for others is made more effective through a proper understanding of their needs. Needs and moral motivations become linked.

In July 2005, the editors of *Science* declared that the explanation of the evolution of cooperative behavior was one of the top 25 questions facing all scientists. In recent years, there has been an explosion of articles and books on the topic. Our understanding of the evolution of cooperation has developed enormously. There are many powerful models and simulations exploring mechanisms and conditions under which altruistic or cooperative individuals can become established in a population.

What does a focus on morality add to this? How would the models and simulations have to be changed to accommodate ethical norms? It will be argued in chapter 5 that prominent models of the evolution of altruism pay insufficient attention to why an intelligent individual should bear costs to help others, even if she was genetically and emotionally disposed to do so. Morality helps to explain why. Although the modelers of cooperation often mention morality, they fail to illuminate its crucial role, typically by lumping matters of ethics and preference altogether in one box.

Chapter 5 includes a simulation that gives a different output when moral algorithms are switched on or off, thus illustrating the distinctiveness of moral systems.

Another reason morality is important is that when we turn our attention from the past evolution of morality in humans to the consideration of economic and social policies for the present, a deeper and more detailed understanding of human motivation is required. By treating motivation as all stemming from blandly described "preferences"—as is typical in much of the literature on the evolution of human cooperation—approaches to policy are more easily diverted into the narrower channels of material or pecuniary incentives, neglecting moral motivation and an appeal to ethical values.

This book is divided into two parts. The first part establishes the nature and importance of moral principles and shows that we must treat morality as a social phenomenon rather than a property of individuals alone. The second part visits different economic contexts and shows that morality has to be taken into account, including in policy design. In chapters 6 and 7, on business and corruption, I show how morality relates to organizations. Chapters 8 and 9 focus on the special but vital cases of health and ecological economics. These provide theoretical cases of where moral motivations matter and the outline of needs-based approaches in each case. The final chapter sketches some general principles. Again, I use evolutionary ideas in an alternative approach.

I bring no fresh empirical evidence. But fortunately, there has been an explosion of empirical inquiry in experimental economics, psychology, anthropology, and elsewhere that I use to substantiate the key claims of this book. I make reference to much of this evidence, but without dissection of it in detail. In many cases, a consensus exists on the interpretation of the evidence. I rely on such consensual positions and draw out the implications.

An aim of this book is to help to reinstate economics as a moral and political science. After the corporate scandals and financial gluttony that led to the Great Crash of 2008, this goal has become even more urgent. The moral failures of economists in this context were documented in the 2010 movie *Inside Job*, which showed leading economists pandering after large consultancy fees relating to a bloated financial sector at the cost of their personal and academic integrity. There are rising demands that economists should take morality seriously, not only in their theories of individual motivation but also in their own behavior.

ACKNOWLEDGMENTS

One of the disadvantages of maintaining an interest in the history of ideas is that one too frequently discovers the long lineage of an argument that might otherwise be promoted as original. Studying the history of thought helps cultivate an intellectual modesty. But it ill-fits an era in which highly specialized and research-targeted subdisciplines have to proclaim their predictive virtues and display their scientific prowess, rather than follow liberal, skeptical, and open-ended inquiry. That may help to explain why the history of a science so rarely appears on any academic curriculum. This book is not a history of ideas, but it could not have been written without detailed reading of classic works by Charles Darwin, John Dewey, Friedrich Hayek, John A. Hobson, John Maynard Keynes, Alfred Marshall, Karl Marx, John Stuart Mill, Adam Smith, Thorstein Veblen, and many others. I am additionally indebted to many recent authors mentioned in the text.

Special thanks are due to Glen Atkinson, Markus Becker, John Davis, Alex Field, Ian Gough, Helena Lopes, Valeria Mosini, Richard Nelson, Peter Richerson, Ernesto Screpanti, Patrick Spread, Wolfgang Streeck, and anonymous referees for commenting so helpfully on major portions of this text. Also I am very grateful to Richie Adelstein, André Ariew, Jürgen Backhaus, Christian Barrère, Jens Beckert, Eric Beinhocker, Mark Blaug, Jitendralal Borkakoti, Béatrice Boulu-Resheff, Samuel Bowles, Graham Brownlow, Robbie Butler, Bruce Caldwell, Ana Celia Castro, Ha-Joon Chang, Simon Deakin, Michael Dietrich, Stephen Dunn, Steven Durlauf, David Elder-Vass, Christoph Engel, Bo Eriksen, Teppo Felin, Nicolai Foss, John Foster, Julien-François Gerber, Jayati Ghosh, David Gindis, Herbert Gintis, Jane Hardy, Rachel Harvey, Chris Hope, Kainan Huang, Geoff Ingham, Michael Jacobs, Shuxia Jiang, Thorbjørn Knudsen, Tony Lawson, Peter Leeson, John Linarelli, Maria Lissowska, Vinny Logan, Uskali Mäki, Gerardo Marletto,

J. Stanley Metcalfe, Bart Nooteboom, Adam Oliver, Susumu Ono, Ugo Pagano, Gabriel Palma, Stephen Parsons, Pavel Pelikan, Stephen Pratten, David Reisman, Jochen Runde, Itai Sened, Clive Spash, Irene van Staveren, Achim Stephan, Rolf Steppacher, Nils Stieglitz, Lars Udéhn, Viktor Vanberg, Jack Vromen, David Sloan Wilson, Ulrich Witt, anonymous referees, and many others for critical comments, stimulating discussions, and other help. I am privileged to have access to such a wonderful community of scholars.

I am especially indebted to Shuxia Jiang, coauthor of the previously published version of chapter 7, and to Thorbjørn Knudsen, who helped develop some ideas used in chapters 6 and 10. An earlier version of chapter 2 was published in the *Journal of Economic Methodology*, and of chapter 8 in the *Cambridge Journal of Economics*. I am grateful to the journal publishers and the Cambridge Political Economy Society for permission to use this material. A version of chapter 7 was published in the *Journal of Economic Issues*: it is revised and reprinted here by special permission of the copyright holder, the Association for Evolutionary Economics.

Principles

ONE

Introduction: Economic Man and Beyond

No science has been criticized by its own servants as openly and constantly as economics. The motives of dissatisfaction are many, but the most important pertains to the fiction of *Homo oeconomicus*.

—Nicholas Georgescu-Roegen (1971)

The economist . . . keeps the motivations of human beings pure, simple and hard-headed, and not messed up by such things as goodwill or moral sentiments. . . . [T]here is . . . something quite extraordinary in the fact that economics has in fact evolved in this way, characterizing human motivation in such spectacularly narrow terms. One reason why this is extraordinary is that economics is supposed to be concerned with real people.

—Amartya Sen (1987a)

"Greed is good. Greed is right. Greed works." Thus spoke Gordon Gekko, played by Michael Douglas in the 1987 movie *Wall Street*. By the late 1980s leading capitalist economies had entered an era of political individualism, privatization, and deregulation, inspired by the principle—cherished by the real Bernard Mandeville and the fictional Gekko—that from private vices public virtues spring. Individual self-interest is the powerhouse of economic progress: this was the mantra adopted by major varied political parties across the spectrum, from the US Republicans to Tony Blair's New Labour in Britain. They quoted (or misquoted) many economists from Adam Smith to Milton Friedman for support. The "gospel of greed" held sway.[1]

1. This phrase is from Charles Sanders Peirce (1893, p. 184), who criticized the self-interested individualism of Herbert Spencer and others. Incidentally, I henceforth refrain from

That consensus prevailed at least until the Great Crash of 2008, when the Western financial system entered its most serious crisis since the Great Depression of the 1930s. While some economists blamed state meddling and misaligned incentives for the financial bubble that burst that year, others saw part of the problem in economics itself, and in the minimally regulated institutions promoted by economists (Krugman 2009; Soros 2008; Stiglitz 2008). Prominent voices in the economics profession are asking us to reconsider our basic assumptions.

Abandoning a hedonistic view of the individual does not mean adopting an equally naive belief that people are wholly self-disregarding and virtuous. Human beings are often selfish and all-too-frequently capable of morally outrageous acts. This is not a dispute between an "optimistic" and a "pessimistic" view of human nature. For reasons ranging from family honor to religious fanaticism, some people may commit murder and believe that they are acting morally. Obversely, some selfish acts do have social benefits. Instead, the key issues are best put in different terms. First, human motivation is complex and involves more than self-interest. Second, the pursuit of policies based solely on an appeal to self-interest is ultimately self-defeating. Third, because of the role of moral judgments in human activity, economics has to be conceived as a "moral science" and fortified by the critical study of analytical approaches from other relevant disciplines. Economics has mistakenly tried to fashion itself as an exact science akin to physics. Instead, the moral tradition, going back to Adam Smith and Aristotle, has to be highlighted and strengthened.

Contrary to some accounts, morality is more than a matter of preference, convenience, or convention. Moral claims, by their nature, apply to others as well as the claimant. They are outcomes of deliberation and conversation, yet inescapable and emotionally empowered (Mackie 1977; Joyce 2006). As Charles Darwin (1871) argued, our propensities to establish and acknowledge moral claims have evolved over many thousands of years. Their emotional fuel and elements of their rule structure are traceable back to our ape-like ancestors (de Waal 1996, 2006). Our moral nature has evolved because we are a social species, with emotional, linguistic, and deliberative capacities. Morality is a profoundly social phenomenon.

---

using the "dismal science" to describe mainstream economics. It is well known that this phrase originates from Thomas Carlyle, but less so that he first deployed it in an 1849 article proposing the reintroduction of slavery in the West Indies, to replace the allegedly "dismal" outcome of the forces of supply and demand in the voluntary labor market (Dixon 1999).

Morality reflects both our biological inheritance and our embeddedness in society. Morality helped us to survive. Morality helps make us human.[2]

Self-interest can be understood in many ways. Acting out of self-interest is not necessarily immoral. But morality means more than self-interest: it involves rules that also apply to others. Hence exclusively self-interested motivation is amoral (rather than necessarily immoral). By focusing on self-interested agents, economics has become largely an amoral science.

Having adopted the notion of self-interested "economic man," economics has been accused of fashioning the real world in his image. Studies suggest that university courses in mainstream economics have the real effect of discouraging cooperative and considerate behavior in the students. Gerald Marwell and Ruth Ames (1981) found that business and economic students were significantly less cooperative in experiments on human cooperation. Similarly, Robert H. Frank, Thomas Gilovich, and Dennis T. Regan (1993) found evidence that differences in cooperation between economics students and others "are caused in part by training in economics" (p. 170). Somewhat different evidence was presented by Anthony M. Yezer, Robert S. Goldfarb, and Paul J. Poppen (1996), but Frank, Gilovich, and Regan (1996, p. 192) reemphasized the conclusion shared by both groups of authors that "economics training encourages the view that people are motivated primarily by self-interest." This raises a serious question whether economists should be taught exclusively such a narrow view of human motivation (Marglin 2010).

If the Great Crash of 2008 and its aftermath—the greatest global economic crisis since the 1930s—do not give us enough cause to consider what may be wrong at the core of economics, then we should consider the reckless destruction of our planet and the growing threat of catastrophic, human-induced climate change. Yet the underlying assumptions of mainstream economics exclude any considerations other than those that lead to the enhancement of individual happiness or utility. If we do not accept that humans are causing global warming or if the required policy measures reduce our pleasure or (intertemporally discounted) expected overall utility—even by the tiniest amount—then standard welfare economics says that we should do nothing about it. Such a utility-reducing move would not be "Pareto efficient." And if radical measures are necessary—such as

2. Essential features of "moral" or "ethical" (two terms treated here as synonyms) judgments are elaborated in chapter 4. By contrast, I use the term "normative" in a sense that includes, but is not confined to, the ethical or moral. Normative statements are "ought" proclamations of any kind, deriving from morality, duty, efficiency, or mere convenience.

drastic reductions in car use or meat consumption—then it is unlikely that the kind of compensation for the utility losers defined by Nicholas Kaldor (1939) and John Hicks (1939) would be feasible. Hence mainstream economics faces this impending ecological crisis with a conceptual framework that is incapable of recommending the radical measures required.[3]

As if severe financial and ecological crises were not enough to make us look again at the fundamentals taught in Economics 101, then we have other chronic problems such as widespread corruption in developing countries (as well as alarming instances of corruption in some of the developed) and global problems in all healthcare systems that face an aging population alongside a rapidly growing repertoire of expensive pharmacological and technological remedies. Are we really supposed to believe that all these problems can be tackled on the basis of the assumption that every individual is selfishly maximizing her utility?

No. An alternative exists in the literature. It needs critical attention and development, but that task has been given insufficient attention. Part of the problem is that the alternative is more complicated and more difficult to fit into a mathematical model. Economists believe in Max U partly because of their analytically individualist agenda and partly because Max U can be expressed more straightforwardly in equations. These reasons have proved sufficient to consign the alternatives to the dusty shelves of an unvisited library.

In the modern commercial era, where consumers are said to be sovereign and customers always right, the meaning of morality has been likewise devalued in popular discourse. Alasdair MacIntyre (1981) has noted how moral values are often deemed relative and subjective, the gratification of uncultivated emotions is seen as paramount, and the notion of the good is deemed to be a purely private matter. Each person is declared free to judge virtue for himself and is granted liberty to pursue that private vision subject to the constraint that it does not impinge on similar freedoms for others. But this denuded version of morality is of limited effectiveness in promoting social cohesion and collective action.

---

3. "Happiness economics" substitutes survey-based measures of contentment or happiness for intangible utility (Easterlin 1995; Oswald 1997; Frey and Stutzer 2000, 2002, 2005; Layard 2005; Di Tella and MacCulloch 2006). Establishing empirically the declining marginal happiness of wealth and income, some happiness economists recommend redistributive policies that overturn Paretian constraints. Nevertheless, policies that increase happiness are necessarily neither moral nor reflective of genuine need. Mere happiness as a welfare criterion is deficient, especially if founded on public misunderstanding or ignorance. No amount of pushpin can ever surpass great poetry.

Despite prominent voices of dissent, mainstream economics typically downplays or ignores questions of moral value. Anything but the most superficial discussion of ethics is absent from the mainstream textbooks on economic policy. Economists often mistakenly treat moral values as superficial and transient, and search instead for a firmer analytical grounding on self-interested preferences. This book cites abundant evidence to counter this view.

For two centuries, repeated warnings have been raised that an economics purged of wider and deeper moral considerations is blinkered, misconceived, and potentially destructive. It is overlooked that economic activity and policy always depend on evaluative and moral judgments that derive through interaction in structured communities rather than the preferences of isolated individuals (Gui and Sugden 2005).

From the 1870s and at least until recently, neoclassical economics was dominant. The term "neoclassical economics" refers here to approaches that

1 assume rational, utility-maximizing behavior by agents with given and stable preference functions;
2 focus on attained, or movements toward, equilibrium states; and
3 are marked by an absence of chronic information problems.[4]

These three attributes are interconnected. For instance, the attainment of a stable optimum under (1) suggests an equilibrium (2); and rationality under (1) connotes the absence of severe information problems mentioned in (3). Addressing point (3), even if information is imperfect, in neoclassical economics information problems are typically overcome by using the concept of probabilistic risk. Excluded are phenomena such as severe ignorance, uncertainty—where by definition no probability can be calculated (F. Knight 1921; Keynes 1936)—or divergent perceptions by different in-

---

4. This definition of neoclassical economics excludes members of the Austrian school, such as von Mises and Hayek, particularly because of their explicit critique of attributes (2) and (3), and because of their rejection of conceptualizations of rationality under (1). Neoclassical economics has attracted numerous critics, but too many fail to define clearly what they are attacking. There are also widespread misunderstandings, such as that neoclassical economics necessarily supports a pro-market policy stance, or it claims that markets are always efficient. On the contrary, models of socialism have also used neoclassical assumptions (Lange and Taylor 1938), and there is a long history of arguments within neoclassical economics itself, from Pigou (1920) to the literatures on the Prisoner's Dilemma and multiple equilibria, that markets are not always efficient. Most policy biases of neoclassical economists result more from ideology than theory. See Hodgson (1999b, chap. 2).

dividuals of a given reality. It is typically assumed that all individuals will interpret the same information in the same way, ignoring possible variations in the cognitive frameworks that are necessary to make sense of data.

Mainstream economics has developed enormously since 1980. New approaches such as game theory, experimental economics, and behavioral economics have emerged, and modern mainstream economics has to some extent broadened from the neoclassical paradigm (Colander 2005a, 2005b; Colander, Holt, and Rosser 2004a, 2004b; J. Davis 2006). The main outcome has been to modify feature (1) and to some extent (2). Attribute (3) has received less modification: even mainstream behavioral economics does not embrace the kind of radical uncertainty promoted by Herbert Simon (1957) who founded the genre (Earl 2010; Hodgson 2011). And there are some areas of economics—such as health economics, discussed in chapter 8—that remain predominantly neoclassical at their theoretical core.

While acknowledging the changing nature and boundaries of mainstream economics—to the extent that parts of the mainstream are non-neoclassical—much less has changed in welfare economics and at the foundations of economic policy. The standard normative neoclassical approach to economic welfare involves the following assumptions, among others (Little 1950):

1 individuals seek to maximize their utility and the individual is treated as the best judge of whether her utility is maximized, and
2 the Pareto criterion is adopted—changes are acceptable only if they increase the utility of at least one person and decrease the utility of no one.

Mainstream economists still widely consider these two assumptions valid, but both of them are especially problematic in health and environmental economics, an issue we turn to in later chapters.

Overall, acknowledging all the real changes in mainstream economic theory, there is a more durable, individualist, and utilitarian core that is difficult to displace.[5] This book is a small contribution toward the construction of an alternative approach. Before explaining its scope and structure, we may usefully look again at the nature and history of the self-seeking

5. Individualism is defined in the preface, using the words of Hobson. Utilitarianism has many different forms, including act-utilitarianism and rule-utilitarianism. My primary target in this book is the form of utilitarianism that pervades mainstream economics, involving individual utility as the metric of merit. The attempt later to rehabilitate a fuller moral discourse dislodges additional varieties of utilitarianism.

individual in economics. We also address the way that utilitarianism has dominated conceptions of the individual and normative approaches to human welfare.

1.1. The Individual in Contemporary Economics

Many economists are proud of the proclaimed individualist credentials of their discipline. This sentiment spans a number of diverse propositions, from methodological individualism to the acceptance of individuals as the best judges of their welfare.

This individualist legacy is in large part positive, especially insofar as it has underlined the importance, first of individual autonomy and liberty, and second of individual incentives in the understanding and design of economic institutions and policies. Individuals are generally more aware than others of their own circumstances, and can often be the best judges of their own welfare. But they are not omniscient, and their knowledge and judgments are ever-changing as they learn from experience.

Turning to incentives, the failure of many on the political left to acknowledge their significance has gravely weakened their input into policy debates. An understanding of individual incentives is essential both to understand how economic systems work and to venture into problems of legal and organizational design. But, as we shall see later in this book, many economists have mistakenly elevated pecuniary incentives above all others. Incentives can be moral as well as pecuniary.

Mainstream economics has placed subjective preferences and individual choices at the center of its analysis of microeconomic phenomena. No less important is the emphasis by Austrian school economists such as Friedrich Hayek (1948) and Ludwig von Mises (1949) on the subjective and tacit dimensions of individual knowledge. Although mainstream economists have difficulty incorporating such notions in their formal models, these Austrian insights remain vital. If we fail to appreciate the impossibility of accessing and processing all knowledge—much knowledge being irretrievable and tacit—then we shall fail to understand why twentieth-century experiments in comprehensive central planning failed (Murrell 1991; Hodgson 1999a). Individual knowledge and individual incentives are key issues in the understanding of any economic system.

But economists have been deluded by the unattainable goal of explaining all economic phenomena in terms of individuals alone, and by the idea that the subjective preferences of the individual are adequate foundations to establish economic institutions and policies. The individual has become both the claimed basis of explanation and the metric of moral virtue. Methodological individualism is hallowed as a sound and unambiguous methodology, and all policy evaluations are measure in terms of their impacts on individual levels of utility. While retaining the individual as a vital feature of economic analysis, this book challenges these ideas. It is important not only to emphasize relations between individuals but also to adopt an enriched conception of human individuality (J. Davis 2003, 2011). Through a richer awareness of human individuals, and the institutions through which they interact, we can improve our understanding of the nature of human organizations and the role of law and the state.

Who is this individual who features in so many economics texts? Often he is openly selfish, greedy, and self-seeking. But even when orthodox economists admit "altruistic" behavior, it is explained in terms of an individual seeking to maximize his utility, perhaps gaining additional "warm glow" utility by giving to others.[6] The "cooperation" or "altruism" that emerge are still based on the maximization of individual utility. If an individual gains utility by helping or cooperating with others, then he is still self-serving rather than being genuinely altruistic in a more adequate sense. The "altruistic" individual often turns out to be selfish, even when he commits suicide (Hammermesh and Soss 1974). All acts—including altruism—are reduced to self-serving utility maximization. Even in models with interdependent preferences, individual utility maximization remains the rule.

Economic man is a pleasure-maximizing machine rather than a reflective individual capable of addressing moral dilemmas, absorbing moral principles, and performing or refraining from true generosity. For economic man, utility is the only measure of moral worth. Concepts such as self-image, integrity and commitment, which are essential to understand phenomena such as altruism and trust, are excluded (Smart and Williams 1973; Sen and Williams 1982). Furthermore, this individual makes no use of any differences between his conception of welfare, his goals, and the bases of his choices (Sen 1977).

Consequently, despite all the emphasis by mainstream economists on "choice," the kind of "choosing" performed by this hallowed individual has no more moral depth or complexity than a programmed room thermostat sensing a lower temperature and hence "choosing" to switch on the heating. The individual's evaluation of worth is superficial, and his sense of duty or morality inadequate. He is simply a pleasure machine.

6. See Becker (1976a); Collard (1978); and Andreoni (1990).

1.2. Individual Selfishness and Adam Smith

Today the selfish individual is upheld as the centerpiece of economics as a science and the essential foundation stone of all its theoretical achievements. But contrary to those who worship Smith as the patron saint of individual greed and unfettered capitalism, the founder of modern economics had a much more complex view of human nature. We can learn much from studying it, not least to discover how much economists have progressively adopted a more impoverished view of the individual.

It is true that Smith (1976, p. 82) in his *Theory of Moral Sentiments* of 1759 and elsewhere saw self-regard as foremost in human motivation: "Every man is, no doubt, by nature, first and principally recommended to his own care." But the whole purpose of the *Moral Sentiments* is to explore how self-interest is modified by positive feelings toward others. The first chapter of this book is titled "Of Sympathy," and its opening words are:

> How selfish soever man be supposed, there are evidently some principles in his nature, which interest him in the fortune of others, and render their happiness necessary to him, though he derives nothing from it except the pleasure of seeing it. . . . (Smith 1976, p. 9)

Later in this work he warns that self-regarding motives can be extremely negative in their consequences. Smith (1976, p. 157) writes of "self-love," this "self-deceit, this fatal weakness of mankind, is the source of half the disorders of human life." But such egotistical motives are counterbalanced by quite different capacities:

> Nature . . . has not . . . abandoned us entirely to the delusions of self-love. Our continual observations upon the conduct of others, insensibly lead us to form to ourselves certain general rules concerning what is fit and proper to be done or to be avoided. . . . It is thus that the general rules of morality are formed. They are ultimately founded upon experience of what, in particular instances, our moral faculties, our natural sense of merit and propriety, approve, or disapprove of. (Smith 1976, pp. 158–59)

Smith thus considered "our natural sense of merit and propriety" as well as our selfishness. He objected to the Hobbesian and Mandevillian theses that ethical principles arise entirely from self-serving motives. Instead, he wrote of the "conscience" and the "impartial spectator" within. The "spectator within" provides a sense of integrity and self, based on a self-image and the commitment to a system of moral values. Although, for Smith, selfishness is a driver of the market system and a major engine of economic progress, it is generally leavened by feelings of sympathy and principles of morality. Smith also insists on the vital importance of a system of justice based on moral principles. This is a crucial part of the institutional infrastructure of a market society; it enforces rules that establish personal security and curb the excesses of self-regarding individualism. Smith (1976, p. 86) thus wrote in his *Moral Sentiments*:

> Society, however, cannot subsist among those who are at all times ready to hurt and injure one another. The moment that injury begins, the moment that mutual resentment and animosity take place, all the bands of it are broke asunder. . . . Society may subsist, though not in the most comfortable state, without beneficence; but the prevalence of injustice must utterly destroy it. Though Nature, therefore, exhorts mankind to acts of beneficence, by the pleasing consciousness of deserved reward, she has not thought it necessary to guard and enforce the practice of it by the terrors of merited punishment in case it should be neglected. It is the ornament which embellishes, not the foundation which supports the building, and which it was, therefore, sufficient to recommend, but by no means necessary to impose. Justice, on the contrary, is the main pillar that upholds the whole edifice.

Contrary to some accounts, most modern scholars of Smith's writings hold that there is no contradiction between Smith's views in the *Moral Sentiments* and the *Wealth of Nations*.[7] Indeed, in the latter and more famous volume, Smith drives home the same point that the market system depends on effectively functioning judicial and administrative institutions. He exhorts his readers to take heed of these preconditions and makes no suggestion that such institutions will emerge spontaneously without the guidance of enlightened politicians and administrators.

Even Smith's pro-market views were qualified. Although he celebrated

---

7. On how Smith's moral philosophy infuses his economics, see W. Campbell (1967), Coase (1976), Winch (1978), Raphael (1985), Sen (1987a), Fitzgibbons (1995), Young (1997), Rothschild (2001), Montes (2003), Fleischacker (2004), Evensky (2005a, 2005b), Castro Caldas, Narciso Costa, and Burns (2007), and Wight (2009). By contrast, Lux (1990, p. 89) wrote that "Smith's sanctioning of self-interest without any qualifying or restraining force completely eliminated the moral problem in human action." This is incorrect. Smith wrote repeatedly of morality as a qualifying or restraining force. His notion of the natural order admitted strong ethical notions of justice.

the self-regulating and efficiency-enhancing properties of the market system, he regarded these mechanisms as insufficient in themselves. Smith regarded significant taxation and "public works" as crucial and proposed "a wide and elastic range of activity for government" (Viner 1927, p. 231).[8] Adam Smith is too important to be surrendered to the hedonistic individualists.

1.3. How the Individual Became a Pleasure Machine

The subsequent evolution of economics into a discipline dominated by self-seeking individuals, with their own utility or satisfaction as the only standard of morality, is a long and complex story. Only a brief summary is attempted here. Among the factors to take into account are the influence of a utilitarian model of individual behavior and the rising positivistic movement to make political economy or economics more "scientific" and "value-free" with greater use of quantifiable data and mathematical models (Rowthorn 1996; Alvey 2000). Nevertheless, it took two centuries after the *Wealth of Nations* for individualist doctrines on greed and welfare to reach their highest levels of influence within the economics profession.

Jeremy Bentham is an early and important player in this story. Bentham (1789, chap. 1, para. 1) revered individuals but transformed them into servants "under the governance of two sovereign masters, *pain* and *pleasure.*" For Bentham, the individual is a slave of these forces, which override all other moral considerations:

> It is for them alone to point out what we ought to do, as well as to determine what we shall do. On the one hand the standard of right and wrong, on the other the chain of causes and effects, are fastened to their throne.

Morality and society were reduced to the mechanics of individual pain and pleasure. Bentham (1789, para. 4) also wrote: "The community is a fictitious *body,* composed of the individual persons who are considered as constituting as it were its *members.*" This is a statement of ontological individualism.[9] Furthermore, the "interest of the community" is nothing else but "the sum of the interests of the several members who compose it." And these interests were measured in terms of pleasure.

8. On Smith's endorsement of an economic role for the state, see also Viner (1960), Pack (1991), Fitzgibbons (1995), and Rothschild (2001), among others.

9. The difference between ontological and methodological individualism is discussed in chapter 2.

By making individuals the supreme arbiters of their own welfare, Bentham was taking a very radical political stance and challenging governmental, aristocratic, ecclesiastical, and divine authority. For much of the nineteenth century, his ideas were resisted both by political conservatives and social scientists disposed toward a more nuanced view of human nature. Partly for these reasons, the complete triumph of Benthamite utilitarianism had to wait until the more democratic ethos of the twentieth century.

Contrary to Benthamite utilitarianism, classical economists from Smith through Thomas Robert Malthus to John Stuart Mill found a place for "moral sentiments" and higher human values. When Malthus (1820, pp. 3, 518), for example, endorsed the idea popularized by Smith of the collective benefits of selfishness, he systematically adds the reservation that an individual should so act only "while he adheres to the rules of justice."

Following Aristotle in his *Politics*, classical economists such as Smith and David Ricardo made a distinction between use-value and exchange-value. The concept of use-value was quite different from the subjective concept of utility or satisfaction. For Aristotle (1962, p. 41), use-value derived from the "proper use of the article" and not its value in exchange. As Karl Polanyi established, Aristotle saw use-value as an objective quality relating to the usefulness of an item for humankind (Polanyi, Arensberg, and Pearson 1957, pp. 65–67, 80–83).[10] When Adam Smith, Karl Marx (1867), and David Ricardo adopted this Aristotelian term, it had the same connotations. Even when they used the word "utility," it typically meant usefulness in serving human needs rather than subjective satisfaction.

Smith and others compared the use-value and exchange-value of water and diamonds. Irrespective of individual preferences, and because of our physiology, water is objectively vital for humanity and thus has a high use-value, despite its low exchange-value. By contrast, despite being desired for adornment and commanding a high price, diamonds had little use-value in terms of practical human well-being (before their modern technological uses). This only becomes a "paradox" if use-value is reinterpreted as subjective utility. Understood in the terms of Aristotelian philosophy or classical political economy, there is no paradox to be found. The idea that there was a problem in classical value theory, and this "paradox" was later "solved" by marginal utility analysis, is a modern myth (M. V. White 2002).

But within classical economics there were divided views on its status as a moral science. David Ricardo (1951–73, p. 2:338) endorsed the claim

10. Despite Polanyi, other authors have conflated Aristotle's use-value with subjective utility (Soudek 1952; Gordon 1964). Meikle (1995) criticizes these claims.

of Jean-Baptiste Say that political economy was a technical subject, concerned mostly with means rather than ends. For Ricardo (1951–73, pp. 1:5, 8:331), political economy was a strict science, akin to mathematics. But Malthus (1820, p. 1) took a different view, stating that "the science of political economy bears a nearer resemblance to the science of morals and politics than to that of mathematics."[11]

On many issues, Marx was closer to Ricardo than to Malthus. Marx reprimanded socialists who appealed to morality rather than the material interests of the working class to bring about the new order. Socialism would be achieved not by a moral crusade but by the workers struggling and uniting to pursue their material interests. Marxism eschews all moral appeals for socialism, to focus instead on proletarian self-interest. Marx and Engels (1976, p. 504) even proclaimed in the *Communist Manifesto* of 1848 that communism "abolishes . . . all morality . . . in contradiction to all past historical experience." Like the utilitarians, Marx separated ends from means. The end of socialism was proclaimed as both desirable and inevitable, and all means toward that end were justified.[12]

The similarities with subsequent mainstream economics are too close for comfort. Thorstein Veblen (1909, p. 623) thus criticized the Marxist use of the "hedonistic calculus," whereby "human conduct is conceived of and interpreted as a rational response to the exigencies of the situation in which mankind is placed."[13] Similarly, Talcott Parsons (1937, p. 110) described Marx's historical materialism as "fundamentally, a version of utilitarian individualism."

Although Marx was strongly influenced by G. W. F. Hegel and other German thinkers, his views on the role of morality in economics contrast with another prominent German intellectual tradition. From the 1840s until the First World War, the largest and most influential school of economics in the world was the German historical school. Generally critical of laissez-

11. Veblen (1899a, p. 411) noted astutely that "Malthus may well be accounted the truest continuer of Adam Smith," but "it was the undevout utilitarians that became the spokesmen of the science after Adam Smith's time." Keynes (1933, pp. 100–101) lamented: "If only Malthus, instead of Ricardo, had been the parent stem from which nineteenth-century economics proceeded, what a much wiser and richer place the world would be today."

12. Lukes (1985) forcefully criticizes Marx's "extreme consequentialism"—which amounts to a neglect of any moral evaluation of the means, as long as they serve the ends. Screpanti (2007, chap. 2) documents the reluctance of Marx and Engels to take a moral stance. Doyal and Gough (1991) criticize Marxists who try to abandon a concept of objective need, arguing that a reliance on such a category is unavoidable.

13. Veblen famously (1898, p. 389) lampooned the utilitarian individual as a "lightning calculator of pleasures and pains . . . a homogeneous globule of desire."

faire policies, this school saw economics as linked to moral philosophy (Koslowski 1995, 1997). But their work is too copious to be discussed here, and their invocation of morality had little effect on post-1945 economics (Hodgson 2001).

Like many subsequent economists, John Stuart Mill (1844, p. 139) defended utility maximization as a useful but strictly false simplification, while recognizing that no "political economist was ever so absurd as to suppose that mankind are really thus constituted."[14] But in other important respects, his approach differed from later neoclassical economics. In his *Principles of Political Economy* (1848), Mill argued that every act of free-market exchange increases the sum of utility. He suggested that a policy outcome should be assessed in terms of the sum of utilities rather than the later and more restrictive Pareto criterion, where no improvement can make anyone worse off. In contrast, Mill's criterion allowed for significant redistribution of wealth and income.

Despite his devotion to some form of utilitarianism, Mill refrained from reducing all human welfare to individual satisfaction. While Bentham had treated all forms of happiness as equal, Mill (1863) argued that intellectual and moral pleasures are superior to physical and other forms of satisfaction. Mill upheld that people who have experienced both the higher and lower forms of happiness tend to prefer the higher. In Mill's modified utilitarianism, the individual does not always know best, unless she has sufficient experience of all feasible options.

But there are severe problems in this modified approach, particularly regarding the difficulty of rendering qualitatively different types of utility rankable or commensurable (Bronk 2009, pp. 51–52). In any case, Mill's radical elaboration of utilitarianism is absent from his own seminal *Principles of Political Economy* (1848). Influential economists from William Stanley Jevons (1871) to Arthur Pigou (1920) made wealth, measured in monetary terms, the practical yardstick of economic value. By the time that Lionel Robbins (1932) jettisoned monetary measures of wealth in favor of straightforward utility, all Millian qualms concerning the commensura-

14. To some extent Mill foreshadowed writers who argue that the maximization postulate may be adopted even if it is not empirically accurate, as long as it sustains theories that make "valid and meaningful predictions" (M. Friedman 1953, p. 7) or that it was simply necessary "for the theoretical system in which it is employed" (Machlup 1972, p. 114). In part following Boland (1981), my position outlined below (and as early as Hodgson 1988) is that the maximization postulate, in principle, can fit every empirical observation, so the first problem is that it is not as much empirically wrong as ultimately empty. It also lacks an adequate causal account of human motivation, informed by our understanding of our evolution. And at best, it is morally insipid.

bility of all pleasure or utility had been forgotten. They rarely surfaced in economics in the succeeding eighty years.

After Mill, John Ruskin made a more radical plea for the insertion of moral values into economic theory. Ruskin (1866, p. 17) attacked the idea that the social affections "are accidental and disturbing elements in human nature; but avarice and the desire of progress are constant elements." For him, faith, generosity, honesty, and self-sacrifice were just as real and potentially durable. Influenced by both Ruskin and the German historical school, the sidelined British economist John A. Hobson's (1901, 1921, 1929) sustained emphasis on ethical issues made him exceptional among Anglophone economists. But the influence of Hobson on economics remained minimal.[15]

For a while, even after the 1870s, when the concept of use-value was displaced within economics by the subjective concept of utility, concerns about objective human needs lingered at the center of economics. For Alfred Marshall (1920, p. 1), economics was devoted to "the attainment and with the use of the material requisites of wellbeing." Even Carl Menger (1871, 1981), who promoted a seminal individualist methodology against the then-prevailing orthodoxy of the German historical school, listed a number of objective needs, including the need for food and shelter.

Jevons represented a different view. He embraced the Benthamite calculus of pleasure and pain and developed it significantly in mathematical terms. For Jevons (1871, pp. 50, 52), economics "must be pervaded by . . . the tracing out of the mechanics of self-interest and utility." He believed that "all economic writers must be mathematical so far as they are scientific at all." It was precisely in this enthusiasm for mathematical expression that the moral dimension of human motivation was subdued.

Francis Edgeworth followed Jevons, embracing both Benthamism and mathematics. Edgeworth (1881, p. 16) wrote: "The first principle of Economics is that every agent is actuated only by self-interest." Edgeworth's (1881, p. 15) additional choices of words and argument were illuminating: "*the conception of Man as a pleasure machine* may justify and facilitate the employment of mechanical terms and Mathematical reasoning in social science."

Jevons and Edgeworth set the tone for later developments in economics, but their conceptions were resisted by many in Marshall's time. In

15. Hobson visited the United States and was regarded as an institutional economist (Rutherford 2011). For general accounts of his work, see Allett (1981), Schneider (1996), and Townshend (1990). His combined emphasis on ethical and evolutionary ideas makes his work especially prescient.

many ways, Marshall remained the preeminent figure in microeconomics until the 1940s, which saw the rise of general equilibrium theory and mathematical economics. He saw mathematics as being of limited value in economics (Whitaker 1996, 2:256, 280, 393). Marshall (1920, pp. 17, 89, 764) also defended a more sophisticated view of the individual than a mere "pleasure machine." Marshall (1885, p. 160) wrote: "Whenever we get a glimpse of the economic man he is not selfish." Marshall (1920, p. 25) also considered that "the life of society is something more than the sum of the lives of its individual members," thus seeing the economy as more than an aggregate of individuals.

Menger emphasized individual self-interest but did not follow the Jevons-Edgeworth advice to put this assumption in a mathematical model. Menger (1985, p. 86) wrote in 1883 in his opening salvo in the *Methoden-streit* that self-interest was part of "the most original and the most general forces and impulses of human nature" and placed its study at the center of economics. He thus laid the foundations of the Austrian school, combining the emerging emphasis on individual self-interest with an increasingly unfashionable discourse that generally avoided mathematics.[16]

1.4. The Rise and Decline of Welfare Economics

From the 1870s, the hedonistic individual played a prominent role in economics. Focusing on the individual sustained the entirely laudable aim of understanding the role of individual incentives. Taking incentives seriously means looking at the perceptions and preferences of individuals. But it is possible to take incentives seriously and also bring objective human needs as well as complex motives into consideration. It took a long time for mainstream economists to entirely abandon the concept of objective need and to embrace subjective utility as the exclusive metrical basis of value and virtue.

The story of how this happened is too complicated to relate in detail here, and it is the subject of much writing and debate in the history of economic thought. Nevertheless, we may mention a few important milestones.

In line with Marshall's (1920) view that economics should consider

16. Menger (1883) wrote after Darwin's *Descent of Man* (1871) and its evolutionary explanation of altruism and cooperation. Ironically, as the Austrian school became still more evolutionary, culminating in Hayek's (1988) somewhat grudging adoption of loosely Darwinian principles to analyze social evolution, the clash between their evolutionary and individualistic sentiments became more apparent (Hodgson 1993).

how wants are formed, and not always take them as given, early articles in the *Economic Journal* discussed the interdependence and social formation of consumer demands (Cunynghame 1892; Foley 1893). Pigou (1903, 1913) made two important attempts to incorporate interdependent and intersubjective aspects of consumer demand into neoclassical analysis. But Pigou (1913, p. 24) himself came to the conclusion that these attempts were "wholly inadequate." Not readily formalized as mathematical models, these issues were eventually to slip off the agenda of mainstream economists (Mason 1995; Fullbrook 1998). It became standard practice to take individual preferences as given.

Pigou (1920) established the mainstream subdiscipline of welfare economics, where welfare was evaluated entirely in terms of individual utility. Within this theoretical edifice, the individual alone became the supreme judge of her own welfare. But Pigou argued that his welfare analysis could not provide the complete and final basis for economic policy. For instance, Pigou (1937, p. 138) favored "the weapon of graduated death duties and graduated income tax . . . with the deliberate purpose of diminishing the glaring inequalities of fortune and opportunity which deface our present civilisation." He further declared that "the most important investment of all is investment in the health, intelligence and character of the people." Despite his solid neoclassical credentials, Pigou was a slave of neither hedonism nor the Pareto criterion.

When Lionel Robbins (1932) redefined the nature and scope of economics as the universal "science of choice," the nature of the individual and the place of morality within economics changed further. Economics would exclude any investigation into the psychological origins or institutional molding of individual preferences or goals. The nature and morality of individual ends were beyond its inquiry. Instead, economics was about the rational choice of means to serve *given* ends. The "economic problem" was then to determine the best means available to meet those ends. It applied to all economic systems, as long as there were choices to be made and a scarcity of resources. Robbins provided the methodological counterpart to Pigou's formal welfare analysis.

But Robbins's view of economics took some time to be accepted. Roger Backhouse and Stephen Medema (2009) show that it faced some resistance until the 1970s. Nevertheless, Paul Samuelson's (1947, 1948) definition of economics was strongly influenced by Robbins, and he adopted a version of Pigou's welfare analysis. The influence of Samuelson in recasting neoclassical economics in his best-selling postwar textbook was crucial. Although other economists disagreed with Samuelson on both theoretical and policy issues, the entire discipline was eventually recast in these utilitarian terms. Morality was brushed aside.

Following Robbins, economists became increasing skeptical of the possibility of meaningful interpersonal comparisons of utility. In contrast to the criteria adopted by earlier utilitarians, that welfare was assessed by the sum of all utilities, the Pareto criterion became so pervasive that economists saw welfare in no other terms. This remained true after the establishment of the Kaldor-Hicks compensation criterion (Kaldor 1939; Hicks 1939). The Kaldor-Hicks amendment was that a change had to be potentially Pareto efficient, in that all losers could be compensated, without necessarily doing so. Influential economists such as Kenneth Arrow (1951) found limitations in an exclusive reliance on standard utility analysis and the Pareto criterion, but sought to supplement rather than to replace them. The individual was still taken as the ultimate arbiter of welfare.

To this day, most economists treat the individual as always the best judge of his welfare and refrain from alternative welfare criteria. Technical problems with this approach are familiar, including the Arrow impossibility theorem, the theory of second best, and the complications imposed by endogenous or interdependent preferences.[17] When the idea that the individual is the best judge of his welfare is criticized, the typical response is mock the notion that anyone, including the government, could know better than the individual himself. But this book is written in the belief that alternative and more sophisticated positions are possible.

In the 1960s, welfare economics seemed a lively field with a rich future. But a combination of technical problems and irrepressible moral dilemmas resulted in paralysis rather than innovation. This was partly because the use of mathematical techniques was becoming the universal requirement of theoretical inquiry, journal publication, and professional advancement. Because mathematics offers little ethical guidance, the moral issues were sidelined. As Anthony Atkinson (2009, p. 792) notes, the subdiscipline of welfare economics "went quiet" after 1970. Today the Pareto criterion is ritualistically observed but rarely questioned.[18] Deeper reflection or criticism is avoided. While the Pareto criterion is taken for granted, welfare economics has suffered. It is absent from entire annual volumes of leading journals of economics and few textbooks on the theme appear (Atkinson

17. See Little (1950), Arrow (1951), Lipsey and Lancaster (1956), Graaff (1957), Mishan (1960), Sen (1970, 1979, 1982), Gintis (1972, 1974), Gowdy and Iorgulescu Polimeni (2005).

18. Several exceptions are cited by Hausman and McPherson (1993, 1996).

2009, p. 793). The subdiscipline is at best taught as a minor appendix to microeconomic theory, with little enrichment from moral philosophy.

But there is at least one important exception to this trend. Pioneering a different approach based on individual capabilities, Amartya Sen has long been a critic of the utilitarian and Paretian foundations of welfare economics (Klamer 1989; Sen 1973, 1987a; Sen and Williams, 1982). For Sen, the reduction of human motivation to utility maximization neglects crucial issues surrounding individual capabilities, agency, and choice. The award of the Nobel Prize in Economics to Sen in 1998 signals a different direction.[19] But otherwise, in terms of its ethical stance and its elemental welfare criteria, and in contrast to enormous advances in theory and technique, contemporary mainstream economics has progressed little from the Benthamism of the early nineteenth century.

Within economics, the core idea of the pleasure machine has survived major ideological shifts. Utilitarianism is flexible, having both radical and conservative faces. The abstract utilitarian calculus is more tractable than most alternatives, and it thus benefited from the growing prestige of mathematics in the discipline. Utility reduces the complex panoply of human sentiments and beliefs to preference rankings, which are amenable to mathematical treatment. The rise of mathematics as the sole standard of economic rigor meant the decline in moral philosophizing for economists. Both utility and the Pareto criterion were taken for granted.

Ironically, classic defenses of socialism against the Austrian critics also used neoclassical theoretical models (Dickenson 1933, 1939; Lerner 1934; Lange and Taylor 1938). Most models of both planned and market economies are populated by self-regarding, utility-maximizing individuals. Particularly in its Marxist form, socialist theory has also relied on narrow self-interest. The ideologically contrasting promoters of free markets and central planning have shared a flawed theoretical foundation.

While some Marxists have used neoclassical theoretical tools (Roemer 1982; Elster 1985), pro-market economists rely additionally on the claim that the individual always knows best. The same theoretical apparatus of preferences and utility maximization are given a contrasting ideological thrust by the addition of one important but challengeable welfare assumption.

---

19. Hausman and McPherson (1993, 1996) argue persuasively that ethical issues are important, both to understand individual motivation and to provide a better grounding for economic policy. Etzioni (1988) and Davis (2003) have also observed that the standard individual in economics pays inadequate attention to personal and moral values. See also Mansbridge (1990).

But in practice, even pro-market governments override the individual. Governments never fully follow the advice of economists that individuals are the best judges of their own welfare. Instead, many possible choices are declared illegal, even when there is mutual consent by those directly concerned. Hence there are commonplace restrictions or prohibitions on the use or sale of drugs, on bribery, on child labor, on futures markets for labor, on the buying or selling of votes, on prostitution, on incest, and on sex with children. Even the most individualist of governments refrains from complete liberalization. They legislate extensively to prevent food adulteration and to maintain public health. Child education in most developed countries is compulsory. Sufferers of severe mental illness can be deprived of their liberty. The state retains a monopoly in the use of much legitimate force—through the police and armed forces—and controls the rights of citizens to bear arms.

Much economic theory neglects the vital role of the state in buttressing essential institutions of the market economy, including law, property, corporations and money. An often overlooked but major reason why the state is important is that—for good or ill—it is recognized as a moral force. As such, it encapsulates political authority and power.[20] An understanding of the role of morality can help us appreciate the roles and limits of both the market and the state.[21]

The analytical problems surrounding morality and human cooperation require insights from multiple disciplines. In mainstream economics, the individual is too "undersocialized" (Granovetter 1985) to explain moral systems and moral motivation. The untenable devotion to a detached individual in mainstream economics is buttressed by genuflections to a vague and rarely defined "methodological individualism." Obversely, while sociology pays more explicit attention to social structures, individual socialization, and roles, it often neglects the biological underpinnings of human

20. With the evidence of his famous experiments, Milgram (1974, pp. 124–25, 131) argues that inherited dispositions to respect authority have evolved because they aid cohesion and enhance group survival. Haidt and Joseph (2008) claim that respect for authority is an evolved value-intuition.

21. Key capitalist institutions depend on the state and its moral authority. Law is more than custom and necessarily involves the state. See Seagle (1941), Redfield (1950, 1957), and Hodgson (2009). On the distinction between possession and property, and the dependence of the latter on the state, see Sened (1997), Pipes (1999), Heinsohn and Steiger (2000), and Steiger (2008). On the dependence of the business corporation on law, see Phillips (1994), Blair (1999, 2003), Iwai (1999), Hodgson (2002), Hansmann, Kraakman, and Squire (2006), and Gindis (2007, 2009). On the modern state theory of money, see Smithin (2000), Bell (2001), and Ingham (2004). There is insufficient space to discuss these wide-ranging issues in the present volume.

sentiment and motivation. Some social scientists have reified structures to the neglect of individuals.[22] Despite some notable exceptions, workers in both disciplines still pay inadequate attention to psychology.[23] To understand how moral communities work, we have to transcend (often outdated) disciplinary boundaries.

We need an economics that builds on scientific studies of human nature in other disciplines, including psychology, neuroscience, and anthropology. These disciplines have recently made huge strides by incorporating insights from evolutionary theory. In the light of these studies, the critique of economic man has become irresistible. With the guidance of evolutionary theory, we need to understand how individuals develop and form their preferences and dispositions. Moral values have to be placed alongside self-interest and self-gratification. The understanding of individuality is too important to be left to individualists. Individuals have to be considered as actors within moral systems.

Figure 1 shows how the usage of terms beginning in "ethic" or "moral" (but excluding appearances of "moral hazard") has declined in articles in ten leading Anglophone journals of economics relative to the use of the term "utility."[24] The number of articles containing terms beginning in "ethic" or "moral" were searched, and the number of articles containing the word "utility," were also found. The graph shows the former figure divided by the latter for each decade. Before 1910 terms such as "ethics" or "morality" were more common than "utility." After the First World War, "utility" took the lead. By the 1970s, articles with "moral" terms were less than 20 percent as frequent as those with "utility," and from the 1980s they were around 10 percent. In an era where mathematical expression matters most, morality had been largely subsumed under utility.

22. Examples downplaying the individual include Ayres (1918, p. 57; 1961, p. 175) and Althusser and Balibar (1970, p. 180). In his excellent introduction to Durkheim's (1982) classic work, Lukes exposes the limitations of this more complex account of individual and structure. See also Hodgson (2004b).

23. Pieters and Baumgartner (2002, p. 504) examined interjournal citation patterns in the mid-1990s and found that "economics builds only slightly on knowledge from its sister disciplines." In the period and data under investigation, citations across disciplinary frontiers were relatively infrequent with, for example, no citations from economics to psychology journals, or vice versa.

24. The ten journals are *American Economic Review, Econometrica, Economic Journal, Economica, Journal of Political Economy, Oxford Economic Papers, Quarterly Journal of Economics, Review of Economic Studies, Review of Economics and Statistics,* and *Southern Economic Journal.* The oldest of these journals started in 1886 and the newest in 1938. Economists use the term "moral hazard" to describe inefficiencies that occur when risks are displaced. It has minimal resemblance to the concept of morality in ethics.

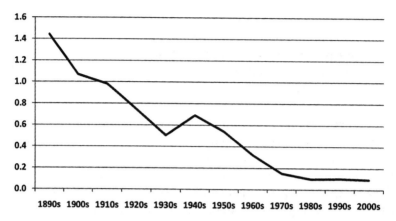

Figure 1. The Decline of "Morality" Relative to "Utility" in
Leading Journals of Economics

1.5. Aims and Outline of This Book

Social relations are as necessary for explanations of economic phenomena as individuals. Consequently, we cannot ignore the structures of power and position in society, and the role of culture as well as biology in forming human nature (Ehrlich 2000). The picture of utility-maximizing agents—in both self-regarding and other-regarding versions—should also be replaced by a richer, multidimensional, and developmental version of the individual, which includes biologically grounded and culturally enhanced moral motivations. The importance of deep-rooted ethical motivations and values—including sympathy and respect for authority—are illustrated in several contexts. The individual is not taken as given, but situated within an interactive social context that enables her education and development. Finally, the book sketches an approach to economic welfare and policy entailing an institutional system for establishing and evaluating human needs in an ongoing and evolutionary manner.

Chapter 2 discusses methodological individualism. A favored slogan of mainstream economics, it turns out to be ambiguous and problematic. One version of methodological individualism, requiring explanation in terms of individuals alone, is untenable. The defensible claim that social phenomena should be explained in terms of social relations *and* individuals would be mislabeled as methodological individualism because the label reveals only part of the story. Whatever label we use, social relations between individuals always have to be brought into the explanation. Because of social relations, society is always more than the mere aggregate of the individuals comprising it. Understanding this is key to understanding moral systems in society.

Chapter 3 tackles the economists' notion of rationality and the evidence of altruism and cooperation. Rationality can be defined in terms of maximizing explicit payoffs. But a large amount of experimental evidence shows that individuals are often not rational in this sense. In response, rationality is defined by some economists in terms of utility maximization or the consistency of preferences.[25] A problem with this revised definition, as shown in the chapter, is that no possible piece of evidence can refute the proposition that people are behaving consistently or maximizing an undetectable variable such as utility. The revised notion of rationality fits everything and explains nothing. After considering the evidence on human altruism and cooperation, the chapter argues that both their origin and persistence must be explained. While persistence may be explicable partly in terms of culture, the origins of that culture must also be understood. Argument and evidence suggest that biologically inherited dispositions are part of the story. Given the complex and multileveled sources of human personality, summary treatments of humans as "preference functions" are inadequate.

After establishing both cultural and biological sources for human dispositions, chapter 4 brings morality into the picture. The first problem is to establish the nature or meaning of morality. Using the work of John L. Mackie (1977), Richard Joyce (2006) and others, I propose that moral claims are inescapable, involve emotions and beliefs, transcend conventions that are established out of convenience, and rely on language, communication, and deliberation. Following Charles Darwin (1871) and others, I uphold that morality has evolved by natural selection of groups: it governs interpersonal relations and counters self-centered individualism. This evolutionary analysis differs from Richard Dawkins (1976) and others. Taking into account both the nature and evolution of morality, I also find limitations in the analyses of a number of leading thinkers, including Amartya Sen, Amitai Etzioni, Robert Frank, and Kenneth Binmore. For example, morals must be more than game equilibria established simply through convenience or utility maximization. The moral naturalist claim that the search for a true morality can also be guided by scientific principles, in the manner of the natural sciences, is found to be unconvincing.

Chapter 5 considers how morality has evolved in human society. Although morality is a relatively recent phenomenon and depends on the

---

25. Preference consistency can itself be approached in different ways (Sen 1987b).

emergence of human language, it is argued along with Frans de Waal (1996, 2006) and others that basic moral feelings have a much longer evolutionary history and stretch back to the social groups of our ape-like ancestors. On the basis of evidence from human psychology, we can establish some near-universal moral disposition, found in almost all human cultures. An illustrative agent-based model shows that morality is different from altruism and is irreducible to it. Consequently, the analytical literature on human cooperation must be broadened to include morality.

The remaining chapters consider applications of the ideas developed in the first part of the book. Chapter 6 considers morality and cooperation in business. The standard literature in economics on the theory of the firm has ignored the possibility that moral or prosocial motivations play an important part in establishing cooperation and facilitating management in business organizations. The operation of markets also depends on moral values (Schultz 2001), but social interactions in firms are typically deeper and more enduring. Partly because of relatively intensive and long-lasting social interactions, people in business organizations often identify with their workgroup and are disposed to accept its values. Given these possibilities for enhanced intrinsic and extrinsic motivation, productivity can be enhanced by bringing production under the organizational umbrella of the firm. Consequently, there are additional reasons for firms to exist, as well as possible reductions in transaction costs.

Chapter 7 addresses the globally pervasive problem of corruption. It reveals a severe problem in dominant definitions of corruption by economists, which often define corruption in terms of "the misuse of public office for private gain." In a gross exhibition of ideological bias, this *by definition* rules out the possibility of corruption in the private sector. A major task of the chapter is to define organizational corruption more adequately. The definition amounts to the conscious breach of ethical rules with the involvement of multiple agents. Corruption is regarded as primarily a moral failure. Addressing the social costs of corruption, it is shown that well-defined property rights cannot be an effective solution to the problem because corruption can disrupt the whole institutional system of private property and contract.

Chapter 8 considers some of the shortcomings of mainstream health economics. Strangely, while retaining most neoclassical credentials, much of mainstream health economics has abandoned the Pareto criterion and has adopted some notions of need. The appropriate next step would be to ditch the rest of the neoclassical utilitarian apparatus as well and embrace a more thoroughgoing discourse of need. By considering healthcare as a need, and the particular characteristics of this necessity, an enhanced understanding can be acquired of the possible motivations of healthcare workers. This undermines such health management approaches as individual "payment by results." Hence a link is made between a needs-based approach to welfare and the analysis of moral motivation.

Chapter 9 considers environmental issues in general and human-induced climate change in particular. Climate change has potentially catastrophic consequences. It forcefully challenges the dogma that the individual is always the best judge of her interests. Sadly, many people neither understand nor accept the science of climate change. Mainstream approaches also take individual preferences as given, when a goal of organizations involved in promoting a sustainable environment must be to educate the population and enhance their capacity to evaluate key problems. Despite the claims of many environmental economists, policies should focus on moral values as well as pecuniary incentives. Moral values are not ephemeral—they are rooted in human evolution.

The final chapter briefly and tentatively sketches a radically different approach to problems of human welfare. Breaking from the utility-based model of neoclassical economics, the design of institutional mechanisms to evaluate and improve assessments of need becomes central. A major inspiration here is the experimental policy approach of John Dewey (1916, 1929, 1935, 1938, 1939; Dewey and Tufts, 1932). As with Dewey, the role and moral authority of democratic institutions become crucial. Economics thus has to return to its former glory as a moral and a political science.

TWO

Meanings of Methodological Individualism

Methodological individualism starts with an ultimate unanalyzable factor, the rational being sovereign over his own choices. This starting point gets in the way of any attempt to relate the structure of individual goals to the goals of an organized social environment.

—Mary T. Douglas (1990)

The recognition that a methodological individualist strategy necessarily incorporates references to social relations, situations, unintended consequences, and even beliefs in social aggregates makes one wonder about the robustness and prospects of this program.

—Kyriakos M. Kontopoulos (1993)

As in most sciences, the majority of economists do their work with little explicit reflection on the philosophical assumptions that underlie their research. But when economists make their philosophical views explicit, advocacy of "methodological individualism" is uppermost.[1]

But the term is rarely defined with adequate precision. Some crucial ambiguities are explored in this chapter. Among these is the commonplace ambivalence over whether explanations should be in terms of individuals alone, or in terms of individuals plus relations between them. It is shown that a great deal hinges on this subtle and often overlooked distinction in *explanantia*. In particular, explanations in terms of individuals alone have never, as yet, been achieved. Furthermore, the more feasible version (explanations in terms of individuals plus relations between them) amounts to

---

1. This chapter is a revised and extended version of Hodgson (2007b). See also Hodgson (2007a).

the introduction of social structures alongside individuals in the *explanantia*. Serious questions remain whether this version warrants the one-sided emphasis on individuals in the term "methodological individualism."

It is necessary to dispose of the myth that economic phenomena can be analyzed in terms of individuals alone, and of any "methodological individualism" that might support this myth. Economies in general and the moral ties that bind people together cannot be understood without an appreciation of the nature of individuals and of social relations.

Although there are different meanings of the term "methodological individualism," they generally insist on the importance of individuals and their purposeful behavior. An emphasis on the individual in the analysis of socioeconomic phenomena became prominent with the Enlightenment, and it is found in the works of numerous authors, including John Locke and Jeremy Bentham (Udéhn 2001). Accordingly, some key ideas behind the term have a much longer history than the term itself.

The term was not invented by a philosopher but by a leading economist. A book in German published by Joseph Schumpeter (1908) has a chapter entitled "Der methodologische Individualismus."[2] Schumpeter (1909) distilled some of the ideas in his 1908 text into an article published in the *Quarterly Journal of Economics*. Here the term "methodological individualism" first appears in an academic work in English.[3]

The term itself does not reemerge in a large database of leading academic journals until the 1930s, when it received very brief favorable mentions by John Hicks (1934), Fritz Machlup 1937), and Alfred Stonier and Karl Bode (1937).[4] In the 1940s, Austrian school economists such as Friedrich Hayek (1942) and Ludwig von Mises (1949) linked the phrase to their own methodological positions. Perhaps influenced by his friendship with Hayek, Karl Popper (1945b) mentioned the term briefly in an article in *Economica*.[5] Popper (1945a) developed his interpretation and brought the concept to the attention of philosophers.

Ironically (but no causal connection is suggested) after Schumpeter's death in 1950 the term began to be used more frequently. Popper's student

---

2. An English version of *Das Wesen* appeared in 2010, but the translation has been criticized.

3. Max Weber (1968) outlined a doctrine in the first chapter of his *Economy and Society* (originally published posthumously in 1920) that has since been described as methodological individualism.

4. I refer to the JSTOR database, which covers economics and other social sciences and includes leading journals in economics.

5. Popper's *Economica* essays on "historicism" were eventually worked up into a book (Popper 1960).

John W. N. Watkins (1952a, 1952b) advocated a version of the doctrine and stimulated a protracted controversy in the philosophical literature. In the 1960s, the phrase made its first appearance in a leading sociological journal (Dore 1961). Accordingly, through the Austrian trinity of Schumpeter, Hayek, and von Mises, the term "methodological individualism" was exported from economics into other disciplines.

But overviews of the history and controversies surrounding the term establish that it has no single accepted meaning (Lukes 1969, 1973; O'Neill 1973; Udéhn 2001, 2002). Despite its frequent appearance, there is no consensus on its sense and usage. Hence there is no warrant for the incantation of the two words without reference to an adequate definition.

The next two sections explore critically some major ambiguities in the use of the term. The ambiguity discussed in the section thereafter is the most pertinent. The subsequent section proposes the "folk theorem" that in practice explanations of social phenomena are never in terms of individuals alone. Another section refocuses on the crucial ambivalence in the use of the term. It shows that the two possible interpretations of the idea that social phenomena must be explained in terms of individuals either violate the folk theorem or do not warrant the label of methodological individualism.

Note that the critique here is essentially internal: it explores inner ambiguities and the logic of current usage. It obliges methodological individualists to clarify or (preferably) abandon the term. It is important, but beyond the nature and scope of the internal argument here, to explore the nature of individuality itself. Given that this is largely an internal critique of methodological individualism, all is required is to use the term "individual" as a placeholder for what methodological individualists might reasonably mean by the term. Of course, focusing on the individual begs questions concerning the social nature of individuality. But for the purposes of the internal critique in this chapter, we can leave these issues temporarily to one side. Contributions to the broader and vital project of exploring individuality are found elsewhere (O'Neill 1973; Hodgson 1988; J. Davis 2003, 2011) and in later chapters of this book.

2.1. First Ambiguity—Methodological Imperative or Demarcation Device?

For Schumpeter (1908, p. 91), methodological individualism "just means that one starts from the individual in order to describe certain economic relationships." He was emphatic that this statement of methodological conduct implies no political alignment; methodological and political individualism are logically separate and propositionally distinct. Subsequent authors have repeated this point, but in some accounts these analytical and normative issues have been confused.[6]

For Schumpeter, methodological individualism was no universal injunction or principle from which we depart at our scientific peril. Instead for him it was an attempt to demarcate the "pure theory" of economics from other approaches and methods of scientific inquiry. For "pure theory," according to Schumpeter (1909, p. 216), "it is irrelevant *why* people demand certain goods: the only important point is that all things are demanded, produced, and paid for because individuals want them." He fully admitted that individual preferences could be malleable, but investigations into the causes of those preference changes were outside the scope of "pure theory." Hence an explanatory division of labor existed between the "pure theory" of economics, and other scientific approaches (Schumpeter 1954, p. 889).

For Schumpeter, this proposal for a division of labor was a means of reconciling the two sides in the ongoing *Methodenstreit*.[7] One side was seen as concerned with "pure theory" and the other addressed broader issues, including the explanation of individual tastes and the evolution of institutions. As Schumpeter (1908, pp. 6–7) wrote: "both sides are mostly right . . . their sole difference lies in their interests in different problems." Hence Schumpeter upheld methodological individualism as neither a universal principle of social scientific research nor an obligatory rule for all social scientists.

Remarkably, Schumpeter (1954, p. 888) coined the different term "sociological individualism" to describe the doctrine that

> the self-governing individual constitutes the ultimate unit of the social sciences; and that all social phenomena resolve themselves into decisions and actions of individuals that need not or cannot be further analysed in terms of superindividual factors.

This "sociological individualism" seems close to what many people today describe as "methodological individualism." But Schumpeter (1954,

---

6. This applies to both critics and exponents. Hayek (1948) used the term "individualism" to refer to both political and methodological doctrines.

7. The *Methodenstreit* (clash of methods) erupted between Gustav Schmoller (of the German historical school) and Carl Menger in the 1880s. Contrary to a widespread myth, the debate between the historical and the Austrian schools endured for several decades and no side was widely acknowledged at that time as a clear victor. Alfred Marshall, for example, enduringly praised the historical school (Hodgson 2001, 2005).

pp. 888–89) immediately rejected sociological individualism as unviable as a complete explanation: "This view is, of course, untenable so far as it implies a theory of the social process." Unfortunately he did not expand further on this point, other than contrasting "sociological individualism" with "methodological individualism." The wording and context suggests that Schumpeter meant that "sociological individualism" was limited because it failed to explain the "decisions and actions of individuals" themselves. Given this criticism by Schumpeter, and the fact that his definition of "sociological individualism" is close to what many people mean by "methodological individualism," it is clear that he should not be associated with many prominent versions of "methodological individualism" that are promoted today.

Schumpeter regarded "methodological individualism" as a limited analytical option, characteristic of "pure economics." By contrast, since his death, "methodological individualism" has been treated as a universal principle for the social sciences. We now turn to some examples of such usages.

2.2. Second Ambiguity—Ontology or Explanation?

Statements about what exists, or concerning the nature of reality, are very different in character from statements on how one should explain phenomena. The first kind of statement is ontological, the latter is methodological. But several authors confuse ontological with methodological individualism.[8]

For example, in a section in his book *Human Action* entitled "the principle of methodological individualism," von Mises (1949, pp. 41–43) provides no clear definition of the term and includes statements such as: "The hangman, not the state, executes a criminal. . . . For a social collective has no existence and reality outside of the individual members' actions. The life of a collective is lived in the actions of individuals constituting its body. . . . There is no substratum of society other than the actions of individuals." All of these quoted statements are ontological rather than methodological in character.

The philosopher Watkins (1957, pp. 105–6) conflates both ontologi-

---

8. Ontological suppositions may limit but do not require any claims concerning explanation. Obversely, methodological individualism by many accounts does not necessitate a purely individualist ontology because many methodological individualists accept that the social world consists not only of individuals, but also of interactive relations between them, and that social entities such as institutions exist.

cal and methodological individualism in a single passage. He upholds that "the principle of methodological individualism" means that "the ultimate constituents of the world are individual people who act more or less appropriately in the light of their dispositions and understanding of their situation." And "we shall not have arrived at rock-bottom explanations of such large-scale [social] phenomena until we have deduced an account of them from statements about the dispositions, beliefs, resources and interrelations of individuals." Statements concerning "the ultimate constituents of the world" are ontological in character. Watkins then moves on to make a methodological statement concerning "rock-bottom explanations."

This frequent conflation by enthusiasts of "methodological individualism" may indicate an allegiance to ontological individualism as well. But a further ontological ambiguity arises. For reasons that will become clearer below, it is crucial whether it is claimed that the social world simply consists of individuals, or of individuals plus *interactive relations between them*. The social world, by virtue of the fact that it is social, must involve such interactive relations.[9] As Hobson (1901, p. 146) wrote: "The real underlying error of Mr. Spencer and his legion of followers is that they persist in regarding society as an aggregate of individuals. . . . If society is a composition, it must have a unity consisting in the relations of its members." Hayek (1967, pp. 70–71), who is often (but questionably) described as an advocate of methodological individualism, makes strikingly similar and additional points:[10]

> The overall order of actions in a group is in two respects more than the totality of regularities observable in the actions of the individuals and cannot be wholly reduced to them. It is so not only in the trivial sense in which the whole is more than the mere *sum* of its parts but presupposes also that these elements are related to each other in a particular manner. It is more also because the existence of those relations which are essential for the existence of the whole cannot be accounted for wholly by the interaction of the parts but

9. The term "social" is used in this book in a broad sense, to encompass phenomena that are examined in economics, as well as other social sciences. In the social context, all relations between individuals are causal and interactive, at least in the sense that in maintaining these relations with others, individuals are affected by their (partial) awareness of them and different actions may be enabled.

10. Udéhn (2001), Caldwell (2004), and Zwirn (2007) argue that Hayek—at least in his mature works—implicitly abandoned dominant contemporary interpretations of methodological individualism.

only by their interaction with an outside world both of the individual parts
and the whole.

Following Hobson and Hayek, society consists not merely of individuals, but also of interactions between individuals, plus interactions between
individuals and other aspects of their environment including, presumably,
both the natural world and other socioeconomic systems.[11]

The brief discussion of social ontology in this subsection has emphasized the difference between ontological and methodological individualism, and also identified an additional ambiguity that becomes crucial at the
methodological level. As shown below, some versions of methodological
individualism require that social phenomena be fully explained in terms
of individuals alone, while other versions require that they be explained in
terms of individuals plus other critical factors, including interactions between individuals. A great deal hinges on this distinction.

2.3. Third Ambiguity—Explanation
in Terms of Individuals *Alone*?

Consider the following selected attempts to define methodological
individualism: For Popper (1945a, p. 2:87), "'methodological individualism' . . . rightly insists that the 'behaviour' and the 'actions' of collectives,
such as states or social groups, must be reduced to the behaviour and to
the actions of human individuals." The use of the term "reduced" here
suggests that explanations should consist *exclusively* of statements about
individuals.

But Popper (1945a, p. 2:91) goes on to modify this significantly, by seeing methodological individualism more fully as "the important doctrine
that all social phenomena, and especially the functioning of all social institutions, should always be understood as resulting from the decisions,
actions, attitudes, etc., of human individuals, and that we should never be
satisfied by an explanation in terms of so-called 'collectives' (states, nations,
races, etc.)." This omits the requirement of complete explanatory reduction
to individuals and does not imply that explanations should be in terms of
individuals alone. Instead, he claims that explanations (exclusively or otherwise) in terms of collectives are unsatisfactory.

11. The role of interactive relations between individuals is clarified in modern accounts of
social ontology (Bunge 2000; Weissman 2000; Sawyer 2005; Elder-Vass 2010a).

As quoted above, the definition of methodological individualism by Watkins (1957, p. 106) is broad in that it does not reduce explanations of social phenomena to individuals alone, but also includes "resources and inter-relations of individuals." The latter term admits a huge class of phenomena, including social relations.

For Ludwig Lachmann (1969, p. 94), methodological individualism means "that we shall not be satisfied with any type of explanation of social phenomena which does not lead us ultimately to a human plan." But few social scientists would deny the role of individual plans in the explanation of social phenomena. Again, this definition is so broad that it would be difficult to find a social scientist who disagrees.

Jon Elster (1982, p. 453) defines methodological individualism as "the doctrine that all social phenomena (their structure and their change) are in principle explicable only in terms of individuals—their properties, goals, and beliefs." Although less banal, this definition is also insufficiently precise, as it fails to clarify whether interactions between individuals or social relations are "properties . . . of individuals." If neither individual interactions nor social relations are "properties of individuals," then this narrower and more meaningful notion of methodological individualism points to explanations in terms of individuals alone. But it is unclear whether Elster means this.

Geoffrey Brennan and Gordon Tullock (1982, p. 225) advocate a methodological individualism in which "the *ultimate* unit of analysis is always the individual; more aggregative analysis must be regarded as only provisionally legitimate." Again it is insufficiently clear, but the exclusive emphasis on individuals as the *"ultimate"* unit seems to uphold the final aim of explanation in terms of individuals alone.

A great deal hinges on this issue: does methodological individualism simply point to the importance of individuals in explanations of social phenomena, or does it insist that explanations should be reduced to individuals alone? Clearly, there is no consensus among advocates of methodological individualism on this crucial point concerning the *explanantia*.[12] As Udéhn (2002, p. 498) puts it: "The doctrine of methodological individualism, then, ranges from versions requiring that social phenomena be fully explained in terms of individuals, to versions requiring only that they be partly explained in terms of individuals."[13]

---

12. An *explanans* (plural, *explanantia*) is an element that purportedly helps to explain something else, namely the *explanandum* (plural, *explananda*). Apologies to those who already know their Latin.

13. See also Kincaid (1997) for a dissection of this and further ambiguities.

2.4. A Folk Theorem Concerning Explanations of Social Phenomena

The key proposition to be discussed in this section is that all adequate and successful motivational explanations of social phenomena (including in economics) involve interactive relations between individuals.[14] In other words, when explanations are reduced to individuals, interactive relations between individuals are also always involved. Because no formal proof of this proposition will be offered, it will be referred to as a "folk theorem." Nevertheless, there are strong arguments in its favor.

By assumption, this folk theorem is confined to social situations. Some economists have been enamored by the example of Robinson Crusoe (before the arrival of Friday) allocating his scarce resources between competing ends, but the social characteristics of such a situation are highly limited. We are concerned with social phenomena, which necessarily involve more than one individual.

In the social sciences, are there any successful explanations of social phenomena in terms of individuals alone? Udéhn (2001) claims that social contract theory and general equilibrium theory are examples of explanations that involve individuals alone, without social relations or institutions. But Kenneth Arrow (1994) denies this, pointing out that price mechanisms involve social interactions and structures, and social phenomena that cannot be reduced entirely to individuals alone. Arrow (1994, pp.4–5) remarks that

> economic theories require social elements as well even under the strictest acceptance of standard economic assumptions. . . . [I]ndividual behavior is always mediated by social relations. These are as much part of the description of reality as is individual behavior.[15]

Arrow is right. All versions of social contract theory and general equilibrium theory involve individuals communicating with others or, at least,

14. With large-scale events, it would be impossible to analyze every individual involved. But we do need a plausible summary explanation of individual motivations in such cases. In part it depends on what is meant by an "adequate" explanation. Once we get to the individual level, individual interactions are always involved.

15. Ten years earlier, Arrow (1984, p. 80) had put a different view, writing: "Society, after all, is just a convenient label for the totality of individuals." This ontological individualism is mistaken. Society consists of individuals *plus* interactive relations (including intersubjective perceptions) between individuals.

adopting tacit presumptions of the intentions and stances of others. All such interactions presume rules of interaction or interpretation. Trading in models of market interaction presumes some form of communication over prices or quantities. Communication involves some form of language, and languages by their nature are systems of rules. Furthermore, exchange involves the transfer of property rights, with rules established through prior social interactions. Similarly, all contracts rely on social structures of enforcement. Hence social contract theory and general equilibrium theory both presume structured relations between individuals rather than individuals in isolation. They also presume social institutions. For example, property rights require some system of enforcement. These things may not be stated explicitly in the models, but they must be presupposed in any meaningful application of the models to economic phenomena.

Individual choice requires a conceptual framework to make sense of the world. The reception of information by an individual requires a paradigm or cognitive frame to process and make sense of that information. The acquisition of this cognitive apparatus involves processes of socialization and education, involving extensive interaction with others (Douglas 1986; Hodgson 1988; Bogdan 2000). The means of understanding the world are necessarily acquired through social relationships and interactions. Cognition is a social as well as an individual process. Individual choice is impossible without these institutions and interactions.

Alexander Field (1979, 1981, 1984, 1991, 2001) has shown that key attempts by economists to explain the origin of social institutions presume individuals acting in a particular context, with rules of behavior governing their interaction. In the presumed "state of nature" from which institutions are seen to have emerged, a number of rules, structures, and cultural and social norms have already been (implicitly or explicitly) assumed. Accordingly, with explanations of the origin of institutions through game theory, Field pointed out that several norms or rules must inevitably be presumed at the start. There can be no games without norms or rules, and thus game theory can never explain the elemental norms or rules themselves. Even in a sequence of repeated games, or of games about other (nested) games, at least one game or meta-game, with a structure and payoffs, must be assumed at the outset.

Similarly, social theorist Kyriakos Kontopoulos (1993, p. 79) notes that "a methodological individualist strategy necessarily incorporates references to social relations." As these critics have showed, methodological individualists never start from individuals alone. For example, Steven Lukes (1973, pp. 121–22) shows that in the claimed "methodological individualism" of

Karl Popper, "the social phenomena have not really been eliminated; they have been swept under the carpet." To get anywhere, we always have to assume relations between individuals, as well as individuals themselves. No counterexample is evident.

The realization that explanations cannot be reduced to individuals alone has now taken hold in the new institutional economics. Jack Knight (1992) criticizes the preceding literature for neglecting the importance of distributional and power considerations in the emergence and development of institutions. Masahiko Aoki (2001) argues that always and unavoidably, analysis must start from individuals plus some institutions, however primitive. With these studies, the goal of narrowly defined methodological individualism is abandoned.

Narrow methodological individualism has a problem of infinite regress: attempts to explain each emergent layer of institutions always rely on previous institutions and rules. If institutional influences on individuals are admitted, then these too are worthy of investigation. In turn, the explanation of those may be partly in terms of other purposeful individuals. But where should the analysis stop? The purposes of an individual could be partly explained by relevant institutions, culture, and so on. These, in their turn, would be partly explained in terms of other individuals. But these individual purposes and actions could then be partly explained by cultural and institutional factors, and so on, indefinitely. As long as we are addressing social phenomena, we never reach an end point where there are isolated individuals and nothing more. In this infinite regress, neither individual nor institutional factors have legitimate explanatory primacy (Nozick 1977; Hodgson 1988).[16]

All theories must first build from elements that are taken as given. But the particular problems identified here undermine any claim that the explanation of the emergence of institutions can start from some kind of institution-free ensemble of (rational) individuals in which there is supposedly no rule or institution to be explained. Consequently, the project to explain the emergence of institutions on the basis of given individuals runs into difficulties, particularly with regard to the conceptualization of the initial state of nature from which institutions are supposed to emerge (Hodgson 1998a).

A powerful body of evidence and argument supports the folk theorem.

---

16. This problem has a parallel in biology: it is like trying to talk about the effects of genes without environments, which is commonly recognized to be a dead end (Jaenisch and Bird 2003). Social scientists should likewise acknowledge that consideration of individuals without an institutional context is also a nonstarter.

One counterexample would be sufficient to undermine it. None has yet emerged.[17]

2.5. The Crucial Ambivalence

As emphasized above, much of the confusion in the debate over methodological individualism stems from whether methodological individualism means one or other of the following:

(a) social phenomena should be explained entirely in terms of individuals *alone*; or
(b) social phenomena should be explained in terms of individuals *plus* relations between individuals.

The first of these versions (a) has never been achieved in practice, for reasons given above. It has been also shown above that many advocates of methodological individualism fail to specify this doctrine clearly in such narrow terms. It is just as well, as version (a) is unattainable in practice.

By contrast, the problem with the second version (b) is not that it is wrong but the term "methodological individualism" is unwarranted. In modern social theory, structures are typically defined as sets of interactive relations between individuals. Crucially, if social structures are definitionally equivalent to relations between individuals, then (b) is equivalent to:

(b*) social phenomena should be explained in terms of individuals and social structures.

The problem then becomes one more of labels than of content. Although (b) and (b*) are both acceptable statements, there is no good reason why they should be described as methodological *individualism*. It would be equally illegitimate to describe them as "methodological structuralism" or "methodological institutionalism." *All* such descriptions are misleading. We *always* have to start from structures *and* individuals. There is no other viable explanatory strategy.

---

17. In apparently conciliatory statements, Sober (1981) and Kincaid (1997) argue that the validity or invalidity of methodological individualism is ultimately an empirical issue. Given this, existing evidence is entirely against the narrow version. No significant explanation of social phenomena in terms of individuals alone has yet been advanced. In practice, there is always a social and relational residual that is not reduced entirely to individual terms.

Some social scientists may uphold that social structures involve more than relations between individuals. If this were true, then (b) and (b*) would no longer be equivalent. But it is not true. The mistake here would be to reify social structure as something more than an interacting pattern of individuals, which would somehow exist even if the individuals all disappeared. Social structures are essentially relations within groups of interacting social individuals, possibly including social positions, and with emergent properties resulting from this interaction (Weissman 2000).

Some methodological individualists target this error of reification of structure. But to endorse the view that explanations must unavoidably involve structures as well as individuals does not mean that the former are independent of the latter. Everyone knows that if all individuals disappeared, then all social structures would disappear as well.

Recognition of the danger of reification of structure does not mean that explanations of social phenomena can or should be reduced to individuals alone. Structures and isolated individuals are different things because interacting and isolated individuals are different things. By definition, isolated individuals have no causal interaction with other individuals. Structures depend on interacting individuals. But when a few people die, many social structures remain in existence. The difference between structures and isolated individuals is also confirmed by the fact that every human individual is born into a world where structures already exist. Then individuals engage with this world and play their part in supporting or changing these structures, while interacting with others.

Sophisticated advocates of methodological individualism are aware that the individual is a social being, enmeshed in relations with others. They are aware of the importance of culture, and that communication and language are deeply involved in constituting individuality (Ehrlich 2000). Consequently, the idea of a genuinely isolated individual, free of all social relations, is untenable (J. Davis 2003, 2011). Many methodological individualists seem reluctant to use this awareness to rule out such isolated individuals in the *explanantia*. Those who understand that explanations of type (a) are impossible, and of types (b) or (b*) only are possible, are eventually impelled like Hayek to abandon the term, or they relapse into vagueness concerning the critical difference between the options (a) and (b).

Joseph Agassi's (1960, 1975) term "institutional individualism" is better. But it gives one half of the story adjectival status while the other half has the prestige of being the noun. It thus carries a bias. Why not "individualistic institutionalism"? Both parts of the story are indispensable, and no good reason has been provided to give one explanatory priority over the other.

The question is then raised why the term "methodological individualism" is so popular, especially when the broader version (b) involves both individuals and social relations. Perhaps there are several motives for the pursuit of "methodological individualism." Some may involve the mistaken idea that it is a necessary corollary or component of political individualism. This would confuse ideology with analysis. Others seem to stem from a more creditable notion that explanation in terms of microcomponents is a key aim of science. But as the examples of genes in biology and atomic particles in physics both illustrate, explanations in science are never in terms of microcomponents alone: they always additionally involve interactive relations. Furthermore, if explanatory reduction to microcomponents were the legitimate aim, then this would be no justification for claiming that rock-bottom explanations are in terms of individuals. Instead, we would face the daunting task of attempting to explain all social phenomena exclusively in terms of the most elementary subatomic particles. The very existence of social entities, and the social sciences devoted to their study, counters such an extreme reductionist agenda.

2.6. Conclusion: Escaping the Mire

Methodological individualism has no single consensus definition. Furthermore, it is typically used in ways that differ from the meaning given to it by Schumpeter, who coined the term.

Among several attributed meanings, the idea of "explanations in terms of individuals" is identified here as problematic. It is unclear whether it means that explanations should be in terms of individuals plus relations between individuals, or in terms of individuals alone. This difference in *explanantia* turns out to be critical.

According to the folk theorem proposed above, narrower explanations in terms of individuals alone have never actually been achieved. Attempts to start simply from individuals must actually start from individuals plus institutions or social relations. All theories must first build from elements that are taken as given. But the explanation of the emergence of institutions cannot start from some kind of institution-free gathering of (rational) individuals in which there is supposedly no rule or institution to be explained. Some institutions and relations—including rules of interaction and communication—are always there at the beginning.

The broader version, where explanations are supposed to be in terms of individuals and relations between them, is definitionally equivalent to the proposition that explanations of social phenomena should be in terms of both individuals and social structures. There is nothing wrong with this proposition. But why call it methodological individualism, when structures and individuals are given equal status as elements in the explanation? If we wish to criticize notions that adequate explanations should be in terms of structures alone, then we should not adopt a term that connotes the mistaken idea that explanations can or should be in terms of individuals alone.

Advocates of methodological individualism are faced with a choice between untenable and maldescriptive definitions of their credo. At the very minimum, the term "methodological individualism" should not be used as an ill-defined mantra. If it is to be employed, then it must be much more clearly defined, overcoming the ambiguities in past usage. After over fifty years of widespread use of the term, advocates of "methodological individualism" have been remarkably negligent in explaining its meaning. In fact, its usage is plagued by deep contradictions and persistent vagueness. Given the deep conceptual problems and confusions surrounding the term, it would best be abandoned.

The lessons here are ontological as well as methodological. Society consists not only of individuals but also relations between individuals (Hobson 1901; Hayek 1967; Kontopoulos 1993; Weissman 2000; Sawyer 2005; Elder-Vass 2010a). Society has emergent properties that are not held by individuals, taken severally. It is more than the sum of individuals, and to understand that social reality we have to consider social relations as well. Economics must unavoidably be about social structures of power and position, as well as the properties of individuals.

This basic truth is important for this book. Consider rationality and preferences, which are typically but misleadingly treated as properties of individuals taken in isolation. No manifestation of reason or preference takes place apart from the social context in which humans operate. And the advancement of human welfare must improve social relations as well as outcomes at an individual level. Economics must be a social as well as an individual science.

The implications of this are enormous, especially for the research agenda of economics. No social science can derive its explanations from the properties of individuals alone, from individual preferences, individual neurology, individual psychology, individual genes, or any other individual attribute—alone. Notwithstanding the importance of these features of individuals, a social science must also address relations between individuals and the particular forms of these relations. These forms include social institutions, organizations, positions, and other structures. These entities are sustained through individuals interacting with some shared meanings and understandings, in part built on precedent and derived from practices in the past. These entities are irreducible to individuals, just as real as individuals themselves, and unavoidable among the *explanantia*.

In chapters 4 and 5 it is argued that morality has to be considered as a group and relational rather than simply an individual phenomenon. Despite its vagueness and ambiguity, the term "methodological individualism" may act as a mental road sign—an imprecise injunction that to understand economies, all that we need is to understand individuals alone. When faced with the vital problem of explaining cooperation in human society, the confusing road sign has helped to confine investigations and simulations to the apparent properties of individuals, thereby neglecting the institutional role and evolution of moral systems. But before we tackle the question of morality, the similarly diversionary concept of rationality is addressed in the next chapter.

THREE

Rationality and Cooperation

The self is not something ready-made, but something in continuous formation through choice of action.

—John Dewey (1916)

I do now regard that [Benthamite] tradition as the worm which has been gnawing the insides of civilisation and is responsible for the present moral decay. . . . We used to regard the Christians as the enemy, because they appeared as the representatives of tradition, convention and hocus pocus. In truth it was the Benthamite calculus based on an over-valuation of the economic criterion, which was destroying the quality of the popular ideal.

—John Maynard Keynes (1933)

Most economists make the assumption that man is a rational utility maximiser. This seems to me both unnecessary and misleading. . . . Let us also start with man as he is . . . acting within the constraints imposed by real institutions.

—Ronald H. Coase (1984)

Much ink and paper have been spent by economists and critics on the elusive concept of rationality. This chapter will not end this output, but it will hopefully divert some of the wasted energy into more useful occupations. There are multiple prominent versions of rationality, not one (Sen 1987b). One version upholds that rationality is essentially about consistency of behavior. Another sees rationality as the maximization of explicit (typically pecuniary) rewards. So much empirical and experimental evidence has been marshaled against the second (more restrictive) version that a significant number of economists have now abandoned the idea, and at least six critics of rationality (Friedrich Hayek, Gunnar Myrdal, Herbert Simon, Ronald Coase, Amartya Sen, and Daniel Kahneman) have been awarded Nobel Prizes in Economics. Whether the existence of altruistic behavior challenges the idea of rationality depends on the definition that is adopted. Definitions of rationality that accommodate altruism end up being unfalsifiable.

This chapter moves on to discuss explanations of altruism or cooperation. A crucial distinction is made between explanations of origin and explanations of persistence. With regard to explanations of origin, some reference to biological factors is unavoidable. But the details remain problematic and controversial. The additional role of culture is undeniable. An alternative construct to the mainstream rationality assumption is proposed at the end of the chapter.

3.1. The Slippery Concept of Rationality

One popular notion of rationality is *thoughtful deliberation*. This is not the meaning that is associated with the "choice" concept of Lionel Robbins (1932) or the "as if" methodology of Milton Friedman (1953). But when Herbert Simon (1957) argued that rationality was "bounded," he sometimes used this term to refer to limited computational and deliberative capacity.

A similar meaning of rationality is the notion of *acting for reasons*. Although etymologically accurate, this is alternatively described as the *rationalist concept of action* and criticized in a different manner (Hindess 1977; Hodgson 1988). The use of different meanings by economists has confused much of the debate surrounding the concept of rationality.

Another prominent notion of rationality is that people try to do the best they can in their circumstances. An important corollary is that agents respond to incentives. There is nothing wrong with this notion. But it fails to tell us how people interpret their situations or identify "the best" goals. It does not acknowledge that different interpretations of situations and hence different goals are often possible. The problem with this "doing one's best" notion of rationality is that it lacks the necessary explanatory detail concerning agent cognition and goal formation. It might also be used to buttress self-interested notions of "the best" that are in fact undermined by the evidence. The "doing one's best" notion of rationality is not entirely vacuous because it does point to the necessity of problem solving. But it lacks vital detail. To avoid confusion, the "doing one's best" notion would better be described as *following incentives* or *adapting to circumstances*. But more specific detail would also be required.

We now highlight notions of rationality that dominate modern mainstream economics. I define some additional terms. A "payoff" is a reward in a game that *has an explicit expected worth* (such as a declared monetary reward) *that is known to the analysts of the game and to all of its players.*[1] By "payoff rationality" or "payoff maximization," I mean the maximization of such explicit payoffs by players, given the information available to them plus their assumption that other players are also payoff maximizers. If one is committed to the axioms of payoff rationality, then logically one is also committed to the idea that rationality involves consistent behavior. But utility maximization is not necessarily payoff maximization, unless there is a monotonic relation between utilities and payoffs.

Vernon Smith (1982) and others have addressed the problem of the possible absence of a monotonic relation or "parallelism" between overall utility and monetary payoffs. To relate payoffs to utilities, the possibility of additional, subjective utilities that are unrelated to one's own monetary payoffs, such as utility derived from the satisfaction of others or from taking risks, has to be substantially diminished. The player's own money payoffs have to "dominate" his decisions. To make experiments "work" in this sense, Smith proposes a number of "precepts" of experimental assumption and design constituting an "induced value procedure." These precepts include nonsatiation, sufficiently large and obvious rewards, restriction of communication between subjects, and so on. But Smith (1982, p. 929) is the first to admit that these precepts cannot *guarantee* any monotonic correspondence between observable monetary rewards and preferences, which are "not directly observable." In fact, we can never know if the precept has been effectively applied. The idea that Smith's precepts "work" is an article of faith, placed up to now under surprisingly little methodological scrutiny.[2]

Some economists retain a notion of payoff rationality, despite any objections from critics. They argue that while there are empirical deviations

---

1. Note that the definition of "payoff" includes those formulated in probabilistic terms. For simplicity I shall ignore games where possible payoffs are known to some players but not others. Including this possibility would not change the principal conclusions below. In fact, it would make the concept of rationality more difficult to define straightforwardly, as in some types of game theory (Sugden 1991).

2. For a critical methodological discussion of Smith's precept of parallelism, see Siakantaris (2000).

from its norms, if pecuniary rewards are sufficiently large and agents are given long enough to learn the game, then payoff maximization will become established as an approximate behavioral rule (Harrison 1989; Binmore 1994, 1998b, 1999; Binmore and Shaked 2010).

By contrast, others follow "behavioral economists" and argue that the evidence is sufficient to undermine payoff rationality. Behavioral economics has now spread to the mainstream and is evident in some of the most prestigious journals in the discipline. Payoff rationality and self-interest were regarded as articles of faith among mainstream economists from the 1950s to the 1990s, and to question them was enough to lose one's credentials as an economist. Subsequently, in the face of massive, accumulating evidence of agents who do not maximize pecuniary rewards, economics has changed.

It is impossible to review all the evidence here.[3] "Framing effects" result when rankings of options change when equivalent choices are presented in different terms. Although payoff rationality means that bygones should be ignored, people often take them into account. Individuals are presented with two gambles—one with a certainty of winning a modest sum of money and the other with a low probability of winning a large sum of money. Even when the expected value of the risky option is greater, people often prefer the certain reward (Slovic and Lichtenstein 1983). In the face of such evidence, strict payoff rationality has been abandoned by many.[4]

Although the axioms of payoff rationality imply consistency of behavior, the reverse is not true. Without logical contradiction, one can abandon payoff rationality and still uphold that behavior is consistent, and even utility-maximizing. Herbert Gintis (2007, 2009) is an exponent of this position.

Gintis is a coauthor of a fascinating set of cross-cultural studies that show that players rarely reach a Nash payoff solution in ultimatum games (Henrich et al. 2001, 2004). One of two players in an ultimatum game is asked to divide an amount of money between herself and the other player. If the second player rejects the division, then both players get nothing; but

3. See the extensive works of Nobel Laureate Daniel Kahneman and his colleagues (Kahneman 1994, 2003a, 2003b; Kahneman, Slovic, and Tversky 1982; Kahneman, Knetsch, and Thaler 1986a, 1986b). Bowles and Gintis (2011) provide an excellent overview of the evidence.
4. But controversy has not ended. For example, different results—sometimes closer to payoff maximization—are obtained from some field experiments (Gneezy and List 2006). The contrasting outcomes of laboratory and field experiments underline a theme of this book: the social and institutional context matters, and individuals cannot be taken in isolation (List 2006).

if he accepts, then they each receive their allocated amounts. If the second player is a payoff maximizer, then he will accept the lowest possible positive allocation when it is offered: payoff maximizers always prefer something to nothing. This is a subgame perfect Nash equilibrium; it gives the best expected payoff outcome for both players, each assuming that the other player is also a payoff maximizer. Consequently, no player has anything to gain by unilaterally changing strategy on her own. But experiments often do not lead to this Nash payoff outcome: players do not always maximize payoffs in this way. Instead, their behavior is consistent with taking additional, intangible, nonpecuniary factors into account, such as honor, custom, and fairness, even when they cannot bargain with one another and the game is not repeated. The cross-cultural studies of Joseph Henrich and his colleagues also showed that the actual pattern of play can vary significantly from one cultural setting to another.

While abandoning payoff rationality, Gintis defends a broader concept of rationality, defined as consistency of behavior. Given behavioral consistency (or transitivity)—along with the other standard assumptions such as independence and continuity (von Neumann and Morgenstern 1944; Fishburn 1970)—it is possible to construct a standard ordinal utility function where behavior is consistent with expected utility maximization. Gintis (2007, 2009) considers much of the experimental evidence and points out that the absence of payoff maximization does not mean that these players are behaving inconsistently or failing to maximize utility.[5] For Gintis (2006, p. 17), this behavioral consistency is rooted in genetically rooted instincts and drives that have evolved over the millennia and dispose us to respond in specific ways to specific cues. Consequently, Gintis (2006, p. 7) argues that "utility maximization should be a central tool in analyzing human behavior, even if humans are not self-regarding."[6]

---

5. Consider the experimental evidence that people are not very good at logical problems, especially when they are posed in abstract terms or involve probabilities. Gintis (2007, pp. 11–12) brushes this evidence aside with the questionable conclusion that "most individuals do not appear to have difficulty making and understanding logical arguments everyday life." The evidence of Wason (1983), Cosmides (1989), and Cosmides and Tooby (1994a, 1994b) suggests otherwise. Even from Gintis's standpoint, this argument seems somewhat superfluous because if an individual made the same logical errors over and over, then she might be behaving consistently and might be "rational" by Gintis's criterion.

6. Gintis distinguishes between "self-regarding" and "self-interested" preferences. With "self-regarding" preferences, one takes account of one's own situation only. Hence for Gintis, a charitable act is not self-regarding, but it may be self-interested because of increased utility gained by the "warm glow" or satisfaction of giving. By contrast, it is argued here that notions of utility maximization or "self-interested" behavior are in principle unfalsifiable and of little use.

3.2. Fitting Everything and Explaining Nothing

Gintis does not acknowledge the following key difficulty. When the young Paul Samuelson (1937, p. 156) discussed utility maximization, he understood that "all types of observable behavior might conceivably result from such an assumption." Because utility is unobservable, all kinds of behavior can be "explained" in terms of the idea, without fear of refutation. As Sidney Winter (1964, pp. 309, 315) and Lawrence Boland (1981) have also remarked, no evidence can possibly refute the theory that agents are maximizing some hidden or unknown variable (such as utility). Amartya Sen (1977, p. 325) has similarly pointed to the circularity of explaining behavior "in terms of preferences, which are in turn defined only by behaviour." Sen (1987b, p. 73) notes elsewhere that the description of choices in terms of utility "does not give any independent evidence on what the person is aiming to do or trying to achieve."

Defending "self-interest, rightly understood" against its critics, Teppo Felin and Nicolai Foss (2009, p. 662) say it is consistent with "cooperation, organization, community-building, trust, or for that matter, any other individual, relational, or organizational virtue." Rather than selling the assumption, this rather gives the game away. An assumption that is consistent with everything describes little and delimits nothing.[7]

If experiments show that some consumers appear to prefer a monetary reward that is less than the expected outcome, or appear to have intransitive preference orderings, or defy the independence axiom, then we can always get round these problems, and make the evidence consistent with utility maximization, by introducing other explanatory variables.[8]

For example, preference reversals can be regarded as consistent with expected utility theory. Assume that a subject is faced with a choice between $10 with certainty and $1,000 with a probability of 2 percent. Experiments with real subjects indicate that in such situations the $10 option is sometimes chosen, despite the fact that the expected value of the second option is higher at $20 (Slovic and Lichtenstein 1983). But preference reversals

---

7. Significantly, Felin and Foss (2009, p. 622) continue: "the type of 'enlightened' self-interest we have in mind should be completely decoupled from ethics." In contrast to their defense of the self-interest assumption, their critique of social constructivist and performativity arguments in their article is much more robust.

8. Hausman (1992, chap. 13) documents several attempts to explain the apparent anomalies that have been revealed by the experimenters, notably by pointing to other possible sources of utility. But in some of these cases, the independence axiom is abandoned in attempts to rescue the idea of utility maximization.

also fail to falsify expected utility theory, once we accept that (expected) utility is not necessarily measured in terms of the monetary payoffs in the experiment. If we assume an added disutility associated with involvement in a risky and low-probability choice, then the theory that people are maximizing their utility is not overturned by these experiments. A risk-averse actor may not maximize expected monetary value but still be maximizing expected utility. By appropriate functional manipulation, the choice of $10 can be made perfectly consistent with the maximization of expected utility rather than the maximization of the expected monetary value of the payoff.

Gintis and others might respond that inconsistent behavior would refute utility maximization. The problem here is one of identifying inconsistent behavior in empirical terms. Note that the utility maximand is unobservable. For example, if an experiment shows that option A with an expected value of $4 is preferred to option B with an expected value of $5, then we can simply assume that there are additional attributes of option A (for example, we may enjoy losing or gain pleasure from seeing others win) that are consistent with the view that it yields higher overall expected utility for the subject.

On repeated visits to the same restaurant, we may prefer steak to fish one day, and fish to steak on another. Is this behavior inconsistent? Maybe. Maybe not. We may discover that the steak is not as good as expected. Or we may have seen an alarming television report about mad cow disease that causes us to switch to fish. The two choice occasions were different in terms of circumstances and knowledge. Hence they do not necessarily imply inconsistency.

The empirical detection of preference intransitivity is also problematic. An experiment may seem to reveal preference intransitivity, by showing that while X is preferred to Y, and Y is preferred to Z, Z is preferred to X. But this result can be explained away by showing that the three pairwise comparisons did not take place under identical conditions or were separated in time or space. Extraneous factors may account for the apparent intransitivity. All we have to do is indicate in some way that the two Zs in the above comparisons are not quite identical. The two Zs could be slightly different in timing, substance, or their informational or other contexts. We then get the result: X is preferred to Y, Y is preferred to $Z1$, and $Z2$ is preferred to X. In these circumstances, transitivity is no longer violated. The defender of utility maximization may conflate $Z1$ with $Z2$, whereas they were in fact different.

It may be objected that if preferences are assumed stable, then evidence on revealed preference could reveal inconsistent preferences. But this would not be the case if utility depended on other factors in the environment. Consider the utility function $U = f(X, E)$, where X is a vector of consumption inputs and E is a vector of environmental or contextual conditions. Assume the function f is perfectly stable. But E can never be strictly held constant. Some part of the environment, however remotely or slightly, will inevitably alter. Hence, in practice, intransitivity (or intertemporal inconsistency) in the rankings of the elements of vector X alone would not reveal preference inconsistency because some elements in the vector E would also have changed, even by the tiniest amount. Strictly, the environment is never constant. Consequently, because we cannot strictly and identically replicate the E conditions, intransitivity or inconsistency of X choices can never falsify the assumption of fixed preferences.[9]

Given that we can never in principle demonstrate that some unobserved variable (like utility) is not being maximized, then the theory is invulnerable to any empirical attack. No amount of evidence can establish nonexistence. Hence the standard core of expected utility theory is *unfalsifiable*.[10]

The utility-maximization assumption is unfalsifiable, but it is not a tautology in the logical sense because it is *conceivably false*.[11] Logical tautologies—such as a triangle has three sides—are true by definition. By contrast, it might be the case that individuals are not maximizing anything. But we can never establish this on the basis of empirical evidence.

This does not necessarily mean that the utility maximization framework is useless or wrong. We do not have to uphold falsifiability as the mark of science—a criterion attributed to Karl Popper, who in fact adopted a more nuanced position (Ackerman 1976). Neither tautological nor nonfalsifiable statements are necessarily meaningless or unscientific.[12]

9. There is a standard argument that intransitive preferences would involve a "money pump"—an agent with intransitive preferences would accept a series of trade offers that leaves her worse off to the benefit of the other trader. But given the sequential separation of each choice in time, strict intransitivity may never apply. This becomes evident when we leave the timeless world of neoclassical economics for the real world with historical time.

10. This argument is redolent of the so-called Duhem-Quine thesis, which claims that it is generally impossible to falsify any single hypothesis because we always have to adopt additional hypotheses in the analysis of any set of observations (Harding 1976). Consequently, we can never be sure that the main hypothesis is being targeted and tested on its own, and that other auxiliary hypotheses are not complicating the picture.

11. Several important authors, from Simon (1986, p. S222) to Field (2001, p. 6), mistakenly confuse tautological with nonfalsifiable propositions.

12. Indeed, it is widely accepted in the philosophy of science—including by Popper—that some unfalsifiable propositions are necessary for science itself. These include the principle of determinancy (every event has a cause) and the assumption of the uniformity of nature. Without these prior assumptions, science is impossible.

A key problem with utility maximization is that it is so general that it can explain anything; consequently, its explanatory power in specific instances is dramatically diminished. Its explanatory success is an illusion. Close inspection of its proclaimed achievements reveal that the results always depend on additional assumptions. For example, Gary Becker (1976b, 1991, 1996) contends that standard rationality assumptions generate a number of testable predictions concerning human behavior. But all of Becker's "predictions" depend on assumptions *additional* to his core axioms of utility maximization. Indeed, because it is difficult to conceive of evidence that falsifies these axioms, such models must depend on auxiliary assumptions to generate specific results. As Mark Blaug (1992, p. 232) puts it: "The rationality hypothesis by itself is rather weak. To make it yield interesting implications, we need to add auxiliary assumptions."

The notion of utility maximization is so capacious that it goes beyond the parameters of human decision. Experimental work with rats and other animals (Kagel et al. 1981; Kagel, Battalio, and Green 1995) has "revealed" that animals have downward-sloping demand curves, supposedly just like humans. Becker (1991, p. 307) proposes that "economic analysis is a powerful tool not only in understanding human behavior but also in understanding the behavior of other species." Similarly, Gordon Tullock (1994) has claimed that organisms—from bacteria to bears—can be treated as if they have the same general type of utility function that is attributed to humans in the microeconomics textbooks. Utility maximization is applied to humans in all forms of society since the origin of our species, and to a large portion of the animal kingdom as well. Seemingly, we now have "evidence" of the "rationality" of everything in evolution from the amoeba onward. As a consequence, such assumptions are telling us very little about what is specific to human nature and human society.

Arguably, human societies are partly differentiated from other animals in terms of developed institutions and cultures. The authors cited in the preceding paragraph thus demonstrate that these distinctive elements are effectively separated from the utility-maximizing picture of "rational economic man." Consequently "rational economic man" bears no mark of any specifically human culture or institution. The causal mechanisms through which culture and institutions mold and constrain human agents remain unexplored in their paradigm. Human psychology is likewise neglected. Essentially, there is no adequate and substantial theory of *human* agency at the core of the standard theory. It tells us nothing of significance that is specific to the human psyche, human interaction, human nature, or human society. With respect to specifically human characteristics, it is causally vacuous. Its very weakness, when applied to the human domain, stems from its excessive scope.

The nonfalsifiability of the concept of rationality-as-behavioral-consistency-or-utility-maximization sustains an *epistemic* critique. It does not clinch the matter. One has also to consider the *theoretical* limitations of this stance. Here rationality-as-behavioral-consistency-or-utility-maximization falls down for at least two reasons. First, it neglects the problem of *explaining the causes* of behavior. Second, it fudges the question of the individual *development* of capacities and dispositions.

In a prominent defense of rationally, Richard Posner makes his neglect of psychological or other causes of behavior explicit. Posner (1980, p. 5) sees the "rationality of 'economic man'" as "a matter of consequences, not states of mind." In discussing "economically rational" human agents, he declines "any statement about their conscious state. . . . [B]ehavior to an economist is a matter of consequences rather than intentions" (p. 53n). Here the problem of explaining behavior, by reference to psychology or other matters, is openly abandoned.

For related reasons, claims that there is an evolutionary basis for utility maximization (Robson 2001; Gintis 2006, p. 17) do not pass muster. It is insufficient to show that the behavioral outcomes of evolution are consistent with some utility function. Ultimately, this claim is trivially true because one can always find a function that fits. One has to show that utility maximization is useful causal account of behavioral motivation. This is problematic, for reasons elaborated below.

Indeed, it is rather odd to claim simultaneously that evolution has produced individuals who maximize utility and are also capable of altruism, as a consequence of inclusive fitness or whatever. Altruism is typically defined as costly for the individual concerned but beneficial for others. This sits uneasily with a utilitarian framework, and consequently the definition of altruism is out of equilibrium and has to be constantly clarified (e.g., Bowles and Gintis 2011, pp. 201–2). Utilitarians working in an evolutionary framework might awkwardly depict altruism as simultaneously involving a fitness cost and a utility gain for the agent, to preserve the near-vacuous dogma that all agents are utility maximizers.

Other defenders of rational economic man—notably Becker (1996)—treat the individual "as if" she is born with a sophisticated but fixed meta-preference function. The process of human development is then regarded as a matter of gradually acquiring information about underlying "true" tastes. Sure enough, some such meta-preference function can always be stretched and twisted to fit the data. But as an account of the developmental process, it is untenable. The fixed meta-preference function has no place in our current understanding of the neural system. Although many dispositions are inherited biologically, our further development from birth depends on the formation of many neural structures and connections, which are contingent on our environment and our past development. Although there is dispute concerning the details, psychologists and neuroscientists agree that there is considerable flexibility and plasticity in the developing brain (Penn and Shatz 1999; Marcus 2004; Sarnecki 2007). This neural flexibility and plasticity goes against the idea of an entirely inherited and fixed meta-preference function.

Placed within some versions of modern game theory, the "as if" argument is stretched beyond the limits of credulity. It is not simply assumed that agents act "as if" they are rational, but also that they act "as if" they consider the rationality of others, and "as if" others respond rationally with such common knowledge (and so on), somehow without necessarily making any assumptions about their deliberative behavior. Retaining the "as if" argument in this context requires us to treat individuals as capable of emulating incredible supercalculators with unbounded cognitive capacities, without any consideration of how they would manage to do this.

Past economists have tolerated the "as if" neglect of real phenomena, but it no longer satisfies scholars in this new age of exploration for evolutionary understandings of origin and development. We are interested specifically in the human mind and human social organization. We obtain little insight in this respect from overly capacious and unfalsifiable principles that apply to any organism or behavioral entity.

On the basis of experimental evidence, some neuroeconomists (Platt and Glimcher 1999; Glimcher, Dorris, and Bayer 2005) make the strong claim that the utility function exists as a physiological reality inside the brain. This claim is scrutinized by Jack Vromen (2010), who argues that at best the neurological evidence exhibits consistency with the predictions of expected utility theory. There is no evidence of actual computation of utility. Given the argument here that any observed outcomes can be made consistent with some utility function, the consistency claim is hardly powerful or surprising. But existence claims are unsupported. After an extensive review of the evidence, Colin F. Camerer, George Loewenstein, and Drazen Prelec (2005, pp. 54–55) are also skeptical of the claim that neuroscience supports a standard model of rational choice. The evidence that carries some weight relates to simple decisions only, not the "abstract, complex, long-term tradeoffs which are the traditional province of economic theory."

Overall, the long debate about whether behavior is "rational" has generated more heat than light. Sometimes the antagonists have misunderstood one another, particularly by confusing the falsifiable notion of payoff maximization with the unfalsifiable propositions of utility maximization or behavioral consistency. Since 1990, many leading members of the economics profession have abandoned payoff maximization. Yet the credo of rationality is preserved in the empty mantra of utility. In these terms, it tells us very little. Faced with this explanatory agenda, "rationality" in the broader sense of utility maximization is but a word of little consequence. By contrast, payoff rationality is more meaningful. But it turns out to be wrong.

The important task is to understand the nature and evolutionary origins of our human dispositions. Both genetic inheritance and cultural transmission are relevant to this quest. To understand the motion of the planets or the nature of matter is to comprehend the structures and forces that lie behind events, not to imagine spirits or gods that create every eventuality. To understand human nature and society is to appreciate human dispositions and interactions, not to fit all observations of behavior to imagined mathematical functions of ever-expandable correlative capacity. Rationality in the broader sense serves an ex post rationalization—rather than a materially grounded causal explanation. A utility function may serve a limited purpose as a formalized preference ordering. Such formal constructions have some benefits. They can be useful shortcuts for modeling or explanatory purposes. But they do not enhance our understanding of human motivation. Utility theory is an elegant way of summarizing what we don't know about human psychology.

Q: Why did the chicken cross the road? A: To maximize its utility. Some economists may be satisfied with this answer. But it tells us nothing about chickens, roads, specific motives, developmental histories, or detailed causal mechanisms. We should also be dissatisfied with summarizing all the complexities of human motivation in terms of a relatively simple preference function. As Sen (1977, pp. 335–36) has famously argued:[13]

> A person is given a preference ordering [that] is supposed to reflect his interests, represent his welfare, summarize his idea of what should be done, and describe his actual choices and behaviour. Can one preference ordering do all these things? A person thus described may be "rational" in the limited sense of revealing no inconsistencies in his choice behaviour, but if he has

13. Sen (1977, 1979, 1982, 1985a, 1985b, 1987a) argues for a complex meta-ranking of action sets. This differs from the evolution-driven, modular, habit- or program-based psychology adopted below.

no use for these distinctions between different concepts, he must be a bit of a fool.

3.3. The Games People Play

Game theory is a valuable heuristic tool. But ironically, predictions based on payoff rationality are often disconfirmed. This has profound implications for economics and the other social sciences.[14]

In 1950 at the RAND Corporation in Santa Monica, California, Melvin Dresher and Merrill Flood first described formally the Prisoner's Dilemma game (Flood 1958; Poundstone 1992; Field 2001). It was given its famous name by Albert W. Tucker. Its details are familiar.

Imagine that a Latin American revolution has been defeated, and Che and Fidel are imprisoned, isolated, and interrogated pending trial. Their known options are shown in table 1. Assume that each player regards death as the worst option, otherwise wishes to minimize his time in prison, and assumes that the other thinks accordingly.[15] Revolutionary ideals and self-sacrifice have been left behind on the barricades. Each prisoner knows that if he remains silent, then it is in the interests of the other to confess and go free, in which case the one who does not confess will be executed. Reasoning in these terms, they both confess and spend five years in jail. This is the Nash equilibrium. But if both players had remained silent, then both would have served lesser terms of two years. The Nash equilibrium does not yield optimal individual or collective benefits.

Does the Prisoner's Dilemma reflect genuine real-world predicaments? Arguably, it is representative of many social interactions. For example, traffic congestion is suboptimal and often it would be better to use public transport, but people continue to drive their cars, knowing that others are likely to do the same. This is similar to the famous "tragedy of the commons" (Hardin 1968). The employment contract has also been modeled as a Prisoner's Dilemma (Leibenstein 1982).

Imagine that you are transported to an extremely dangerous and lawless part of the world. Murders are frequent, and people are very suspicious of one another. You take a gun for your protection and leave all consid-

14. Sections 3.3 and 3.4 draw much from Field (2001). But in section 3.6, I question Field's explanatory reliance on genetic group selection.

15. Game theorists often assume that agents not only act to maximize their payoffs, but also assume that others will do the same. This is the "common knowledge of rationality" assumption. Aumann and Brandenburger (1995) show that the common knowledge of rationality assumption is not strictly necessary for a Nash equilibrium.

Table 1 Prisoner's Dilemma

	Outcome for Che	Outcome for Fidel
Both Che and Fidel remain silent	2 years in jail	2 years in jail
Che remains silent; Fidel confesses	Death	Freedom
Che confesses; Fidel remains silent	Freedom	Death
Both Che and Fidel confess	5 years in jail	5 years in jail

erations of morality in your home country; you are simply concerned to maximize your chances of survival. You assume that everyone else has the same sole objective. One foolhardy night, you walk alone down a street and dimly observe a stranger coming toward you. What should you do? You might speak and establish a rapport, but that would be too risky. Having dispensed with trust and morality, the solution is obvious—shoot the stranger because of the risk that he is about to kill you. You may also surmise that the stranger may fear what you might do to him, and it is thus doubly necessary for you to act immediately. This "game" is a form of the Prisoner's Dilemma, and the Nash strategy is "strike first."

If you believe that this is mere fiction, then consider the Cold War from 1949 to 1991. Both the West and East had nuclear weapons. The situation was similar to the fictional story in the previous paragraph. Leaving aside trust and morality, each side might maximize its chances of survival by the strategy of a first nuclear strike to eliminate the nuclear capacity of the other. John von Neumann, one of the pioneers of game theory, advocated this option. Von Neumann and Bertrand Russell joined military and political leaders in the "preventive war" movement, which advocated a nuclear first strike against the Soviet Union (Poundstone 1992). But the world was not plunged into nuclear war. This is chilling testimony that people and governments do not always play the Nash payoff solution (Field 2001).

A less chilling but equally important body of evidence comes from the first-ever laboratory experiment with the Prisoner's Dilemma using human subjects. Dresher and Flood wanted to know how intelligent humans would play this game. The subjects they chose were no less than the economist Armen Alchian and John Williams, chair of the mathematics department at RAND. They were offered two strategies: they could "cooperate" (equivalent to "remain silent" in table 1) or "defect" (equivalent to "confess" in table 1). Together they played one hundred sequential games.

Game theorists argue that the best strategy on the 100th game is to defect because the last game gives the other player no chance to retaliate. The strategic reasoning is thus identical on the 100th game to a one-shot play of the game. Having established this strategy for the 100th game, the line of attack for the 99th follows. Because each player assumes that the other will defect on the next game, the best strategy is to also defect on the current one. And so on. By so-called backward induction, the Nash solution for both players is to defect on *every* game.

Remarkably, these two highly intelligent players failed as rational payoff maximizers. Although Alchian defected on the first game, he cooperated 68 times. Mathematician Williams cooperated 78 times out of the 100. In reporting these results, Flood (1958, p. 16) remarked that "there was no tendency to seek as the final solution . . . the Nash equilibrium point." John Nash remarked "how inefficient" the two players were: "One would have thought them more rational" (quoted in ibid.).

Of course, one can pick holes in this early trial—the protocols of experimental design much improved in the following half century—but the early results remain compelling, particularly given the intellectual stature of the participants. Subsequent trials have also shown that many people do not defect, even when players are anonymous and the game is played once.[16] In an analysis of 37 different studies involving 130 experiments from 1958 to 1992, David Sally (1995) found an overall rate of cooperation of 47.4 percent of the entire pooled sample.

It is important to distinguish between experiments with a finite and indefinite number of repeated plays. Using indefinite repeated plays of the Prisoner's Dilemma, Robert Axelrod (1984) famously demonstrated the strength of a "tit-for-tat" strategy, where cooperation is met by a subsequent cooperation and defection punished by a subsequent defection. Tit-for-tat won in a tournament with leading game theorists and mathematicians as players. But the tit-for-tat strategy is neither dominant nor evolutionarily stable (Kitcher 1987; Lindgren 1992; Binmore 1998c). Nevertheless, tit-for-tat performed better than several strategies devised by economists seeking a rational maximization of payoffs.

The Prisoner's Dilemma contrasts in several ways from coordination games, which typically provide incentives for everyone to cooperate (Schotter 1981). Consequently, coordination equilibria can be self-policing and stable. Language is an example. In communication, we have strong incentives to use words in a way that conforms as closely as possible to the norm (Quine 1960). There are obvious incentives (apart from avoiding legal sanctions) to stop at red traffic lights and to drive on the same side of the road

16. See, for example, Marwell and Ames (1981), Schneider and Pommerehne (1981), Caporael et al. (1989), Davis and Holt (1993), Frey and Bohnet (1995), and Ledyard (1995).

as others. A coordination equilibrium can be sustained by self-regarding players. But once we leave the world of coordination games, self-regarding preferences are often not enough. Viktor Vanberg (1994, p. 65) has rightly pointed out that writers in the spontaneous order tradition—from Hume and Smith through Menger to Hayek—inadequately acknowledge the additional moral and legal mechanisms that are required for enforcement in noncoordination games.

Significantly, some animals have shown a greater disposition than humans to defect in Prisoner's Dilemma experiments. David W. Stephens, C. M. McLinn, and J. R. Stevens (2002) conducted experiments with blue jays. They are intelligent birds that cooperate within family groups. Two unrelated birds were paired and could repeatedly peck a "cooperative" or a "defect" key for food. Food payoffs followed the form of the Prisoner's Dilemma. The jays cooperated in limited circumstances only. Comparing this experiment with those involving humans, an orthodox economist must conclude that blue jays are more intelligent and rational!

Keith Jensen, Joseph Call, and Michael Tomasello (2007) conducted ultimatum game experiments with chimpanzees. They found that these social primates tended to play a Nash strategy and have much less inclination than humans to norms of sharing or fairness. Hence are chimpanzees more intelligent and rational than humans?

What these interspecies comparisons do show, in fact, is that something special about our species gives us a greater disposition to cooperate. This "something special" is not found in economists' general notions of rationality or utility maximization. The best that can be done with these is to bend the utility function to fit the specific facts.

In 1988, the *Journal of Economic Perspectives* published an article on cooperation by Robyn Dawes and Richard Thaler in its "Anomalies" section. Even then there was extensive evidence that people cooperate much more often than theories with rational payoff maximizers predict. This evidence covered Prisoner's Dilemma and other games. For example, in a Public Goods game, individuals in a group (of say ten) are each given (say) $10 and offered the choice of keeping the money for themselves or investing it for the public good. All the money invested is multiplied by (say) two and distributed equally to all the members of the group, whether they contributed or not. If everyone contributes, then each person will received $20. If only one contributes, then she will receive $2. If no one contributes, each member gets $10. A payoff maximizer will invest nothing because of the risk that less than five people will contribute. In the Nash equilibrium, there is no investor, and everyone takes $10. By contrast, Dawes and Thaler

(1988, p. 189) note that in a series of experiments about half the participants contributed. Subsequent work (Hoffman, McCabe, and Smith 1998; Ostrom 1998) yields varied results, but no experimental study confirms the Nash prediction of an overall zero contribution.

Since the 1988 article by Dawes and Thaler, an enormous amount of experimental evidence has accumulated to undermine the idea that individuals are generally payoff maximizers (e.g., Bowles and Gintis 2005b, 2011; Camerer 2003; Henrich et al. 2001, 2004; Gowdy 2004; Gintis et al. 2005; Camerer and Fehr 2006). This evidence is so overwhelming that any social scientist should seek an alternative to the payoff maximization model of individual behavior.[17] Many economists have abandoned "economic man" and joined in the quest.[18]

3.4. The Inadequacy of Biology-Free Explanations

Many social scientists claim that altruism and associated values such as sympathy are acquired culturally: we learn them through the process of socialization. Can the social sciences step in to provide adequate explanations of the high degree of cooperation—including with nonkin—observed within human societies? Economics has often sidestepped such problems by simply taking our preferences as given. Can sociology, cultural anthropology, or social psychology fill the breach?

A traditional sociological and anthropological tenet is that any altruistic dispositions are learned in cultural settings. Our dispositions are products of our cultural circumstances, which include constraints on behavior, forms of punishment including disapproval, and rewards such as status and power. Social psychologists provide rich experimental evidence of how our preferences and beliefs can be molded by social circumstances.

These explanations are not necessarily wrong. Substantial evidence supports the role of culture, particularly when we look at behavioral phenomena that vary greatly from one culture to another (Ehrlich 2000). The difficulty is that cultural explanations of cooperation assume at the outset the

---

17. A possible exception is Bruce Bueno de Mesquita's (2009) allegedly successful use of game theory and the assumption of self-interest to predict political and international developments. But even if valid, his models generally apply to groups rather than individuals. As explained below, there are good evolutionary reasons why groups may be selfish but individuals within them are more altruistic. Properties of groups are not necessarily individual properties writ large.

18. Notably Akerlof and Shiller (2009) and Thaler and Sunstein (2008) rely on psychological insights rather than bland "rationality."

existence of a social culture with norms conducive to cooperation. It is not shown how such a culture becomes established in the first place. Much of cooperation is an outcome of enculturation, but we cannot simply assume a culture with cooperative norms. We need an explanation of the origin of that culture. Before such a culture existed, it would be highly unlikely for a critical mass of cooperating individuals to become established. Any such emergent group would be highly vulnerable to invasion by free riders, cheats, or opportunists. A wholly cultural explanation cannot get off the ground.

In his perceptive study of Émile Durkheim, Paul Q. Hirst (1975) reminds us that explanations of origin and of persistence are both required and should not be conflated. Similarly, Alexander Field (2001, p. 49n) criticizes "the inappropriate attribution of mechanisms that may be sustaining cooperation to the explanation of its origin." Much of sociology and cultural anthropology is about the explanation of persistence: the focus is on how particular structures and norms are sustained and how they may develop thereafter. Social psychology considers our minds and behavior in the context of an assumed cultural configuration. As well as understanding how individuals are influenced by culture, we need an explanation of how particular cultures originated.

Explanations of origin are not simply relevant for the evolutionary long ago. Numerous natural and human disasters in our history have led to local collapses in social institutions, where people have resorted to brutish and less cooperative behavior. The factors that led to the original evolution of a cooperative culture also become relevant when that culture breaks down and has to be restored.

But some social scientists resist explanations of origin, and we need to deal briefly with their objections. All science is about explanation. Underlying our quest for explanations is the *principle of determinacy*. It means: "*Everything is determined in accordance with laws by something else*" (Bunge 1959, p. 26). This ontological statement cannot itself be verified by observation or experiment. Yet it is central to all science. If science admits the possibility of an event without a cause, then it has abandoned its own mission.[19]

Why would social scientists resist the principle of determinacy and the

19. Bunge (1959) argues that stochastic determination—as in quantum physics—is also causal determination. The "principle of determinacy" is sometimes described as "determinism." But this word has other very different meanings, and sloppy and undefined accusations of "determinism" plague the social sciences. Hodgson (2004a, 2004b, pp. 57–62) identifies three distinct varieties of "determinism" and argues that one (the "principle of determinacy") is true; that "predictability determinism" (the future is predictable) is generally false; and "reg-

search for causal explanations in the social sciences? One problem is a reluctance to consider the causes of human choices or dispositions because of a belief in human autonomy, agency, and responsibility, and a further belief that these are inconsistent with causation. But if our choices were uncaused, then they would be no more under our conscious control. It is unconvincing to suggest that individual agency or choice is incompatible with its own causation. It is also unpersuasive to suggest that human agency could somehow emerge in evolution via the creation of a miraculous, causality-free zone.[20]

By asserting that culture provides a sufficient explanation, some social scientists claim that biology has no part to play in the explanation of human cooperation. But they fail to explain the very origins of cultural norms. We have to explain how culture evolves and what precultural dispositions gave it initial form. In part, emergence of culture must have relied on biologically transmitted dispositions. These dispositions would have evolved over millions of years, and they must remain with us today, notwithstanding the additional importance of culture.

Consider the evidence of human cultural and normative universals (Roberts 1979; Haidt and Joseph 2004; Nichols 2004). Donald E. Brown (1991) describes more than 400 statistical regularities in every known culture. These include ideas of fairness and taking turns, admiration for generosity, condemnation of murder and rape, restrictions on violence, concepts of property and inheritance, and distinctions between actions that are willed and actions that are not under self-control. Similarly, Shalom H. Schwartz (1994) identified a set of values that were nearly universal in 44 countries. The idea that lying is wrong is found in virtually all religions (S. Bok 1978). Michael Walzer (1994) and Sissela Bok (1995) thus propose that there is a universal minimal morality. These human universals endure despite the power of culture and immense cultural variation in

---

ularity determinism" (event X is always followed by event Y) is strictly of little practical use, even if true, because then X would have to describe a complete state of the universe.

20. Rejecting what he vaguely describes as "determinism," Lanse Minkler (2008, p. 21) writes: "Determinism is the opposite of autonomy, which means free of external causes." His "autonomy" implies that there are no external causes acting on human volitions: they are purely spontaneous developments within the individual's mind. Vromen (2001) shows that the fact that intentions are caused does not mean that human agency is any less substantial or real. Some argue that if our will is determined, then we cannot be held responsible for our choices and actions, and hence there can be no basis for morality or law. But if our will is determined, then moral pressure and legal sanctions still can have an effect on our actions. Consequently, there is no ground for abandoning morality or law. Even if our will was an "uncaused cause," we would be no more responsible for the capricious and spontaneous processes that led to our actions.

other respects. Given that they are not mere coincidence, we may consider that these universals are longstanding and have had some fitness value for humans. If so, they may also have acquired some biological roots through natural selection.

In a related vein, the human ethologist Irenäus Eibl-Eibesfeldt (1989) has documented the universality of many human facial expressions and gestures across different cultures, confirming the pioneering work of Charles Darwin in his *Expression of the Emotions in Man and Animals* (1872). Just as Darwin believed that this evidence supports the idea of human descent from a common ancestor, it also supports the notion of a common biological basis of many emotions. Our capacity to reason requires emotional input (Damasio 1994; Bechara and Damasio 2005). Some emotions, in turn, act as forces to sustain moral judgments, as discussed in the following chapter.

Studies of the human brain offer more evidence. The neuroeconomist Paul J. Zak (2004) has shown that oxytocin levels in the brain are related to levels of trust. Studies have also identified the neural processes associated with prosocial dispositions (Fehr and Camerer 2007; Vercoe and Zak 2010). There is also evidence that human decision making in social dilemmas relies on areas of the brain connected with emotions, as well as in the prefrontal cortex. Moral judgments are not exclusive to the deliberative prefrontal cortex but relate also to several other brain areas, some of early evolutionary origin (Greene and Haidt 2002; Tancredi 2005).

All this growing evidence suggests that there are some neural, biological, and evolutionary foundations for our dispositions to cooperate. It should lead us to consider evolutionary explanations of the human propensity to cooperate in specific situations.

Both selfish *homo economicus* and culturally driven *homo sociologicus* are challenged by recent research. Human nature is not a tabula rasa on which cultures write values and goals. Neither does society cohere simply on the basis of self-interest. No single discipline is able unaided to solve the problem of cooperation. Explaining human cooperation involves multidisciplinary cooperation.

3.5. Biological Explanations: Kin Altruism and Reciprocity

The biologist William Hamilton (1964) famously proposed a theory of kin-based altruism using the idea of "inclusive fitness." If natural selection operates principally on genes, then a gene that disposed the individual to altruism—even when there was a cost or risk for that individual—could be selected as long as the altruistic behavior aided sufficient relatives sharing enough of the same genes. Two (nonidentical) brothers share half their genes. Consequently, a person who risked his life to save two of his brothers would not be reducing the frequency of his genes in the overall population.

Kin altruism seems to be a major reason why many animals look after their young, and helps to explain the caring affection that humans have for members of their own family. But altruism in human society goes much further. Kin altruism alone cannot explain the huge degree of cooperation in very large and diverse human societies and the many specific acts of generosity and self-sacrifice toward people who are not closely related (Frank 1988; Field 2001, 2007, 2008; Henrich 2004).

A prominent additional gene-based explanation is *reciprocal altruism*: dispositions to aid others evolve when there is a sufficiently high probability that such acts will be reciprocated (J. Friedman 1971; Trivers 1971). Reciprocal altruism has been modeled in various ways. To work it requires a sufficiently high probability that individuals will repeat their interaction and also often a critical mass of cooperators to get the process going. Robert Trivers (1971) and others have argued that kin groups may provide this critical mass and then trigger more widespread cooperative behavior through reciprocal altruism.

But researchers point to relatively few examples of reciprocal altruism in the animal world (Hammerstein 2003a, 2003b). By contrast, strong evidence supports the "you scratch my back, I'll scratch yours" disposition in human society. Note also Robert Axelrod's (1984) demonstration of the frequent viability of the tit-for-tat strategy within the Prisoner's Dilemma.

While reciprocal altruism may account for the maintenance and spread of human cooperation between neighbors in small communities or groups, it cannot explain large-scale cooperation in modern, complex societies. Some limited but significant degree of large-scale cooperation is evident in cohesive national units, in large corporations, armies, and other organizations. This cannot be entirely caused by reciprocal altruism because with random meetings in large populations the probability of meeting the same person again is small. Warranted expectations of reciprocal reward are low. Despite this, people still leave tips in restaurants that they are unlikely to visit again, and they help strangers in infrequently visited locations a long way from home. It is difficult to explain such commonplace behavior through reciprocal altruism.

Robert Sugden (1986) and Richard Alexander (1987) independently proposed a more general mechanism to maintain cooperation, usually termed *indirect reciprocity*, which takes account of the reputations of individuals for cooperation or selfishness in a group. It is assumed that individuals will cooperate with members of their group only if other members have a sufficiently strong reputation for cooperating. There is both theoretical and empirical evidence that under some conditions this group mechanism may help to sustain cooperation in human societies (Milinski, Semmann, and Krambeck 2002; Panchanathan and Boyd 2003, 2004; Nowak and Sigmund 2005; Nowak 2006).

But generally the simulations involved show that the conditions to establish and maintain cooperative reputations are quite stringent. There are many different systems of assessing other individuals and developing their reputations (Uchida and Sigmund 2009). The results of simulations depend crucially on the rules used to establish a reputation and what behaviors are remembered by others. In some simulations, errors and incomplete information make the group vulnerable to invasion by defectors, who exploit the goodwill of others and swamp the group. In these cases, the mechanism of indirect reciprocity depends on adequate and reliable information that may not be obtained in many interactions. Experiments by Dirk Engelman and Urs Fischbacher (2009, p. 399) consider the possibility that a limited number of individuals may act strategically to build up a cooperative reputation. In these circumstances, they find that strategic do better than nonstrategic players and nonreciprocating do better than reciprocating players, thus "casting doubt on previously proposed evolutionary explanations for indirect reciprocity."

It is too early to pass a final judgment on this rapidly expanding literature on indirect reciprocity. But the overall impression is that the outcomes of the theoretical models vary enormously according to the chosen assumptions. And as yet, there is inadequate evidence or protocol to discriminate between one set of assumptions and another. The models that establish the evolution of cooperation through indirect reciprocity depend critically on particular assumptions, and the validation of these assumptions is often rudimentary.

Given that there must be a biological mechanism to explain a critical mass of cooperators, the most straightforward possibilities are kin selection and direct reciprocity. The problem is that these alone cannot explain cooperation in large groups. Can group selection provide the answer? This is the topic of the next section.

3.6. Prosocial Preferences and Group Selection

A number of experiments provide evidence for "social preferences" or "other-regarding preferences" in large groups (Bowles 1998, 2004; Field 2001; Fehr and Fischbacher 2002; Bowles and Gintis 2005a, 2005b, 2011; Charness and Rabin 2002). As Samuel Bowles (2004, p. 109, emphasis removed) elaborates: "The key aspect of other other-regarding preferences is that one's evaluation of a state depends on how it is experienced by others." The experiments reveal other-regarding preferences beyond kin and other small groups. So how can such prosocial behavior be explained?

A crucial issue is whether dispositions to cooperate are inherited biologically, as well as enhanced culturally. Alexander Field (2001, 2007, 2008) argues that altruistic and cooperative dispositions must have a biological origin. Without this, they could not become established. He argues convincingly that culture may explain the persistence of cooperation but cannot show how a critical mass of cooperators among a population of selfish individuals emerged. Field concludes that cooperation must have a biological basis and that the mechanism involved is genetic group selection. Samuel Bowles and Herbert Gintis (2005a, 2005b, 2011) reach a similar conclusion, both by asserting a biological foundation for prosocial dispositions and by invoking group selection as the mechanism by which it emerged.

Is group selection viable in principle? Darwin (1871) originally promoted the idea. Much later it fell out of favor, after criticisms by George C. Williams (1966), Richard Dawkins (1976), and others. If individuals had dispositions to cooperate in a group, then that group could be invaded by free riders who would benefit from this cooperation but fail to reciprocate themselves. The free riders would not bear the costs of cooperation, and natural selection would mean that they would eventually drive out the cooperators.

It is important to distinguish between *genetic group selection* and *cultural group selection* (Henrich 2004). *Genetic* group selection is a process where groups are the objects of selection, and genes are addressed as the causes of variation. *Cultural* group selection is a process where groups are also the objects of selection, but cultural and informational mechanisms (such as individual habits and social customs) are addressed as the sources of variation.

The distinction between replicators and interactors—developed by David Hull (1988) from Dawkins's (1976) replicator-vehicle distinction—is useful to help understand the two different types of selection. Interactors are objects of selection in a population, and changes in the gene pool are among the outcomes of such selection.[21] Replicators are essentially informational mechanisms. Interactors are relatively cohesive entities that host replicators. In the biological struggle for existence, the selection of organisms (interactors) as objects leads to differential selection of genes (replicators) as outcomes. With genetic group selection, the selection of groups (interactors) as objects leads to selection of genes (replicators) as outcomes. With cultural group selection, the selection of groups (interactors) as objects leads to selection of *sociocultural replicators* as outcomes. Sociocultural replicators include habits, customs, and organizational routines (Aldrich et al. 2008; Hodgson and Knudsen 2010).

In his rigorous analysis of genetic and cultural group selection, Joseph Henrich (2004) shows that the process of genetic group selection can be partitioned into the effects of between-group variation and the effects of within-group variation caused by individual migration or other factors that tend to increase variation within groups. Consequently, genetic group selection becomes a stronger force when migration is limited or when other constraints maintain or enhance between-group variation.[22]

In principle, both genetic and cultural group selection are possible. It depends on the relative effects of inter- and intragroup variation. Many former arguments against genetic group selection relied on overly restrictive assumptions.[23] But admitting such a possibility in principle does not mean that it is significant in (past or present) reality.

Powerful arguments suggest that cultural group selection has been a major factor in the development of human cooperation (Boyd and Richerson 1985; Henrich 2004). The key point is that cultural transmission effects can generate high degrees of conformism and cooperation within groups and overcome factors, such as individual migration, that tend to increase variation within groups.

21. Sober (1984) established the distinction between selection *of* and selection *for*, where he considered selection *for* traits and selection *of* genes. But in Hodgson and Knudsen (2010), we relate Sober's terms more closely to the replicator-interactor distinction. Accordingly, we wrote of selection *of* interactors and selection *for* replicators such as genes. Jack Vromen noted this divergence, and we should have made our different usage more explicit. Richard Goode and Paul E. Griffiths (1995) argue that Sober's distinction has been misused by other authors.

22. Wilson and Wilson (2007) show that group selection arguments share many key features with theories of both kin altruism and reciprocal altruism.

23. See Wade (1976, 1978), Wilson (1980, 1983, 1999), Wilson and Sober (1994), Sober and Wilson (1998), and Wilson and Wilson (2007). In particular, it was assumed that migration into groups was unrestricted and that the selection of individuals is insensitive to the fitness of the population as a whole.

But our search here is for a genetic foundation for the emergence of altruism. Because we cannot take cultural conditions as given, we must turn to their biological and psychological underpinnings. So in this context, we must consider the viability of genetic group selection.

Individual migration between groups, and other processes that diminish the genetic variation between groups or increase variation within groups, tend to undermine the effectiveness of genetic group selection. If migration were unbounded and extensive, then extensive genetic mixing would occur, and the genetic variation within groups would approach the level of genetic variation in the population as a whole. In these circumstances, the groups would have few differentiating genetic features, and genetic group selection would be a weak force. By contrast, if migration is constrained, then genetic differences between groups can be maintained. This is a necessary but insufficient condition for genetic group selection to occur.

Has genetic group selection occurred among humans in a way that would allow genetic prosocial dispositions to evolve? Field (2001) claims that group selection must have occurred, but does not consider the conditions for its operation. Bowles and Gintis (2005b, 2011) consider mathematical models and refer to some evidence (Bowles 2006), but they do not demonstrate decisively that genetic group selection of prosocial dispositions has occurred.

While genetic group selection is theoretically possible, so far we lack clear empirical evidence on the extent of its operation and on whether it is the foundation of human cooperation. We have very little direct evidence on the composition of groups of early humanoids and of migration patterns between these groups. But the evidence from living primates is powerful. Frans de Waal (2006, p. 16) points out that

> in all of the primates, the younger generation of one sex or another (males in many monkeys, females in chimpanzees and bonobos) tends to leave the group and join neighboring groups. . . . This means that primate groups are far from genetically isolated, which makes [genetic] group selection unlikely.

This evidence from primates undermines the idea that we have genetic prosocial dispositions acquired through genetic group selection from our ape-like past.

A study of contemporary human hunter-gatherer groups (Hill et al. 2011) revealed migration patterns where either sex may disperse or remain in their natal group. It also established a relatively low level of genetic relatedness within groups. Although inclusive fitness would help to explain cooperation between closely related family members within groups, it does not seem viable as an explanation at the group level, where learning and culture must be relied on to do much of the explanatory work.

Overall, the evidence we have from primates and contemporary hunter-gatherers undermines genetic group selection as an explanation of the origins of cooperation. But the question is still open because evidence on primates or humans today is not evidence about prehistoric humans.

Numerous conjectures are possible. The reasons why primates of one sex migrate from one group to another may not be genetic. They could be the result of protocultural influences that were absent or suppressed in early human societies. Bowles and Gintis (2011, pp. 51–52) consider other possibilities, including "tribe splitting" where subgroups with larger numbers of altruists split off and reduced within-group variation. They also hypothesize that fatalities from intergroup warfare increased as humans developed weapons, thus enhancing the survival advantages of group cooperation (pp. 102–6). But much of this is speculative. With the present level of knowledge and understanding, it is unwarranted to explain cooperation principally on the basis of genetic group selection.[24]

We are left with a conundrum. With empirically grounded doubts about the degree of genetic group selection in this context, it may seem that we have reached an impasse. Biology-free explanations cannot account for a critical mass of cooperators. Mechanisms leading to the genetic group selection of cooperative behaviors are speculative. Forms of reciprocity may be relevant, but they depend critically on assumed parameters. Cultural group selection gives us a good explanation of how cooperation may be sustained and reinforced, but it cannot explain the emergence of a critical mass of cooperators.

It seems warranted to suppose that cultural group selection was an important force, and genetic group selection was undermined by migration between groups of early humans. But there must be some biological triggers for cooperative behavior that help explain both the existence of cultural universals and the emergence of a critical mass of cooperation in human groups.

Craig T. Palmer and Lyle B. Steadman (1997), Frans de Waal (2006), and others have suggested that mechanisms of kin altruism and then recip-

---

24. Bowles and Gintis (2011) often conflate genetic and cultural group selection, partly because they fail to deploy key concepts developed by philosophers of biology such as the replicator-interactor distinction (Hull 1988), or the differences between *causes, objects* and *outcomes* of selection (Sober 1984, Hodgson and Knudsen 2010). When it comes to the crunch (e.g., Bowles and Gintis 2011, pp. 126–28, 197–98), they deploy a combination of genetic and cultural mechanisms and do not rely on genetic group selection alone.

rocal altruism account for levels of cooperation that spread further through cultural means, particularly through the inculcation of behavioral norms in children by parents. This suggests that there are genetic triggers for cooperative behavior, which are selected among individuals who are closely related genetically. But once these triggers are present in a wider group, cultural transmission leads to their enhancement and dispersion. Mechanisms of cooperation are part inherited and part developed in cultural settings (Simon 1990). The idea that the explanation of cooperation or morality must be *either* cultural *or* biological is flawed. An adequate explanation of these phenomena must involve both.[25]

The experiments on chimpanzees by Jensen, Call, and Tomasello (2007) suggest that our ape-like ancestors may have made less use of norms of sharing or fairness, despite living in relatively cohesive social groups. A crucial factor may have been the specific development within human societies of durable family groups, where kin altruism would have developed more strongly.[26] The evolution of a sophisticated human culture also would be vital for the establishment of these norms. But we must also explain their earlier evolutionary origins in supportive, instinctive emotions. Here we must turn to explanations based on inclusive fitness and reciprocity in smaller family units.

Both genetic and cultural mechanisms are required to explain the evolution of cooperation, although there is no consensus yet on the details. The deployment of universal and purportedly explanatory notions, such as rationality or preference functions, masks the plurality of mechanisms and distracts us from their examination. We need to consider more directly the social, psychological, and evolutionary mechanisms involved.

3.7. Beyond Preferences: Modularity and Program-Based Behavior

Cooperative dispositions are a consequence of a long evolutionary history (over millions of years) and the rapid development and enculturation of

25. J. McKenzie Alexander (2007) seems to make this flawed either-or presumption in his discussion of the evolution of morality.

26. Rodseth et al. (1991, p. 221) propose on the basis of comparative anthropological and primatological evidence that "the human social pattern unites conjugal families within 'atomistic' communities. Humans are the only primates that maintain lifelong relationships with dispersing offspring; both sexes therefore remain embedded in networks of consanguineal kin." Migration and dispersion still increase within-group variation, and alliances between groups become more likely.

each individual from birth (typically within two decades), involving both inherited and context-dependent developments in the brain, and multiple mechanisms and levels. This sits very uneasily with the concept of all-purpose rationality based on a fixed and encompassing preference function.

We need to seek inspiration from different perspectives. Evolutionary psychologists argue that the evolution of the human brain over millions of years in social and hunter-gatherer contexts has equipped the brain with specific mental modules that apply to specific problems and circumstances. Rather than an all-purpose calculator, this evolutionary perspective points to a modular brain consisting of many special-purpose and domain-specific mechanisms (Fodor 1983; Cosmides 1989; Cosmides and Tooby 1994a, 1994b; Carruthers and Chamberlain 2000). The work of anthropologist Dan Sperber (2005) and philosopher John Sarnecki (2007) also provides strong support to the notion of evolved mental modules. There is a dispute within this field on the number and nature of the modules involved, but we do not need to adjudicate on this here. What is important is to accept that evolution has not provided all with all-purpose, context independent, deliberative capacities. Instead, natural selection has equipped us with a number of modules for specific circumstances. The modern modularity literature is redolent of the instinct-habit psychology of William James (1890) and others, who also viewed the human mind from a Darwinian evolutionary perspective (Richards 1987; Barbalet 2008).

Another way of describing these modules is *programs*. The biologist Ernst Mayr (1988, p. 45) defines "teleonomic" or "program-based" behavior as that which *"owes its goal-directedness to the operation of a program."* Such behavior is governed by connected, rule-like dispositions, similar to a computer program. There remain enormous differences between a human mind and a computer, but they share this common, rule-driven or program-based characteristic. Vanberg (2000, 2002, 2004) elaborates Mayr's argument and shows that it provides a powerful alternative to the rationality concept. The assumption that human behavior is determined by a rational appraisal of interests or a given preference function lacks an adequate scientific explanation of the origin or operation of these rational capacities or preferences. The mental technology of rationality is assumed rather than explained.

By contrast, the program-based approach relies on evolutionary theory to explain the origin of systems of rule-like dispositions, which are either inherited as instincts or acquired as habits in a historically specific cultural setting. Generally, the human problem-solving capacity that rational choice theory attributes to "rationality" is explained in the Darwinian terms by the knowledge of the world that is incorporated in rules or programs that guide behavior. This knowledge has been accumulated through trial and error in the processes of human evolution and individual learning.

Understanding the human mind in terms of multiple modules or programs, which are part inherited and part developed in a cultural context, provides a perspective that is very different from the preference function of the pleasure machine. In the following chapter, we consider particular, morally salient modules that are vital in establishing social cohesion. A key difference between the preference function and program-based perspectives is that the former upholds a singular objective, whereas the latter sustains multiple incommensurable motives. The individual is no longer a utility maximizer. She becomes a conscious being, adjudicating between often-conflicting dispositions, where conversation and deliberative judgment are often vital in making a choice between conflicting sentiments or considerations (Dewey 1922).

The response of the utilitarian economist is predictable. He would argue that as long as behavior is consistent, then it can be "explained" in terms of a single preference function. One response, as elaborated above, is to point out that such a claim is unfalsifiable. The preference function can always be stretched to fit the data. Unfalsifiability means that in principle all behavioral outcomes—including the behavior of robots or other organisms—can fit the theory. The illusory triumph of this theory provides an excuse to ignore psychology. In turn, this means that key features of the *human* psyche, including the capacity for conscious deliberation and the mechanisms of social cooperation, are omitted.

Another problem worth emphasizing is the failure of the unitary, preference-based approach to capture adequately the development of each individual, as she learns and adapts in the light of experience. Because the preference function can fit every eventuality, the tendency has been to abandon any notion of changing preferences and to suppose that we are all born with super-duper meta-preference functions that serve us adequately for the rest of our lives (Becker 1976b, 1996). In more ways than one, preference functions are insufficiently evolutionary.

Crucially, these defective perspectives focus on manifest behavior rather than the dispositions and mechanisms that cause behavior. The utility function—with or without other-regarding preferences—is an ex post rationalization of behavior rather than an explanation of its causes.

For these reasons, "other-regarding preferences" is an inadequate concept to deal with the problem of explaining human cooperation. Furthermore, the language of preference is always vulnerable to a hedonist counterattack. "Other-regarding" preferences are still preferences and interpreted in terms of utility maximization. The "other-regarding" individual is still maximizing *his own* utility. It is but a tiny step to claim that "other-regarding" behavior is also a form of selfish, utility-maximizing behavior. This is a major weakness: the very ideas of cooperative or altruistic behavior are robbed of much of their meaning. By contrast, the modular and program-based perspective provides a niche for layered dispositions and acquired moral sentiments, as particular modules, programs, or rules (Vanberg 2008). Morality is not reduced to utility.

At least so far, attempts to explain human cooperation in terms of utility or preferences have been found wanting. We are led to the conclusion that the explanation of cooperation and social order requires additional ingredients. The foremost of these is morality. The nature and function of moral sentiments is the subject of the next chapter.

FOUR

The Nature of Morality

A moral being is one who is capable of comparing his past and future actions or motives, and of approving or disapproving of them. We have no reason to suppose that any of the lower animals have this capacity. . . . [M]an . . . alone can be certainty be ranked as a moral being.

—Charles Darwin (1871)

Construction of a persuasive rational basis for behaving morally has been the problem on which most moral philosophers have stubbed their toes. I believe they will continue to do so until they recognize what Chinese philosophers have known for a long time: namely feeling, not logic, sustains the superego.

—Jerome Kagan (1984)

The two quotations that begin this chapter highlight important issues concerning morality: its emotional fuel, and its transcendence of pure emotion through its dependence on deliberative evaluation and communication. The quotation from Darwin, whose work remains an inspiration for an evolutionary analysis of morality, points to a crucial feature of morality proper. Darwin understood that some social "lower animals" have proto-moral sentiments. Nature does not make leaps, and morality must have evolved from something. But without language and extensive deliberative evaluation, a fully developed moral capacity is impossible. The second quotation emphasizes the emotional impulses behind moral sentiments, which must partly involve inherited dispositions that are likely to be partially sustained through inclusive fitness and reciprocity, before being vastly enhanced cultural settings.

Regarding ethics, between Darwin and Adam Smith lies an important connection. Although the popular view is that both Smith and Darwin were apologists for self-interested individualism and market competition, they both stressed sympathy and the role of morality. Darwin's early notebooks (Gruber 1974; Vorzimmer 1977) show that in 1838 and 1839 he read Adam Smith's *Theory of Moral Sentiments*. (But there is no evidence that he ever read the *Wealth of Nations*.) The moral side of Smith's economics inspired Darwin. Furthermore, a forensic reading of Smith's work reveals harbingers of Darwin's evolutionary argument (Wight 2009). Both Smith and Darwin are icons for twenty-first-century work on the origins of morality.

As noted in previous chapters, much of the recent theoretical work by economists that attempts to explain cooperation in the real world conflates issues of morality with altruism or cooperation under the description of "social" or "other-regarding" preferences (Bowles and Gintis 2011; Camerer and Fehr 2006; Charness and Rabin 2002; Fehr and Camerer 2007). To some extent, Bruno Frey (1992, 1997a, 1997b) undermines this with his distinction between extrinsic and intrinsic motivation. Morality seems to relate more closely to the latter than the former—although it also relates to (extrinsic) outcomes, it is primarily about the action itself. Morally "doing the right thing" is more about the doing than what is done. As Viktor Vanberg (2008, p. 608) shows, once we distinguish between preferences over outcomes and preferences over actions, then morally motivated behavior cannot fit into the former category:

> There is . . . a significant difference between claiming, on the one hand, that agents evaluate outcomes not only in terms of their own narrowly defined interests but also in terms of how they affect the well-being of other persons, and claiming, on the other hand, that agents are motivated to act in accordance with ethical rules or principles of fairness.

The incapacity of the standard utilitarian calculus—or even the language of preferences—to depict adequately the nature of morality becomes even more evident if we consult ethical philosophy.

I shall rely on extensive discussions of philosophers such as John L. Mackie (1977) and Richard Joyce (2006) to sketch the meaning of moral judgment. Emphatically, the aim here is neither to establish nor promote a *valid* morality. Instead, the goal in the following section is to identify the features of what may be described as a moral judgment, whether agreeable, defensible or otherwise.

These criteria provide a benchmark against which some other approaches are briefly compared. Further sections of this chapter consider the evolution of a moral sense among humans. Doctrines of *moral naturalism* and *moral realism* are then scrutinized, leading to a rejection of the former and an open verdict on the latter.

4.1. What Is Morality?

Students of economics are taught in best-selling textbooks that "normative economics . . . involves ethical precepts and norms of fairness," but regarding these "ethics and values" there are "no right or wrong answers" (Samuelson and Nordhaus 2001, pp. 7–8). It is all a matter of taste or preference. Ethics and morality are thus doubly degraded. First, they are rendered indistinguishable from any other kind of normative claim: injunctions against murder are given the same moral status as table manners. Second, the possibility that one system of morality is superior to another is ruled out. Anything goes. And gone, for example, is any claim that legislation on vital matters such as human rights can have ethical grounding.

Morality is complex and controversial.[1] Many issues of dispute divide moral philosophers, and modern meta-ethics reveals a tangled web of classifications. The best we can do here is to pick up rather selectively some relevant threads in some prominent descriptions of the nature of moral judgment.

The leading moral philosopher Richard M. Hare (1952) argued that morality was subject to reason and one cannot hold contradictory ethical judgments. He also maintained that any normative judgment was inherently universalizable in the context to which it pertained, in the sense that anyone proclaiming an "ought" in a particular context was committed to prescribing a similar normative judgment for anyone in any relevantly similar situation. As Mackie (1977, p. 33) put it in his classic account, a moral judgment

---

1. Some academic writers draw a difference between *ethics* and *morality*, where morality is based on notions such as duty and obligation, reserving ethics for more practical matters concerning virtue. Nevertheless, throughout this book I treat them as synonyms. All moral or ethical values are *normative*. But the latter term has also the weaker meaning of following a rule because it is convenient or more efficient, without any imputation of duty, obligation, or moral virtue. I follow most moral philosophers in regarding these special attributes of morality as important. But beyond this, it is unnecessary for the purposes of this work to take sides on the different ways in which ethical principles may be justified, such as the distinction between deontic ethics and virtue ethics (Staveren 2007).

is not purely descriptive, certainly not inert, but something that involves a call for action or for the refraining from action, and one that is absolute, not contingent upon any desire or preference or policy or choice, his own or anyone else's.

In his major philosophical account of the *Evolution of Morality*, Joyce (2006, p. 70) argues on the basis of considerations in the philosophical literature that morality has most or all of the following characteristics.[2]

1   Moral judgments express attitudes (such as approval or contempt) and also express beliefs.
2   The emotion of guilt is an important mechanism for regulating moral conduct.
3   Moral judgments transcend the interests or ends of those concerned.
4   Moral judgments imply notions of desert and justice.
5   Moral judgments are inescapable.[3]
6   Moral judgments transcend human conventions.
7   Moral judgments govern interpersonal relations and counter self-regarding individualism.

These characteristics do not establish a *valid* morality; they instead help us to identify what is a *moral judgment*, whether acceptable or otherwise. Most religions involve moral claims, but that does not make them right or just. Point (1) establishes that a moral judgment must involve both beliefs and sentiments, and is not reducible to either alone. If an action is impelled purely by emotion and sentiment, then—as Darwin understood—it cannot amount to moral motivation. Deliberations and beliefs are also vital, but are themselves insufficient because they must be backed by sentiments or emotions: acting morally is more than conscious conformity to moral rules.[4]

2. For a much fuller discussion, see Joyce (2006, chap. 2), on which this section relies.

3. Joyce does not explain whether "inescapable" can apply to judgments that are group-specific. Can a normative rule in a community that is applied exclusively to one gender, age range, or ethnic group be a *moral* claim? (We are not requiring it to be a *valid* moral claim.) Many religions have gender-specific injunctions in their codes of morality. Broadening the criteria of what is a moral claim to include group-specific injunctions does little damage to the argument that follows. We may believe in moralities that treat all people equally, but that is a statement about what is *morally valid*, not a definition or description of *possible moralities*.

4. Economists and other social scientists have become interested in the general role of emotions. See Frank (1988, 1993), Elster (1998), Loewenstein (2000), Barbalet (2001, 2008), Bechara and Damasio (2005), Cohen (2005), Zizzo (2008).

Moral judgments may be rationalized in various ways, but they are more than matters of propositional belief or logical syllogism. Defiance of moral rules is often met with emotional hostility. Conformity to them may sometimes bring a warm affective glow. The emotional dimension of moral rules plays an important role in their evolution and their survival, as I shall discuss further below. Guilt is a particularly important emotion that sometimes emerges after breaches of moral rules; it too plays a part in the evolutionary process.

Joyce's points (3) through (7) reveal the limitations of typical utilitarian approaches. Moral judgments are not simply expressions of an individual's interests, preferences, sentiments, or beliefs. They are also claims to universality in their context, which would apply irrespective of the interests, preferences, sentiments, or beliefs of those to whom they are supposed to apply. "Thou shalt not kill" applies even to those who take pleasure out of killing or to a victim considering escape from a mugger. If it is modified by a conditional clause, allowing killing in some circumstances such as self-defense, then the modified rule remains an inescapable moral claim in cases where self-defense does not apply.

As both Mackie and Joyce insist, morality surpasses matters of preference. It is a matter of right or wrong, or of duty, irrespective of whether we like it. This is part of what makes us human. We are capable of considering moral rules. We understand that their observance is more than a matter of personal whim or satisfaction. As Darwin noted, other animals do not have this capacity.

In mainstream economics, moral values are either ignored or subsumed under matters of utility or preference. Utilitarianism is an example of an axiological and extrinsic approach to morality, where actions are assessed on the grounds of the deemed value of their motives or consequences. Utilitarians may justify an action in terms of an increase in happiness, for example. Despite the historical importance of work in the utilitarian tradition, including its deployment of universal meta-principles, it retains an inadequate form of morality.

The kind of morality that has evolved culturally (on an emotional and biological foundation) in Darwinian terms is more likely to be deontic rather than axiological, with explicit, emotionally buttressed obligations rather than more complex, extrinsic, second-order principles of evaluation. Selection acts on groups according to features such as group cohesion. The evolutionary outcomes of selection in the population will be changing frequencies or dispositions that help generate these features. For the same reasons that evolutionary psychologists conclude that the brain is modular rather than an all-purpose calculator, specific context-dependent emotional and deontic drives are more likely to be favored by selection than an all-purpose, general inclination to seek happiness or utility (Cosmides and Tooby 1994a, 1994b; Wright 1994).

It is notable that many prominent moral principles in different cultures have a straightforward deontic character. Consider the biblical Ten Commandments and the culturally widespread Golden Rule ("do unto others as you would have them do unto you"). The typical claim is that specific actions are morally right or wrong, often without further explanation or consequential evaluation.

Modern society establishes a fundamental difference between moral rules and other (normative) rules. "Rape is wrong" does not carry the same connotations as "splitting infinitives is wrong" or "in America one must drive on the right side of the road." Linguistic and traffic rules are matters of convention; they are nonuniversal and do not apply to all languages or countries. But punishment may still occur when some conventions are breached. Rape is also punishable, but it is more than a breach of convention.

Threat of punishment or respect for the law are each insufficient to explain the relatively low frequency of rape. Most of us abstain from rape not simply because the probability of severe punishment outweighs any expected benefit or because we have a distaste for illegality. Most of us refrain from rape because we believe that it is *morally wrong*; we would desist even if we lived in a country where we regarded the legal system as illegitimate or where rape went unpunished. We believe that rape is universally immoral and unjust.

While there is a difference between morality and mere convention, some conventional rules seem to acquire a moral imperative when they become laws. But they often inherit the force of morality from other purportedly universal moral rules, particularly the need to respect others and to obey the law. While conventions often vary from culture to culture, we often conform to them, partly out of mutual respect or legal responsibility. Hence matters of mere convention can acquire some moral force if they become enshrined in law. If so, they do not necessarily become moral issues themselves, but their observance may acquire moral substance by virtue of their legal status. Consequently, the legitimacy (or otherwise) and moral stature of the legal system in the eyes of citizens is crucial.

Illustrations of this point are found in studies of why people evade taxes. Standard neoclassical models of tax evasion in particular and criminality in general treat such behavior as simply a result of cost-benefit calculations involving assessments of pecuniary benefits and probabilities of punishment. Tax evasion is seen principally as a gamble (Becker 1968; Allingham and Sandmo 1972; Lemieux, Fortin, and Frechette 1994). But critics such as Jonathan C. Baldry (1986) and Joel Slemrod (2003) challenge the assumption in standard models that taxpayers are entirely amoral. They point out that tax evasion involves the unethical shirking of social obligations. Obeying the law is not simply a matter of appreciating the risks and costs of criminality. James Andreoni et al. (1998) and Joseph G. Eisenhauer (2008) point out that standard neoclassical models with plausible parameters have greatly overestimated the amount of tax evasion in real life. From experimental data, Eisenhauer, Geide-Stevenson, and Ferro (2011) estimate that much tax compliance is motivated by moral considerations and matters of conscience, as well as by the perceived risks of tax evasion.[5]

It is a commonplace observation that what may be a moral rule for one culture may not be so for another. But this does not mean that moral rules are reducible to conventions. They become moral rules because many people believe in them as such and uphold them as more than matters of convenience, self-interest, or convention. But counting as a moral rule is not the same thing as being a *valid* moral rule. The cultural specificity of some moral judgments does not justify a *normative moral relativism*, where one person's morality is deemed as good as any other's.

By contrast, the uncontroversial observation that different cultures have ethical codes that are different in some respects may be described as *descriptive moral relativism*. More disputable are conclusions drawn from this observation. For example, based on his extensive anthropological studies, Edward Westermarck (1932) concluded that there was no foundation for an objective morality. But he accepted the objective claims of moral judgments and denied that they were simply expressions of personal preference.[6]

---

5. These results do not mean that the standard neoclassical approach is falsified—standard preference functions can be adjusted to fit the experimental data. But adding endless modifications to a model to fit the data is often a sign that a paradigm is degenerate rather than progressive. The Eisenhauer, Geide-Stevenson, and Ferro (2011) concept of "ethical preferences" treats morality as a matter of preference and utility maximization. But maximizing one's own utility is different from acting ethically, which may mean countering one's own interests or preferences. An advantage of the "ethical preferences" approach is that it more readily leads to tractable models and empirical estimates of the degree of "ethical" behavior. But the sacrificial cost may be too great.

6. As Stroup (1984) points out, there are resemblances between the works of Westermarck (1932) and Mackie (1977). From descriptive moral relativism, Mackie rejects both the real ex-

His empirically driven argument could be seen more as a critique of moral naturalism than a thorough case for ethical relativism. While stressing the emotional foundations of moral judgments, Westermarck placed too little emphasis on the reflective and discursive processes behind moral evaluations. Although emotions are vital, they are insufficient.

Advocates of normative moral relativism take a further step and uphold that if an act is regarded as morally permissible in a culture, then it must be deemed acceptable, even if it is regarded as wrong elsewhere. To accept such a version of moral relativism is to undermine an essential feature of morality itself—that it is absolute and inescapable. Because this feature is denied, such a moral relativist cannot believe in *any* moral judgment as defined above. Hence normative moral relativists are obliged to become moral nihilists or amoralists.

Moral relativism is not the same thing as cultural relativism—the view that any culture must be understood in its own terms. But they are linked and sometimes conflated. For example, the cultural relativist and influential anthropologist Ruth Benedict (1934b, p. 278) was apparently indifferent between "equally valid patterns of life." She suggested that we refrain from criticizing the morality of any culture. Yet this ethical tolerance in the field is inconsistent with her noted intolerance of racism and sexism in Western society. And her global opposition to discrimination and injustice would be devalued if it were simply regarded—in morally relativist terms—as the product of her own culture.[7]

Just as there are unavoidable ontological commitments in any process of inquiry, for humans there are unavoidable moral commitments. And some moral rules are ethically superior to others. Moral relativists respond that there is no way of knowing what the superior moral rules are. But even if there were no way of finding them, this argument is invalid. As with the epistemic error in ontology (the fact that we can never prove that the real world exists does not mean that there is not a real world outside our senses[8]), there is a similar error in ethics (the fact that we may be unable to identify a superior moral code or prove that it is valid does not mean that

---

istence and sustainability of moral judgments. But his careful account of the nature of morality can be rescued from the flames of his moral nihilism. See Honderich (1985).

7. Benedict (1934a, p. 73) also wrote that "morality differs in every society, and is a convenient term for socially approved habits." This reduction of morality to "socially approved habits" is morally moribund rather than morally relativist.

8. Bhaskar (1975, p. 36) describes the "epistemic fallacy" as "the view that statements about being can be reduced or analysed in terms of statements about knowledge, i.e. that ontological questions can always be transposed into epistemological terms."

a morally superior code does not exist). Ignorance of a valid morality does not mean that it is nonexistent.

Notwithstanding important cultural diversities, studies show a number of common features of moralities across cultures.[9] All cultures regard some acts of harm against others as immoral and invest some acts of reciprocity and fairness with moral virtue. Moral codes restraining individual selfishness also have universal prevalence. As Darwin understood, human societies where such prosocial dispositions prevail and replicate will engender greater cooperation and have an evolutionary selection advantage over competing societies where these dispositions are relatively weak. While there is also enormous cultural diversity, genetic and cultural coevolution have ensured that some specific types of prosocial moral rule have endured.

4.2. Moral Sentiments in Some Recent Accounts

Having sketched the nature of moral rules, we are now in a position to review some literature in economics and sociology on the topic. While there are several milestone contributions, relatively little of the work in the problem of explaining human cooperation combines all three of the following features:

1 an acknowledgment of the crucial role of morality in sustaining social cooperation with
2 an understanding of the nature of morality that transcends convention or preference and
3 an adequate evolutionary account of both the origin and persistence of morality.

Underlining the third feature, there must be an attempt to explain assumed moral attributes in evolutionary terms. Are the assumptions consistent with our knowledge and understanding of human evolution? Elsewhere I have called this the *principle of evolutionary explanation* (Hodgson 2004b).

The selective reviews below omit several major authors. I briefly address the works of Amartya Sen, Amitai Etzioni, Robert Frank, and Kenneth Binmore, all of whom have made their important contributions in this area since 1970.

---

9. S. Bok (1978), Roberts (1979), D. Brown (1991), Schwartz (1994), Haidt and Joseph (2004), Nichols (2004).

Amartya Sen

One of the most eloquent critics of self-interested "economic man" is the Nobel Laureate Amartya Sen. In a series of works dating back to the 1970s, Sen (1977, 1979, 1982, 1985b, 1987a) has argued—following Adam Smith—that human agents are not purely self-interested but have a measure of *sympathy* for others. Sen also stresses the concept of *commitment*, which is defined as a practical reason for an action that is independent of any gains or losses for that actor. Sen (2002, 2004) later adds the concept of *identity* to his multifaceted view of human nature. For Sen, identity is a vital chosen categorization and sense of self.

Although for Sen (1977, p. 327) commitment "is closely connected with . . . morals," it is itself broader than moral obligation. Obeying a moral rule is but one type of commitment. One can be committed to rules that are not moral rules, such as the grammatical rules of a language. Commitment is not defined in moral terms but through its detachment from any individual gain or loss. In this sense, it is defined negatively. Despite Sen's extensive discussion of the role of morality, he subsumes it under the notion of commitment, which is itself defined negatively in terms of the absence of losses or benefits for an individual (Pettit 2005; Pauer-Studer 2006).

Sen's separation of morality and commitment, on the one hand, from preferences and interests, on the other, is powerful and important. For Sen (1977, p. 329), the distinction between commitment and preferences "drives a wedge between personal choice and personal welfare, and much of traditional economic theory relies on the identity of the two." He argues that commitment is particularly important in labor markets and in choices concerning public goods. His work has persuaded some economists and other social scientists to abandon the narrow framework of preferences as an explanation of human behavior and as the exclusive normative basis for welfare economics. But partly for reasons of mathematical tractability, others remain tied to the conventional utilitarian framework of individual preferences.

Sen has made forceful appeals for the rejoining of ethics with economics. To his great credit, he shows the limits of utilitarianism. But by overlaying morals by individually oriented terms such as commitment, he gives less relative emphasis to the social fabric that sustains any morality.

In his rather speculative picture of human agency, Sen makes his overarching principle the sovereignty of individual choice: we *choose* our commitments and our identity on the basis of a Smithian mixture of sympathy and self-interest. In his concern to keep the choosing individual in the driving seat, Sen pays less attention to the function of social positions and institutions in providing the repertoire of choice and molding choices themselves. Sometimes it seems that he has been deluded by the slogan of methodological individualism to attempt to locate the origins of all social phenomena in individuals alone.

Although Sen refers to psychology, it provides relatively little guidance in his exploration of human motivation. Above all what is lacking here is a Darwinian evolutionary perspective. We have to explain how capacities for conscious reflection evolved.

We need to examine the causal motors behind choice itself, and to consider whether supposed attributes of human nature could have had an evolutionary selection advantage. We must apply the Darwinian rule: if no such selection advantage can be identified, then an assumed attribute must be considered implausible. The discipline of evolutionary thinking, based on at least the selection of individuals and the genetic outcomes, and the cultural selection of groups, can guide our speculations into fruitful channels. Sen has yet to employ such thinking in an extensive way.

Amitai Etzioni

The Moral Dimension (1988) by sociologist Amitai Etzioni gave enhanced attention to social structure while accenting the moral aspect of commitment. Did he fill gaps in Sen's account? Etzioni's picture is relatively simple. Etzioni (1988, p. 254) argues that all choices have a moral component: "All items have at least two valuations: their ability to generate pleasure and their moral standing." Moral standings arise through interactions between agents in social communities. Etzioni frequently but loosely writes of the "I & We paradigm" and adds a moral dimension as orthogonal to the rational utilitarian calculus.[10] In this two-dimensional evaluative space, we rarely reach the axes of pure utilitarianism or pure moralism: most "rational" decisions are informed with normative considerations.

---

10. Margolis (1982) offered a more rigorous account, foreshadowing later work in the area. Within each person he saw two selves, one selfish and the other with group-oriented "social preferences." Individual selection favors the first trait, and group selection the second. What Margolis and Etzioni both fail to explain is the evolutionary origin of the multifaceted personality, but Margolis does offer a pioneering and intriguing explanation of why a mix of selfish and cooperative dispositions is sustained. Unfortunately, the notion of morality in Margolis's analysis is analytically underdeveloped, and his argument is generally couched in the language of preferences.

He nevertheless finds a sizeable place for standard neoclassical economics. It becomes relevant to a specific domain of analysis. Etzioni (1988, p. 3) declares that "rather than abandon neoclassical concepts and findings, they are viewed here as dealing with subsystems within society (markets)." For him, neoclassical economics is appropriate for the domain of the market, where rational self-interest is deemed more prevalent.

There are a number of problems with this. First, it assumes that neoclassical economics offers a basically valid analysis of market systems, contrary to a host of powerful critics including Thorstein Veblen, Friedrich Hayek, and Herbert Simon. They all argue that the neoclassical depiction of individuals and markets is deeply flawed.[11] Second, Etzioni suggests that the market as an ideal type has minimal morality beyond self-interest and pleasure. Although Etzioni argues at length that all market systems in reality involve agents who make moral as well as purely self-interested decisions, it is his depiction of the Weberian "ideal type" of the market that is open to dispute (Staveren 2009). An ideal type must be plausible, at least in the sense that if real-world markets necessary involve morality, then the market ideal type must involve morality as well.

Etzioni's position is very close to that of the precursors and pioneers of neoclassical theory. John Stuart Mill (1848) argued that "political economy" applied to the sphere of business, where the acquisition of wealth was paramount, whereas other motives were relatively more pronounced elsewhere in society. Neoclassical writers such as William Stanley Jevons (1871) and Francis Edgeworth (1881), and Austrian school founder Carl Menger (1883), defined economics in terms of self-interested behavior. Philip Wicksteed (1910) argued that neoclassical economics applied to the sphere where concern for the welfare of others was overshadowed by self-interest. This line of argument was further developed in the 1920s in the writings of Vilfredo Pareto (1935, 1971). Despite their differences, all these economists saw economics as applicable not to the whole of society but to those zones most connected to markets, business, and money, where calculative and self-interested motives are allegedly most important. This is in contrast to the later positions of Lionel Robbins (1932) and Gary Becker (1976b), who considerably broadened the scope of neoclassical economics and applied utility maximization to every sphere of behavior.

Accordingly, Etzioni's argument is an attempt to undo the Robbins-Becker revolution and to juxtapose two parallel lines of inquiry. A pre-Robbins neoclassical economics that focuses on supposed self-interest in

---

11. See, for example, Veblen (1909), Hayek (1948), Simon (1957), Murrell (1991).

business and markets is placed alongside "sociological" considerations concerning morality, emotions, and values, which are regarded as ubiquitous but more prominent in some spheres than others. As Michael Piore (2003) argues, the thrust of Etzioni's approach "is to preserve the core of the neoclassical paradigm and to add on to it, or to modify it, at several key points."

Placed in a historical context, Etzioni's (1988) work represents a relatively small additional advance.[12] It faces the same enduring conceptual problems involved in its juxtaposition of fundamentally different theoretical frameworks. This juxtaposition ends up denuding the concept of morality itself, by suggesting that moral values can themselves be traded off with one another (Etzioni 1999). Hence the notion of morality advanced by Etzioni seems to have more to do with personal values than universal claims relating to human progress and well-being (Lutz 2000).

Despite its subtitle, Etzioni's 1988 book has not yet led to discernable progress *Toward a New Economics*. Significant changes have occurred within mainstream economics since 1988, but it is difficult to detect any significant influence of Etzioni's thinking on economic theory. While Etzioni has captured the attention of several influential politicians and policymakers and been influential in bringing some sociologists and economists together, his impact on economics itself has been slight. Furthermore, Etzioni's socioeconomic analytical framework has not exhibited a "positive heuristic" of significant further theoretical development in the succeeding years. It appears simultaneously as too radical and too conservative: it points back to a confined utilitarianism of the early neoclassical era while exhorting economists to take on board moral considerations that many believe are either irrelevant or may be accommodated within a post-Robbins "science of choice."[13]

Like Sen, Etzioni also makes relatively little use of psychology. He tends to associate emotions with values rather than rationality and does not acknowledge sufficiently that all rational deliberation must have an emotional basis as well. Without emotion, the human agent would have

12. Nevertheless, as Castro Caldas, Narciso Costa, and Burns (2007) demonstrate, a return to pre-Robbins perspectives on human motivation would represent a considerable advance over the prevailing subsequent reduction of all motivation to individual preferences and utility.

13. Etzioni is the key founder of the Society for the Advancement of Socio-Economics. But this has served more as a multidisciplinary forum than a crucible for further theoretical advance along the detailed lines of Etzioni's (1988) book. Unclear are the differences between socioeconomics and other similar transdisciplinary movements, including economic sociology (now a division within the American Sociological Association) and social economics (long organized under the Association for Social Economics). See Hodgson (2008c).

no impetus to categorize or calculate (James 1890; Barbalet 2001, 2008; Nussbaum 2001; Cohen 2005). Rational utility maximization is a form of evaluation. Etzioni thus sustains an untenable dichotomy between the rational, on the one hand, and the emotional and evaluative on the other. His view is very similar to that of the sociologist Talcott Parsons (1937), by whom he was strongly influenced. Like Parsons, Etzioni tries to develop an all-embracing theoretical framework that nevertheless retains within it a subservient place for neoclassical economics. Also like Parsons, the fault line between the sociology and economics is drawn with "values," on the one side, and "rationality," on the other. And from the viewpoint of moral philosophy, there is little exploration of the nature of the moral content of such values.

Furthermore, reflecting the strong aversion to biological ideas that dominated sociology for much of the twentieth century, Etzioni makes no use of Darwinian evolutionary theory in his analysis.[14] Like Sen, his schema remains much in the realm of speculation, without the explanatory power of evolutionary survival to help sustain it. It is attractive to a few mainstream economists because it retains a qualified place for utilitarianism, but this doctrine cannot comply with the full requirements of evolutionary and causal explanation.

Robert H. Frank

Unlike Sen and Etzioni, Robert H. Frank (1987, 1988, 1993) attempts a Darwinian justification for his assumptions about the human agent. Although Frank does discuss the matter of conscience, he is less concerned about morality as such and more about the origins of altruism and the more general role of the emotions. For Frank, emotions like love, sympathy, and hate are also "rational" in that they serve to substantiate commitments and to make them credible for others. Pursuing self-interest may be self-defeating unless there is a sense of our commitment to our declarations, so that others may take us seriously. The possibility of pretence arises, but we are honed by evolutionary selection over millennia to detect cheaters. Frank argues that under certain conditions the agents with genuine emo-

---

14. As shown in Hodgson (2004b, 2006a), Anglophone sociology cut loose from biology after the First World War. From the 1930s, Parsons played a major role in this disciplinary reconstruction (Camic 1987, 1989), which involved the jettisoning and subsequent neglect of earlier important American sociologists such as Franklin Giddings, Edward Ross, and Lester Frank Ward, as well as a hasty rejection of Veblenian institutional economics, partly because of its Darwinian associations.

tions will have individual advantages. He sees fine-tuned emotional capacities as arising through both cultural and genetic evolution, where they give a selection advantage to the individual.

Frank (1993, p. 168) applies this argument to cases of altruistic and self-sacrificial behavior: "Unlike the self-interest version of traditional rational choice theory . . . it is . . . able to accommodate cases in which individuals willingly subordinate their own interest to the interest of social groups." Redolent of Sen, Frank (1993, p. 162) upholds that

> there is an important class of problems in economic and social interaction that cannot easily be solved by persons known to have narrowly self-interested preferences. Problems in this class, which I call *commitment problems*, have the common feature that their solution requires people to commit themselves to behave in ways that will later conflict with their material self-interest.

He argues that emotions are an important way of effecting such commitments. At the same time, Frank retains much of the mainstream apparatus of individual choice and upholds that behavior, even if powered by emotions, is nevertheless rational. A problem here is that Frank is unclear whether deliberation or emotion is in ultimate command of our behavior. Is reason or emotion the true sovereign of our acts? As Alexander Field (2001, p. 160) puts it in his critique of Frank:[15]

> But he never satisfactorily explains whether emotional behavior is ultimately under the control of reason, and thus can be considered truly strategic, or whether it is not. If emotions are truly under the control of reason, then a tendency to exhibit emotional behavior cannot serve its appointed role of giving credibility to commitments or threats.

If reason controlled all passions, and this were common knowledge, then a rational player would see through any emotional ruse, and emotion would serve no useful function. So is emotion in command? Frank (1988, p. 2) defines rationality in terms of self-interest (and assumes in his models that individual payoffs are equivalents to interests) but brings in the emotions to attempt to explain why people often fail to act in their inter-

---

15. I agree with most of Field's (2001, chap. 4) critique of Frank. But Field relies on genetic group selection to explain altruism. I find no compelling evidence for the conditions necessary for genetic group selection to lead to altruism. Cultural group selection has occurred, but this explains the persistence not the origin of these traits. Field (2001, pp. 44–45, 107, 136) also adopts an inadequately defined notion of "methodological individualism."

ests. This would suggest that people often act irrationally (in terms of their interests) because of their emotions. But Frank argues differently: he suggests that emotions can serve our rational pursuit of our interests. As Field (2001) establishes at length, this argument is internally contradictory: one cannot logically uphold that people are both rational (serve their interests) and irrational (do not serve their interests).

Facing such dilemmas, Frank (1988, pp. 12, 16) ultimately opts for the supremacy of rationality and self-interest: "the logic of self interest . . . ultimately sustains these emotions," and the presence of emotions "is in perfect harmony with the underlying requirements of a coherent theory of rational behavior." So rationality and self-interest are ultimately in command after all.

Frank assumes that evolution selects self-interested individuals, but in fact he is torn between two modes of argument: evolutionary selection and appeals to individual self-interest. Contrary to the pop Darwinism that is found in some quarters of the social sciences, the two do not lead to equivalent outcomes. One does not have to appeal to group selection to show this.[16] Even from a gene-centered perspective, both inclusive fitness and reciprocal altruism establish that an individual may sacrifice her benefits— even to the point of her death—in a plausible evolutionary process (W. D. Hamilton 1964; Trivers 1971). Frank (1988, p. 24) even quotes Dawkins (1976) and acknowledges kin selection, but Frank does not seem to appreciate that gene-centered theorists emphasize the survival of genes over individuals.[17] As Samuel Bowles and Herbert Gintis (2011, p. 45) demonstrate, "the idea that selfish genes must produce selfish individuals is false."

Frank (1988, p. 23) also upholds that the evolution of a trait depends on its enhancement of "the reproductive fitness of the *individuals* who bear it" but does not acknowledge that biological reproductive fitness is essentially the capacity to pass on one's genes (De Jong 1994). Consequently, reproductive fitness is consistent with self-sacrifice by parents on behalf of their offspring. Self-interest and reproductive fitness are not necessarily

16. In 1988, Frank (1994, p. 620) was "a committed individual selectionist" who rejected group selection. But he was persuaded by David Sloan Wilson and Elliot Sober (1994) to join the now near-consensus view that both genetic and cultural group selection are theoretically possible under specific conditions. Field (2001, pp. 205–6) also shows that the formal model in an appendix to Frank (1988) relies on assumptions that are sufficient to establish genetic group selection. Group selection is also implicit in a later work (Frank 2011). From multilevel selection perspectives (including group selection), there are abundant reasons why evolution does not optimize individual gains (Dupré 1987; Hodgson 1993).

17. Individuals struggle for survival, but the decisive evolutionary outcome is the change in the gene pool–selection *of* individuals leading to selection *for* genes.

equivalent, yet Frank generally assumes self-interest, payoff maximization, and reproductive fitness all amount to the same thing.

Contrary to the famous account by Milton Friedman (1953), there are many reasons why evolutionary selection at the social level does not necessarily lead to individual payoff maximization (Winter 1964; Boyd and Richerson 1980; Schaffer 1989; Hodgson 1993, 1994). In fact, the evolutionary selection of payoff maximizers depends on a number of highly restrictive conditions. If they are violated, the outcome may be different. For example, individual payoffs may correlate positively with the proportion of similar individuals in the population, but this virtuous circle never gets established because the population is more vulnerable to invasion by individuals of a different type. Violations may occur when the criteria of selection depend on the context, including where performance depends on complementarities with or numbers of other entities (Lewontin 1974).[18]

Consequently, contra Frank (1988, pp. 58, 63) and many other evolutionary models, one cannot generally assume that self-interested payoff maximization will emerge through evolutionary selection. Darwin himself was aware of this when he argued that evolution had created humans with cooperative rather than self-regarding dispositions. Although Frank refers often to morality, he does not much explore its meaning and significance, although he rightly insists that morality is in part sustained through emotion.

In sum, although Frank should be given credit for attempting an evolutionary explanation and highlighting the importance of emotions, his account of prosocial behavior is compromised by mainstream notions of rationality and a flawed use of evolutionary theory.

Kenneth Binmore

Like Frank, Kenneth Binmore (1994, 1998b, 2005) defends both rationality and a Darwinian approach. His employment of evolutionary ideas is extensive and highly instructive. Even more emphatically than Frank, he believes that social cooperation can be explained in largely self-interested terms. Although for Binmore preference functions are "empathetic," they still involve the maximization of individual utility: "each citizen honors the social contract because it is in his own self-interest to do so, provided

---

18. This applies to the payoffs of firms as well as individuals (Winter 1964). There is a growing theoretical and empirical literature on institutional complementarities that lock economic evolution into specific and possibly suboptimal paths (Amable 2000, 2003; Aoki 2001; Hall and Soskice 2001; Boyer 2005; Kenworthy 2006; Gagliardi 2009).

that enough of his fellow citizens do the same" (Binmore 1998b, p. 5). In-spired more by David Hume than Immanuel Kant, Binmore seeks founda-tions for Rawlsian ideas about fairness in biological and social evolution. Binmore uses evolutionary game theory to show how social conventions emerge. He treats moral rules as solutions to Nash bargaining problems with payoff-maximizing agents.

In Binmore's analysis, possible moral norms emerge as multiple equi-librium solutions to repeated games. Given this, he promotes a normative moral relativism, entertaining no justification for regarding one cultural set of moral norms as superior to another. He further describes his approach to ethics as *naturalist*, by which he means that morality can be grounded entirely on scientific principles, in the manner of the natural sciences. Bin-more (1998a, p. 278) writes: "those who wish to enter the pulpit to preach that one society is better than another are not entitled to appeal to natural-istic theories of ethics." But the next section examines alternative natural-ist accounts of morality that reject normative moral relativism. Binmore's normative moral relativism arises from his particular utilitarian version of moral naturalism based on equilibrium outcomes.

The normative force of Binmore's argument emanates from models involving structured interaction and communication between individu-als. They do not derive from individuals alone. Indeed, because of his in-sistence on self-regarding individual preferences, Binmore is obliged to ground his notion of morality on structured social interactions. Implicitly, his work testifies that while morality relates to individuals, it is not reduc-ible to the properties or sentiments of individuals alone.

There are several criticisms of Binmore's theory. One is to challenge the realism and efficacy of Binmore's assumption of individual payoff maxi-mization or self-regarding preferences. His game-theoretic demonstrations of high levels of cooperation with payoff-maximizing individuals assume that information is mostly unambiguous and public, that most signals and interpretations are accurate, and that individuals are generally patient and educable when faced with error. Critics point out that these assumptions are often implausible and their explanatory relevance is confined to rela-tively small groups. As Herbert Gintis (2006, p. 8) argues: "highly coopera-tive equilibria among self-regarding agents are both evolutionary inacces-sible and unstable."

Although Binmore's theory has prominent evolutionary dynamics, there is no evolutionary explanation of the origin of self-regarding preferences. Evidence cited elsewhere in this book concurs with Darwin's (1871) view that human evolution has created individuals who are not entirely selfish.

Consequently, to use the words of Thorstein Veblen (1898, p. 188), "if this economic man is to serve as a lay figure upon which to fit the garment of economic doctrines, it is incumbent upon the science to explain . . . his emancipation from the law of natural selection." The self-regarding individual is assumed by Binmore, rather than explained in evolutionary terms.

Binmore's conception of morality is also deficient. As argued above, moral rules are much more than stable social conventions and they transcend the interests or ends of those concerned. At root here are problems with all naturalist accounts of ethics, of which Binmore's is but one example.[19] For the naturalist moral philosopher, "doing the right thing" is ultimately no more than a matter of utility, efficacy, or expediency. For Binmore in particular, the immoral is little more than a defiance of convention. Joyce (2006, p. 207) puts the following question to the moral naturalist:

> Why, according to your theory, do we need a distinct moral discourse at all? . . . Why not just talk openly about what we like and dislike, what is conducive to social harmony and what is not, what we will tolerate and what we will punish?

Although Joyce does not address Binmore, these questions apply perfectly. It is difficult to find an adequate answer within Binmore's framework that would avoid the reduction of morality to matters of taste or convention.

Unlike Binmore, many moral naturalists are not normative moral relativists. Although he does note the de facto universality of some basic moral values such as fairness, he stresses that their norms of implementation vary greatly from culture to culture. But that is insufficient to establish normative moral relativism. The fact that moral codes vary does not mean that they are equally valid. As noted above, the absoluteness and inescapability of moral judgments is difficult to reconcile with a normative moral relativism. Binmore is able to overlook this problem because, like many moral naturalists, when he writes of morality he means convention.[20]

---

19. Moral naturalism is discussed in the following section. Several prominent moral naturalist accounts rely on evolutionary modes of explanation, some are inspired by sociobiology and some use evolutionary game theory (R. Alexander 1987; Wright 1994; Ridley 1996; Skyrms 1996, 2004; Casebeer 2003; Nichols 2004). Dennett (1995) asks whether ethics can be "naturalized," but his ultimate answer is unclear, and on some readings his argument leads to a moral nihilism (Joyce 2006, pp. 163–68).

20. For a comparison of evolutionary game theory and modern evolutionary economics see Hodgson and Huang (2012).

In a powerful critique of Binmore, Robert Sugden (2001) argues that if normative principles are to be deduced in a naturalist manner from an analysis of evolutionary processes and outcomes, then there must be considerable appeal to the facts concerning human social evolution. Yet Binmore's two-volume treatise is instead dominated by a priori assumptions, including a standard view of human agents as expected-utility maximizers. Despite Binmore's own contribution to experimental economics, there is relatively little use of results from this field. Sugden (2001, p. F242) concludes that Binmore has unintentionally performed a service by exposing the limitations of evolutionary game theory as a foundation for moral theory: "a genuinely evolutionary approach to economics may have to diverge much further from the conventional, rationality-based approach than most theorists so far been willing to countenance." This hits the nail on its head.

In his *Moral Sentiments* of 1759, Adam Smith (1976, p. 13) warned against "deducing all our sentiments from certain refinements of self love." This counsel retains its relevance today. Moral views are shared among (some or all) members of a community, and they are irreducible to matters of individual pleasure, convenience, or utility. For this reason, despite its sophisticated evolutionary and game-theoretic structure, Binmore's attempted naturalistic foundation for ethics fails to support much moral weight. It is an interesting and well-crafted line of argument that sustains at best a limited notion of morality.

4.3. Varieties of Ethical Naturalism

Binmore raised the question of naturalism. By definition, *ethical naturalism* upholds that the search for a true morality can also be guided by scientific principles, in the manner of the natural sciences. The term *naturalism* is also applied to versions of philosophical realism and monism, which claim that phenomena are susceptible to scientific explanation. I believe that it is possible to be a nonnaturalist in ethics and otherwise a naturalist in a realist and monist sense. Consider some illustrations of ethical naturalism.

Clarence Ayres

The influential American institutional economist Clarence Ayres promoted a version of moral naturalism. He claimed that it was possible to identify universal ethical values through the norms of scientific and technological progress. Ayres (1952, p. 15) wrote that "doing-and-knowing, science-and-technology, is the real life process of mankind. This is the process from which modern industrial civilization has resulted, and it is the process in terms of which men have always judged things good and bad, and actions right and wrong." For Ayres, problems of moral valuation are resolved by the ongoing accumulation of scientific knowledge relating to the provisioning of human needs. Science and technology are the source and bases of moral evaluation: their progress is ethically good, and ungrounded superstitions or worthless ceremonies that get in their way are ethically bad.

Hence for Ayres, the discovery of moral values is nothing more than the revelation of the scientific and technological means of human life. As James Webb (2002, p. 991) noted: "Ayres argued that moral questions can be treated in about the same way that positivists treat factual questions. That is, the positivist principle of verification is not rejected but extended to the realm of values, where it is presumed to operate in the same unproblematic way as it does on factual issues."

But the proposal to use technology or science as standards of moral value is problematic. In the face of awesome twentieth-century developments, such as nuclear, chemical, and biological warfare, and the increasing pollution of the planet, it appeared that Ayres had given a positive evaluation to *all* technology. Many scientific and technological developments, such as nuclear physics and the internal combustion engine, can be used destructively as well as for the flourishing of human life. Especially after the rise of the antiwar and green movements in the 1960s and 1970s, even Ayres's followers were obliged to modify his evaluative scheme. They incorporated a deeper reading of the work of John Dewey.[21] The result was a developed notion of "instrumental valuation" in terms of the capacity of proposals or arrangements to sustain or enhance the means and quality of human life (Dewey 1939).

Sustaining and enhancing the quality of human life can be taken as a fundamental need and policy objective. But that is not necessarily the same thing as morality. As explained below, there are prominent moral dilemmas that cannot convincingly be resolved using criteria of need or well-being. And if morality were simply a matter of need or well-being, then it would lose much of its essential nature, as defined in section 4.1 above. Moral questions would be reducible to matters of human survival and development and a separate moral discourse would be unnecessary.

A moral question would remain: why should human need or well-being

---

21. Notably Foster (1981), Bush (1987), and Tool (1995). Webb (2002) criticizes Ayres's selective interpretation of Dewey.

be universally valued? The moral assumption that all humans should be supremely valued cannot be deduced from science alone. For example, science cannot tell us why humans should be valued more than whales or pandas. We have to accept or reject (without much aid from science) the moral premise that humans are ultimately to be valued more than other species.

Roy Bhaskar

Roy Bhaskar (1979, 1986, 1989) promotes an explicit version of moral naturalism. Against David Hume and many others, Bhaskar argues explicitly that an "ought" may be derived from an "is." For him, social science is essentially emancipatory: social-scientific explanations of what "is" lead logically at some point to undeniable claims concerning what "ought" or "ought not" to exist.[22]

His argument contains several steps. Bhaskar (1989, p. 101) claims that "the subject matter of the human sciences includes both social objects (including beliefs) and beliefs about those objects." The next step is also reasonable. Bhaskar argues that false beliefs (sometimes described by Marxists as "false consciousness") help to sustain some institutions. Consequently, to counter such false beliefs is to undermine these institutions.

To obtain a moral evaluation, Bhaskar (1991, pp. 155–56) has to push the argument further. According to him, from a true theory that explains how particular false beliefs help sustain some institutions "one can pass immediately, without the addition of any extraneous value judgement, to a negative evaluation on the object that makes such consciousness necessary and to a positive evaluation on action rationally directed at removing it." This, according to Bhaskar (1986, p. 169), is the "essential emancipatory impulse" of the social sciences, amounting to an "explanatory critique."

But an "extraneous value judgement" *is* required to make such a move. For Bhaskar, it is that falsehood is bad and the revelation of truth is good. Clearly, the scientific pursuit of truth will undermine support for those social institutions that are sustained by false beliefs. If the truth is of overrid-

---

22. Much confusion exists on this issue. Claims that science is unavoidably infused with value judgments are defensible. But one should not go so far as to regard judgments of fact and value as the *same thing* or *indistinguishable*. As Irene van Staveren (2007, pp. 21–22) rightly argues, "there is a fundamental difference between distinguishing facts and values (which is necessary for conceptual reasons as well as for doing justice to the different meanings of these concepts) and placing them in a dichotomous relation."

ing moral value, then it should be pursued, even if the result is a challenge to the existing social order. But this involves a value judgment.

Bhaskar's argument boils down to the following: (1) some false beliefs help to sustain some social institutions, (2) in confronting false beliefs and their explanations, we are challenging these beliefs and confronting the institutions that are sustained by them. Again there is an implicit value judgment that false beliefs should be confronted. Bhaskar has to add an "ought" to an "is" to obtain an "ought."[23]

Like others, Hugh Lacey (1997, p. 238) argues that Bhaskar's proposed "quick rational move from coming to accept theories in the social sciences to adopting value judgements partial to emancipation" depends on "the mediation of value judgements" or on "value-impregnated theoretical terms" and hence the theoretical explanation itself is insufficient to establish emancipatory moral values. Consequently, Hume's postulate is not refuted by Bhaskar and his argument for moral naturalism is unconvincing.[24]

The universal moral worth of truth is by no means self-evident. For example, under a totalitarian regime it may be morally unacceptable to proclaim to the authorities the names of those that are working clandestinely to establish democracy. And if a mother is dying, there could be a strong moral case to conceal some unpalatable truths, such as the infidelity of her husband or the sins of her children. In such circumstances, other moral values, such as democratic rights or the personal feelings of a dying person, may outweigh the moral good of truth.

Sam Harris

In an argument for moral naturalism, Sam Harris (2010) argues that, in principle, science can uncover the conditions for individual well-being or

---

23. More accurately, in most cases, Bhaskar's conclusion is an "ought not," in the sense of reaching a negative evaluation of capitalist institutions. As I argue elsewhere (Hodgson 2006a, chap. 5), Bhaskar and other "critical realists" are vigorous in their critique of the capitalist order, but extraordinarily weak in proposing feasible social and political alternatives grounded in current adequate understandings (from economics or other social sciences) of how socioeconomic systems actually work. In particular, they make the untenable and extreme claim that markets should not simply be minimized but *entirely abolished* in modern complex societies (Bhaskar 1989, p. 6; Collier 1994, p. 195; Bhaskar and Collier 1998, p. 392). Their realism is somewhat unrealistic.

24. Hammersley (2002) and Elder-Vass (2010b) make similar points. Sayer (1997, p. 486) observes: "The resulting impression is one of pulling global salvation out of the critical realist hat."

human flourishing. But (unlike Ayres and Bhaskar) he seems to straddle both utilitarian and needs-oriented horses. When asked in an interview how his advocacy of "well-being" squared with utilitarianism, he expanded his notion of "well-being" to include "utility, pleasure" and "short-term happiness" as well as "truth, justice, fairness, intellectual pleasure, courage, creativity and having a clear conscience" (Gefter and Harris, 2010, p. 45). The notion of "well-being" is doing a lot of work here. His narrative oscillates from subjective experiences such as happiness to the struggle for objective goals such as sustenance, shelter, or education. Either way there are problems.

On the subjective side, even if we knew how to make people happy, we would face the familiar utilitarian dilemmas of how to compare the happiness of different people and how to construct our objective happiness function for society as a whole. Is the aim to maximize mean or median happiness and ignore the extremes, or is some redistribution of happiness required (in which case, the happiest will be less happy), or in Paretian mode do we refuse to reduce the happiness of anyone? It is doubtful whether science can ever resolve such normative questions.

On the objective side, we have come a long way in outlining the human needs that are required for survival and beneficial development.[25] While this knowledge is vital and important, and should certainly help to shape our moral goals, it is not equivalent to morality itself. Needs-provision and morality are not necessarily the same.

Furthermore, knowledge of individual or social needs does not help us resolve many moral dilemmas. Consider the famous "trolley problem" where someone is faced with the choice of diverting a runaway railway vehicle at a manually operated switch point, from a track where it would kill five people to another track where it would kill just one (J. Thomson 1976; Hauser 2006). How can such killing be moral? But failing to act would involve complicity in the death of the greater number. The choice to arrange the death of one to save five others cannot be sustained by science alone. It would involve an overriding moral criterion, such as the minimization of the number of human deaths.

As another example, the moral dilemmas with abortion are familiar, where advocates accept the killing of a living fetus partly on the grounds of the choice and well-being of the mother. Unlike the trolley problem, here

---

25. Hobson (1929), Maslow (1954), Sen (1985a, 1999), G. Thomson (1987), Doyal and Gough (1991), Nussbaum and Sen (1993), Corning (2000, 2011), Gough (2000, 2004), Nussbaum (2000, 2003).

the choice to kill by abortion is not balanced by a greater number of alternative deaths: one possible option is not to kill at all. But moral defenses of abortion are commonplace (Foot 1976). Moral dilemmas often involve the choice of the lesser of apparent evils, and science alone seems generally unable to rank or quantify many harmful acts.

One has only to peruse an adequately intelligent national newspaper to find controversies that are difficult to resolve with the use of present or conceivable scientific knowledge. What kind of voting system is best? Should there be publicly funded faith schools? Should monarchies become republics? Should prisoners be allowed to vote in governmental elections? These are all ethical dilemmas of importance, but science in principle may not be able to help us here. Harris's argument is based on the faith that eventually science will be able to resolve these dilemmas.

Merely to raise these problems is to expose the limitations of the naturalist approach to ethics. Science can tell us much about the requirements for human well-being and flourishing. It thus may inform us of the possibilities and constraints that surround impending moral choices. It is an ally of an enlightened morality; but when it comes to many real dilemmas, science alone cannot teach us right or wrong. Understanding the conditions for human flourishing does not provide us with a full moral code. Science may be able to tell us about mechanisms or outcomes, but it tells us much less about how we should evaluate them.

Outside morality, we can be naturalists in other domains of inquiry—where naturalism upholds the possibility of explanation in terms of scientific methods. Consistent with this, an ethical nonnaturalist could argue that there can be scientific explanations of how morality works, but not of why any particular moral judgment is ethically valid. Science is generally about causal explanation and sometimes about prediction, but it is insufficient for ethical justification.

Whatever the value of science in guiding our current moral choices, we should not overlook the functional role of morality in the past evolution of the human species, particularly in providing forms of motivation and control for individuals to enhance the cohesion and survival chances of their group. Some naturalist accounts of morality would ignore this evolutionary function and sweep such consideration of past moral rules away, as mumbo-jumbo or religion. But an understanding of how morality works—in motivational, group survival, and evolutionary terms—can help us when making practical judgments, even though we cannot derive morality directly from science.

4.4. Moral Realism and the Search for a Justifiable Morality

Another meta-ethical dilemma has to be addressed. Moral realism is typically defined as the claim that all moral beliefs are objectively true or false. Accordingly, there may be a valid, objective, and universal morality, whether known or otherwise. A prominent contrary view is that moral values are outcomes of individual, social, or biological circumstances and their validity depends on these. Hence an ethical claim may be *considered* true in a given social context, but this does not mean that it is universally or timelessly true. Moral realists uphold an objective and universal morality; their opponents typically argue that the validity of a morality depends on the overall circumstances in which it is advanced.

Moral realism is defended by some philosophers (Moore 1903; Sayre-McCord 1988; Bhaskar 1993; Shafer-Landau 2003) but opposed by others (Mackie 1977; Elder-Vass 2010b). Philosophers also differ on whether moral naturalism necessarily implies moral realism (compare Moore with Bhaskar). But in any case, rejecting moral naturalism does not mean that we have to reject moral realism.

Although the philosophical debate over moral realism is important for understanding the nature of morality, for the purposes of the present work it does not have to be resolved. In making this claim I rely on a key argument by Mackie. While opposing moral realism, Mackie (1977, p. 35) argues that "ordinary moral judgements include a claim to objectivity, an assumption that there are objective values," and this assumption is in the everyday established interpretation of moral terms. Mackie (1977, pp. 42–43) elaborates:

> Moral attitudes themselves are at least partly social in origin: socially established—and socially necessary—patterns of behaviour put pressure on individuals, and each individual tends to internalise these pressures and to join in requiring these patterns of behaviour of himself and of others. The attitudes that are objectified into moral values have indeed an external source, though not the one assigned to them by the belief in their absolute authority.

Moreover, this objectification of moral judgments serves a vital purpose: it gives them an air of authority that is essential if morality is to be effective in its social task of regulating our behavior.

What matters here is not whether moral values are objectively true, but how they function as purported objective truths, irrespective of Mackie's additional claim that they are all false. Both advocates and opponents of moral realism can accept that claims to objectivity and universality are essential to empower moral beliefs in social contexts. Hence the debate over moral realism need not be resolved here.

Likewise, although the role of morality is highlighted, the establishment of a universal system of acceptable moral principles is not achieved in this work. That would be a Herculean and very different project. The appeal to evolutionary biology in this volume—alongside insights from social science—is not intended as a moral quick fix, in the manner of some populist writing in sociobiology. As Elliott Sober (1980, p. 379) laments: "Perhaps it is a sign of our crumbling moral confidence that we no longer find it possible to separate questions of what is natural from what is good." But we must. Nature does not tell us what is right. Instead we turn in part to evolution to understand the origins of our moral propensities. In this regard, as Jürgen Habermas (1993, p. 84) puts it: "An ultimate justification of ethics is neither possible nor necessary."

But this does not mean that we should downplay morality or uphold that any one moral claim is as good as any other. Instead we focus on the importance of moral motivation, even in economic settings. Some people are motivated by a notion of "doing the right thing," even in the greedy world of capitalist business. It is one thing to acknowledge the importance of moral motivation and another to determine whether particular morals are justified. The latter task is difficult; but that is no excuse to ignore the former fact.

We shall concern ourselves with the way that morality has evolved as an essential social phenomenon and consider the institutional conditions under which morality can be scrutinized and developed. The evolution of morality is the subject of the next chapter.

FIVE

The Evolution of Morality

All this implies some degree of sympathy, fidelity, and courage. Such social qualities . . . were no doubt acquired by the progenitors of man . . . through natural selection, aided by inherited habit. . . . Obedience . . . is [also] of the highest value,
for any form of government is better than none. Selfish and contentious people
will not cohere, and without coherence nothing can be effected. A tribe possessing the above qualities in a high degree would spread and be victorious over other
tribes . . . although a high standard of morality gives but a slight or no advantage
to each individual man and his children over the other men of the same tribe, yet
that an advancement in the standard of morality and an increase in the number
of well-endowed men will certainly give an immense advantage to one tribe over
another. There can be no doubt that a tribe including many members who, from
possessing in a high degree the spirit of patriotism, fidelity, obedience, courage,
and sympathy, were always ready to give aid to each other and to sacrifice themselves for the common good, would be victorious over most other tribes; and this
would be natural selection.

—Charles Darwin (1871)

We require evolutionary explanations of the origin and persistence of
morality. In the quotation that heads this chapter, Darwin proposes that
groups containing individuals who devote themselves to the interests of
their group will have an advantage in the struggle for survival. Among humans, binding sentiments of sympathy and solidarity are strengthened by
a moral code, typically transmitted by instruction and often sanctified by
religion (Wilson 2002).

For some time Darwin's account of the evolution of morality was pushed
to one side, even with the growing popularity of the Darwinian theory of
natural selection. Among his fellow Victorians his account suffered because

of a contrary view that the foundations of human morality are of very recent origin—due perhaps to Christianity or modern civilization—rather than based on "social qualities . . . acquired by the progenitors of man." As noted below, even Darwin's supporters saw morality as something that runs counter to natural selection.

Darwin's evolutionary explanation of morality relies to some degree on a notion of group selection, where individual traits that benefit the group are automatically assumed to prosper. Darwin did not consider the objection that selfish individuals would be able to free ride within an altruistic group and eventually outbreed the unselfish (Williams 1966; Dawkins 1976). This apparently powerful attack on group selection theory seemed to undermine Darwin's account. Before the theory of group selection was rehabilitated through the meticulous efforts of several scholars (Wade 1976, 1978; Wilson 1980, 1983, 1999; Wilson and Sober 1994; Sober and Wilson 1998; Wilson and Wilson 2007), Darwin's theory of the evolution of morality was regarded as quaint and outmoded.

As noted in chapter 3, genetics must be distinguished from cultural group selection (Henrich 2004). They differ because they focus on separate levels and mechanisms of inheritance, while the group is the object of selection in both cases. This conceptual distinction does not mean that the interaction between the genetic and cultural levels is ruled out. On the contrary, culture provides part of the environment in which genes are selected, and our genetic endowment influences cultural evolution (Boyd and Richerson 1985; Durham 1991).

As previously noted, strong arguments sustain the notion of cultural group selection among humans. Genetic group selection is more problematic. Although it is possible in principle, it depends on the restriction of intergroup migration and the limitation of genetic mixing between groups. But the evidence among primates is that significant group-to-group migration does occur (de Waal 2006, p. 16). Some contemporary human hunter-gatherer groups reveal intergroup migration and relatively low levels of genetic relatedness within groups (Hill et al. 2011). We lack evidence on the degree of intergroup migration among early humans, but we have no reason to presume that they differed radically from primates in this respect. Consequently, the genetic foundations of altruistic and moral feelings seem more likely to have evolved through mechanisms of kin altruism and then reciprocal altruism, and morality then spread further through cultural means, particularly through the inculcation of behavioral norms in children by parents (Palmer and Steadman 1997).

Some moral feelings have a genetic basis and have evolved in family and kin groups. Because reciprocity and cooperation in such circumstances enhance the fitness of the genes, emotional and other dispositions that aided cooperation and family cohesion also had a survival advantage. Moral sentiments evolved on a genetic foundation, but they required social interaction to become expressed and channeled. Culture enhanced and refined expressions of these sentiments into a transmitted moral code. Morality evolved through the interplay of genetic and cultural factors.

Darwin hints at this with his reference in the above quotation to "inherited habit." But although he hints at both mechanisms, he often conflates cultural and biological inheritance. Nevertheless, his stress on habit is apposite, and it turns out to be a far better concept than the nonmaterial "meme." Habits are socially transmitted dispositions necessarily underlying thoughts, beliefs, and deliberations.[1]

We need to consider the interplay of biological, social, and linguistic factors in the evolution of moral capacities, both in phylogeny of the human species as a whole and the ontogeny (or development) of human individuals. Although Darwin's account of the evolution of morality has its limitations, it deserves more attention than it has been given in the past. Darwin sketches how morality has evolved and traces its origins way back into our prehuman past.

The biological foundation of morality is discussed below in more depth. But prominent Darwinians from Thomas Henry Huxley to Richard Dawkins have failed to appreciate this foundation and contradicted their own evolutionary principles as a consequence. It is argued in the second section that the evolution of morality combined moral feelings that evolved among our ape-like ancestors with discursive capacities that are much more recent. Some research that illuminates specific, evolved, moral dispositions is discussed in the third section. The individual development of moral sentiments is discussed in the fourth section. The fifth section underlines that, notwithstanding its genetic foundation, morality and its evolution have to be understood also as social phenomena. It is shown more specifically that morality is much more than collections of individuals with moral or coop-

---

1. After criticizing Darwin for failing to distinguish adequately between the two modes of inheritance, James (1890) developed the concept of habit in a more rigorous manner. This became a major inspiration for Veblen (1899b, 1914, 1919). See Hodgson and Knudsen (2010) for a critique of the meme concept and an instatement of habit as a social replicator. Instead of focusing on the levels of ideas or behaviors—as with the meme—we point to the underlying, materially based replicators at the social level. The material basis of these social replicators is not simply the neural connections in the brain. It also includes the structured, communicative, and causal interactions between individuals.

erative attributes, and typical models of the evolution of altruism or cooperation are inadequate in their treatment of morality. Reference to moral
systems is required to explain the persistence of moral or cooperative attributes, especially when we acknowledge that humans can resist emotions
and reflect on their interests.

5.1. Morality Is More Than Skin-Deep

Is morality something that emerged only after the development of human
civilization? Is it a recent innovation that has to be instilled into everyone
against their rude and selfish nature? Or is it more than skin-deep?

Darwin was amazingly prescient and perceptive on this topic. In a quotation that heads the preceding chapter, Darwin (1871, pp. 88–89) upheld
that morality involves "comparing . . . past and future actions or motives,
and of approving or disapproving of them." Hence the actions of other animals do not derive from a sense of morality, and humans alone have this
capacity. But at the same time, Darwin saw the biological roots of morality
as a product of natural selection. Humans were the first species to develop
and articulate moral codes; but the foundations of morality go back into
our prehuman past.

But evolution and morality have often been regarded as separate, even
by Darwin's disciples. In 1893, Darwin's friend Thomas Henry Huxley famously argued that "the ethical progress of society" depends on not ignoring, accepting, or imitating natural selection in that sphere "but [on]
combating it" (Huxley and Huxley 1947, p. 82). This severance of the evolution of ethics from the evolution of humanity was criticized by a number of writers including Edward Westermarck (1891) and Petr Kropotkin
(1902). Likewise refusing such a separation, the British heterodox economist John A. Hobson (1921, p. 132) wrote:

> The importance of retaining in moral and political philosophy the clear rec-
> ognition that we are dealing with conduct which continues ever to be di-
> rected by biological considerations of survival is that only thus can we grasp
> the substance and vitality of ideals. For if we regard them as pure products of
> rational consciousness, of a moral and intellectual nature supervening upon
> our animal inheritance, it is easy . . . to dismiss them as illusions or shadowy
> epiphenomena. But if we recognize that the stuff out of which these ideals,
> even the loftiest and most spiritual, have been generated is not of ultimately
> diverse nature from the animal desires and the selfish cravings with which
> these ideals seem to conflict, the charge of unreality collapses.

Hobson (1929, p. 13) argued that it would be better to "search for values not in the high abstractions of philosophic thought but in the lower levels of human nature—the instincts, appetites, and behaviour of the animal man." In contrast, by pressing the point that nature herself has no morals, and thus dismissing "an 'ethics of evolution' . . . Huxley had missed the opportunity to discuss an 'evolution of ethics'" (Allett 1981, p. 21).

Richard Dawkins (1976, pp. 2–4, 215) describes the "ruthless selfishness" of our genes. He also claims that "we are born selfish" and "anything that has evolved by natural selection should be selfish." Genes *and* individuals are described as selfish.[2] Similar claims that evolution gives rise to the self-interested human individual are found in works by Michael Ghiselin (1974) and Richard Alexander (1987).

But Dawkins adds in a contradictory and Huxleyan manner: "Let us try to teach generosity and altruism. . . . We, alone on earth, can rebel against the tyranny of the selfish replicators." It is supposed that we can rebel against our congenital selfishness with the aid of the "meme." We are born selfish but somehow we can choose to be otherwise. The contrasts with Darwin's (1871) views on human nature and morality are graphic.

There are many problems with the Huxley-Dawkins separation of our evolutionary legacy from our current choices and capacities (Midgley 2003; de Waal 2006; Joyce 2006). Above all, if natural selection provides us with selfish dispositions, then why should we be inclined to "combat" selfishness or "teach generosity and altruism," unless they are some sort of elaborate selfish ruse to get the upper hand? Why should nature-red-in-tooth-and-claw rule in one sphere but not another? Furthermore, any inclination "to teach generosity and altruism" and any capacity to "rebel" against our own selfishness is unexplained. We are asked to overturn natural selection in our domain, but with unspecified human powers whose evolution is a mystery. What evolved dispositions would we recruit in this rebellion against evolution?

Dawkins (1976) invented the "meme" to do the moral work and "rebel" against the genes. But where do memes themselves come from and how do they evolve? How do we explain the evolutionary selection and survival of unselfish memes when all other evolutionary processes are supposed to lead to selfishness? The capacities to store, copy, and respond to memes must have themselves evolved. Or are we in a dualist or Platonic universe

---

2. But the concept of inclusive fitness demonstrates that "selfish" genes do not necessarily put the interests of their host organism first, giving rise to observed "altruistic" behavior among some animals (W. D. Hamilton 1964; Trivers 1971). Even a gene-centered approach must deny that individuals are necessarily self-seeking.

where memes are simply disconnected "ideas" that float above the material world and may rebel against its natural laws?[3]

Dawkins's implicit claim that memes are somehow themselves absolved from the laws of evolution is exemplified by his characterization of religion as a dysfunctional memetic "virus" (Dawkins 2006).[4] By contrast, David Sloan Wilson (2002) has argued that religion has historically played a role of enhancing the cohesion and survival of social groups. This is not to defend religious ideas as such, but to understand part of their evolutionary function. An understanding of their nature and function can help the construction of moral systems that do not rely on religious beliefs.

Frans de Waal (2006, p. 10) criticizes the Huxley-Dawkins view where "morality is presented as a thin crust underneath which boil antisocial, amoral and egotistic passions." He describes this as the "veneer theory" of morality and presents contrary evidence from his study of primates that they are capable of feeling sympathetic and cooperative emotions and committing emotionally to social rules. Hence our moral capacities are grounded in our evolution as a social species over many millions of years. While characterizing and criticizing this veneer theory, de Waal names Thomas Hobbes, Thomas Henry Huxley, George C. Williams, and Richard Dawkins among its advocates. Against them is Darwin himself, allied with such writers as Edward Westermarck, Edward O. Wilson, Jonathan Haidt, and de Waal.

On one side is the "veneer theory" view that evolution leads to individual selfishness, and morality is a possible overlay. On the other side, the critics argue that our long survival as a social species has meant the evolution of social instincts such as fairness and sympathy and the emotional capacity for guilt, and these form part of the foundations for morality. The critics cite evidence from the study of primate behavior, from psychology,

---

3. There is more than a hint of ontological dualism here: minds and ideas stand separate from matter and nature. Problems arise because Dawkins and others define memes as ideas. Philosophers have grappled with the reconciliation of the ideal and material for millennia. Unless we conceive of ideas as based on habits, emotions, or other similar, materially grounded dispositions, then the slide into dualism is difficult to resist.

4. As Susan Blackmore (1999) and others note, meme enthusiasts have typically been unclear or ambivalent whether memes are replicators or interactors (i.e., Dawkins's "vehicles"). Biological viruses host genomes (which are replicators), and hence viruses must be interactors not replicators (Hodgson and Knudsen 2010, p. 125). Hence Dawkins's (2003) depiction of religion memes as "viruses" effectively abandons his original description of memes as replicators. There may be a case for depicting (some) religions as social viruses that damage human society, but if so, they are not meme replicators.

from neuroscience, and from experimental economics.[5] They argue that morality is a product of evolution and is more than skin-deep.

The evidence of the critics is compelling. But we may not conclude that a fully developed morality has existed for millions of years. On this point Darwin is right: morality proper requires the capacity to compare and deliberate on actions and motives. It requires communication with others and a highly developed language (Joyce 2006). As Darwin (1871, p. 1:72) wrote: "after the power of language had been acquired and the wishes of the same community could be distinctly expressed, the common opinion how each member ought to act for the public good, would naturally become to a large extent the guide to action." Given that the evolution of morality depends on the emergence of a sophisticated language, "man . . . alone can be certainty be ranked as a moral being" (Darwin 1871, p. 1:89).

Morality proper, involving articulated abstract rules, could not have developed earlier than language. A language sufficiently well developed to sustain morality is of fairly recent origin—the earliest estimates being hundreds of thousands of years (Oppenheimer 2004) and the more recent being around 50,000 years ago (Diamond 1991). By contrast, the human species has been in existence for several million years. So is morality a recently acquired "veneer" after all? To answer this question, we need to distinguish between, on the one hand, the evolution of the preconditions for the development of moral systems and, on the other hand, the full emergence of morality itself. As outlined in the next section, some of the preconditions of our morality evolved as early as our ape-like ancestors.

5.2. How Morality Evolved

The nuts and bolts of morality include capacities for sympathy and cooperation that we share with the primates. The evidence suggests that much of this is biologically inherited as social instincts. But long before the evolution of human language, a form of protocultural and nongenetic transmission occurs. De Waal (1996, 2006) argues that primates can read or even transmit emotional states such as approval, empathy, and fear through sounds, body language, facial expressions, and pheromonal excretions. This "emotional contagion" (Hatfield, Cacioppo, and Rapson 1993) lies at

---

5. See, for example, de Waal (1982, 1996), Goodall (1986), Güth (1995), Greene and Haidt (2002), Zak (2004), Tancredi (2005), Hauser (2006), Fehr and Camerer (2007).

the core of the capacity for empathy: apes can understand and even share the joys or sufferings of others.[6]

The possibility of reading emotions in others, and even replicating emotional states, is a crucial inheritance mechanism for transmitting useful information and enhancing social cohesion. For example, the transmission of fear in the group can lead to collective flight from a predator. Such mechanisms are ubiquitous in nature. They have a long evolutionary history, and the capacities to respond to such signals are genetically inherited as instincts. Most organisms are genetically programmed to respond to signals that are relevant for their survival. If these include responses to the behavior of others in the same species, then this amounts to an additional level of information inheritance, above the gene. But if phenomena such as ritual or language are lacking, then this additional level does not amount to a developed culture.[7]

Among the repertoires of response for sophisticated organisms is the imitation of the behavior of others. Humans and primates use at least two types of imitation. The first is conformist transmission (Boyd and Richerson 1985). It has been shown that genes disposing individuals to such conformism would be selected in some contexts (Henrich and Boyd 1998). A second psychological mechanism is prestige-based imitation (Henrich and Gil-White 2001; Henrich 2004), where individuals learn advantageously from the more successful. Clearly this second mechanism must involve capabilities to recognize social hierarchy and prestige. In any social species, such instinctive propensities are likely to be selected over time; they would bestow survival advantages for the individual and the group.

There is also evidence for learned or inherited dispositions, which are triggered in specific contexts, to punish those who break the rules or fail to enforce them.[8] The relevant inherited dispositions have evolved in our social species over millions of years. Some such punishment involves "strong reciprocity" (Gintis 2000) where there is a propensity not only to punish

6. Consider also the phenomenon of *neural mirroring* where emotional contagion is shown to be a result of "mirror neurons" in the brain (Rizzolatti, Sinigaglia, and Anderson 2007).

7. See Hodgson and Knudsen (2010, chap. 8) for a discussion of how different levels of supra-genetic information transmission evolve and what may or may not be regarded as fully fledged cultural inheritance.

8. See Boyd and Richerson (1992), Andreoni (1995), de Waal (1996), Ben-Ner and Putterman (2000), Fehr and Gächter (2000a, 2000b, 2002), Gintis (2000), Field (2001), Price, Cosmides, and Tooby (2002), Boyd et al. (2003), Carpenter, Matthews, and Ong'ong'a (2004), Gintis et al. (2005), Wiessner (2005), Henrich et al. (2006), Fehr and Gintis (2007), Guzmán, Rodriguez-Sicken, and Rowthorn (2007), Carpenter and Matthews (2009), Henrich et al. (2010), Bowles and Gintis (2011).

cheats, free riders, rule breakers and self-aggrandizers, but also to punish others who fail to punish the offenders. Especially within small groups, these propensities are driven by strong feelings of anger. Primates also show evidence of such dispositions (de Waal 1996). On the other hand, the evidence of Keith Jensen, Joseph Call and Michael Tomasello (2007) shows that chimpanzees are less inclined to norms of sharing or fairness. Primate societies show evidence of social rules and supportive emotions, but these are more developed in some arreas than others. The more developed emotional dispositions include respect for authority and for the enforcement of rules.

No doubt these rule-following dispositions—and supportive emotions such as guilt or anger—were well developed when *Homo sapiens* evolved. As a more complex culture evolved with the development of language, the repertoire of rules would include sharing and fairness beyond the immediacy of the family group. Some of the more longstanding cultural developments would have led to the selection of consonant genetic dispositions. In a complex culture, emotionally empowered rules can help to enhance notions of justice and morality (Darwin 1871; de Waal 2006; Robinson, Kurzban, and Jones 2007). Overall, morality must have a genetic as well as a cultural foundation. This does not mean that genes are sufficient to generate a moral system, but that the cultural phenomenon of morality is fueled by biologically grounded emotions and value impulses.

Support for this view comes from experiments showing that preverbal babies assess individuals in the light of their behavior toward others. Studies of six- and ten-month-old infants show that they prefer an individual who helps over one who hinders another, prefer a helping individual to a neutral individual, and prefer a neutral to a hindering individual (Hamlin, Wynn, and Bloom 2007). Such inclinations may serve as a foundation for later moral thought and action, and their early developmental emergence indicates that these capacities have an inherited biological grounding. Other studies show that children as young as four years have a sense of fairness (McCrink, Bloom, and Santos 2010). Michael Tomasello (2009) provides evidence that children as young as two years have dispositions to cooperate and help others. Yet although we have such inherited dispositions, he shows how they are later shaped by culture.

Every human has a rudimentary sense of morality. It may develop in a social environment without much formal instruction. Young children are capable of distinguishing moral from prudential norms (Tisak and Turiel 1984), although many adults would have difficulty articulating the distinction. Moral development starts in very young children and is subject to abrupt developmental leaps. For example, ideas concerning fairness tend to emerge around the age of four years, to be applied wildly to multiple contexts (Fiske 1991). As Jonathan Haidt (2001, p. 827) concludes: "This pattern of sudden similarly timed emergence with overgeneralization suggest the maturation of an endogenous ability rather than the learning of a set of cultural norms."

Through our genes we inherit the capacity to quickly respond to social dilemmas by developing emotions. These dispose us to make choices and help us to form rapid judgments concerning what is morally right or wrong. In social settings, the moral judgments help us justify our actions to others and to exhort others to approve or imitate. Genetic dispositions to deal with social dilemmas by developing emotionally charged value-intuitions can thus have strong survival value. These emotional capacities evolve by natural selection.

But our genes do not tell us what is moral or immoral. We have to learn that through engagement in a social culture. The foundations of our moral capacity have evolved over the millions of years that we have been a social species. But in the last one or two hundred thousand years, the development of human moral capacities has been dependent on particular cultural settings, allowing for multiple and contrasting moral systems on the basis of largely shared instinctive bedrock.

Tomasello (2009) uses experiments with young children to show how their innate desire to help others becomes shaped by culture. They become more aware of their membership of a group and of its rules. Groups convey shared expectations and may encourage or discourage cooperation in specific circumstances.

Given that we also inherit genetically a long-evolved capacity to imitate others and a capacity for empathy, we are likely to conform to strong moral claims, especially when made by high-status or numerous individuals. Cultural mechanisms lead to conformity within the group. Although rebellion against the prevailing rules is possible, clashes are more likely between groups with different cultures. Hence cooperation emerges as a distinctly human combination of innate and learned behavior.

The evolution of moral capacities is much like the evolution of linguistic ability, as well as depending on language itself. Darwin (1871, p. 1:106) referred to the "half-art and half-instinct of language." Because it would be impossible for an infant to learn all the rules of a complex language solely by reinforcement learning and cultural transmission, some very basic linguistic capacities must be inherited as instincts. But the nature and extent of this instinctive legacy is a matter of current dispute among psychologists and linguists, with the more recent contributions emphasizing the learned and cultural component (Pinker 1994; Deacon 1997; Sampson 2005; Evans and Levinson 2009). In any case, language acquisition depends on both inherited genetic capacities and interaction with others in specific cultural contexts. Similarly, the evolution of morality is "half-art and half-instinct." As Marc Hauser (2006, pp. 419–20) argues:

> Our expressed languages differ, but we generate each one on the basis of a universal set of principles. . . . Underlying the extensive cross-cultural variation we observe in our expressed social norms is a universal moral grammar that enables each child to grow a narrow range of possible moral systems. When we judge an action as morally right or wrong, we do so instinctively, tapping a system of unconsciously operative and inaccessible moral knowledge. Variation between cultures in their expressed moral norms is like variation between cultures in their spoken languages.

This view is consistent with recent studies of how each brain develops into a highly complex organ on the basis of a limited set of genetic instructions. Gary Marcus (2004, p. 12) outlines the developmental pathways by which genes guide the construction of brains. For Marcus, genes create the *first draft* of the brain, and experience later *edits* it: "Nature bestows upon the newborn a considerably complex brain, but one that is best seen as prewired—flexible and subject to change—rather than hardwired, fixed, and immutable."

Although most of our genetic endowment changes much more slowly than human culture, in the hundred thousand years or so that human language and morality have developed, some culture-led gene-culture coevolution has been likely. As culture evolves, it creates a new environment for genetic selection. Hence over tens of thousands of years, the cultural evolution of morality is likely to have led to some slight consonant genetic change.[9]

In sum, morality depends on language, communication of abstract concepts, discussion and reflection on them, and the derivation of principles that are general (at least for the group). We inherit some core moral capacities genetically, but not morality as a whole. The development of morality proper depends on interaction with others in a social context.

9. There is evidence for the relatively rapid gene-culture coevolution of some traits, including the classic case of adult lactose tolerance (Durham 1991; Richerson, Boyd, and Henrich 2011). But much of the human genetic endowment has changed very little in millions of years. Culture evolves much more rapidly.

5.3. The Evolution of Prominent Moral Universals

Thanks to the work of several researchers, we now have a sketch of the components of morality that have evolved through a combination of genetically acquired value dispositions and developmental and discursive processes within cultures. Some important contributions in this area have been made by Jonathan Haidt and his colleagues. Haidt and Craig Joseph (2004, 2008) propose that five sets of innate value-intuitions are found in all human cultures and guide the development of many culturally specific moral dispositions (Haidt et al.'s key defining terms appear in bold):

1 **Care** for others, protecting them from harm.
2 **Fairness**, justice, treating others equally, **reciprocity**.
3 **Loyalty** to your group, family, nation, or **ingroup**.
4 **Respect** for tradition and legitimate **authority**.
5 **Purity**, avoiding disgusting things, foods, or actions.

Excepting purity, the other four are present to some degree in other primates (de Waal 1996). This strengthens the claim that some foundations of moral learning are inherited in advance of experience. Each of these five value-intuitions is a good candidate for a Sperber-style learning module that impels development of a valuation capacity in a cultural setting. Dan Sperber's (2005) modules are not themselves innate; they are generated during development by a smaller set of "learning modules" that are innate templates or "learning instincts."

There are good reasons why every one of these moral intuitions has been favored by natural selection, at least among closely related kin. Caring for others evolves originally from a shared genetic endowment with offspring and relatives. Fairness and reciprocity can bring the benefits of social cooperation. Ingroup loyalty helps to improve the cohesion of the group. Authority and respect lead to valuation of the adaptations of successful leaders, as well as providing a further mechanism for group cohesion. Intuitions of purity and sanctity help promote efficacious improvements in diet and hygiene.

Our inclinations to respect those in authority were dramatized by the experiments of Stanley Milgram (1974). Milgram invited members of the public to help in a laboratory study ostensibly about learning. A "scientist" asked these recruits to administer electric shocks to a subject, to punish wrong answers to questions. Milgram found that a majority of adults would administer shocks that were apparently painful, dangerous, or even fatal if ordered to do so by the person in authority. In fact, there were no shocks and the subject was an actor, feigning agony or even death. This experiment shows that people can willingly accept the orders of perceived authority figures, even when their own moral feelings are violated.[10] Milgram (1974, pp. 124–25, 131) argues that our disposition to respect authority emanates from the evolutionary survival advantages of cohesive social groups. He proposes that the human species has evolved an inherited, instinctive, propensity for obedience that is triggered by specific social circumstances. In accord with Haidt and Joseph (2004, 2008), Milgram suggests that dispositions to respect authority have genetic and cultural foundations.

Given the evolution of these five emotionally laden intuitions, a tribe that encoded them in a system of explicit moral rules would enhance the processes of enculturation and moral development, even at the risk of some social rigidity. Teaching children explicitly a set of moral rules that prevail in the specific culture is more reliable and forceful than relying on intuitions and feelings alone. Such didactic routines would have survival value for the group.

Haidt and Joseph (2008) regard moral traits as relatively flexible capacities to interpret and act in different circumstances. They conceive of such capacities in the manner of John Dewey (1922), as dynamic patternings of perception, emotion, judgment, and action. Moral virtues are social skills involving the perception of morally relevant information and the potential to respond accordingly in the cultural context.

They argue that the moral development of an individual is a movement from crude judgments and feelings based on a small number of innate moral intuitions to highly sophisticated and differentiated perceptions, emotions, beliefs, valuations and judgments. Mature moral functioning is much more than emotional or intuitive reactions to social stimuli. Disgust, for example, is not a moral judgment. Morality also depends on the acquisition and use of moral concepts. As we interact with others in a specific culture, domain-specific, module-like, intuitive mini-programs give rise to a flexible set of moral modules that are more powerful and subtle than the innate intuitions. The five foundations are multiplied, expanded, and

---

10. Perhaps because of the challenge in Milgram's work to conventional ideas of the autonomous individual, these striking experiments have had less impact on the social sciences than one might expect. Relatively rare exceptions include Akerlof (1991), who emphasizes their challenge to mainstream assumptions in economics. Although scrutiny of the results of Milgram experiments reveals a more complex interaction of situation and personality than in some interpretations (Blass 1991), their replication shows similar outcomes across several different cultures (Smith and Bond 1993).

refined to the point where we acquire a variety of codifiable moral beliefs (Haidt and Joseph 2008).

5.4. Individual Moral Development

Inspired by Jean Piaget's (1965) studies of the moral development of children, Lawrence Kohlberg and his colleagues elaborated several key stages of individual moral development, involving three levels and two developmental stages at each level (Colby and Kohlberg 1987). At the first *preconditional* level, children take their own interests as central and regard rules as imposed from outside. Two stages within this level center on avoiding punishment and on meeting personal desires. From his empirical studies, Kohlberg (1969) estimated that the preconditional level characterizes most children under nine, many adolescents, and some criminals.

Ironically this level is also the highest moral development of "economic man." As Lanse Minkler (2008, p. 46) wittily observes, the familiar individual of the economics textbooks would primarily "pursue his or her own interests" and "maximize satisfaction" (to use the words of Colby and Kohlberg 1986, p. 26). Economic man is clearly stuck at the first and preconditional level, with a highly underdeveloped morality. Lynne A. Stout (2008, pp. 158–59) goes further: given his selfishness and deceitfulness "*Homo economicus* is a sociopath."

At the second, *conventional* level, stage three involves mutual interpersonal expectations, relationships, and interpersonal conformity, while at stage four individuals assimilate their status as members of society and develop a conscience. They identify with others and base their morality on social norms. At the third, *postconventional* level, stage five is characterized by social contract and individual rights, while stage six is characterized by purportedly universal ethical principles. Kohlberg (1969) estimates that only a minority of adults reach this third level of moral development. While Kohlberg's classification is not the only one available, it clearly is useful in delineating differences and stages between self-interest and full moral development.

Moral development depends on others and is highly sensitive to cultural conditions. Among the many forms of social interaction promoting the development of morality, Haidt and Joseph (2004, 2008) highlight storytelling and gossip. For them, narrative is a major cultural tool for the socialization and development of the fundamental moral intuitions. Stories tell us what is noble and valuable, and sometimes help to legitimate authority figures. Gossip can check or reinforce our moral feelings in local contexts. Religion is typically a major vehicle for conveying morally loaded narratives. The modern mass media widens the scope by capturing regional, national, and international events, as well as fictional tales.[11]

This is not to deny a substantial element of self-construction in moral development (Piaget 1965; Kohlberg 1969). We are not passive receptors of cultural norms. Through an "internal conversation" involving conflicting habits, feelings, and judgments (Dewey 1922), we develop our own distinctive moral personalities. It is unnecessary and unacceptable to assume that individual agency is uncaused or free of cultural pressures. Variations in both genetic endowment and personal circumstances account for huge variations in individuality, especially when the resolution of inner conversations and conflicts is often sensitive to small cognitive triggers or events.

5.5. Modeling the Evolution of Moral Systems

The development of moral dispositions in individuals is necessarily a matter of both inherited value-intuitions and a unique personal developmental process within a social culture and community. Hence, contrary to some authors, morality cannot be understood simply as individual attributes or dispositions, however complex or multidimensional. Morality also depends on social relations—it is a social system as well as an individual evaluation.[12] Morality cannot be encompassed by the social preferences of an individual or by a "multiple self" with plural preference functions (Margolis 1982; Elster 1986). Morality is both a biological and a social phenomenon, and is irreducible to either individual preferences or genetic endowments. A century of utilitarianism, biological reductionism, analytical individualism, and the terminology of preferences have thwarted this realization.

Furthermore, as a social system, morality depends on social positions and relations of authority. Morality is sustained not merely through genetic and cultural transmission, but through the replication of structures of authority and power (Milgram 1974; Haidt and Joseph 2008). Hence what is involved is imitation or learning and the reproduction of institutions and

11. There are even narratives within academia itself, which help to frame political attitudes of researchers, teachers, and students (Haidt and Joseph 2008; Graham, Haidt, and Nosek 2009).

12. The interesting attempts to model morality by Danielson (1992, 1998) are defective in that respect. Alexander (2007) also makes the error of regarding morality as purely a property of individuals rather than a social system.

cultural mechanisms for legitimating positions of authority (Runciman 2002).

Morality is an emergent property of interactions between individuals in structured groups. Groups can be interactors and objects of selection in a process of evolutionary selection. A system of morality—enhancing rule enforcement and social cohesion—is a typical property of such human groups.

Although it relates to individual fitness, the evolution of morality cannot be specified simply in individual terms. The evolution and sustenance of moral systems involves a battle between the selfish inclinations of individuals and group moral pressure to conform and cooperate. If the group pressure is insufficient, then individual fitness will be enhanced by acting selfishly. If the group moral pressure restrains selfishness sufficiently, then individual fitness will be enhanced by cooperating with others. It is a classic case of individual fitness being context dependent. In such circumstances, we can also speak of group fitness.

Given these complexities, to what extent is it possible to model the evolution of moral communities? Because morality depends on both biologically inherited feelings and cultural transmission, we are reminded of the models of *dual inheritance* pioneered by Robert Boyd and Peter Richerson (1980, 1985) and others. Richerson and some coresearchers have turned to the task of modeling the evolution of business organizations and their internal cultures (Cordes et al. 2008, 2011). Samuel Bowles and Herbert Gintis (2011) have also developed several useful models, particularly concerning the evolution of cooperative and altruistic behavior. But Bowles and Gintis (2011, p. 125) also rightly point out that when evolutionary processes involve multiple and complex interacting levels, then analytically soluble models are out of reach:

> Because this process [of the coevolution of altruism with institutions] involves highly complex selection processes operating at two levels—individual and group—in which the magnitude of within-group and between-group selection effects are endogenously determined by the evolution of group-level institutions, the dynamic is not amenable to mathematical analysis . . . capable of analytical solution.

The only other modeling options here are agent-based simulations. Samuel Bowles, Jung-Kyoo Choi, and Astrid Hopfensitz (2003) simulate the coevolution of altruism and cooperation-enhancing institutions in a population of agents. This is very useful, but it needs to be enhanced by an understanding of moral motivation.

Morality exposes a serious gap in the hitherto predominant models in this research area. Typically it is assumed that there two types of agent: altruistic cooperators versus self-interested egoists. Initially there is often a low or zero frequency of altruists, and more come into existence by selective replication or low-probability random mutation. Altruists help others at their own cost, in terms of their expected fitness. Even with low initial frequencies and relatively high costs, these models and simulations show that a population with a much higher frequency of altruists can evolve. But what these models do not show is why any intelligent and reflective individual should continue to act in accordance with any inherited disposition toward altruism or cooperation. Why should altruists remain altruists or cooperators remain cooperators? Apart from the low-probability random mutation, individuals in these models are assumed to remain as one type or the other.

Biological models of the evolution of altruism were developed to apply to nonhuman species, with illustrative examples such as the alarm call of an individual bird that warns the flock of the approach of a predator, thereby placing itself at greater risk. These models typically assume a close correlation between genetic dispositions and actual behavior. But in the case of humans, this close connection is even less tenable. Apart from the fact that culture plays a more important role, humans have much greater capacity to reflect on their circumstances and consider the consequences of their actions. Although culture is a major influence, we are neither cultural nor biological puppets. We can reflect on our situation and even resist our emotions. Some people may rebel against prevailing norms.

This exposes a major limitation in typical models of the evolution of altruism or cooperation. They fail to take into account that emotions such as sympathy, anger, or guilt can be countered by deliberation on our self-interest. If an individual experiences (genetically or culturally acquired) feelings of sympathy for an orphaned child or a destitute beggar, or anticipates the warm inner glow of satisfaction from the envisaged act of giving, he can reflect on his costly sacrifice and override these emotions (and perhaps in favor of contrary feelings related to self-interest). Why not? We are deliberative and thoughtful, so we do not always follow our emotions. For example, we do not always answer the call of sexual lust by making advances on an attractive partner. Although we have urges to copulate, we do not act like dogs in the park. So why shouldn't we also resist the pangs of sympathy and maintain our bank balance? If we can resist such animal desires, then why cannot we resist altruistic urges as well? Genes or culture cannot overcome the fragility of altruism among species that are capable of reflecting on its costs. Some additional factor is required to explain the enduring frequency of altruistic or cooperative behavior. Morality is this missing ingredient.

Consider acts of charity. A number of explanations make sense of altruism and charitable giving, including status-seeking, sociability, self-esteem, guilt, identity construction, and much else (Bourdieu 1977, 1990; Collins and Hickman 1991; Eckstein 2001; Osteen 2002). The evidence suggests that people act altruistically for a number of motives, including perceptions of moral obligation. Notwithstanding the existence of baser motivations, a shared code of philanthropic morality is a powerful social mechanism for keeping emergent altruists on track. The whole point of a moral system, and a reason for its evolution and survival, is that it acts partly at the discursive level to restrain all persuasive rationalizations of self-interest. This does not mean that it always works in this way. But it can be a powerful social mechanism to restrain deliberative revelations of self-interest.

A system of morality will work best when it dovetails with altruistic emotions. Insofar as these emotions have a genetic foundation, they will reflect communalities of human evolution and sustain some ethical universals. Other emotions will reflect specific cultural settings. A disposition to respond to all such value-laden emotions by reflecting in terms of "doing the right thing" or "do unto others as you would have them do unto you" would help to sustain altruistic sentiments and counter selfish thoughts about personal costs and benefits. Habits of thought that underpinned and retained such moral sentiments would also come into play.

Groups with strong moral systems that enhance cohesion and cooperation can have fitness advantage over other groups with less effective moral systems. This would aid a process of cultural group selection. It would be the selection of groups as objects in a population, with selection outcomes favoring particular customs and habits that sustained fitness-enhancing ethical principles. At the same time, this cultural process depends on the prior and sustained evolution of particular genetic dispositions and capacities. These evolved initially as a result of inclusive fitness, and they were then enhanced by procultural developments in our early ancestors. Our morally discursive evolution over one or two hundred thousand years has provided sufficient time for moral systems to have some slight feedback on genetic evolution as well. But the most important drivers in this process are institutions and culture.

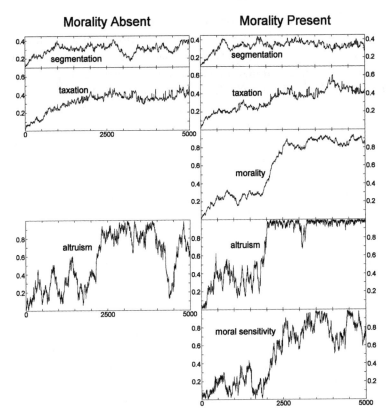

Figure 2. The Evolution of Altruism, Morality, and Institutions. The figure shows the results of two runs of an agent-based model, with 200 replicating heterogeneous agents and 10 varied groups, each run being 5,000 generations (horizontal axes). Panels for segmentation (the tendency to interact with similar individuals in the group), taxation (group sharing), and morality show the average of these group institutional variables. Panels for altruism (the basic tendency to cooperate in a Prisoner's Dilemma game) and moral sensitivity (the additional tendency to take group morality into account when playing the game) show the averages through time for these individual attributes in the whole population. The three panels on the left show outputs for a run when moral institutions were absent, as in the Bowles, Choi, and Hopfensitz (2003) model. The five panels on the right show outputs for a simulation when the morality algorithms in the program are switched on and the moral variables are allowed to change and take effect.

Figure 2 shows the results from an agent-based model that can incorporate both altruism and morality. Like the Bowles, Choi, and Hopfensitz (2003)—henceforth BCH-2003—model, it is meant to address the evolution of cooperation and altruistic dispositions among humans in the last few hundred thousand years. The model here is very similar to BCH-2003, except that instead of being altruists or nonaltruists, agents have altruistic dispositions on a scale from zero to unity. But this model explicitly adds the effects of morality, which is absent or subsumed under altruism in BCH-2003. As in their model, agents are place randomly in several groups. The simulation goes through several generational cycles. At the start of the simulation, the levels of individual altruism, individual moral sensitivity, group segmentation, group taxation, and group morality are set at zero for all individuals and groups.

In my model, at the beginning of each generational cycle, each individual's altruistic disposition is increased by a small, randomized increment that is proportional to the group level of morality.[13] This top-down process represents institutional processes of individual instruction in groups with some positive level of morality. Each individual's moral sensitivity is raised or lowered by a small randomized increment depending on whether its value is respectively below or above the group level of morality. An upward movement would correspond to socialization or instruction. But as with the BCH-2003 model, all institutions are maintained at a cost to each group's fitness.

Then, as with BCH-2003, individuals within each group are paired randomly to play a Prisoner's Dilemma game. Also as with BCH-2003, the group's segmentation value is the probability that two identical agents will be paired, and if an agent fails to find a close match, then it pairs randomly in the group. But in the present model, two similar and nonidentical agents also have a chance of pairing, while higher segmentation makes the similarity conditions more stringent.

The chances of cooperating in the game are related to the individual's altruistic disposition, enhanced by a term involving the product of individual moral sensitivity and the (institutional) level of morality in the group as a whole. The game is then played and the payoffs determined. As in BCH-2003, it is assumed that the fitness of every agent is the sum of its game payoff and ten baseline units representing further resources acquired by other means.

As in BCH-2003, each group has a taxation level. This is the proportion of the group's resources that is shared equally between all group members. Set initially at zero, each group's taxation level is altered (up or down) each generation by a small random mutation. Also set initially at zero, each group's segmentation level is altered (up or down) each generation by a

---

13. Devotees of some version of methodological individualism may worry about this. But it is not being suggested that real institutions can affect individuals directly without the mediation of other individuals. The institutional variables are condensed descriptions of group rules and norms that are effective for individuals within the group.

small random mutation. But in the present model, each group's morality level is altered (up or down) by a random mutation adjusted by the average levels of morality and altruism in the group.

The following steps are again similar to the BCH-2003 model. Every agent replicates, and their copies are more likely to be similar to the fitter members of their group, plus small random mutations. The new generation replaces the old. Then with probability 0.2, each agent migrates to another randomly chosen group. Subsequently, with probability 0.25, each group engages in lethal combat with another randomly chosen group. The weaker group in terms of aggregate fitness is exterminated. Members of the winning group then replicate to fill the population gaps left by the losers. After that, the winning group splits randomly into two, subject to a minimum group size of four.

The most significant differences between the present and the BCH-2003 model are the addition of scaled rather than binary altruistic dispositions, the top-down effects of group morality levels on group member altruism and individual moral sensitivity, and the bottom-up effect of average individual altruism and average moral sensitivity on group morality. In some circumstances, this combination of top-down and bottom-up feedback effects can lead to virtuous circles of moral development in the group.

In figure 2, compare the results for the simulations without and with moral systems in place. As with the published results for BCH-2003, the three panels on the left show cycles of boom and bust for altruism and other variables. Altruism reaches high levels for several generations, and then crashes again.[14] If most people are altruistically disposed, then maverick nonaltruists can exploit the situation and reap higher rewards. The mavericks will then reproduce more rapidly and bring the average level of altruism crashing down. By contrast, the panels on the right-hand side of the figure show that when the moral system is in operation, then once a high level of average altruism is maintained, it can be sustained by moral imperatives. In these circumstances, individual moral sensitivity and group taxation also reach higher levels. But given that taxation—like segmentation and morality—is a costly institution for the group to maintain, there are limits to its rise.

To obtain a more robust comparison of runs with and without the morality component, 40 runs in each mode were averaged. The results (not reproduced here) show that mean altruism reaches significantly higher lev-

---

14. See in particular the results in Bowles, Choi, and Hopfensitz (2003, pp. 142–43).

els with the moral system operative. When morality is not operative, after 1,300 generations the altruism level stabilizes at about 0.5. But when morality is operative, after 2,300 generations the altruism level remains above 0.9. When operative, the global morality level on average rises and stays above 0.8 after about 2,500 generations. Consequently the patterns in figure 2 are quite typical of runs with the same parameter values.

All these runs are merely illustrative and not meant to reproduce anything like the exact course of human evolution. The evolution of moral systems in this model is also sensitive to parameter values. The point of the exercise is not to predict actual outcomes but to indicate how the evolution of moral systems may begin to be modeled and to show that moral factors are irreducible to altruism. This is an important agenda for future research that has previously concentrated on the evolution of altruism and cooperation to the relative neglect of morality.

I raised my suspicion at the end of chapter 2 that the slogan of "methodological individualism" has helped to confine investigations and simulations of the evolution of cooperation to the apparent properties of individuals, thereby neglecting the institutional evolution of moral systems. The arguments in this and the preceding chapter establish that morality has also to be considered as a group and relational phenomenon rather than simply an individual one.

The evolution of morality shows that the biological and the social are so deeply entwined, it is difficult to confine powerful general principles to one domain alone. The valid assertion of biosocial continuity, when considered in its details, has to rely on generalized Darwinian principles, as well as an understanding of specific detailed mechanisms. The Darwinian concepts of variation, selection, and replication apply to both the genetic and social levels. Genes, habits, and customs are relevant replicators. The evolution of morality is a specific illustration of the organizing value of the principles of generalized Darwinism (Aldrich et al. 2008; Hodgson and Knudsen 2010).

5.6. The Bottom Line: Humans Combine Morality with Self-Interest

We are born neither moral nor immoral. We are born with the capacity to develop a moral sense and to act morally, subject to sufficient cultural and institutional supports. But we are also self-interested. Evolution has provided us with instincts that trigger our moral development in a suitable sociocultural setting and with basic instincts such as hunger and lust that can be spurs to egoism. Through our socialization, we typically develop into complex personalities where all biologically inherited impulses are extended or constrained to different degrees and in different ways.

The sometimes diverging inner impulses that we bring into the world play out their conflict as our personality grows, in the institutional settings of parental care, peer group interaction, and organized education. All these institutional settings have major effects on how the moral and self-interested aspects of our personalities develop. Given our declining potential for adaptation as we get older, the earliest years are the most formative. Guided by inherited impulses, we learn much of our morality from our parents or guardians.

Preceding chapters have considered the hardwired elements of human nature that are necessary for humans to cooperate in various ways and to develop complex and diverse social cultures and structures. But the structures themselves are not hardwired, and the long "genetic leash" has permitted a lot of variety, notwithstanding some important communalities. Both individuals and societies can develop in many different ways.

The mistake of influential neoclassical economists was to assume that in the economic sphere self-interest was overwhelming, and our altruistic and moral tendencies could be ignored as we entered the world of contract and business (Jevons 1871; Edgeworth 1881; Wicksteed 1910; Pareto 1935, 1971). Later writers such as Gary Becker (1976b, 1991, 1996) made it less complicated, with the claim that the mechanics of individual utility maximization, developed in the neoclassical analysis of business life, applies generally to all social interactions. Becker ignored any moral dimension that could not be captured in a utility function. But even the earlier view that moral propensities were real but can be safely ignored in the economic sphere is profoundly mistaken. Business, in the firm and the market, is unavoidably infused with moral considerations. This argument is developed in the next chapter.

Applications

SIX

Morality and Cooperation in Business

Organizations endure, however, in proportion to the breadth of the morality by which they are governed. This is only to say that foresight, long purposes, high ideals, are the basis for the persistence of cooperation.

—Chester I. Barnard (1938)

"Economic man" has been characterized as greedy or selfish. His sole ethical commitment is to himself and his own pleasure. The Nobel economist Oliver Williamson (1975, p. 255) goes further in his work on business firms, to underline "self-interest seeking with guile. . . . Economic man is a much more subtle and devious creature than the usual self-interest seeking assumption reveals." Although he later seems to dilute this assumption, to stress the significant contractual effects of the minority threat of opportunism rather than its supposed universality, he still upholds opportunism as a foundational assumption of transaction cost economics.[1] Williamson thus enhances a longstanding belief among many economists that business is an amoral arena of self-interest. Accordingly, Williamson (1985, p. 122) treats culture and ethical values as external constraints on business transactions rather than intrinsic parts of economic activity.

Williamson's amoral view of the capitalist economy partly overlaps with many on the left who find little virtue in the system and believe that capitalists as forced by competition to seek profit to the point of oblitera-

---

1. Compare, for example, Williamson (1993, 2002). Elsewhere I show that—independently of its prevalence in the real world—the assumption of opportunism is logically unnecessary to sustain the transaction cost argument. Other factors, including morally innocent misunderstandings, can lead in principle to potential noncompliance and the requirement of monitoring (Hodgson 2004c). Determination of the actual frequency of any such behavior is a matter of empirical investigation rather than a priori assumption.

tion of any ethical sentiment. As Karl Marx and Frederick Engels (1976, pp. 486–87) wrote in the *Communist Manifesto*: "The bourgeoisie, wherever it has got the upper hand . . . has left remaining no other nexus between man and man than naked self-interest, then callous 'cash payment.'" It has drowned chivalry and sentimentalism "in the icy water of egotistical calculation." Although they differ greatly in their analyses, Marx and Williamson share the view that capitalist businesses exhibit self-interest and opportunism rather than morality. They both theorize individual motivations as mostly selfish. Shared theoretical preconceptions span different disciplines and divergent ideologies.

In proposing a different view, I do not claim that capitalism is a noble example of ethical achievement. On the contrary, we have abundant evidence of corruption and injustice under capitalism. Capitalism has exploited the weak and driven many into a life of mind-numbing labor. Bankers are rewarded for their recklessness while ordinary people suffer austerity. It is predominantly a system of getting and spending, driven by greed. In the absence of enforceable rules to the contrary, greed can lead to corruption and injustice. But whatever their failings, humans are not *entirely* motivated by self-interest, even under a social order that encourages and depends on private acquisition and consumption. Consequently, it is analytically unsound to treat business agents as totally amoral, even as a conceptual "ideal type." Business strategies are touched by ethical impulses of some kind, even if these drives are deleterious or narrowly applied. Competition does not extinguish moral sentiment. Capitalism depends on significant residues of morality for its very existence.

This is neither a novel observation nor one confined to apologists of the status quo. Several prominent writers in the German historical school—which flourished from the 1840s to the 1920s—argued that economic activities of individuals are not motivated by self-interest alone. They included Wilhelm Roscher, Adolph Wagner, Karl Knies, and Gustav Schmoller. Michael Pickhardt (2005) notes that while modern experimental economics has cast considerable doubt on the pure self-interest hypothesis, several current speculations concerning nonselfish motives in economics were foreshadowed by members of the German historical school. That school influenced leading British and American economists including Alfred Marshall, Thorstein Veblen, and John R. Commons, who also adopted a more complex view of individual motivation in business.[2]

2. The myth that Marshall was an antagonist of the historical school can be refuted simply by reading his *Principles* (Hodgson 2001, 2005). For example, Marshall (1920, p. 784) noted

Joseph A. Schumpeter (1942, p. 423) was also strongly influenced by the German historical school and argued accordingly that "no social system can work which is based exclusively upon a network of free contracts between (legally) equal contracting parties and in which everyone is supposed to be guided by nothing except his own (short-run) utilitarian ends." A few years later, Polanyi (1947, p. 114) argued that economic man "was never as selfish as the theory demanded." Even in the business sphere "he was still found to be acting on remarkably 'mixed' motives, not excluding those of duty towards himself and others—and maybe, secretly, even enjoying work for its own sake."

Similarly Amartya Sen (in Klamer 1989, p. 147) opined: "If now within the firm you were to pursue only your interests and goals, if you were trying to get away with as much cheating as you could manage, the productive efficiency of that firm would be deeply problematic." Joseph Stiglitz (1994, p. 271) has also warned: "Capitalism, as it promotes self-interested behavior, may create an environment less conducive to efficiency." Abandoning a hedonistic view of the individual does not mean adopting an equally naive belief that people are wholly virtuous. Human beings are often selfish and sometimes capable of morally outrageous acts. What is required is a more complex theory of motivation that takes both moral and selfish motivations into account.

The following section addresses an ancient and elemental form of human interaction—the conversation. From the claim that such communication must entail some ethical principles, it is established that business contracts also depend on ethical considerations. This leads to a discussion in the second section of the role of morality within the firm. The third section shows that ethical issues must be taken on board in discussion of the nature of the firm.

6.1. Ethics, Conversations, and Contracts

A basic and omnipresent feature of human relationships is conversation. As Jürgen Habermas argues at length, important ethical values including

---

without dissent that Adolph Wagner installed both egoism and altruism as actual business motives, including moral motivations involving perceived duty and the approval of others. Reviewing Schmoller's (1900) *Grundriss*, Veblen (1901, p. 92) noted approvingly that "Professor Schmoller shows . . . that this self-seeking motive is hemmed in and guided at all points in the course of its development by considerations and conventions that are not of a primarily self-seeking kind." Schmoller engaged in controversy with Menger in the famous *Methodenstreit*. Commons (1934, p. 720) opined that "Schmoller might have gone further in his criticism of Menger's method. . . . Menger . . . eliminated all such motives as ethical feelings of right, wrong, justice, duty." This criticism of Menger remains relevant for much of subsequent Austrian school economics.

truth, sincerity, and normative appropriateness, are implicit in dialogue. Habermas (1991, p. 1) defines "communicative action" as "the type of action aimed at reaching understanding." According to this definition, all contractual negotiations in business and trade are communicative acts. Consequently, there is an unavoidable ethical dimension to the negotiation of all contracts, including on product and labor markets. Even when the contractual conversation is far from "ideal" in Habermas's sense—that is, honest, participatory, and unmanipulative—ethical issues are ineradicable in business life.

Contract and trade raise matters of honesty, trust, and rights. A contract involves a mutual recognition of rights. It involves agreed obligations and invokes general (tacit or explicit) principles concerning different eventualities (including noncompliance) and rights of ownership. Given the complexities and uncertainties, some degree of trust is unavoidable. Given that trade in some form has existed for tens of thousands of years—albeit originally between tribes rather than individuals (Weber 1927)—commercial rules invoking basic moral precepts have a very long pedigree.

The formation of a contract is a matter of integrity and not merely self-interest. People who made an agreement with little intention of honoring it would be liars. As Lanse Minkler (2008, p. 2) observes: "This simple but powerful fact seems to have eluded most economic analyses." And if our choice to tell the truth is simply a contingent, utilitarian outcome of our preferences and current circumstances, then it hardly signals an honest and reliable personality. We may be selfish and opportunistic in other respects, but if we are identified as a cheater or a liar, then our self-seeking mission is typically undermined, as we rely continually on conversation and negotiation with others.

Of course, we are not saints. Everyone who has bought a secondhand car knows that dishonesty and withholding of crucial information are commonplace. Deception is widespread in contracts and markets (Gerschlager 2005). But that is not the point. Even if lying is widespread, some norms and expectations of honesty are necessary to make the contract system work.

Knowing that opportunism does exist, contracts are often drawn up to protect traders from possible shortcomings, and legal or other penalties of some kind are relied on to ensure compliance. But there are limits to these protective devices. Contracts typically involve problems of radical uncertainty and incomplete knowledge. The world is complex and unpredictable. Consequently, full contractual specification to deal with all possible eventualities in all possible circumstances is impossible. We must rely to some degree on custom and precedent. Furthermore, although contract depends on will, it presumes the legal status and rights of the parties and a set of other complex precedents and institutions inherited from the past. These are always too lengthy and complex to be fully specified.[3] For these reasons, Émile Durkheim (1984, p. 158) proposed in 1893 that "in a contract not everything is contractual"—unavoidably there are factors, irreducible to the intentions or agreements of individuals, that potentially have regulatory and binding functions for the contract itself. These consist of rules and norms that cannot be completely codified in law. The parties to the agreement have no alternative but to rely on customary rules and standard patterns of behavior, which cannot for practical reasons be established or confirmed by detailed negotiation. Consequently, to some degree, all business deals have in part to rely on fragile mechanisms of honesty and trust. That is why reputation and "goodwill" in business are so important and widely appraised (Commons 1924). Contract, so central to modern economic life, presumes some honest intention to honor an agreement.[4]

Yet honesty would be an alien concept in a world of pleasure machines; their only possible standard of morality would be their own satisfaction. Knowing that it was simply maximizing its own utility, few people would enter into a contract with a pleasure machine. If things went wrong or were unexpected, then there could be no higher appeal to justice, ethical practice, or its better nature.

It is thus no accident that the elevation of honesty as a virtue and the disapproval of lying are found in almost all human cultures, and a prohibition of lying is present in almost all religions (S. Bok 1978). Whatever the veracity or otherwise of their tenets, religions are important cultural adaptations that have helped to sustain some moral principles that enhance social cohesion, regulate human interaction and help commerce, notwithstanding the fact that some religious practices are useless, discriminatory, or harmful (Wilson 2002).

Chapter 3 noted neurological research showing that activities involving bonding and trust are associated with higher oxytocin levels (Zak 2004;

3. It is possible that an overreliance on contractual details will undermine these uncodified mechanisms. As Hirsch (1977, p. 88) suggests: "the more that is in the contracts, the less can be expected without them." Overspecification of contractual details undermines perceptions of trust.

4. Economists and others who have considered the importance of honesty or trust in agreements include Sen (1977), Adler (1992), Bowles (1998), and Minkler (1999, 2004a, 2004b, 2008). On trust, see Lorenz (1999) and Nooteboom (2002), among many others. But trust is neither a panacea nor an alternative to sanctions. Lascaux (2008) argues forcefully that trust itself has to be buttressed to some extent by institutional rules.

Vercoe and Zak 2010). Experimental studies indicate that significant degrees of trust and cooperation are normal outcomes of human interaction, including in market settings. Paul Zak (2008, p. 261) concludes that "most people, most of the time, behave ethically, and a set of shared values is essential to the functioning of modern economies." Albert O. Hirschman (1982) and Deirdre McCloskey (2006) have discussed how private property and commerce depend on and promote moral development. Economics cannot legitimately simplify human motivation by concentrating on self-interest alone. Rather than a pleasure machine, the economic agent is a person of significant integrity; although looking after herself and capable of deceit, she upholds some moral rules and has some disposition to honesty.

Honesty and integrity are important, even (or especially) in a world of regular contracting. Our moral makeup is an important part of our identity (Sen 1985b; Davis 2003, 2007, 2011; Akerlof and Kranton 2005). Yet some formulations treat identity principally as a matter of choice, treating integrity and honesty as a matter of preference. But would we trust someone whose honesty was simply the outcome of the self-interested maximization of their own utility? We need more fundamental explanations for our propensities for honest and moral behavior. The social and cultural conditions under which our inherited value-impulses are nurtured have to be taken into account.

But while elements of deliberation and choice are involved in the construction of our identity, we should not ignore the extent and role of the unconscious processes involved. Work in cognitive psychology and elsewhere shows that many of our cognitive and behavioral tendencies are the product of processes that occur outside our awareness.[5] This is one reason why we have to consider the cultural circumstances under which morality is engendered, as well as understanding its biological roots. It is also a reason why we have to go beyond the explicit formalities of the contract itself.

The acquisition of identity involves interactions with leaders, peers, and role models. Experimental psychology shows that learning through identifying is more powerful than attempts to teach individuals through incentives, punishments, or didactic discourse (Bandura and Walters 1963). Social relations within the group enhance individual learning and contribute to the survival capacity of the group as a whole. Learning involves the con-

---

5. See Regan (2007) and Hodgson (2010a) for citations and discussions.

struction of identities within communities of practice. Thus identity, knowing, and group membership entail one another (Lave and Wenger 1991).

6.2. Firms, Employment, and Morality

People are typically more caring and trusting with family and friends. Such intimate settings—many involving young children—require considerable openness and sympathy. But when we move away from close and caring relationships, into the competitive business world of power and acquisition, to what degree should we expect the amoral, opportunistic, and self-seeking side of our personalities to be unleashed? And when we enter a capitalist firm, to what extent do workers have the propensity to shirk or be opportunistic, and what measures are required to combat these tendencies?[6]

The empirical evidence within firms tells a story of human nature that is very different from the pictures in Williamson's (1975, 1985) transaction cost economics and in principal-agent theory (J. Brown 1954; Rees 1985; Stiglitz 1987; Sappington 1991). In a comprehensive literature review of empirical tests of the assumptions underlying principal-agent theory, Canice Prendergast (1999) found widespread evidence that pecuniary incentives matter. But the predictions of principal-agent theory on how contracts will be designed to deal with self-interested behavior received little confirmation. Furthermore, the evidence also revealed that the relative effectiveness of individual incentives is diminished with jobs requiring close cooperation or teamwork.

Even when principal-agent theory predicts correctly, it is not necessarily validated because similar predictions can be derived from other theories. Several other predictions of principal-agent theory and the opportunism assumption are consistent with alternative personalities that are sometimes honest or dutiful (Hendry 2002; Hodgson 2004c). The theory needs to be grounded on a plausible causal account, informed by our knowledge of human nature and evolution. It is not.

If shirking was a ubiquitous problem, as mainstream economists assume, then we would expect to see the widespread use of pecuniary and other incentive mechanisms in business firms, as predicted in the literature. But this is not the case. Studies show that the majority of employers avoid individual payment-by-results and use subjective performance evaluations to determine pay and promotion (Macleod and Parent 1999; Pren-

---

6. This section draws heavily on Minkler (2008), among others.

dergast 1999; Ichniowski and Shaw 2003). The contract-design outcomes predicted by models involving agents who are self-interestedly focused on pecuniary payoff are unconfirmed in the real capitalist world.

There is strong evidence of more complex motivations in business contexts, including the interplay of incentives, motivations, and commitments (Locke and Latham 2004; Meyer, Becker, and Vandenberghe 2004; Meyer, Becker, and Van Dick 2006). For example, Minkler (2004b) commissioned an extensive US national survey of employees on shirking and its determinants. Subjects were asked:

> Suppose that it is almost impossible for your employer to check up on you. Would you say that you are very likely, somewhat likely, somewhat unlikely, or very unlikely to work hard if you agreed to?

In response to that question, 82.7 percent responded "very likely," 12.1 percent "somewhat likely," 1.9 percent "somewhat unlikely," and 1.6 percent "very unlikely." This is clear evidence that most people would not shirk, or at least would not admit to it. Minkler probed their incentives further and asked:

> Now we want to ask why you would be likely to work hard. On a scale of 0–10, with 0 being not important at all, and 10 being very important, how important is each of the following in determining why it is likely you would work hard?

Of the options presented, "It is the morally right thing to do" ranked highest, scoring an average of 9.10. This is strong evidence of moral motivation in the workplace.

The second-highest average score (8.59) was given to "I enjoy my work." This captures the notion of intrinsic motivation: motives related to the task itself rather than its payoff outcomes. Intrinsic motivation means that people work hard because they enjoy their jobs.[7] This goes against the long tradition in economics of regarding work as a disutility.[8] Bruno Frey (1992, 1997a, 1997b) places the distinction between intrinsic and extrinsic rewards at the center of his theory of motivation. According to his argument, backed by impressive empirical and experimental evidence, intrin-

---

7. See Herzberg, Mausner, and Snyderman (1959), Vroom (1964), Deci (1975), Steers and Porter (1991), Deci and Ryan (2000a, 2000b).

8. See Lutz and Lux (1979), Lane (1992), and Spencer (2003) for critical histories of this tenet.

sic motives as well as monetary and other incentives affect behavior. But the degree of intrinsic motivation is influenced by other factors and can be "crowded out" if too much emphasis is placed on extrinsic penalties or rewards (Ostrom 2000; Frey and Jegen 2001; Vollan 2008).

Ironically, there is evidence that strategies typically recommended by economists, including monitoring and individual payment-by-results, act to crowd out intrinsic and moral motivation and diminish effort (Bowles 2008). By highlighting and extending the powers of the manager, the worker is demotivated. Conversely, management policies that acknowledge intrinsic motivation and enhance the self-determination of workers help to "crowd in" intrinsic motivation and improve performance.

It seems that both moral and intrinsic motivations are very important for workers. Minkler (2008, p. 94) reports that these two factors are significant in regression on measurements of the propensity to shirk.

The third-highest average score (6.95) was given to "I wouldn't want to let down my coworkers or get them mad at me." This captures notions of peer pressure and reciprocity within a group. The worker wants to feel part of that group and to avoid ostracism and disapproval. This is consistent with the considerable evidence, cited previously, that actors take into account the dispositions of others in their group to scorn or punish anyone who violates group norms.[9]

Much lower average scores were given to negative motives such as "My employer might catch me" (3.08) and "My employer has convinced me to feel guilty if I don't work hard" (2.37).

There is also evidence that employees care about fairness. What seems to matter is whether the employer is perceived to use fair processes to determine tasks and rewards, and whether the outcomes are perceived to be fair.[10] Minkler's (2008, p. 95) evidence indicates a greater willingness by employees to keep agreements with honest rather than dishonest employers.

---

9. In their study of the management of common-pool resources, Ostrom (1990) and her colleagues (Ostrom, Gardner, and Walker 1992, 1994) showed that people established social rules to exploit a shared resource and regarded rule breaches as unfair or unjust. As noted in the previous chapter, dispositions to punish rule breakers probably have biologically as well as culturally transmitted components. See Boyd and Richerson (1992), Andreoni (1995), de Waal (1996), Fehr and Gächter (2000a, 2000b, 2002), Gintis (2000), Boyd et al. (2003), Field (2001), Price, Cosmides, and Tooby (2002), Gintis et al. (2005), Henrich et al. (2006), Fehr and Gintis (2007), Guzmán, Rodriguez-Sicken, and Rowthorn (2007), and Henrich and Boyd (2001).

10. See the evidence in Cohen-Charash and Spector (2001) and Fehr and Falk (2002a, 2002b).

Studies indicate that fairness can involve much more than mere reciprocity. Psychologists typically deploy three different types of justice or fairness: distributive, procedural, and interactional.[11] Distributive justice is about the perceived fairness of outcomes, such as wages, bonuses, and promotion. If outcomes are regarded as unjust, then resentment or anger provoke uncooperative behavior. By contrast, procedural justice refers to the perceived fairness of the processes that determine the outcomes. A fair process is typically regarded as ethical, inclusive, consistent, unbiased, accurate, and open to correction. Finally, interactional justice means that the people affected by decision are treated with dignity and respect.

Theoretical argument and pooled data analyses suggest that each type of justice is conceptually distinct, notwithstanding that each is correlated with the others.[12] Crucially, the pooled data also show a correlation between perceived procedural justice and work performance. Evidence indicates that two factors are crucial in influencing workers' perception of procedural justice: whether the organization gives the employee "voice" to explain their wishes or concerns, and whether managers explain and justify their acts and decisions (Rotemberg 2006). Employee motivation is enhanced when employers act justly and fairly.

Some people identify closely with their employers and their fellow workers. Such identification shapes their values. Through sustained interaction, people develop a cooperative discourse and engender a smoother coordination of knowledge than would apply if they were an episodic collection of self-interested individuals. Hence Bruce Kogut and Udo Zander (1996, pp. 502–6) argue that firms can "provide a sense of community by which discourse, coordination, and learning are structured by identity." Hence the firm "changes the character and quality of human discourse and behavior." Accordingly, firms "provide the normative territory to which members identify." This defines the conventions and rules by which individuals coordinate their decisions and behavior. Experimental work also shows that cooperative behavior may be elicited by promoting both social proximity between subjects and participation in decision-making processes (Frey and Bohnet 1995). As Helena Lopes, Ana C. Santos, and Nuno Teles (2009, p. 332) put it: "There thus seems to be overwhelming evidence that relational and moral considerations are significantly correlated with cooperation."

---

11. See Skarlicki and Folger (1997), Cohen-Charash and Spector (2001), and Cropanzano, Prehar, and Chen (2002).

12. See Tyler and Blader (2000) and the references in the preceding footnote.

Consequently, the development of firm capabilities through learning is enhanced through identification and the formation of common values. Moral commitment helps to promote teamwork and respect for authority within the firm. By developing its internal morality, a firm can raise productivity and enhance capabilities (Bowie 1991).

The advantage of the firm is more than a governance mechanism to reduce transaction costs: the firm has the potential for an enhanced, innovative, and dynamic organizational learning capability empowered by intrinsic motivation. But Kogut and Zander (1996) are also careful to point out the downside of this process of integration: the creation of closely knit teams is likely to limit positive interchanges with outsiders.

Much motivation is endogenous within organizations. The combined use of intrinsic and extrinsic motivation helps to overcome social dilemmas in firms that are not solvable by hierarchical authority (Osterloh, Frost, and Frey 2002). Managers need to foster an organizational environment that enhances intrinsic motivation. This may include such measures as employee participation in some decision making and the nurturing of cooperative personal relationships, as well as the establishment of fairness and justice in internal procedures.

But this does not mean that even the most virtuous capitalist firms are paragons of high morality. Linda K. Trevino (1992) reviewed applications of Kohlberg's (1969) stages of moral development to managers and workers in business situations. Using the scores with individuals facing nonbusiness dilemmas as a benchmark, she noted that levels of moral reasoning were significantly lower in business situations than with problems involving compassionate dilemmas in more personal contexts. But that does not mean that morality is absent in the business world. The degree of moral variation between different organizational cultures suggests that significant improvement is possible. There is significant evidence that levels of moral reasoning are context dependent. Trevino and many others have made a number of suggestions on how a moral culture in a firm can be enhanced (Vidaver-Cohen 1998). But clearly, the possibilities in the corporate zone also depend very much on the level of moral culture in the society as a whole.

The exercise of employer authority depends on it being accepted as legitimate. But as Hannah Arendt (1958) pointed out, a form of authority can only be legitimated in the eyes of those involved by invoking a source beyond the authorities themselves. Hence capitalism throughout its history has relied to some degree on noncontractarian norms of obligation, whether of religious or secular origin. The legitimacy of the contractual system cannot itself be established by an appeal to the force or veracity of contract. Hence culturally molded moral values play a vital role in the functioning of business organizations.

6.3. The Nature of the Firm Revisited

The "theory of the firm" has been a lively area of research among economists for more than a hundred years. But strangely there is still no agreement on why firms exist. And even more scandalously, economists have yet to agree on what a firm is. In this section, after defining firms as legal and contracting organizations, we reconsider why they may exist. The key argument is that the firm increases productivity by providing a relatively sheltered organizational environment that enhances social cohesion and fruitful interaction among workers. And in particular, a firm that cultivates a suitable moral culture among its managers and employees is likely to enjoy greater commitment and cooperation among its workforce. Ethical codes within the firm can play a necessary part in enhancing organizational cohesion. The firm exists for reasons in addition to any lowering of transaction costs.

Prominent studies within economics fail to address the organizational and cultural aspects of the firm. Armen Alchian and Harold Demsetz (1972) see teamwork as an important feature, which then requires an overall monitor to reduce shirking. But they also emphasize that there is otherwise no difference between an employment contract and any other commodity exchange. Sanford J. Grossman and Oliver D. Hart (1986) define a firm as a set of owned assets, ownership in turn being defined as the power to exercise control. Here it is difficult to see the difference between a firm and an individual with property. Michael C. Jensen and William H. Meckling (1976) propose that the firm is basically a "nexus of contracts." It is. But so too are contracting adults. Jensen and Meckling (1976) insist that the firm is not an individual human being, so that we have to elaborate their "nexus of contracts" definition by adding other terms such as a "framework of contractual relations." But we are not told clearly what this framework is or what holds it together. Similarly endorsing the "nexus of contracts" view, Eugene Fama (1980, p. 290) writes: "The firm is just the set of contracts covering the way inputs are joined to create outputs and the way receipts from outputs are shared among inputs." But any random collection of individuals—including those participating in a market—would also involve a "set of contracts" governing inputs and outputs. Again, the definition fails to specify what holds the firm together to establish its contingent superiority over alternative governance modes.

Ronald Coase (1937) argued in his classic paper that firms exist because they lower the costs of devising and enforcing contracts, compared with the market and the price mechanism. Coase (1937, pp. 388–90) clearly demarcated the market from the firm, with the "price mechanism" on the one hand and its "supersession" on the other. But the internal organization of the firm was largely unexplored. To his great credit, Williamson opened the "black box" of the firm. Using transaction cost analysis, Williamson (1975, 1985) probed much more deeply into the nature of firm organization. He gave explanations of different organizational and contracting forms.

But as Williamson gazed into the black box with his opportunism-detecting but law-obfuscating spectacles, the distinction between the firm and the market began to disappear. Negating his earlier sharp distinction between markets and hierarchies, Williamson (1985, p. 83) was "persuaded that transactions in the middle range are much more common." But both the nature of the "middle range" and the definition of the "firm" extremity remain insufficiently clear. For Williamson (1991, p. 271), hierarchies (or firms) are "a continuation of market relations by other means." Sometime after it was opened, the black box dissolved into the background of market relations.

It became popular for both economists and sociologists to argue that the boundaries of the firm were fuzzy and indistinct. Some wrote of "internal markets" within firms (Doeringer and Piore 1971), of the "quasifirm" (Eccles 1981), of "hybrid firms" or "hybrid forms" (Cheung 1983; Williamson 1985; Ménard 1995, 1996), and of "quasi-markets" (Ménard 1995). Even Coase (1988b, p. 27) himself revised his earlier view and perceived previously invisible "markets" *within* firms. Richard Langlois (1995a, p. 72) observed that "much of transaction-cost economics has reached the conclusion that the distinction between firm and market is little more than semantics." Similarly, most other approaches to the theory of the firm have failed to establish a clear boundary between the firm and the market, or to proclaim a clear definition of the firm. Coming a long way since Coase's (1937) clear distinction between firm and market, in many accounts the theory of the firm remains little more than an ornamented theory of the market itself.[13]

The essence of the firm has still to be properly identified by economists.

---

13. See Foss (1993), Montgomery (1995), Hodgson (1998b), and Garrouste and Saussier (2005) for fuller overviews of theories and definitions of the firm.

Two important ingredients, missing in most preceding accounts, need to be placed at the center of its definition. First, the firm is an entity granted by some state authority to act as a legal person. This is known as a "legal fiction"—an organization is treated in law as a single individual. The "fictional" nature of this construct is that contractual considerations that apply to individuals also apply to partnerships or incorporated firms. But it does not mean that the application or legal status is imaginary or false. On the contrary, the law has to establish analogous tests of contractual offer and agreement to apply to firms as well as individuals. *Legal fictions are not false* (Fuller 1967).

The firm is not simply constituted through agreements between individuals; its structure and assets are protected through legal authority, which itself involves moral rules and values. Legal factors are important because they invoke authority and power. Law and the state depend on mechanisms of legitimation, and through this process these institutions gain moral authority. Partly through law, moral issues infuse the firm.[14]

Although they are not the entire story, legal factors are crucial for understanding the nature, boundaries, and dynamism of the firm. Its legal status means it has the capacity to attract and "lock in" capital, to shield it from any debt claims made on firm owners, and to protect firm owners from debt claims made on it beyond the scope of their equity in the firm (Blair 1999, 2003; Hansmann, Kraakman, and Squire 2006). Its legal status is crucial in cohering its interactions with a market environment and its competition or cooperation with other firms. In legal and meaningful sense, it is firms, not teams or divisions, that contract with customers or suppliers. The firm has a degree of cohesion resulting from its unitary legal status as a single legal person, which provides a legal basis for integrated and bounded procedures of delegation and command. The singularity of legal personhood is a key demarcating feature for the firm. Generally, the criterion of legal personhood is helpful in identifying the relevant boundaries between the firm and its socioeconomic environment.

---

14. On the legal nature of the firm, see Soderquist (2000), Hodgson (2002), and Gindis (2007, 2009). The importance of legal forms was acknowledged by original institutionalists. Veblen (1904, p. 141) argued that "with the assumption of the corporate form is associated a more modern method of capitalization and a freer use of credit." Commons (1925, p. 682) claimed that "general incorporation laws" had facilitated innovation and growth. For Commons, these legal institutions simultaneously enabled "the concentration of capital and the deconcentration of ownership." Both authors upheld that the legal structure of the corporation helps to explain its nature and behavior. But there are several possible corporate forms, and the predominant corporate framework is not necessarily ideal (Ireland 2010; Muchlinski 2010; Toporowski 2010).

Second, the firm is an organization. Definitionally, an organization is an integrated system of ingrained social rules involving

(a) criteria to establish its boundaries and to distinguish its members from its nonmembers,
(b) principles of sovereignty concerning who is in charge, and
(c) a structure of command and responsibility delineating roles within the organization.

These conditions imply the existence of social roles or positions that have properties irreducible to those who occupy them. These social positions (such as prime minister, production manager, or university professor) carry some rights, powers, and duties that are independent of characteristics or preferences of their incumbents (Runciman 2001, 2002).

The legal and organizational aspects are clearly complementary. Legal rules emanating from the legal incorporation of the firm help empower additional rules within the organization. By entering into an employment contract, employees take on legal responsibilities that are further interpreted and augmented by internal rules. Obversely, internal organizational rules are necessary to establish how the legal personhood of the firm is operationalized in contracts between the firm and other legal entities. The two aspects of the firm come into play when the organization interacts and contracts with individuals and other firms.[15]

Durable organizations have some capacity to bind individuals together in groups where people identify with each other and with the organization as a whole. Capitalist firms are characterized by employment contracts (unlike company partnerships or worker cooperatives). Employment relationships provide the legal right of exit by the employee, after a period of notice is served. In modern capitalism, lengthy confinement in an employment contract is legally forbidden because it is "tantamount to slavery."[16]

Especially in dynamic, knowledge-intensive industries, employers often have an incentive to retain employees because they have acquired valuable

15. Accordingly, Argyris and Schön (1996, p. 8) argue that organizations, by their nature, "1. devise agreed-upon procedures for making decisions in the name of the collectivity, 2. delegate to individuals the authority to act for the collectivity, and 3. set boundaries between the collectivity and the rest of the world."

16. Steinfeld (2001) provides a rich account of coerced and bonded employment in Britain in the nineteenth century. Even after the abolition of slavery, it took some time for such other coercive labor institutions to be declared illegal. Deakin (1997) examines the late development of the employment contract.

skills during their period of employment. Without additional measures, employment relationships might be casual and result in limited personal integration into the organization. Workers are likely to remain with an employer for longer periods when no known alternative employment or income is available, wages for equivalent work are perceived as higher than elsewhere, working conditions are perceived as better than elsewhere, or an effective culture of loyalty and commitment to the firm is present. Often two or more of these incentives are in play.

To some extent, the firm may increase productivity by exercising disciplinary control over the pace and manner of work.[17] Stephen Marglin (1974) famously argued that the emergence of the firm during the Industrial Revolution was a result of the exercise of the power of the capitalist over the workers. Although workers could in principle leave and work elsewhere, outside options were generally limited and poorly remunerated. Consequently, workers had little option but to accept managerial power. Managers established habits of punctuality and diligence and instilled norms of compliance. Productivity was thus increased.

But firms do not rely on discipline alone. In modern capitalism, particularly with skilled workers, a moral culture of commitment is often crucial in retaining and integrating a workforce. Cultural mechanisms of corporate identification, moral duty, involvement, and trust may often be important in creating the learning environment. Once this is achieved, skill development and learning can be enhanced. The firm can thus provide an organizational environment consisting of routines, images, artifacts, and information that can enhance the capabilities of workers.

Organizations provide structured environments with interactions and routinized practices that can augment individual skills. The organizational whole is more than the sum of its individual parts. Consequently, through individual relations and interactions, the collective dimension of the organization can enhance overall productivity, more than the total productivity of workers performing in isolation. Some particular routines, images, and stored information depend on the existence of the organization per se, and hence may not be found in the episodic context of exchange or markets.

Expanding on the role of organizations as repositories of knowledge, Chris Argyris and Donald Schön (1996, pp. 12–13) write:

First, organizations function in several ways as *holding environments for knowledge* . . . in an organization's files, which record its actions, decisions, regula-

17. Pages 144–48 draw on ideas in Hodgson and Knudsen (2007).

tions, and policies. . . . Second, *organizations directly represent knowledge* in the sense that they embody strategies for performing complex tasks.

Accordingly, organizational learning is enabled by the structures, files, or routines of the organization itself. The mark of organizational learning is a change in the environment in which the individuals operate, leading to enhanced individual or organizational capabilities.

Scott Cook and Dvora Yanow (1993) develop a similar argument, focusing also on the capacity of corporate culture to preserve and enhance capabilities. For them, organizational learning is more than the cognitions of individuals. It involves the development of cultural features, constituted in intersubjective meanings and expressed in common practices. Through such meaning-bearing activities, languages, and objects, knowledge is reproduced and transmitted in the firm. Much of this knowledge is tacit and uncodified.

Armen Alchian (1991, p. 233) argues that "cooperative activity with a 'firm' yields an output greater than could otherwise be achieved and . . . the underlying factor in that source of gain in the firm is 'teamwork.'" We might add that one reason teamwork sometimes promotes a greater output is that the team may provide a cohesive and value-infused environment that enhances individual learning and overall productivity.

Nicolai Foss (1996, p. 18) suggests that "firms exist because they can more efficiently coordinate collective learning processes than market organization is able to." One reason why intrafirm coordination is more effective in this respect is that the moral ethos of cooperation engendered by individuals working in close and ongoing collaboration with others helps enhance motivation and productivity (Bowie 1991).

What is common to many "competence-based" or "capabilities" perspectives on firms is the proposition that the average productivity of individuals can be enhanced in specific organizational and cultural contexts.[18] Some organizational environments can enhance individual productivity through learning, as well as the incentive effects and contracting economies that are at the center of the transaction cost explanation of Coase (1937) and Williamson (1975, 1985). Despite differences on points of analytical detail, we may extract from this body of work an important core argument. It depends on the following minimal assumptions:

18. Such perspectives include competence, capabilities, dynamic capabilities, knowledge-based, resource-based, and evolutionary approaches (Penrose 1959; Nelson and Winter 1982; Rumelt 1984; Marengo 1992; Foss 1993; Dosi and Marengo 1994; Conner and Prahalad 1996; Foss and Knudsen 1996; Hodgson 1998b; Nooteboom 2000, 2004b).

1 Individual capabilities are not fixed but are, in part, *adaptations to an environment*. Individual skills are in part a function of past and present environmental conditions and cues, including aspects of the organizational and cultural environment.

2 The organizational and cultural environment facing individuals within a firm is *different from* the organizational and cultural environment found in the market. These differences typically concern organizational structures and routines and the development and uses of different types of knowledge.

3 The *possibility* exists that under certain conditions individual skill enhancements (resulting from adaptations to an environment) can be greater in a firm environment than in a market environment.

The core proposition is that the firm can provide an environment that enhances worker skills and performance, and in some circumstances this enhancement will be greater than cases where the coordination of production is through commodity exchanges outside the firm.

Typically, transaction cost economics is overly focused on the aggregate costs and benefits of individual, atomistic transactions. Transaction costs are defined as the costs of formulating, negotiating, monitoring, and enforcing contracts. But the costs and benefits of any governance structure amount to more than this aggregate. This is because the structure—consisting of interactive causal relations between individuals—itself affects individuals and their transactions. Firm-specific learning is a case where the emergent properties of firm organization lead to enhanced individual learning capacities.

Of course, some forms of learning are specific to markets rather than firms. The market also has emergent properties and can foster learning capabilities. People adapt to a market environment by learning specific skills, such as pecuniary judgment, risk taking, marketing technique, or innovative foresight. Furthermore, some learning found in organizations can be transferred to market or network contexts. Crucially, under some conditions, the firm may have the capacity to enlarge average individual capabilities more than they are enlarged through market or commodity exchange relations. Part of this is explained by the ability of the firm to generate greater moral commitment due to more longstanding relations within groups. The degree to which this possibility is found in reality is a matter of empirical investigation.

In a way, the structure of this argument is similar to the transaction cost theory. Transaction cost analysis does *not* predict that the creation of a firm will *always* lower transaction costs. In a comparable argument, the creation of a firm does not always lead to firm-specific learning effects that are greater than corresponding effects provided by a market. Like transaction cost theory, it is argued that firms are likely to survive when the net benefits of firm organization are greater than the net benefits of using the market. But typical presentations of transaction cost theory fail to specify adequately all the possible net benefits of any governance system.

As long as there is a possibility of firm-specific learning, the existence of some firms might be explained even if transaction costs have no significant effect. This would be an explanation and formalization of the mechanism that can sometimes give rise to this firm-based advantage under specific conditions. Consequently, the general explanation of the existence of the firm cannot be based on transaction costs alone.

Thorbjørn Knudsen and I (Hodgson and Knudsen 2007) devised heuristic models to illustrate such effects. Our models assume a firm-specific learning effect that is strictly dependent on the number of workers in the firm. The argument is that the existence of the firm can enhance individual skills or capabilities by providing a repository of tacit and codifiable knowledge, embodied in organizational structures and routines. In short, the firm may provide a learning environment in which individual skills may be enhanced.

The models suggest that there are possible reasons for firms to exist even if transaction costs are zero or insignificant.[19] Furthermore, dynamic learning effects may enhance these factors. This does not mean that transaction costs are unimportant in the real world, but that they may provide only part of the explanation for the existence of some firms. This explanatory shortfall is likely to be greater in contexts where firm-specific learning is significant.

Markets exist for good reasons too. But comparisons of the net benefits of firms and markets have to take into account the learning effects of both market and firm institutions, as well as transaction costs. In the heuristic models, the existence of a firm depends on the supposition of the firm-specific effects captured in a function, as a necessary but insufficient condition. We assert that *if* such effects exist, *then* they may be sufficient to explain the existence of the firm. If such effects are small, then the burden

---

19. One critic has objected that if transaction costs are zero, then market-like (individual to individual) contracts could invade and dissolve the firm. This Coase-like argument depends solely on allocative and ignores possible productive efficiency. It overlooks possible collective benefits that may be indivisible within the organization itself. We suggest that some productive benefits may be inseparable from firm organization and would disappear if the firm was dissolved. Similar objections to a pure transaction cost approach are made by Milgrom and Roberts (1992, pp. 33–34).

of the explanation for the existence of the firm may shift back to transaction costs. The onus is on supporters of the argument that all firms are *always* explained by transaction costs *alone* to show that effects depending on such a function are *generally* insignificant. We see no basis for such a general statement.

Firms may exist for multiple reasons. We need to develop and test "hybrid" theories of the firm in which capabilities and transaction cost elements are combined. This means that both transaction costs and capabilities would come into the explanation of the existence of the firm.[20]

The extent of the learning effects is an empirical issue. One exceptional study that provides econometric evidence on the relative impact of productive capabilities and transaction costs as drivers of vertical scope (Jacobides and Hitt 2005) supports our argument that firm-specific learning may sometimes be of even greater significance than transaction costs.

We can now see why ethical issues are important within the firm. Under appropriate conditions, particular moral values can be enhanced in enduring groups with high levels of ongoing interpersonal interaction. In turn, these values help to further promote cohesion and performance, just as moral feelings have helped to enhance group cohesion in tribal bands for hundreds of thousands of years. Morality can act as a social glue, bringing groups together and focusing them on shared goals. Morality makes economic sense: it should not be sidelined by an individualist concentration on opportunism alone. Opportunism and selfishness are real, but they are far from the whole story.

Empirical evidence supports these arguments. A meta-analysis of all 52 known quantitative studies of the relationship between corporate ethical "social responsibility" and financial performance, yielding a total sample size of 33,878 observations, found that "corporate virtue in the form of social responsibility and, to a lesser extent, environmental responsibility is likely to pay off" (Orlitzky, Schmidt, and Rynes 2003, p. 404). It seems that acting ethically can help the firm's bottom line. While ethical corporate behavior can help a corporate image and promote sales, it is also likely that a public ethical stance has to be supported by an internal corporate culture where moral issues are taken seriously, especially when they foster employee cooperation. When the leadership of the firm acts morally, then

---

20. See, for example, Langlois (1992), Teece and Pisano (1994), and Nooteboom (2004a). Hybrid theoretical approaches receive some support from the empirical research of Argyres (1996), Poppo and Zenger (1998), Combs and Ketchen (1999), and Whinston (2003). David and Han (2004) and Carter and Hodgson (2006) provide meta-studies of the empirical research in this area.

teams within the firm are more likely to cohere and become more productive. When senior managers are racked by scandal and accused of acting unethically, then morale and productivity are likely to suffer throughout the organization.

The internal moral values of the firm would be important even if the firm was seeking maximum profits or shareholder value. But often firms have moral as well as pecuniary objectives, which can help to enhance their internal moral cultures. To some degree, the adoption of broader moral objectives has been undermined by legal and ideological moves toward the maximization of shareholder value (Froud et al. 2000). The concern here is that the exclusive pursuit of profit in turn may undermine the capacity of a firm to mobilize its human resources to productive effect and unwittingly confound the firm's own performance. Just as with the "hedonistic paradox"—the more one seeks pleasure, the less likely one is to find it— the "paradox of profit" means that the more a business becomes obsessed with profits, the less likely it is to achieve them (Bowie 1988). A policy implication here is that legal and accounting drives toward shareholder value maximization as an exclusive objective should be replaced by the more traditional notion of a firm adopting a number of diverse objectives, with an open debate about what those objectives should be.[21]

6.4. Concluding Remarks

In highlighting the role of morality, cooperation, and commitment within the firm, we should not forget the evolutionary origins of such traits. At the genetic level, altruism can provide a survival advantage among kin, *in competition with others*. At the cultural level, cooperation and morality are selected because they bestow the advantages of group cohesion, *in competition with other groups*. Evolutionary analysis shows that *competition is the spur for cooperation*. Consequently, an evolutionary perspective challenges both the individualist depiction of the economy as a self-interested struggle of each against all and the rose-tinted leftist utopia of unbounded amity and cooperation without effective incentives to cooperate. Although not necessarily in an optimal form, modern capitalism exhibits the creative tension between organizational cooperation and market competition. Competition and cooperation are synergetic phenomena.

21. Khurana (2007) describes at length how from the 1970s the assumption of narrow self-interest and "agency theory" drove out notions of professional managerial commitment in American business schools.

One limitation of the argument so far in this chapter is that we have considered merely two contracting contexts: the firm and the market. This neglects important additional cases. The market is best defined as a system of recurrent, organized exchange involving multiple buyers or sellers (Hodgson 2008b, 2008c). Consequently, not all commodity exchange takes place on markets. In three seminal and influential works, George B. Richardson (1972), Victor P. Goldberg (1980), and Ronald Dore (1983) point out that many real-world commercial transactions involve firms in an ongoing relationship, in which they exchange relevant information before, during, and after the contract itself. This is often described as *relational exchange*.

Studies of relational exchange show that ongoing contact and communication, and enhanced cooperation and trust, are important in such contexts. Consequently, we should expect some of the mechanisms that help to build up firms as moral communities to be found in relational contracts, albeit typically in a weakened form. Relational contracts become important with more complex transactions involving knowledge sharing and information transfer. They are less integrative than organized contracts within a firm, and they often have advantages over the price-driven and short-term relations in the market. In fact, only a minority of transactions in modern economies take place in open markets (Simon 1991).

Moral norms operate in all these contexts: the firm, markets, and relational contracting. The nature and durability of these norms requires much further investigation in each case. The argument in this chapter is that the modern firm provides a forum of close, ongoing, and intensive interpersonal interaction that would sustain a relatively powerful moral environment conducive to greater productivity. By contrast, the mainstream economic theory of the firm adopts a one-sided conception of the individual who is prone to greed, shirking, and opportunism. We do not have to be utopian idealists to question such an extreme and unwarranted depiction. And if we were to take the existence of some moral motivation on board, the consequences for the theory of the firm would be enormous.

SEVEN

The Economics of Corruption and the Corruption of Economics

Corruption? Corruption is government intrusion into market efficiencies in the form of regulations. That's Milton Friedman. He got a goddamn Nobel Prize. We have laws against it precisely so we can get away with it. Corruption is our protection. Corruption keeps us safe and warm. Corruption is why you and I are prancing around in here instead of fighting over scraps of meat out in the streets. Corruption is why we win.

—Danny Dalton, *played by Tim Blake Nelson, in Syriana (2005)*

Corruption is now a popular topic in the social sciences.[1] In economics and elsewhere, a large number of articles on this theme have been published in leading journals. Some organizations produce indicative data on corruption. For example, Transparency International publishes a widely cited "Corruption Perceptions Index" for most countries, and these data are frequently used in statistical analyses of economic performance. Corruption raises issues of both morality and economic performance.

The World Bank (1997) sees corruption as a major obstacle to economic and social development. According to the 2010 report of Transparency International, "corruption remains an obstacle to achieving much needed progress." Its 2010 Corruption Perceptions Index shows that nearly three-quarters of the 178 countries sampled have high levels of corruption by the organization's measure, indicating globally "a serious corruption problem" (Transparency International 2010). These include massive and fast-growing economies such as those in China, India, and Brazil, which account for a large and rapidly increasing share of the world economy.

Several empirical studies indicate that corruption has negative effects on

1. This chapter is a revised version of Hodgson and Jiang (2007).

economic performance.[2] Despite this, corruption has its apologists on the left and right of the political spectrum. Especially in the context of bureaucracy and underdevelopment, corruption may seem to be the only way to get things done. But it also has strong institutional and moral externalities. The pooled evidence shows that it stultifies effective economic competition, undermines investment, inhibits the rule of law, undermines effective state administration, and promotes political instability.

Although modern economists rarely discuss morality, corruption is now being taken seriously. But most anti-corruption programs in developing countries promote the cleansing virtues of privatization and market liberalization. This ideological stance is grounded on a faulty analysis, has little empirical support, and typically relies on a definition of corruption that is intrinsically biased against the state. Reacting against the privatization and market-liberalization agenda of much anti-corruption discourse, some critics on the left have attempted to play down the evil of corruption itself or to diminish its stature as an immediate obstacle to development (Bukovansky 2006; Khan 2006). The critics overlook the neoliberal bias in the predominant conception of corruption, and they mistakenly react against the flaws in anti-corruption policies by downplaying the significance of corruption as a brake on economic development. All sides give insufficient attention to the importance of a moral social fabric for economic development.

More attention needs to be devoted to the concept of corruption, its meaning, and its definition. This is much more than a matter of tidy terminology. As Arvind Jain (2001, p. 73) observes: "While it may appear to be a semantic issue, how corruption is defined actually ends up determining what gets modelled and measured." Similarly, Toke Aidt (2003, p. F632) remarks that "the definition of the concept determines what gets modelled and what empiricists look for in the data." It is argued here that this conceptual lacuna in the literature has led some authors—particularly economists—to adopt a narrow and inadequate definition of corruption that has led to skewed empirical measures and ideologically biased policy recommendations.

It is shown below that prevailing definitions of corruption unwarrantedly and misleadingly confine the phenomenon to the public sector, not-

2. See Shleifer and Vishny (1993), Mauro (1995), Jain (2001), Mo (2001), Aidt (2003), and Pellegrini and Gerlagh (2004). But indices of corruption are higher in countries such as China and India than in some less-developed countries with lower growth rates. Rather than negating the importance of corruption, this suggests that corruption is not the only variable affecting growth. Serious empirical studies examine corruption conjointly with other variables. The balance of evidence is that corruption undermines prosperity.

withstanding well-known reports of private sector corruption. In addition, the rare but real phenomenon of "noble cause corruption" suggests that corruption is not strictly and universally for private gain, despite selfish motives typically being involved. Another distorting factor that pervades the literature on corruption is the utilitarian reduction of all morality to matters of utility or satisfaction. Consequently, the moral dimension of corruption has been dissolved into the hedonic calculus of individual pleasure. Ideological and theoretical biases, prevalent in mainstream economics and elsewhere, have corrupted the concept of corruption.

With the exception of the rhetorical allusion to the "corruption of economics," this chapter is concerned with organizational corruption, rather than corruption in a broader sense, such as the corruption of language or of an individual. The following section criticizes the idea that organizational corruption can be definitionally or otherwise confined to the public sector only. A much shorter subsequent section briefly establishes that corruption need not always be for private gain. Another section criticizes utilitarian treatments of corruption and establishes its immoral character, leading to a specific definition of *organizational corruption* involving the violation of established ethical rules. From this perspective, it is argued in the penultimate section that organizational corruption incurs social costs that cannot fully be internalized.

7.1. Corruption—Confined to the Public Sector?

The root of the word "corruption" is in the Latin adjective *corruptus*, meaning spoiled, broken or destroyed. According to the *Concise Oxford English Dictionary*, a meaning of "to corrupt" in the social context is to bribe, and *corruption* amounts to "moral deterioration." Neither these definitions nor the Latin etymology of the word confines the notion of corruption to the public sector.

Prominent international organizations adopt an inclusive definition of corruption. The United Nations Office on Drugs and Crime (2011) emphasizes that corruption can occur in both the public and private domains. Similarly, the World Bank does not regard corruption as confined to the public sector and has identified several cases of corruption among private corporations. For Transparency International (2007), corruption is operationally defined as "the misuse of entrusted power for private gain." This too covers individuals in both the private and public sectors.

But among economists, a different consensus prevails. In his overview article, Jain (2001, p. 73) declares "there is a consensus that corruption refers to acts in which the power of public office is used for personal gain in a manner that contravenes the rules of the game." In another major survey article in a journal of economics, Aidt (2003, p. F632) writes: "Corruption is an act in which the power of public office is used for personal gain in a manner that contravenes the rules of the game."[3]

The survey articles by Jain (2001) and Aidt (2003) accurately report and endorse the tendency of most economists to confine their definition of corruption to the public sphere. For example, in a widely cited article simply titled "Corruption," Andrei Shleifer and Robert Vishny (1993, p. 599) confine their attention to government corruption only, defining it as "the sale by government officials of government property for personal gain." The influential study of the negative effects of corruption on economic growth by Paolo Mauro (1995) has the unqualified word "corruption" in its title but in the text mentions government corruption only. Likewise, Daron Acemoglu and Thierry Verdier (2000) also have the unqualified word "corruption" in their title, but in their analysis they confine themselves entirely to the corruption of government officials. Like many others, Daniel Treisman (2000, p. 399) defines corruption as "the misuse of public office for private gain." A. Mitchell Polinsky and Steven Shavell (2001) confine their study to corruption in law enforcement. By definition or default, many economists confine their attention to corruption in the public sector. There are exceptions, and there is some discussion of private sector corruption in the literature, but a pronounced and questionable bias remains.

This bias is not confined to economics. An influential article by political scientist Joseph Nye (1967, p. 419) defined corruption as the deviation from the formal duties of a public role for private gain. Subsequently, in one of the few articles devoted entirely to the definition of corruption in the literature, John Gardiner (1993, p. 112) proclaimed approvingly: "All probably would agree with Nye's emphasis on *public roles*." Similarly, Daniel Kaufmann (1997, p. 114) is among the many social scientists who define corruption as "the misuse of public office for private gain." He is followed by Wayne Sandholtz and William Koetzle (2000, p. 31) and numerous others. Mark Warren (2004, pp. 328–29) asks "what does corruption mean in a democracy?" and then confines himself to political corruption and "the misuse of public office for private gain." The analysis in

---

3. There are exceptions. Lambsdorff, Taube, and Schramm (2004) provide a set of essays on the "new institutional economics" of corruption, where commendably, several of the authors stress occurrences in the private as well as the public sector. Also to their credit, Bardhan (1997), Svensson (2005), and Pellegrini (2011) point out that corruption takes place in the private as well as the public sector.

Susan Rose-Ackerman's (1999, p. 9) influential book is deliberately confined to government corruption, which is defined as payments "illegally made to public agents with the goal of obtaining a benefit or avoiding a cost." A major part of the literature on corruption in the social sciences has restricted itself to the public sector.

Consider two possible sources of this bias. The first is to *define* corruption in terms that confine it explicitly to the public sector. Accordingly, malpractice that is outside the public sector would not be regarded as corruption. The second would admit a broader definition, but for some reason to bias research toward corruption in the public sphere. Examples of both stances are found in the literature. Neither is acceptable. The pitfalls of an overly narrow definition are criticized below. And any ideologically-biased research program—even with a broader definition—would obviously be flawed.

The problems with the narrow definition are manifold. First, the narrow definition ignores similar malpractices in the private sphere. One need only mention the name Enron. There are well-known instances of corruption in trade unions, including the US Teamsters Union (Friedman and Schwarz 1989). Corruption has also been found in sport, including the bribing of players or challengers to "throw" contests. Several serious corruption and bribery allegations were made against FIFA (Fédération Internationale de Football Association) officials in 2010 and 2011, particularly concerning its choices of future locations for the lucrative World Cup.

Terms such as "corporate corruption" and "business corruption" are in widespread use in popular and even legislative discourse. There are several studies of corporate fraud and corruption, including that by Marshall Clinard (1990). The more restrictive "public sector" definitions are far from universal.

For example, in 1997 the Organisation for Economic Cooperation and Development (OECD) member states adopted a convention making business bribery abroad a criminal offense in the home country of the bribing firm. Major cases of corporate fraud involve US-based companies such as Enron, WorldCom, Adelphia, and Parmalat. Alarm about corporate fraud and corrupt accounting practices fueled political pressure in the US Congress. In response, President George W. Bush signed the Corporate Corruption Bill in 2002, thus endorsing the notion that corruption is more than a purely governmental phenomenon. It is strange that Bush was less blind to corruption in the private sector than were many economists.

Another problem with the narrow definition is that there are several ways of defining the boundary between the public and private sectors, leading to classificatory problems if corruption is definitionally restricted to the public sphere. Consider a private corporation of which the state owns 51 percent of its share capital. Is it part of the public or the private sector? Does corruption within it magically cease if this state ownership drops from 51 to 49 percent? Some organizations—including nearly all British universities and "foundation hospitals" in England—are formally private but largely dependent on state funding and consequently come to some degree under state control. Are these in the public or the private sector? In response, one can refine the definition of the public or private sector, but that is beyond the point. We should be interested in the reality of corruption, whether these institutions are formally defined as public or private.

This problem of defining the public-private boundary is "fiendishly difficult" in one of the world's largest and most corrupt economies—China (Huang 2008, p. 13). There is a plethora of business types, including nationally owned, local government–owned, nationally controlled private, local government–controlled private, and privately owned and controlled firms. Consequently, recent estimates of the size of the private sector in China range from as much as 71 to as little as 21 percent or even less (Huang 2008, pp. 13–26). In this maze of public-private entanglement, the definitional confinement of corruption to the "public sector" is ludicrous and analytically dysfunctional.

Institutions that in some nations are private can be public elsewhere. In some countries, postal services, railways, and universities are run entirely by the state. University professors and other functionaries can essentially be civil servants or state officials. Yet elsewhere these services are privatized. An act of bribery involving an official within the French university, postal service, or railway system would be corruption by most definitions. But would it cease to be corruption if it occurred in the private equivalents of these institutions elsewhere, in say the United States? An affirmative answer would be absurd. Furthermore, France might have more corruption than another country with similar levels of dishonesty, simply because the public sector is larger. Once again, restricting the definition of corruption to the public sector leads to severe anomalies.

Finally, corruption is typically contagious and does not respect sectoral boundaries.[4] Corruption involves rule breaking and duplicity, and it reduces levels of morality and trust. Once it takes root, it tempts others with

---

4. There are several models of corruption, treating it either as a contagion process or as a persistent outcome in models with multiple equilibria (Andvig and Moene 1990; Mishra 2006; Sah 1991; Tirole 1996). See Cartier-Bresson (1997) on "corruption networks."

its pecuniary gains, lowers ethical standards, and reduces incentives to conform to the rules. As levels of morality and trust are lowered, it becomes more difficult to resist corrupt practices. Virulent corruption or illegality can spread quite easily from the private to the public sector or vice versa. For example, illegal but lucrative phone-hacking practices in the British *News of the World* newspaper led allegedly to the bribing of some police officers to overlook the offenses (Guardian 2011; Wikipedia 2011c). Corruption involves negative externalities that traverse sectoral boundaries, by undermining legal and moral norms and facilitating further corrupt acts. Consequently, empirical studies of the levels of organizational corruption should be comprehensive and unconfined to the public sphere.

Given the absurdity of restricting the study and definition of corruption to the public sector, one may ask why so many social scientists define it in these limited terms. Political scientists may plead that their role is to study political institutions, but this would not warrant the confinement of the definition. Economists do not even have this excuse. One possible reason for their bias is the widespread influence of pro-market, antistate, libertarian ideology. A primary ideological target is the allegedly systemic abuse of power by politicians. The misuse of power by directors of large corporations—several of which are as big as some national states—does not raise the same level of concern among leading libertarian thinkers. According to this thinking, most voluntary contracts between consenting adults are moral and legitimate, as long as they do not harm others. Ignoring the negative externalities of corruption, libertarians further argue that bribery and other forms of malpractice in the private sphere have potential benefits and are expressions of entrepreneurial activity. In sum, the bias toward public sector malpractice partly reflects an ideological notion that the private sector is the zone of largely unconstrained individual liberty, whereas the state represents its antithesis and must be subject to rigorous scrutiny, confinement, downsizing, and restraint.

From this libertarian perspective, the solution to the problem of corruption is the reduction of the size of the state. Hence Nobel Laureate Gary Becker (1998) wrote: "The only way to reduce corruption permanently is to drastically cut back government's role in the economy."[5] Of course this would be true if corruption was definitionally confined to state institutions—but it is not particularly helpful or feasible. An alternative statement, "if we diminish the state, we diminish corruption," would sus-

---

5. Becker is also quoted in *Business Week* as declaring: "if we abolish the state, we abolish corruption" (Tanzi 2000, p. 112).

tain the view that extensions of privatization and market competition are generally effective cures for a corrupt polity. Is such a proposition tenable?

Evidence of enduring corruption in the transitional economies challenges this stance. Corruption was endemic in the Soviet-type regimes in China and Eastern Europe before they introduced widespread private enterprise. But corruption has also prospered long since 1990. The economic powers of the state have diminished, and markets and private ownership have grown to play much more important roles, but corruption is still rampant.[6] In Russia in particular there is evidence that corruption increased dramatically during the 1990s despite extensive privatization.[7] Extensive corruption has continued in China despite the extension of markets and private enterprise.[8] As Rose-Ackerman (1999) shows, the outcome of privatization in any country may reduce some types of state corruption by diminishing the economic role of the state, but also the process of privatization can enhance some particular opportunities for corruption by state officials. Overall, the evidence does not show that levels of corruption in general, or even public sector corruption in particular, are closely related to the size of the state. Crucially, some of the least corrupt countries according to published indicators, such as Denmark, Finland, Holland, Norway, and Sweden, have the largest levels of public spending as shares of GDP (Lambsdorff 2007).

As Jonathan Hopkins (2002, p. 585) points out, the anticorruption strategies advocated by many mainstream economists consist "of two main planks of reform: reforming the state administration to minimize corrupt incentives, and reducing the role of the state in economic life in order to leave as much economic activity as possible in the hands of the market." Again, the role and extent of corruption in the private sector is largely neglected in these strategies. Instead of cultivating moral values and the rule of law, strategic reliance is put on individual incentives, property rights, and contracts.

There is an alternative view of the state and law, with important implications for the analysis of corruption. It is found within the German his-

---

6. For an overview, see Kaufmann (1997). Bliss and Di Tella (1997) devise a model that shows that increases in competition may not lower corruption.

7. See Levin and Satarov (2000). Russia was described as a virtual "mafia state" by the Spanish National Court Prosecutor and corruption expert José Grinda Gonzalez in January 2010: "Grinda stated that he considers Belarus, Chechnya and Russia to be virtual 'mafia states' and said that Ukraine is going to be one" (quoted from US Embassy cables leaked by Wikileaks on November 28, 2010 (Guardian 2010)).

8. See Manion (1996), Root (1996), G. White (1996), Kwong (1997), He (2000), and Lu (2000).

torical school, the original American institutional economics, parts of the new institutional economics, and elsewhere. The basic proposition is that the state provides an essential social and legal scaffolding for all private enterprise.

Consider property rights. Individual property is not mere individual possession; it involves socially acknowledged and enforced rights.[9] Individual property is not simply a relation between an individual and an object. It requires some kind of customary, legal, and moral apparatus of recognition, adjudication and enforcement. Similar considerations apply to the market: rather than the mere ether of individual interaction, markets are social institutions. Most of them are structured in part by statutory rules.[10]

Contrary to writers such as Friedrich Hayek (1973), law is not equivalent to custom: it is a creature of the state (Seagle 1941; Redfield 1950, 1957). Generally, many important legal rules, enforcements, and structures cannot emerge spontaneously through individual interactions. They require additional third-party enforcement by the state or another strong institution.[11] Many key institutions and legal relations, arguably including property and markets, exist as a result of a combination of spontaneous and statutory mechanisms. Institutions are generally and inevitably intertwined, and often provide essential mutual and moral support for one another. The public and private spheres are inseparable.

These institutionalist propositions concerning the necessary role of the state, and the interpenetration of (public and private) institutions in a market economy, undermine definitions of corruption that limit it to the public sector. They also thwart anticorruption polices aimed primarily at downsizing the state. Corruption is an institutional and moral phenomenon, affecting both private and public spheres.

7.2. Is Corruption Always and Necessarily for Private Gain?

This brief section criticizes the other half of the commonplace definition of corruption as the "misuse of public office for private gain." The idea that corruption *always* involves "private gain" is almost as problematic as the first part of this definition. But this does not mean that we should overlook

9. See Commons (1924), Samuels (1989), Sened (1997), Pipes (1999), Heinsohn and Steiger (2000), Hodgson (2003, 2009), and Steiger (2008).

10. See Lowry (1976), Hodgson (1988, 2008b, 2008c), Fligstein (1996, 2001), Sened (1997), Vanberg (2001), Chang (2002), and McMillan (2002).

11. This point is recognized not only by the original institutionalists but also by "new" institutionalists such as Sened (1997) and Mantzavinos (2001).

the fact that individual gain is typically the motive. It means that that commonplace definition is too restrictive. Definitions represent the essence rather than the majority form of a phenomenon. As John O'Neill (1998, p. 9) puts it: "The essential properties of an entity of a particular kind are those properties of the object that it must have if it is to be an object of that kind. Accidental properties of an entity of a particular kind are those properties it has, but could lack and still be an entity of that kind." In some cases, corruption may not be for personal gain: hence personal gain is not an essential property of corruption.

Of course, if we start from the utilitarian idea that all individual actions are performed to increase individual pleasure or utility, then by assumption all actions—including corrupt deeds—involve individual or private "gains" in that sense. All acts are "explained" in terms of individual utility maximization. But from this unfalsifiable utilitarian perspective, the second half of the commonplace definition is redundant because all acts are seen as motivated by such gains, and actions to the contrary are denied. The "for private gain" addition would serve no function in this case.

By contrast, one may define the phrase "for private gain" more narrowly and confine it to cases where the persons concerned obtain some kind of tangible personal reward, such as the receipt of money, status, goods, or services, rather than intangible and mysterious utility. But although this may cover the majority of cases of corruption in the real world, it excludes some important cases where individuals act corruptly (and immorally) for higher moral ends. This is sometimes called "noble cause corruption" (Miller 2011; Miller, Roberts, and Spence 2005). Examining these (perhaps exceptional) instances helps us further to understand the nature of corruption itself.

Examples include bribing for higher motives officials under a totalitarian or repressive regime. For instance, Oskar Schindler paid Nazi officials to prevent more than a thousand Jews from being sent to the concentration camps, as depicted in the movie *Schindler's List* (and the book *Schindler's Ark* from which it is derived).

Many real-world cases involve a mixture of motives. Consider two police officers, believing that a criminal is guilty (perhaps also having clear evidence of guilt that cannot be used in court), fabricate evidence to secure a conviction. Although this may also improve the police officers' chances for promotion and thereby in part be motivated by "private gain," the moral motive of convicting a dangerous criminal may also be powerful.

Although these actions are not necessarily for material gain, they remain corrupt because they break specific rules and undermine their character and moral justification. On the scales of moral calculus, the immoral act of corruption may be outweighed by the moral outcomes of the noble cause, but corruption remains corruption nevertheless.

It may be objected that motives of personal gain are so commonly behind corruption that this term can be retained in the definition. This argument confuses definition with description. The definition of a mammal does not necessarily include features such as four legs, lungs, and body hair. The role of a definition is to get to the essential distinguishing characteristics, or to "carve" reality "where the joint is" as Plato's Socrates states in *Phaedrus*. Overall, we may conclude that the phrase "for private gain" plays no *vital* role in the definition of corruption, even though private gain is often important.

Both components of the commonplace "misuse of public office for private gain" definition have been undermined. An alternative definition of organizational corruption is required.

7.3. Defining Organizational Corruption

What concerns us here is the nature of corruption within (public and private) organizations. Two propositions are relevant to the conceptual analysis of organizational corruption. The first proposition is that *institutions are the stuff of social life*. Institutions refer to systems of established and embedded social rules that structure social interactions. Organizations are particular kinds of institutions involving rules concerning membership and sovereignty, with examples including states and firms.[12] In this context, the general emphasis on institutions reflects the concern with forms of corruption that corrode the institutional and social fabric. Because of their emphasis on institutions, institutional economists are more alert to rules and their infringement.

This first proposition also invokes a fundamental shift of ontological outlook, where social reality is partly constituted by structures made up of social rules. From Veblenian and similar perspectives, these rules are sustained by psychological habits. Habits themselves are conditional and rule-like.[13] The role of habit is important in this context because corruption

12. In Hodgson (2006b), I quote Douglass North and show that, contrary to a widespread but mistaken interpretation, he also regards organizations as a type of institution. The notion that institutions are basically systems of rules is shared by other authors, including North (1990), J. Knight (1992), and others.

13. On the nature and ubiquity of social rules, see Ostrom (1986), Gilbert (1989, 2001), Crawford and Ostrom (1995), Hodgson (1997b), Potts (2000), Vanberg (2002, 2004), Dop-

typically involves a sustained pattern of imitable corrupt actions that are driven by corrupt habits or dispositions.

The prevailing rule structure provides incentives and constraints for individual actions. Channeling behavior in this way, accordant habits are further developed and reinforced among the population. Habits are the constitutive material of institutions, providing them with enhanced durability, power, and normative authority. In turn, by reproducing shared habits of thought, institutions create strong mechanisms of conformism and normative agreement. As the pragmatist philosopher Charles Sanders Peirce (1878, p. 294) declared, the "essence of belief is the establishment of habit." Accordingly, habit is not the negation of deliberation, but its necessary foundation. Reasons and beliefs are often the rationalizations of deep-seated feelings and emotions that spring from habits laid down by repeated behaviors.

The second proposition concerns the *normative* nature of social rules. The term "rule" is broadly understood as a socially transmitted and customary normative injunction or immanently normative disposition, that in circumstances A do B.[14] The term "socially transmitted" means that the replication of such rules depends on a developed social culture and some use of language. Such dispositions do not appear simply as a result of inherited genes or instincts.

This interplay of behavior, habit, emotion, and rationalization helps to explain the normative power of custom in human society. Hence "custom reconciles us to everything"—as Edmund Burke (1757) wrote—and customary rules can acquire the force of moral authority. In turn, these moral norms help to further reinforce the institution in question.

Adherence to many social rules involves a moral commitment to associated ethical values. This does not mean that all social rules involve morality or that everyone follows rules for moral motives. Some rules, such as the rules of grammar, carry little moral weight. But morality plays an important role in the adherence to many social rules. We are concerned here with morally loaded rules.

---

fer (2004), Dopfer, Foster, and Potts (2004), and Parra (2005). On habits, see Veblen (1914, 1919), Dewey (1922), Ouellette and Wood (1998), Kilpinen (2000), Wood, Quinn, and Kashy (2002), Hodgson and Knudsen (2004, 2010), Wood and Neal (2007), and Hodgson (2010a).

14. As in previous chapters, "normative" is used in a wider sense than "moral." Rules by this definition can be procedural or constitutive. In the latter case, the "do" is primarily about understanding and acknowledging a role or function. In both cases, it carries a normative connotation.

Many professions have established ethical standards, including the medical profession. Moral rules are also important for the conduct of scientific research. The crucial point in these cases is that the manifest adherence to behavioral rules is required, but also the inner moral commitment to appropriate values is necessary. Such moral commitments or habits transcend the calculus of punishments or rewards. In such contexts, rational utilitarian calculations of gains and losses are widely regarded as insufficient for deciding behavior: "Citizens who refrain from treason merely because it is against the law are, by that fact, of questionable loyalty; parents who refrain from incest merely because of fear of community reaction are, by that fact, unfit for parenthood" (Hagstrom 1965, p. 20). Accordingly, there are values or commitments held by individuals that are irreducible to matters of incentive or deterrence. Indeed, their reduction purely to matters of individual incentive or disincentive precisely betrays such values or commitments. The emphasis on moral commitments implies that it is not simply the breach of a rule that is important in defining corruption.

Consider legal rules. The relation between law and morality is a matter of dispute among legal theorists (Hart 1961; Devlin 1965; Fuller 1969). Without resolving the detailed differences, a minimal stance is that the general obligation to obey the law typically carries a moral force. Particular laws themselves are not necessarily moral precepts, but general obeisance to the law is a moral issue based on the acceptance of legitimate authority. This minimal position is consistent with some legal positivists, who insist on the conceptual separation of laws and morals at the level of particularities, and of their critics, who insist that law and morality are somehow connected.

But with organizational corruption, an exclusive focus on law can mislead us. Although much organizational corruption involves breaking the law, there are many crimes other than organizational corruption. More important, corruption is not always unlawful. Until 1977 it was legal for US companies to offer bribes to secure foreign contracts, and in many other countries such inducements were lawful until the OECD convention of 1997. Generally, rules (including laws) can be broken by accident or through ignorance, and the breach of a rule does not necessarily constitute a corrupt act. Corruption "is not at bottom simply a matter of law; rather it is fundamentally a matter of morality" (Miller 2011).

By contrast, in an early and influential paper Nye (1967) attacked "moralistic" stances on corruption and warned against the "moralistic approach." This dismissal of morality is replicated by some on the left who see anticorruption programs as neoliberal plots to privatize and deregulate.

But morality cannot be dismissed. The functioning of many key institutions depends on moral rules and motivations. All acts of corruption violate moral norms associated with rules and despoil the moral character of the social role that is associated with the rule. This does not mean that all moral rules are valid. Corruption may sometimes be justified, as in the case of Oskar Schindler. The point is that the broken rules have a deontic or ethical character.

Utilitarians retort that the uncomfortable feelings caused by the displeasure of others when we break rules simply enter into the calculus of pleasure and pain, alongside the net utility we may gain by breaking the rule. But this reduces the individual to a pleasure machine, thereby dissolving irreducible aspects of individual personality such as dignity and self-regard. Exclusively instrumental utilitarian arguments undermine important ethical values such as respect for the law. Utilitarianism reduces morality to narrower questions of individual pleasure.

We are now in a position to sketch a definition of organizational corruption that acknowledges its ethical and rule-related character:

By definition, *organizational corruption* involves at least two agents, X and Y, where at least Y occupies at least one designated role that is attached to a particular organization. This organizational role obliges Y to follow an established set of ethical rules, at least some of which are consistent with the goals of the organization. X consciously intends an action, which is deliberately designed to cause or persuade Y to breach at least one of these goal-consistent ethical rules, of which X and Y are both aware. With the option of acting otherwise, Y violates this rule in accord with the wishes of X.[15]

What is crucial is that organizational corruption undermines the capacity of the organization to fulfill its own objectives. Note also that moral conditions are vital to this definition. If a rule has no ethical content, then its breach is of no moral consequence and the violation can hardly be regarded as corrupt. Observe also that bribes or payments are strictly inessential to this definition, even if money often changes hands. Corruption can and does occur on the basis of camaraderie, expected reciprocity, family

15. The definition of "institutional corruption" in Miller (2011) and Miller, Roberts, and Spence (2005) inspired the modified formulation here. Organizations are a special kind of institution involving membership, rules, and roles (Hodgson 2006b). Examples of organizations include states, political parties, business corporations, trade unions, and private societies. "Institution" is a broader term, covering additional phenomena such as language (Searle 1995). Hence the term "organizational corruption" is preferred here.

ties, or whatever. Furthermore, dishonesty is also strictly inessential to this definition. Although corrupt agents typically lie to conceal their violations of the rules, there are circumstances where such breaches can be acknowledged and even go unpunished.

If an act involves one person only, then it is not *organizational* corruption, which involves collusion and the violation of organizational rules. If Y acts alone to embezzle funds, then this is not *organizational* corruption because no collusion is involved, notwithstanding the immoral breach of organizational and legal rules. It is unnecessary for our purposes here to define additional forms of corruption: in some general cases, we may rely on the Latin-based etymological meaning, as cited above.

Also there is no specification that X and Y are necessarily principal and agent (or agent and principal) as in some influential studies (Banfield 1975). Corruption can occur when X and Y simply collaborate to break the organizational rules.

The criterion of goal-consistency is important for the following reason. Organizations often lay down particular rules that conflict with other overt goals, such as producing high-quality goods or maximizing shareholder value. For example, rules concerning secrecy may limit scrutiny and discussion. In such cases, X acting to cause Y to breach a secrecy rule would not necessarily be an act of corruption. Organizational corruption refers to the erosion of organizational capacities that are in accord with organizational purposes. Of course, what is and is not goal-consistent is often open to dispute. Consequently, there may be a number of debatable cases concerning what is and what is not corruption. But the fact that the true situation is complex and its investigation leads to disagreement does not mean that that there no single truth to be sought.

The above definition of organizational corruption is in general terms. But because corruption is defined in relation to specific organizational roles and ethical rules, what is organizationally corrupt in one organizational, ethical, and cultural context may not be organizationally corrupt in another. The definition is general, but the results may be historically or geographically specific.[16]

This raises the question of whether it is legitimate today to judge contemporary China or India (for example) by the roles, rules, and ethical standards that are associated with Western countries. Historically, such

---

16. Andvig (2006) treats corruption as the intrusion of norms from family and other social contexts into political and bureaucratic fields. This is often the case, but it is too special to provide an adequate definition of corruption.

differences would have been more relevant, but they are less so today. At least in business and international political relations, some common rules have gained general legitimacy. The basic institutions of property, contract, trade, and political treaty are now global, although nuanced by numerous important variations and peculiarities in different settings. Basic standards concerning commerce and international diplomacy have become global. To this extent, corruption can be appraised by common global criteria.

Finally, how does the definition relate to disparities between codified legal or organizational rules, on the one hand, and prevailing and established practices, on the other? Consider an ethical rule concerning an organizational role that is widely ignored by the people fitting this role. The ethical rule could be specific to the organization or it could be a law. For example, employees may routinely ignore a rule of honesty in their claims for business expenses. The rule is disregarded without collusion, so the breach does not amount to organizational corruption. It is individual fraud. And if daily individual practices contradict ethically important rules, then corruption is often unnecessary to sustain the breach.

The above definition of organizational corruption does not apply to roles and ethical rules that are poorly established in habits and sentiments. Organizational corruption occurs when there is a conflict between (a) morally loaded roles and rules that are established in the habits of thought and behavior of people in the organization, and (b) other emerging or intruding habits that undermine those roles and rules. Corruption is thus a dynamic process involving clashes between different sets of habits and norms.

7.4. Social Costs of Organizational Corruption

Famous studies by Nathaniel Leff (1964) and Samuel Huntington (1968) claimed that the benefits of corruption can exceed the costs. Against the protestations of Nobel economist Gunnar Myrdal (1968) and others, it was said that bribery can reduce delays and provide incentives for officials (Lui 1985). Huntington (1968, p. 386) notoriously declared: "In terms of economic growth, the only thing worse than a society with a rigid, over-centralized, dishonest bureaucracy is one with a rigid, over-centralized, honest bureaucracy." Corruption is regarded as the champion of economic efficiency against stultifying state bureaucracy. These arguments overlook the possibility that the state may be necessary to sustain commerce, protect property, and enforce contracts. Corruption undermines such powers: the outcome may be that it is more difficult to implement contracts, to the detriment of business activity and output.[17]

The utilitarian arguments employed by Leff and Huntington echo Bernard Mandeville in his *Fable of the Bees*: where private vices lead to public virtues. These arguments imply, for example, that the voluntary acceptance of bribes to vote for a person in a democratic election increase the welfare of the briber as well as the bribed. The problem is that the values and institutions of democracy are also corrupted by such actions (Seligson 2002).

In a more balanced mainstream approach, Daron Acemoglu and Thierry Verdier (2000) establish a trade-off between, on the one hand, the benefits of diminishing (public) corruption by reducing state intervention and, on the other hand, the need to retain some state intervention to deal with market failures. Both the benefits and disbenefits of state intervention in the economy are acknowledged. But this analysis ignores corruption in the private sphere and the negative externalities of corruption in any context.

A key question is whether corruption can have social costs. Organizational corruption undermines the capacity of the organization to use or dispose of its property, in accord with the aims and objectives of its owners or managers. When an official is bribed to get something done, both parties may immediately benefit, at least in terms of their own wealth or satisfaction. But an additional outcome may be to erode institutions that support enterprise and undermine the legal and social fabric. Such bribery also encourages the growth of self-serving bureaucracies that sustain themselves through corruption. Is corruption an example of an activity that may have benefits for the individuals involved, but has negative externalities that impose social costs on the community as a whole, by undermining the institutional structures of commercial activity and sustaining bureaucratic quagmires?

Such questions face the problem that the concept of social costs has become less fashionable since the influential critique of Ronald Coase (1960). For example, if it were possible to specify individual property rights in one's environment, then polluters could be sued: the externalities would become internalized, and the social cost of pollution would be transformed into private costs for individuals. Nevertheless, this Coasean solution depends on the full specification of individual property rights and the absence of

---

17. Positive views of corruption as greasing the wheels of economic activity are criticized by Leys (1965), Bardhan (1997), Kaufmann (1997), Shleifer and Vishny (1993), and several others.

transaction costs. The emphases of Coase are often different from many Coasean followers. Many Coaseans uphold that externalities can be internalized, but Coase himself is more circumspect.[18]

Leaving aside many of the conceptual and practical problems involved with this topic and its huge literature, it must be noted that corruption has particular features that place additional difficulties in the way of a Coasean argument. Essentially, is it possible to establish property rights in the institutional fabric through which contracts and property rights are themselves sustained? There are special reasons here for answering in the negative. *Enforceable and well-defined property rights and contracts cannot be an effective solution to the social problem of corruption, when corruption disrupts the whole institutional system of private property and contract.* Within the Coasean argument, corruption establishes a self-referential tangle where the property rights solution is undermined by corruption itself. Corruption creates transaction costs and uncertainties that are absent from the Coasean model. Corruption is thus the nemesis of the Coasean solution.

As far as I am aware, Coase himself has not suggested that the particular externalities involved in corruption can be internalized. Indeed, Coase's testimony can be used to support the contrary stance. He has repeatedly drawn attention to the importance of the institutional structures of economic activity. For example, Coase (1988a, p. 10) insists that "markets require . . . the establishment of legal rules governing the rights and duties of those carrying out transactions." As if he were following original institutionalist maxims (Commons 1924; Samuels 1989), Coase (1988a, p. 10) further argues that these legal rules cannot always emerge privately: they require the sustenance of the state:

> Such legal rules may be made by those who organize the markets, as is the case with most commodity exchanges. The main problems faced by the exchanges in this law making are the securing of the agreement of the members of the exchange and the enforcement of its rules. . . . When the physical facilities are scattered and owned by a vast number of people with very different interests . . . the establishment and administration of a private legal system would be very difficult. Those operating in these markets have to depend, therefore, on the legal system of the State.

18. Important differences between Coase's own position and the ideas of some of his "Coasean" followers are discussed by Medema (1994), Canterbery and Marvasti (1994), Glaeser, Johnson, and Shleifer (2001), and Hahnel and Sheeran (2009). Demsetz (2011) argues persuasively that the logic of Coase's (1960) paper overlooks indivisible benefits such as the rule of law.

It is impossible to dismiss the social costs of corruption by using a Coasean internalization argument. And Coase himself insists that a properly functioning state legal system is necessary to sustain property rights, on which the Coasean argument depends. Although Coase does not mention corruption in this context, it would be consistent with his stance to uphold that when corruption undermines institutional rules that help to sustain economic activity, then it must be regarded as a negative externality or positive social cost.

Corruption is an important area where social costs must be considered, and they cannot be dissolved within a universal Coasean framework of property rights allocation. Nevertheless, this does not mean that property rights are unimportant. While the costs of corruption cannot be entirely internalized by a better assignment of property rights, the minimization of corruption will depend on institutional design, involving matters of incentives and property rights assignment (Lambsdorff 2007). It also depends on morality.

7.5. Conclusion: Addressing Corruption

The central argument in this chapter is that the concept of corruption has been corrupted by the utilitarian underpinnings of mainstream economics and by the ideological prejudices of many economists against state activity. The commonplace definition of corruption as the abuse of public office for private gain itself reflects this conceptual corruption. But there is no good reason why organizational corruption should be definitionally confined to the public sector, especially given the corporate scandals experienced in modern corporations. Furthermore, in exceptional cases, organizational corruption can be motivated other than by private gain.

An alternative approach highlights two issues that are missing from the commonplace definition of corruption. First is the ontological claim that rules are key elements of social being; institutions—defined as systems of established and ingrained social rules—are the stuff of social life. Second, many established and important social rules have a moral character. Organizational corruption by definition involves the breach and moral violation of these rules, with the effect of undermining their future efficacy.

Insofar as these rules contribute to human needs and social welfare, their erosion by organizational corruption means negative externalities and positive social costs, despite the fact that the individuals directly involved may gain from the corrupt act. These externalities and social costs cannot fully be internalized by defining property rights because they erode the institutional fabric of private property rights on which any internalization depends.

Corruption reduces levels of trust in dealing with both business and the state. Consequently, it encourages reliance on ethnic, religious, family, and other ties, where contract enforcement relies on sanctions and reputational effects within a group (Landa 1994). Business life becomes fractured into clans or mafias, thus losing the benefits of wider cooperation and competition. The efficacy of general, inclusive, and nondiscriminatory legal rules is undermined. Such legal rules are necessary for the operation of a modern, complex, market economy (Hayek 1960; Weingast 2005). Furthermore, the enforcement of many legal and other rules throughout society depend on a system of morality.

The essentially immoral nature of corruption means that measures to deal with it must address standards of morality. Mainstream economists are ill equipped in this area because they reduce issues of morality to individual utility. Privatization is not necessarily a solution to corruption, properly defined. Anticorruption programs should recruit social scientists and philosophers with a better understanding of ethical issues. Of course, simply preaching morality would be ineffective. Connection with local cultures and practices would be essential to communicate the moral message, and it would have to be combined with additional incentives or disincentives, whether pecuniary or otherwise.

EIGHT

Human Needs and Moral Motivations in Health Economics

Health economics would seem to be a perfect topic for heterodox dissent. . . . [H]ealth economics is a field which must make the average neoclassical economist squirm because it challenges his or her standard assumptions at every turn. Perhaps that is precisely what makes it so interesting to study.

—Mark Blaug (1998)

[The NHS] is there to improve our health and well-being . . . bringing the highest levels of human knowledge and skill to save lives and improve health. It touches our lives at times of basic human need, when care and compassion are what matter most.

—Constitution of the National Health Service for England (2010)

Healthcare is attracting increasing attention from economists, at least because of its increasing cost in absolute and relative terms. In the United States, healthcare now accounts for about one-sixth of GDP.[1] Neoclassical theoretical concepts—as defined in chapter 1—remain at the core of modern health economics. By contrast, other approaches are relatively underdeveloped and have a marginal influence.[2]

1. The OECD (2010) reports that from 1980 to 2008, total healthcare expenditures as percentages of GDP increased from 8.8 percent to 16.0 percent in the United States, from 7.0 percent to 11.2 percent in France, from 8.2 percent to 10.5 percent in Germany, from 7.1 percent to 10.4 percent in Canada, from 5.6 percent to 8.7 percent in the United Kingdom, and from 6.5 percent to 8.1 percent in Japan. (The 2008 figures for Japan and Canada are estimates.)

2. For overviews of mainstream approaches in health economics, see Culyer (1991), Mooney (1994), Newhouse (1996), Culyer and Newhouse (2000). Nonmainstream contributions include Backhaus (unpublished), Champlin and Knoedler (2008), Davis (2001), Dunn (2006), Hildred and Watkins (1996), Langlois and Savage (2001), McMaster (1995, 2002,

It is argued in this chapter[3] that the peculiar features of the health sector and the special requirements of health policy limit the viability of a neoclassical approach even more severely than elsewhere. Insights from evolutionary and institutional economics have a hitherto unrealized potency in this area. Furthermore, because of the nature of the work and our propensity for sympathy for the afflicted, health systems involve an especially heightened degree of moral motivation on the part of health workers. Yet neoclassical economics has severe limitations when dealing with morality.

Neoclassical welfare economics assumes that individuals are the best judges of their interests, and the Pareto criterion rules out making anyone worse off. But these assumptions jar against much health policy. Often in a non-Paretian manner, smoking is forbidden in public places, many substances are banned, and taxes are imposed to fund healthcare. Consequently, many mainstream health economists are inclined to adopt alternative normative criteria, even focusing on measures of health rather than utility (Hurley 2000). As leading health economist Anthony Culyer (1991, p. ix) puts it:

> In practice, the overwhelming majority of health economists use the familiar tools of neoclassical economics, though no means all (possibly not even a majority) are committed to the welfarist (specifically the Paretian) approach usually adopted by mainstream neoclassicists when addressing normative issues.

One is left wondering why neoclassical theoretical propositions are retained when the standard normative apparatus of neoclassical theory is often abandoned. The adoption of some but not other elements in the standard neoclassical package is a bit odd. This chapter questions the relevance of neoclassical precepts in this context. Following the rejection of the utilitarian calculus by many health economists, the elements of a needs-based approach to policy are outlined here, along with an emphasis on the importance of moral motivation.

Leading health economists suggest that healthcare has special features that make it different from other domains of application, limiting the ap-

---

2003a, 2003b, 2004, 2008), McMaster and Sawkins (1996), Reisman (1993), and Spithoven (2011). The institutional economist Hamilton (1932) raised enduring problems in the economics of healthcare, such as insufficient consumer knowledge and the pitfalls of market provision. He also stressed that healthcare professionals had motivations in addition to money.

3. This chapter is a revised and extended version of Hodgson (2008a). There is significant revision of terminology and key concepts in the present version.

propriateness of neoclassical assumptions. Why is healthcare different? Jeremiah Hurley (2000, p. 67) summarizes its distinctive features as follows:

> (1) demand for health care is derived demand (for health); (2) externalities; (3) informational asymmetries between providers and patients; and (4) uncertainty with respect to both the need for and the effectiveness of health care. Individually, each of these features can be found in other commodities, but no other commodity shares all of these features to the extent found in health care.

But while these four features are important, they are insufficient to characterize the economic features of healthcare. A more adequate listing, with a deeper analysis of its exceptional features, suggests that a different type of economic analysis should be employed.

Another quite different problem is to define the boundaries of healthcare or of a healthcare system. Many aspects of public and corporate policy affect health, from occupational support to the provision of adequate nutrition and clean water. While recognizing the vital importance of all these factors, the focus in this chapter is not on public health policy. Instead it is on essential healthcare services contracted by specific individuals and provided by trained healthcare professionals, including primary, hospital, disability, and other forms of care. These aspects of healthcare provision take up a large and growing part of national income in most developed countries. The distinction between essential and inessential healthcare services is itself problematic and is discussed below, although much of healthcare expenditure is regarded as essential by analysts and policymakers.

While shifting the analysis from a demands-based to a needs-based approach, it is not naively assumed that health authorities or professionals always know best. Indeed, the problem is one of the design of institutions where knowledge is developed and where mistakes become useful cues for learning and adaptation. But the detailed complexities of institutional design would require a whole book. Instead this chapter argues for major shift in approach, to complete the separation of health economics from utility analysis. The overarching paradigm involves a combination of institutional, evolutionary, and needs-based approaches, with an emphasis on the comparative institutional analysis of healthcare systems.

This chapter shows that a needs-based analysis helps to identify distinctive features of healthcare. It also proposes a link between the recognition of needs and personal motivation, and argues that the salience and nature of needs in healthcare is an important motivational factor for healthcare

professionals. Motivation in this context is infused by moral considerations, partly in terms of dilemmas concerning treatment or its termina-
tion, but more universally in terms of sympathetic and moral motives to
care for and help others. This implies a critique of incentive systems that
rely principally on pecuniary rewards.

A critical evaluation below of Hurley's list of healthcare peculiarities
serves as a springboard for the main argument. Four following sections
examine further distinctive features of healthcare. Three of them focus
on peculiar characteristics of healthcare in meeting our health needs. The
needs-based approach is outlined, with a focus on the moral motivation
of healthcare professionals to meet needs. Section four brings in more dynamic, evolutionary, and technology-driven issues. The penultimate section considers the epistemic problem of need appraisal and the creation
of institutions through which needs can best be evaluated. The concluding
section underlines key parts of the argument, including why a needs-based
approach relates to motivation and helps us to understand the distinctiveness of healthcare.

8.1. Derived Demand, Externalities, Information Asymmetries and Uncertainty

Hurley's proposal that derived demand—in the standard sense of a demand that is not for the good or service itself but for its outcomes—is an
important distinguishing feature of healthcare does not stand up to close
scrutiny. Like healthcare services, most goods and services satisfy derived
demands: they are purchased as means to consumption ends (K. Lancaster
1966). Consider, for example, motor cars (supplying a means of transport), housing (supplying shelter and comfort), consumer durables, and
most services.

But goods such as cars and houses have an intrinsic status value and
may serve the purposes of conspicuous consumption (Veblen 1899b) to
a degree that is not found with many healthcare services. With some important exceptions of degree and kind, much demand for healthcare arises
from need rather than from appetite or status. In turn, this points to an important distinctive feature of healthcare that is hinted at in the mainstream
literature but often eludes overt identification: health is an objective, universal need, irrespective of whether it is also a want. The distinction between wants and needs, which is examined below, challenges the utilitarian foundations of neoclassical economics. Because of these limitations,

mainstream health economists are pressured, despite their intellectual origins, to move some way in this direction.

Turning to externalities, the literature on public health widely recognizes their existence. Disease contagion is a prominent example. Hence inoculation against disease does not simply help the patient being inoculated: it also helps prevent the spread of disease to others. Excessive drug or alcohol consumption also incurs costs on others. And so on. The nonexcludable character of some health-related services makes them by definition public goods: public sanitation is a prominent example.

Accordingly, mainstream health economists (including Hurley) take the existence of externalities and public goods on board. In some cases, they become the centerpiece of their argument for some government regulation in the health sector. According to this view, one of the primary roles of government is to use fiscal policy to deal with "market failures" and compensate for externalities associated with individual behaviors. This in economics is the traditional Pigovian justification for government intervention.

But this Pigovian case for government intervention is much stronger in the case of some healthcare services rather than others. Externalities do not apply to an exceptional degree to surgery or palliative care, for example. If the case for government intervention rested to a large degree on the existence of externalities, then it would suggest that the case for intervention would be much stronger in some health service sectors, with a consequent reorganization of the health system to reflect this fact.

The externality-based argument for government intervention is countered by the Coaseans, who claim that the case for government intervention disappears once private property rights are fully specified and externalities become internalized. Accordingly, those infected by a contagious disease would somehow sue those responsible for its outbreak. The practical limitations of such an approach are already evident in Coase's (1960) classic paper: the property rights solution to such problems requires low transaction costs in suing those responsible for causing such harm. Arguably, in the health context these transaction costs will typically be large enough to thwart a Coasean solution. Many mainstream health economists are aligned to Pigou rather than Coase. But another striking point here is that very few health economists take on board the familiar institutional concept of transaction costs. This strange omission is discussed further below.

We now turn to arguments concerning information asymmetries between providers and patients, and uncertainty with respect to the effectiveness of some health treatments.[4] Such considerations are at the center of Kenneth Arrow's (1963, 1965) classic analysis, where he argued that these factors undermine the case for purely market-based provision. Consumers are often unaware of what is best for them and thus depend on expert advice. These information asymmetries are a persistent and warranted feature of the health economics literature.

Among others, Thomas Rice (2001) argues persuasively that the goal of consumer choice in healthcare would be desirable only if the consumer had adequate knowledge and understanding of the viable choices and their consequences. In practice, because of inexpert medical knowledge, healthcare consumers have limited awareness of both. In the real world of imperfect information, if patients deal psychologically with symptoms by denying or underestimating their significance, or exaggerate them to seek personal attention, then the welfare benefits of an entirely voluntary system based on competitive private health insurance can be undermined. Another argument against private health insurance is the possibility of moral hazard: where the insurers have insufficient information to identify and prevent excessive claims for health services.

When modern health economics emerged as a major field in the 1970s, severe problems concerning information and uncertainty were acknowledged. Particular attention was paid to the phenomenon of supplier-induced demand in healthcare.[5] This arises because the identification of required, and the capacity to pay for, healthcare services typically depends on expert advice, diagnoses, and approval from healthcare providers.

Some qualifications must be added to these arguments concerning information asymmetries and uncertainty. First, these features are neither universal in healthcare systems nor unique to them. Information asymmetries are far less severe in peripheral but important aspects of healthcare systems such as waiting times, appointment flexibility, hospital food, and hospital accommodation. Consequently, a stronger case for patient choice can be made in these peripheral areas. By comparison, chronic information asymmetry and uncertainty are also features of other sectors outside healthcare, notably education. While important, these informational features are inadequate as pointers to what is distinctive about health.

Second, the phenomenon of supplier-induced demand is important but

4. Mainstream economists often associate the term "uncertain" with cases in which statistical probabilities can be attributed to outcomes. But for Knight (1921), Keynes (1936), and others, "uncertain" by definition applies to cases in which no probability can be calculated.

5. See R. Evans (1974), Reinhardt (1985), Phelps (1986), Labelle, Stoddart, and Ruffles (1994), Blaug (1998). Supplier-induced demand is absent from Hurley's (2000, p. 67) list.

not unique to healthcare. Institutional economists such as John Kenneth Galbraith (1958) have long argued that consumer demand is often manipulated by advertising. What makes healthcare delivery special in this respect is that the informational and skill asymmetries are so extreme that we are often unable even to specify the detailed healthcare we require, whereas the allegedly manipulated consumers of other items can indicate clearly the product that is the object of their desire. It is the extremity of supplier-induced demand—not any uniqueness of healthcare in this regard—that is significant.

Overall, attempts by mainstream health economists to describe the peculiar features of healthcare systems list some important key points, but are inadequate in several respects. The additional features identified in the following sections derive largely from a deeper consideration of the concept of need.

8.2. Health Is an Objective, Universal Need

Health is an objective, universal need, irrespective of whether it is also a want.[6] Clearly, to make sense of this statement, a distinction must be made between wants and needs, where wants are culturally conditioned subjective desires, and needs are objective conditions of autonomy, survival, well-being, and social interaction. But some social scientists have become suspicious of a separate concept of need.[7] Neoclassical economists focus instead on subjective evaluations of utility. Cultural relativists proclaim that apparent needs are simply reflections of a specific culture. Social constructivists decry any objective foundation for the need concept. Nevertheless,

6. The literature on need includes Hobson (1929), Dewey (1939), Maslow (1954), Boulding (1966), Etzioni (1968), Kapp (1976), Lutz and Lux (1979, 1988), Braybrooke (1987), Thomson (1987), Doyal and Gough (1991), Corning (2000), Lawson (2003), and Gough (2004). Some of the neglected early roots of health economics lie in needs-based approaches, particularly the importance of a healthy population to sustain national industry and the arts, and the need for effective treatments for soldiers to maintain military effectiveness (Backhaus unpublished). Questions of objective need were also central to the thinking of the German historical school of economics in the nineteenth century, and even to Carl Menger, the founder of the contrasting Austrian subjectivist approach. Indeed, the German historical school inspired the first modern welfare state, in Bismarck's Germany in the 1880s, with its provision of accident, health, and pension insurance.

7. A prominent fear is that the discourse of need may overshadow variations between individuals and their rights to make decisions concerning their welfare. I try to alleviate these concerns in the final chapter of this book. Standard neoclassical theory is of little solace as it often requires that individual preference functions are identical (Arrow 1986). By contrast, variation between individuals is essential to a Darwinian perspective (Hodgson 2006a; Hodgson and Knudsen 2010) and is emphasized in regard to healthcare in this chapter.

as Len Doyal and Ian Gough (1991) demonstrate, when confronted with real-world circumstances, these perspectives end up relying on universal or objective standards of evaluation, equivalent to what might be termed needs. Hence all these relativist positions are internally inconsistent since they embody some needs-based principles.

In particular, those who believe that need is equivalent to individual utility or that the individual is always the best judge of her welfare rarely go so far as to condone all voluntary and consensual instances of slavery, prostitution, incest, drug use, vote buying, or sex with children. Even political individualists and subjectivists such as Friedrich Hayek (1960) insist that the goal of individual liberty must be sustained through *needed* general rules and political structures that are not necessarily a matter of individual taste or preference. The establishment of human liberty and the autonomy of choice depend on the *need* for information concerning the choices, some knowledgeable understanding of their consequences, and sufficiently healthy and adequate physical and mental capacities to make an evaluation (Nussbaum and Sen 1993).

Against cultural relativists and subjectivists, Doyal and Gough (1991) and Martha Nussbaum (2000) establish mental and physical health as basic human needs. Their objectivity and universality are grounded on the common biological and social characteristics shared by all humans. Factors such as clean water, shelter, physical security, and appropriate healthcare all contribute to health, and their efficacy can be examined by scientific investigation. Accordingly, most if not all health needs are potentially distinguishable from subjective wants: the latter may vary from individual to individual and culture to culture. As Doyal and Gough (1991, p. 54, emphasis removed) write:

> since physical survival and personal autonomy are the preconditions for any individual action in any culture, they constitute the most basic human needs—those which must be satisfied to some degree before actors can effectively participate in their form of life to achieve any other valued goals.

Definitionally, a need must be satisfied for the individual to avoid serious physical or mental harm. Harm includes impediments to individual development or social involvement. Described in such terms, needs are objective, universal, and transcultural.

There is much in common between Doyal and Gough's theory of needs and the *capabilities approach* of Martha Nussbaum and Amartya Sen (1993). Nussbaum (2000) lists several essential capabilities involving the ability to live a healthy life, move freely, enjoy freedom of thought and expression, and be able to interact with others. These broadly concur with Doyal and Gough's "basic needs."[8]

Of course, investigators who attempt to identify needs will be encumbered by prejudices that derive in part from their own history and culture. But the fact that all statements about needs may be distorted does not mean that objective needs do not exist. Impediments to objective observation are not arguments against the existence of an objective reality. If something is difficult to detect, that does not mean that it does not exist. The problem is to set up scientific procedures and responsive institutions that discern and constantly reevaluate the nature of needs and the efficacy of measures to meet them.

We have to distinguish between the objective and universal need for *health* and the individual's requirement for *healthcare*. Basic needs such as health and autonomy are universal and exist irrespectively of the means to satisfy them. Health is a *need*, but healthcare is a *need satisfier* (Doyal and Gough 1991).[9] When people are hungry or lack treatment for illness, there is a *need satisfier shortfall*. For simplicity, I use the single word "requirement" to refer to what Doyal and Gough identify as a "need satisfier shortfall." Requirements are essential measures to meet basic needs. Hence I write here of health *needs* and the *requirement* for healthcare to meet those needs. Unlike health *needs*, healthcare *requirements* vary enormously among people and through time. These variations are considered below.[10]

A sense in which both health needs and healthcare requirements are objective is that they are largely independent of individual whim or preference. Healthcare requirements apply more or less equally to everyone with

8. Gough (2004, p. 293) writes: "Our theory of human need perhaps sits between the Sen and Nussbaum approaches. . . . By expanding a thin derivation, and by distinguishing autonomy of agency from critical autonomy, it recognizes cultural differences within a universalist framework, but by positing universal satisfier characteristics and recognizing our collective understanding of these it provides a potentially richer framework for conceiving and measuring human need."

9. In Hodgson (2008a), I did not always make this rigorous distinction. I thank Ian Gough for pointing this out to me. See Doyal and Gough (1991, esp. p. 170).

10. Matthew (1971, p. 27) defines healthcare needs as emerging "when an individual has an illness or disability for which there is an effective and acceptable treatment or cure." This differs from the terminology adopted here in two ways. First, this reference to an illness or disability points to a needs satisfier shortfall (or healthcare requirement) rather than a need as such. Second, it is a capacities-dependent definition, where requirements exist only when there are means of meeting them. By contrast, needs satisfier shortfalls (or healthcare requirements) are defined here in a way that is independent of the local or global availability of treatments or cures.

similar physical and mental characteristics, in the same circumstances, and afflicted with the same condition. Everyone with a complex limb fracture needs surgical attention, irrespective of preference or diagnosis.

By contrast, some healthcare demands—such as mostcosmetic surgery— have little relation to survival or the avoidance of harm. But severe disfig- urement can inhibit social participation, and in these cases surgery may help meet a need. As with many classifications, the boundaries are fuzzy. But that does not mean that there is no substance to the distinction be- tween demand and need. Especially with healthcare, the majority of re- quirements are fairly obvious in broad terms. Badly broken bones require surgical treatment, infections require medicines, sicknesses require nurs- ing, and so on, notwithstanding the problems of determining the precise nature of and limits to health provision in all these cases.

Given the subjectivist and utilitarian tradition in mainstream economic thought, one might expect neoclassical economists to focus largely on wants and subjective utility, rather than objective needs. But generally this is not the case. A concept of need relating to the ability to benefit from healthcare interventions, in contrast to demand (which is a function of preferences and the ability to pay), is recognized by several leading main- stream health economists (Culyer 1995; Hurley 2000).

Mainstream health economists often abandon neoclassical welfare analysis to focus instead on more objective measures such as "social indi- cators" (Culyer, Lavers, and Williams 1971) or "Quality Adjusted Life Years (QALYs)" (Maynard 1991). Essentially, these are indicators of treatment priority based on an assessment of healthcare requirements. In practice, such measures of cost effectiveness are used much more widely than at- tempts to measure utility. But claims have been made that the more objec- tive measures are based on a utility analysis (Bleichrodt and Pinto 2006). Such assertions seem academically ceremonial or partly designed to retain respectability among neoclassical colleagues rather than to identify real causal mechanisms or enhance practical criteria.

Perhaps one reason for this exceptional mainstream admission of needs is that health relates closely and obviously to matters of survival, mobil- ity, and autonomy. Health is often a matter of life and death. Some other nonhealth needs can be met by individuals themselves, or the harm that results from them being unmet is sometimes less immediate or obvious. Even rational economic man faces the vital objective problems of physical survival, personal autonomy, and the maintainance of his massive mental calculative capacities. Whatever his subjective preferences, he too objec- tively must be healthy in body and mind.

Compare healthcare with some other basic needs, such as food. Dietary requirements are less complex and include vitamins, energy, fiber, and key chemical elements, while limiting the intake of fats, sugars, salt, and so on. By contrast, as noted above, the identification of healthcare requirements often requires expert diagnosis. Furthermore, much healthcare requires the involvement of skilled healthcare professionals. Health is a basic need, and the diagnosis and provision of healthcare is often sufficiently complex to require the involvement of workers with special training and skills. This combination is one of the key features that makes healthcare special.

The recognition that health needs are universal helps to sustain an ethos of professional commitment and ethical obligation by health workers. They are not producing mere widgets or candy floss. Healthcare work is much more than a source of remuneration. Most health sector workers wish to address objective health needs, and they frequently deploy deepseated moral motivations to care for the welfare of others. It has been noted previously that caring for the needs of others in the same community is an elemental moral universal (Haidt and Joseph 2004, 2008). Like others, health workers also seek status and esteem, but the principal means of achieving this is to serve the health needs of their patients. While mainstream health economists acknowledge the existence of nonpecuniary motivations in the health sector (Scott, Maynard, and Elliott 2003), they retain utilitarian theories of individual motivation. Instead they should accommodate criticisms of individual payments-by-results in the huge literature on motivation in organizational psychology and elsewhere.[11] The intrinsic motivation of work itself is widely considered in this literature, and the significant motivational forces of professional duty and perceived need are acknowledged in studies of healthcare workers.[12]

In sum, the objective and universal character of health needs conflicts with the utilitarian presuppositions at the core of neoclassical economics and helps to explain part of the motivations and professional commitments of healthcare workers. Consequently, a needs-based approach has important implications for the commissioning and provision of healthcare

11. Evidence on the merits of *organizational* payment by results is different. For example, a payment-by-results scheme for English hospitals was introduced in 2002, and there is some evidence of improved performance (Farrar et al. 2009). Given the differences between group and individual motivations (discussed in previous chapters), we should carefully distinguish between organizational and individual payment-by-results schemes.

12. On intrinsic motivation, see Herzberg, Mausner, and Snyderman (1959), Vroom (1964), Deci (1975), Steers and Porter (1991), Frey (1992), Deci and Ryan (2000a, 2000b). Analyses of the motivations of health workers include Janssen, de Jonge, and Bakker (1999), Franco, Bennett, and Kanfer (2002), and Benson and Dundis (2003).

services. Theories and policies that underestimate these factors are likely to be inadequate, at best, and destructive of commitment and morale among health workers, at worst.

8.3. Most Healthcare Requirements are Involuntary and Unequally Distributed

As we continue to consider the peculiarities of healthcare, it is useful to compare it occasionally with other areas of human need. Education is also a universal need, requiring the involvement of skilled professionals. But for reasons given in this and the following section, there is a divergence in other respects between education and health.

The need for health is universal, but the requirement for healthcare services is unequally distributed and depends to a significant degree on factors beyond the control of the individual. Generally you don't choose to be sick. (Although exceptions may exist, such as illnesses related to drugs, smoking, alcohol, or overeating.) Contagions afflict us, despite precautions. People with inherited dispositions toward illness do not choose their plight either. Many requirements for healthcare services result from accidents, for many of which the victim bears little or no responsibility. In short, much requirement for healthcare results from a lottery of misfortune, as if God was playing dice with human health.

Comparing healthcare with education or nutrition, some people do have special educational or nutritional requirements. But general requirements for education or nutrition are much more uniformly distributed than the requirement for healthcare services. Because many healthcare patients are not responsible for their plight, only the most hardened and insensitive of observers can avoid reflecting: "It could have happened to me." This special feature of healthcare requirements has major moral and policy implications.

First, the fact that most people do not willingly cause their health problems generates widespread sympathy from others, including health practitioners. This is another source of the motivational ethos of professional obligation in the health sector. It is another reason that a needs-based approach has implications for the production and commissioning of healthcare services.

Second, this special characteristic of healthcare requirements challenges the Pareto criterion and gives rise instead to concerns regarding equity or universal access to healthcare. Mainstream economists are likewise impelled in this direction: so equity or universal access has become a topic of discussion in both orthodox and heterodox texts alike (Culyer and Wagstaff 1993; Hurley 2000; Reisman 1993).[13] It seems obvious that Paretian norms are less appropriate in this context, and it would be better to turn to alternative ethical traditions, including the intellectual lineage from Adam Smith in the *Moral Sentiments* to John Rawls (1971) and beyond, where moral criteria necessarily involve concern for others as well as oneself.

The involuntary nature of much injury and ill health has enormous normative repercussions. But mainstream health economists seem reluctant to spell this out. Why? Perhaps a focus on involuntariness would dethrone the supreme Robbinsian idol of choice. Many mainstream economists define the subject in these terms and regard dissenters by definition as noneconomists. The core mission and claim of mainstream health economists is to bring the theoretical tools of the "science of choice" to the healthcare domain and thereby demonstrate their value. To downgrade choice as the supreme problem would be to undermine this claim in the health sphere and allow banished heretics with a fundamentally different conception of the discipline to reenter the high temple of economic theory. For the mainstream economist, Pareto can be sacrificed rather than Robbins because more is at stake with the latter. Yet the tension remains within mainstream health economists between devotion to the core precepts of neoclassical theory and their frequent abandonment of the standard normative criteria of neoclassical welfare economics.

8.4. Healthcare Requirements Are Varied and Idiosyncratic

Requirements for healthcare services are unequal in more senses than one. They are unequal because of the random lottery of misfortune, as discussed above. Furthermore, even when affected by a similar injury or infection, the nature and severity of the outcome can vary from individual to individual. Healthcare requirements are idiosyncratic, reflecting substantial physiological and mental variations between individuals. Differences in health problems emanate from differences in past environment and genetic endowment. The peculiarities often vary significantly from person to person; each patient requires an individual diagnosis and remedy.

In comparison, requirements for educational services are also partly idiosyncratic: a significant proportion of students have "special needs." But the degree of heterogeneity and inequality is much less, confirmed by the

---

13. But there are differences between health economics in Europe and the United States, with notions of objective need being more prominent in the former than in the latter.

fact that successful schooling curricula involve a great deal of material and teaching common to all students. Everyone must be taught to read. Most will manage to learn together with others in a classroom. In healthcare, by contrast, even among those patients requiring a simple or standard operation, detailed procedures will vary considerably because of differences in age, weight, allergies, and so on. Drugs, physiotherapy, and aftercare will differ because of varied requirements.

Some operations—such as for cataracts—are now fairly simple and standard. But generally, attempts to treat all patients in exactly the same way would be catastrophic. Even when patients with similar afflictions are brought together to benefit from shared specialist skills and equipment (thus realizing possible economies of scale), their detailed healthcare requirements typically remain highly diverse. Highly standardized mass production of healthcare services is possible in a limited number of cases only. Some significant standardization of medical diagnostic procedures has occurred in healthcare systems, but when effective, this leads to improved individual diagnoses rather than uniform healthcare provision. In contrast to education, there is very little equivalent common provision among patients undergoing healthcare. Healthcare services have to be varied and flexible to reflect idiosyncratic requirements.

With heterogeneous goods or services, economic analysis faces familiar problems of theoretical tractability. Although there is a significant mainstream literature on heterogeneous goods or services, much standard theory assumes relatively few homogeneous products. But the problem here is not simply one of building formal models. Under conditions of limited information, the heterogeneity of goods and services creates a set of operational problems of a contractual and administrative type. Interestingly, these problems appear in both market-based and planned economic systems. They are highly relevant in the healthcare context.

In a market-based system with limited information, the idiosyncrasy and heterogeneity of goods and services is an important source of transaction costs. These are the costs of formulating, negotiating, monitoring, and enforcing contracts. If a set of goods and services were homogeneous, then one standard contract would often do because in all likelihood their characteristics would be widely known. But with heterogeneous goods and services, problems of specification, uncertainty, and complexity confound standardized contracting solutions.

Since the pioneering work of Coase (1937), Williamson (1975) and other "new" institutional economists, the concept of transaction costs has become commonplace in modern economics, although it has proved difficult to incorporate adequately in formal models. By contrast, relatively little attention is paid to the concept and its significance in mainstream health economics. In the *Handbook of Health Economics* (Culyer and New-house 2000), only 2 chapters out of 35 mention transaction costs, and in both cases briefly and without much elaboration. There is no significant discussion of transaction costs in Culyer's (1991) collection of definitive essays in the subdiscipline or in the *Elgar Companion to Health Economics* (Jones 2006). Although transaction costs in health systems are discussed elsewhere (Hsiao 1995; Robinson and Casalino 1996; Ashton 1998; Jan 2000), they have not yet achieved the prominence they deserve in main-stream health economics.[14]

By contrast, transaction costs are highly significant in reality. In health systems that rely more on markets, such as in the United States, it is esti-mated that transaction costs amount to 25 percent or more of health insur-ance premiums (Hsiao 1995, p. 138). Transaction costs impinge on both demand and supply in a system. Information and other problems concern-ing the contracting of insurance affect the demand for healthcare. Com-mercialization and competition in the production of healthcare services enhances possibilities for litigation and contractual dispute. Both commis-sioning and provision are affected.

Transaction cost economics is well established and has gained main-stream respectability. But despite all its concern with problems of micro-measurement, mainstream health economics has paid inadequate atten-tion to the measurement of transaction costs. Yet comparisons of different healthcare systems suggest that high transaction costs is one of the typical downside problems that arise within private and market-based healthcare provision. Although transaction cost economics differs in character from other versions of institutional economics, few institutionalists would deny the reality and importance of transaction costs.

A possible advantage of organized hierarchies is that they may reduce transaction costs, just as they are sometimes reduced by organizing produc-tion under the unitary administrative umbrella of the firm (Coase 1937). Nevertheless, while transaction costs may be reduced in an integrated sys-tem, the planning of heterogeneous goods or services may bring problems of a different kind.

Consider the formerly planned economies in the Soviet Union and

14. Barr (1992) emphasizes information problems without referring to the transaction costs literature. Promotion of "quasi-markets" by social policy theorists such as Le Grand (1993) has led to more discussion of the problem of transaction costs outside mainstream economics. See Hughes, Griffiths, and McHale (1997) and Donato (2010).

China. Faced with product heterogeneity and complexity, the central planning authorities were obliged to fix relatively simple quantitative targets. But firms working to target-based incentives responded by producing inferior products. Planning targets in the textile sector in terms of square meters led to the production of thin, fragile cloth. Changing the target to weight led to useless, sackcloth-like material. Attempts by the planners to deal with the problem of cloth "quality" led to its definition in terms of the absence of a particular type of imperfection. At least one enterprise responded by cutting out all the imperfections so that the cloth was dotted with holes (Ellman 1989, p. 45). Plan-fulfillment targets are bound to cause such distortions when significant variations in product characteristics are typical (Nove 1979, 1983).

The severity of such problems varies from one type of planned system to another. Large corporations are planned to a degree.[15] But most corporations face more competition from outside than large centrally planned economies. Corporations typically respond by building devolved and flexible internal structures. Competitive pressures have less impact on centrally planned economies, especially when they are less engaged in international trade; hence planning distortions can be more enduring.

Historical evidence shows that highly centralized hierarchies settle into established routines, and they lack dynamism, innovation, and growth. Routinized hierarchies cope better within a steady state than with dynamic transformations that necessarily require changes in routine (R. Nelson 1981). But when faced with rapidly changing demands or requirements, such centrally planned systems are deficient. Peter Murrell (1991) demonstrates that the communist countries were no less efficient in allocating resources than capitalist societies. Where they lagged was in terms of dynamic efficiency: the ability to change and innovate.

To what extent have plan-fulfillment problems appeared in centrally planned healthcare systems? They are more likely to emerge if central planners attempt to bring about radical transformations in the system instead of relying mostly on the judgments and habits of healthcare professionals and on the routinized practices of local healthcare organizations. When big changes impact on the system, routines are disrupted by turbulence and uncertainty. Hence serious problems can arise when central healthcare

---

15. Langlois (1995b) argues that the firm is not and cannot be a fully centralized system of planning, at least in the sense of planners adequately envisaging the future and enacting appropriate responses. But few if any sizeable planning systems could function in such a visionary and proactive manner. They are still systems of planning in a meaningful sense, and they are not markets.

authorities, driven by their own strategic agenda, disrupt a planned system that is moving along largely under the impetus of its local routines. In such circumstances, people search for new ways of coping with the changes, some of which malfunction.

Important illustrative examples are found in the British National Health Service (NHS). From its inception in 1948 until the 1980s, there were relatively few attempts at restructuring or reform. While various governments tried to introduce some markets or quasi-markets in the system, the NHS remained a huge, bureaucratic, centrally planned organization. The NHS is frequently cited as being the world's third biggest employer, after the Indian railways and Chinese army.

By 1997 there was public discontent due to delays in treatment and hospital waiting lists. The Labour Party pledged during the 1997 election to deal with this problem. When elected, it controversially chose a target maximum time on a formal waiting list instead of targeting the average length of actual waiting times. In response, hospitals resorted to administrative devices to reach their waiting list targets, reportedly including setting up covert waiting lists to get onto their declared waiting lists.[16]

Hence Labour's 1997–2010 management of the NHS produced some outcomes reminiscent of the centrally planning systems that used to exist in China and the Soviet bloc. There were attempts to reduce waiting times to see general practitioners. Prime Minister Tony Blair set up incentives in 2003 to ensure that general practitioners saw patients within 48 hours. The NHS offered substantial (five-figure) monetary payments to general practices that met this target. Some practices responded simply by refusing to make advance appointments in excess of 48 hours. To get an appointment, a patient had to be among the first to make telephone contact with the appointments office immediately after it opened in the morning. Within minutes, the appointment schedules were filled up for that day and the next, leaving patients who telephoned later without any chance of getting any appointment. The appointment-time target was fulfilled by limiting the possibility of making an appointment.[17]

These examples suggest that target-fulfillment problems similar to those in centrally planned economies can arise in centrally administered healthcare systems. Concerns have been raised that overattention to targeted areas weakened performance in others.

16. See Hansard (1997, 1998, 2002), Green and Casper (2000), BBC News (2001).

17. During the 2005 general election campaign, a woman angrily explained the problem to Blair in front of a televised audience. The Prime Minister conceded that he had no idea that such evasive practices took place (BBC News 2005; Moss 2005).

But as in centrally planned economies, targets may bring benefits as well as problems. There is some evidence for this. Since 1999, management of health systems in the United Kingdom has been devolved to England, Scotland, Wales, and Northern Ireland, each taking a different path. Despite having lower per capita staffing and funding, England has outperformed the other nations in several performance targets, including reduced waiting times. In a detailed study, Sheelagh Connolly, Gwyn Bevan, and Nicholas Mays (2010, pp. 95–102) gave some reasons for these differences in performance:

> Each country had targets for hospital waiting times and ambulance response times; but only in England from 2000 was there a system of public reporting . . . backed up by active performance management. . . . [T]he UK taxpayer funds health services in each country, but only England is held to account for its performance by the UK Treasury.

This suggests that targets can work when backed up by mechanisms of public accountability. On the other hand, there is some survey evidence that Scotland outperformed England in terms of quality of healthcare (Connolly, Bevan, and Mays 2010, p. 96). The extent to which other aspects of healthcare provision have been undermined by even a successful focus on limited targets is inadequately investigated.

Despite the success of publicly accountable targets, the English healthcare system has again seen more attempts to bring in private providers and market incentives, raising the obverse specter of high transaction costs and other problems caused by rapid structural change.[18] Experience from the United Kingdom and elsewhere confirms that both central planning and market mechanisms have advantages and shortfalls.

Although this dilemma is central to much policy discussion, mainstream economics has severe limitations in addressing it. In the 1930s debate over the efficacy of centrally planned systems, the defenders of central planning used neoclassical theoretical tools. Critics such Friedrich Hayek (1945) emphasized that mainstream theory neglected the problems of information, knowledge, heterogeneity, and radical uncertainty that are prevalent in complex economic systems. This goes against the neoclassical theoretical grain, notwithstanding the fact that neoclassical theorists have become more sympathetic to market-based policies. For this reason, the immensely

---

18. See Gorsky (2011). The post-2010 coalition government has moved even further in a market direction (Walshe 2010).

important debate between planning and market-based solutions remains neglected to this day. It is rarely present in the teaching curricula of university departments of economics.[19]

This omission partly accounts for the surprisingly limited discussion within mainstream health economics of the relative virtues of different types of healthcare systems. If mainstream health economists were to pay adequate attention to the problems of knowledge, complexity, heterogeneity, and uncertainty that have to be addressed in such comparative analyses, then they would have to abandon the more optimistic informational assumptions at the core of neoclassical theory.

The argument in this section does not depend on any particular ideological inclination toward either markets or planning. Either way there are problems, due to highly idiosyncratic and heterogeneous requirements in the context of uncertainty. Market-based systems increase contracting activity and may exacerbate the problem of transaction costs. Planned systems face other problems of knowledge, complexity, and uncertainty, identified by Austrian school economists such as Hayek. The inappropriate informational assumptions within mainstream economics lead to a neglect to both types of problem. By contrast, evolutionary and institutional economists are much better equipped to take these issues on board.

In reality we are not faced with a simple dichotomy between market-based and planned systems. In fact, most national healthcare systems involve a complex combination of administration and competition, of public and private provision, and of centralized and decentralized authority.

8.5. The Evolution of Healthcare Requirements and Systems

Recent decades have seen massive ongoing changes in the nature and distribution of healthcare requirements and the capacities of healthcare technologies to meet them. These have put new and changing demands on healthcare systems. When the British NHS was founded in 1948, it was anticipated that the need for healthcare services would diminish as a result of universal provision. This prediction proved to be unfounded as capacities to meet healthcare requirements have increased.

Several factors are changing the scale and nature of healthcare requirements (Towle 1998). The first is growing longevity and the increasing proportion of elderly in the populations of most developed countries. This

---

19. See Lavoie (1985) and Steele (1992), among others. Nove (1983) spells out implications for socialist thought. See also Hodgson (1984, 1999a).

is augmenting the need for healthcare provision for conditions associated with seniority. An increase in the proportion of retired people also creates problems for systems of healthcare funding that rely significantly on taxes or other contributions made during periods of employment.

The second major factor is the increasing availability of new technologies for screening, diagnosis, information analysis, and treatment, including expensive new drugs and diagnostic equipment. Because of the costs involved, it is inconceivable that all relevant available technologies can be employed in all cases. The increase in the capacity to serve needs comes at a cost, and the more this capacity is enhanced, the greater the potential cost involved. In response, there is likely to be an increasing ongoing emphasis on health technology assessment, to determine the benefits of each technique. There is also likely to be the further development of systems of prioritization or rationing. Without such measures, there is the risk of huge cost overruns.

Significantly, new information technologies are giving patients access to new information, leading to a growth in patient awareness and demands for greater empowerment. These additional trends do not themselves increase healthcare *requirements* (which exist whether or not we are aware of them) but can potentially greatly expand healthcare *demands* and put greater consumer pressure on the healthcare system. People become more aware of the possibilities and come to expect solutions. Real healthcare possibilities are enlarged, and healthcare consumers come to believe that they need additional healthcare services. These heightened expectations have major systematic repercussions.

What are the consequences for health economics? In this dynamic context, it becomes increasingly irrelevant to search for optimal equilibria. Even if an optimum policy solution can be found, it will not remain an optimum for long; relentless technological and demographic changes will shift the optimum solution elsewhere. Problems of uncertainty make the identification of any optimum generally problematic; when it is endlessly shifting, then these problems are compounded. Real-world dynamism further undermines the relevance of neoclassical assumptions.

Instead there is scope for evolutionary, Schumpeterian, and Austrian approaches to analysis, which abandon the focus on equilibrium and optimum solutions.[20] In their place, there is analysis of the processes of change

---

20. Classic works include Veblen (1919), Schumpeter (1934), Hayek (1945), Simon (1957), R. Nelson (1981), and R. Nelson and Winter (1982, 2002).

themselves, with a view to understanding what kind of efficacious interventions are possible in a complex, uncertain, and evolving system.

While a detailed discussion of institutional design is impossible here, a few relevant themes can be highlighted. In general policy terms, evolutionary economists have argued for flexible institutional structures, which can accommodate sufficient variety to withstand shocks and fuel the evolutionary process (Hodgson 1984, 1988; Metcalfe 1998; Witt 2003). These ideas have major implications concerning the system of provision of healthcare services, particularly concerning the respective roles of the state and the market. Policy solutions are not straightforward, as there is strong evidence that innovation and growth are best fostered by a *combination* of state regulation and market mechanisms (Nelson 1981, 2003, 2005a; Kenworthy 1995; Moreau 2004; Martinez 2009).

Healthcare decisions by consumers and practitioners are made in a complex, evolving environment. Especially in such contexts, original institutional economists in the Veblenian tradition emphasize the role of habit in decision making (Veblen 1899b, 1919; Hodgson 1997b, 2004b, 2010a). Generally, consumers are myopic rather than globally rational and rely on habits, conventions, and rules of thumb. The relatively extreme conditions of complexity and uncertainty surrounding healthcare make such considerations even more pertinent. With limited understanding of the complexities of healthcare, consumers tend to rely on customs, simple decision rules, and advice from others. Allied studies underlining the roles of habit and rules in healthcare are found in the medical literature (Lindbladh and Lyttkens 2002; Marshall and Biddle 2001; Plsek and Greenhalgh 2001).

Here too is an opening for institutional economists, through the construction of habit-based models of choice and the introduction of the allied concept of organizational routines (M. Becker 2004). These concepts have important implications for the understanding of incentives and institutional design in healthcare systems.

8.6. The Dynamic Evaluation of Healthcare Needs and Requirements

Economists often assume that they are dealing with consumers who know what they want: consumer demands are sovereign. However, since Arrow's (1963) classic paper, mainstream economists have questioned the applicability of standard precepts of consumer demand and sovereignty to healthcare systems. At least in healthcare, the consumer is not necessarily the best judge of her welfare, even after she has received expert advice. Several mainstream economists have instead moved toward a needs-based approach to healthcare evaluation.

The familiar objection to a needs-based approach is that it shifts the decision of what is best for the individual to other individuals or institutions, such as experts or the state. Such a shift is seen as illiberal and dangerous because such alternative individuals or institutions have their own vested interests and are insufficiently familiar with individual preferences and circumstances.

But in proposing a needs-based approach, it is not assumed that needs are readily discernable. Doctors, for example, are often wrong in their diagnoses. The state is incapable of assessing many detailed requirements at the local level. The heterogeneous and idiosyncratic nature of healthcare requirements places further difficulties in the way of centralized assessments. Neither is it proposed here that consumer tastes are irrelevant. Some middle ground must be found between the propositions that the consumer always knows best and the state or the experts always know best: neither extreme is defensible.

Abraham Maslow's (1954) theory of needs is based essentially on psychological considerations. Other theories of need—including Hobson's (1929) and Doyal and Gough's (1991)—involve social as well as psychological needs. Social needs are regarded as the social and institutional preconditions for the achievement of individual needs such as survival, autonomy, and social interaction. The specific mechanisms for satisfying social needs are problematic and open to continuous debate: they occupy a significant part of the disputed agenda of the social sciences.

Neither individuals nor governments always know best. The problem is to design institutions that set up a creative dialogue between individual preferences and expert advice, embody mechanisms to scrutinize the skills and claims of experts, and facilitate the creation and distribution of relevant knowledge concerning healthcare.

Matters of institutional design are highly complex and context dependent. They would be best informed by comparative studies of different national healthcare systems. But some brief general observations are in order. First, the incentives involved in the institutional design of healthcare systems are never entirely pecuniary. Indeed, the nature of healthcare needs inspire a professional ethos of care and obligation that is above and beyond any pecuniary motive for healthcare workers. Healthcare institutions must nurture and harness this ethos of obligation. While pecuniary incentives are also important, they can be undermined by systems that overshadow and may serve to override ethical and other commitments through excessive emphasis on pecuniary rewards.[21]

Second, to cope with complexity and change, systems require adequate internal diversity of institutional forms and structural mechanisms. W. Ross Ashby's "law of requisite variety" is relevant here (Ashby 1956; Beer 1964; Hodgson 1984, 1988). Diversity within a system is necessary so that it deals with complexity, variety, and unforeseeable shocks in the real world. A coexisting variety of healthcare institutions and subsystems provides a nationwide basis for comparative performance evaluation and piecemeal experimentation.

An intellectual mentor for this type of approach is John Dewey, who has been influential for institutionalists in the original American tradition. Dewey favored an experimental approach to policy with democratic involvement. Institutional design had to be cautious and experimental. The primary role of experts is to outline feasible alternatives and their likely consequences (Ryan 1995; Evans 2000). This thinking is highly relevant for healthcare systems, although it awaits much further elaboration and detailed application. Some steps in this direction are made in the final chapter of this book.

8.7. Conclusion: Toward a New Health Economics

In their introduction to the *Handbook of Health Economics*, Anthony Culyer and Joseph Newhouse (2000, p. 1) wrote: "health economics has been a remarkably successful subdiscipline." Indeed, there have been significant achievements. Mark Blaug (1998) argues that health economics is in a much better state than the economics of education.

Nevertheless, mainstream health economics has some severe limitations, as outlined above. The predominant mainstream focus in the literature has been on issues of measurement and quantification, to the relative neglect of the big questions. Much effort has been put into establishing appropriate measures for use in cost-benefit (or cost-effectiveness) analyses, overlooking the inherent limitations of such approaches (Zerbe 2007). Healthcare systems are nonlinear and complex, and have strong interactive effects. Mainstream healthcare economists seem to have set themselves the foremost goal of providing full analytical information in a field where problems of complexity and uncertainty are so extreme that such a goal

---

21. Titmuss's (1970) classic comparison of voluntary and payment-based blood donor schemes illustrates some disadvantages of the latter.

is not remotely achievable. The problems of uncertainty and complexity will not disappear as a result even of titanic efforts of data collection and measurement.

This prognosis is confirmed in practice. Citing studies of the impact of cost-benefit empirical research on health systems, Maria Goddard et al. (2006, p. 81) observes that "despite the best endeavors of economists over many decades, it is widely acknowledged that economic approaches to priority setting have had only limited impact in practice."

Although there is much discussion in the literature of the roles of markets and the state in healthcare, it is often focused on micro instances to the neglect of systemic interactions in a more dynamic context. The theory used to make such evaluations is generally constrained by the protocols of standard neoclassical theory. These approaches are severely challenged by the realities of healthcare. While several mainstream health economists have defied neoclassical welfare norms and embraced other indicators, they have been remarkably deficient in utilizing other relevant concepts, including the highly relevant idea of transaction costs.

The needs-based approach reveals some special qualities of healthcare. These are summarized in table 2 and compared with other requirements, showing why healthcare is special. As argued above, involuntariness and inequality in the distribution of requirements, shown in the first column, affect the intrinsic motivation and commitment of service providers. Healthcare has the highest score in this column.

Considering the second column, a high degree of variety and idiosyncrasy generates transaction cost problems for a market system and incentive specification problems for a centrally planned system. It is likely that planned health systems such as the British NHS have previously been able to mitigate incentive specification problems by maintaining a strong ethic of professional commitment. If true, this has relatively unexplored implications for health policy and the design of healthcare systems. It would mean that some central planning with less market provision is viable, as long as an ethic of professional dedication and commitment is nurtured.

In the third column, the picture is further complicated by the high rate of growth in the healthcare requirements due to an aging population and increasing technological capacities. Although arguments concerning dynamic systems often point to the virtues of market competition, even here Richard Nelson (1981, 2003, 2005a) argues that theory and evidence both suggest a combination of market and state provision.

This framework of needs analysis offers a research agenda for the comparison of different systems of provision. It combines with strong argu-

Table 2 Comparing Healthcare, Educational, and Nutritional Requirements

	Degrees of involuntariness and inequality in distribution	Degrees of variety and idiosyncrasy	Rate of expansion of requirements that in principle can be met
Healthcare requirements	High	High	High
Educational requirements	Low	Medium	Medium
Nutritional requirements	Low	Low	Low

ments in mainstream health economics against a fragmented and competitive system of health insurance, in favor of state or other monopsonistic provision on a universal basis (Arrow 1963; Rice 2001).

In mainstream health economics, there is inadequate comparative discussion of healthcare systems.[22] Some comparative studies focus on estimating the marginal effects of factors such as healthcare expenditure (Evans et al. 2001). Issues of structural and overall institutional design are often neglected. But such comparative system studies seem to provide the most promising route toward an understanding of the merits and demerits of private, public, and mixed provision in this area. Evolutionary and institutional economists would relegate static efficiency comparisons, focus on relevant institutions, and deal with other important matters such as institutional complementarities, technological innovation, and learning (Aoki 2001; Nelson 1993, 2005b). A pressing task is to apply these approaches to the peculiarities of healthcare systems.

The world today provides us with several different types of healthcare system, including the private and market-oriented system in the United States; the publicly financed and planned system in the United Kingdom; the mixed systems based on compulsory insurance in Canada, France, Germany, and Scandinavia; and the more limited systems in poorer economies. There is enough empirical material here to assess the merits, demerits, and systemic characteristics of different types of systems and learn from these existing examples. Both the commissioning of healthcare services and the systems of healthcare provision have to be taken into account.

Health is also an area that dramatically exposes the limitations of util-

22. Exceptions include Dixon and Mossialos (2002), McPake, Kumaranayake, and Normand (2002), and Retziaff-Roberts, Chang, and Rubin (2004). Culyer, Maynard, and Williams (1981) see the key differences between systems in terms of "ideologies," without regard to social structures such as management systems, social positions, markets, contracts, and property rights. By contrast, Connolly, Bevan, and Mays (2010) highlight incentives, responsibilities, and structures and provide a more enlightening comparative analysis.

itarian approaches to motivation and policy. The replacement of utility-maximizing economic man by a more complex individual, motivated by selfish gain but also responsive to moral pressure, can provide a more effect approach to the understanding of individual motivation and the design of appropriate institutions. Instead of Paretian or other utility-based welfare criteria, the focus is on the determination and satisfaction of human needs. Practical discourses on needs and healthcare requirements are used as motivational springs for those working in healthcare.

NINE

From Utilitarianism to Evolution in Ecological Economics

Only so far as current tastes and appetites are reliable indices of human utility, only so far as we can identify the desired with the desirable, is the evolution of customary standards of life a sound human art. But it is needless to cite the ample evidence of the errors and wastes that are represented in every human standard of consumption.

—John A. Hobson (1929)

Indeed the really important problems of economics are questions of collective decision-making which cannot be dealt with in terms of a calculus deductively derived from a formal concept of individual rationality under hypothetically assumed and transparent conditions.

—K. William Kapp (1978)

Global warming is one of the most urgent and serious problems facing humankind. Yet in no other area are the deficiencies of utilitarianism and neoclassical welfare economics so dramatic. Any welfare approach based on the presumption that individuals are the best judges of their own interest falls at the first hurdle: many people neither understand nor accept the conclusions of the science of climate change. Climate change skeptics are prominent in the United States and the United Kingdom (among other countries), with only 49 percent and 48 percent respectively saying in a 2008 poll that rising global average temperatures are a result of human activities (Pelham 2009).

Against this, despite many important differences on details, the scientific community is overwhelmingly of the opinion that human activity is the cause for the increase in global average temperatures over the past century (IPCC 2007). Yet a large number of educated people in developed countries do not accept this conclusion and would oppose costly measures to deal with it. Standard utilitarianism gives low weightings to human needs that are of lesser rank in individual utility functions. Many people oppose, or give a low priority to, the radical measures that are needed to deal with climate change. Consequently, such measures would be Pareto suboptimal.

A problem here is of reconciling subjective utility or individual satisfaction with scientifically grounded policies that address environmental problems. The aim of this chapter is to move beyond such narrow and self-interested considerations and help prepare the foundations of an approach more suitable to deal with environmental issues, including impending climatic disruption.

Of course, the first difficulty facing policymakers is not neoclassical economics but public misunderstanding of the issues. But neoclassical economics plays a role by sustaining sentiments of consumerism and self-interest that have to be challenged if global warming is to be alleviated. The limitations of the neoclassical approach need to be examined, so that the contribution of economics can be reformed in this area.

A vital component must be the reintroduction of moral values into economics and the recognition of moral as well as pecuniary or material motivations. Contrary to some environmental economists cited below, morality is neither skin-deep nor less deeply rooted in human nature than material selfishness. Evolutionary reasons for these assertions have been explored in preceding chapters. A further aim of this chapter is to show how evolutionary theory can help to bridge both economic and ecological concerns. Evolutionary thinking can begin to connect economic and ecological values and vindicate moral motivation as a major element in environmental policy design.

9.1. From Neoclassical Self-Interest to Morality and Need

Neoclassical economics incorporates rational, optimizing agents with exogenously given preference functions; it focuses on the equilibrium outcomes and limited types of information problem associated with such optimizing behavior.[1] From the 1990s, neoclassical economics has been challenged within the mainstream by other approaches, including behavioral economics. But—despite the work of Amartya Sen and others—no

---

1. This section builds on an earlier discussion in Hodgson (1997a).

developed alternative to neoclassical, utility-based welfare approaches has yet prevailed. Even the new institutional economics of Oliver Williamson (1975) and others—which pays attention to information problems and has improved our understanding of institutions—"shares conventional economic assumptions on how agents are motivated by their utility" (Paavola and Adger 2005, p. 358).[2]

Broadly, there are two types of neoclassical approach to environmental policy. The first follows Arthur Pigou (1920) and is based on "market failures." Existing markets may not take into account some environmental costs. A car driver who pollutes the air and adds to road congestion imposes costs on others as externalities. The market-failures approach aims to identify such externalities and to use such measures as road charging and fuel taxes to attempt to alleviate the problem. This approach relies on government legislation, the tax system, and experts to estimate the economic costs and benefits involved.

The second neoclassical approach is associated with the Chicago school and Ronald Coase (1960). It focuses on the creation of clearly defined property rights, thus allowing markets and contracts to deal with problems such as pollution, congestion, and resource depletion.[3] Pigovian externalities are deemed to arise primarily because of the absence of clearly defined and enforceable property rights. Such problems are remedied in practice "by rescinding the institutional barriers preventing the full operation of private ownership" (von Mises 1949, p. 658). If pollution occurs, then the owners of the seas, rivers, or open spaces would have recourse to law to obtain compensation.

Information and enforcement problems arise with each approach. But we need not enter into the controversy between the two perspectives.[4] Of concern here are the assumptions common to both types of policy. Both

2. See Ostrom (1990, 2009), Bromley (1991), Jacobs (1994), Bromley and Paavola (2002), Paavola and Adger (2005), Vatn (2005), and Paavola (2007) for applications of various versions of institutional economics to environmental problems.

3. For example, Block (1989) proposes the fencing of the atmosphere with laser beams to establish and enforce property rights, just as the American range was fenced by barbed wire in the nineteenth century. Demsetz (2011, p. 12) argues that the Coasean logic excludes indivisible benefits where individuals have a strategic interest in underdeclaring their willingness to pay for them, including policies dealing with climate change: "Just as we find the State's ability to coerce legitimately helpful in the maintenance of law and order, so we may find it useful in helping to finance production of goods and services that are important to society but are subject to serious strategic bargaining problems."

4. These issues are discussed in the conventional environmental economics literature (Baumol and Oates 1988; Pearce and Turner 1990; Helm and Pearce 1991; Cropper and Oates 1992). See also Sagoff (2004) and Vatn (2005).

approaches rely on individual utility maximization or self-regarding preferences to solve the problems of environmental degradation and resource depletion.

Consistent with the underlying utilitarian philosophy, moral values and stewardship virtues, such as duty to others, concern for future generations, care for the planet, respect for other species, and so on, are considered only insofar as they yield utility for that individual. Altruism and cooperation are possible, but only insofar as an individual gains utility from such acts (G. Becker 1974, 1976a; Collard 1978; Hirshleifer 1977, 1978). But such an individual is still self-serving rather than being genuinely altruistic in a wider and more adequate sense. Notions of morality or duty that are not incorporated in the utility-maximizing calculus are disregarded.

Once they are incorporated into a preference function, moral issues are stripped of their distinctive meaning. This strategy is adopted by some mainstream environmental economists. For example, in an essay on the evaluation of environmental resources, W. Michael Hanemann (1995, p. 105) notes that the modern theory of social choice is based on individual preferences and "considers it immaterial" whether they reflect "selfish interest or moral judgment." Yet surely it is important whether individual motivation is selfish or moral, especially if we consider the possibility that preferences may change, and we are thus obliged to examine the causes of these changes.

Another mainstream view is that individual self-interest is a much more solid foundation for policy. Moral values or commitments are treated as superficial or transient, ignoring their importance in environmental policy. Thus Dieter Helm—a leading environmental economist and former UK government advisor—claims that "values" are generally "fragile" and "highly uncertain." But if values were potentially variable, that might provide an argument for making them the center of analysis. Overlooking this option, as well as the possibility that moral values have deep biological and cultural foundations, Helm (1991, p. ix) asserts that "environmental policy must largely take values as given, and focus instead on the context within which humans act. Within this framework, the economic process plays a leading role." He thus takes the view that moral values are ephemeral and have little to do with the "context within which humans act" or with the "economic process." Helm goes on to argue that the inclusion of the environment within economic calculations requires that we assign a monetary value to it and "treat it as if is a commodity."

This latter theme is taken up by Partha Dasgupta, who is another leading mainstream economist working on environmental issues. In an essay entitled "The Environment as a Commodity," he considers such environmental problems as the depletion of the Amazonian rain forest. There Dasgupta (1991, p. 31) writes: "I cannot think that it will do to look solemn and utter pious sentiments concerning our moral duty." Discussions of moral values are thus removed from debates on environmental policy, in an unsentimental appeal to self-interest alone. Morality sadly lacks even the durability portrayed in the "veneer theory" (de Waal 2006). In the words of Hobson (1929, p. 132), moral values are treated as "illusions or shadowy epiphenomena."

In sum, moral values and norms are either disregarded in the neoclassical approach or rendered commensurate with everything else via the utilitarian calculus of satisfaction-seeking individuals. Either way, their motivational significance is overlooked. Money value is used as the principal incentive. The well-known neoclassical technique in environmental policy to ask people what they would be willing to pay to maintain an environmental asset. It is assumed that everything—including moral and aesthetic values—can be given a price.[5]

While disregarding morality, neoclassical economists such as Dasgupta and Helm focus on pecuniary and other material incentives to get people to change their behavior. Such incentives are important. But pecuniary and moral incentives can be vital complements and are not necessarily rivals. As Elinor Ostrom (1990) and Michael Taylor (1996) have pointed out, many cases of cooperation in modern societies depend on combinations of normative exhortations, peer pressure, incentives, and sanctions. Moral values typically supplement and enhance other incentives, and in some cases self-interest can be overridden by moral considerations. Moral discourse can also help to educate people and alter their preferences.

A danger in the exclusive focus on extrinsic motivation and pecuniary or material rewards is that intrinsic motivations and moral concerns will be "crowded out" and undermined. Experimental and other evidence supports this (Frey 1992, 1997a, 1997b; Ostrom 2000; Frey and Jegen 2001; Bowles 2008; Vollan 2008).

As argued in the preceding chapter, an alternative to the subjective and utilitarian approach is one based on human needs, including the need to

---

5. The assignment of monetary values to environmental attributes in welfare calculations has been criticized by Martinez Alier (1987, 1991), Sagoff (1988a, 1988b, 2004), Norgaard (1990), Christensen (1991), Jacobs (1991, 1994), Page (1991), Söderbaum (1992), Bergström (1993), Bowers (1993), O'Neill (1993), and Spash (2000, 2002). Martinez Alier, Munda, and O'Neill (1998) propose collective deliberation to open up the debate on environmental policy, followed by a multicriteria technique to close the debate and arrive at final recommendations.

sustain an ecological environment conducive to our well-being. (The question whether we should consider environmental needs more broadly is raised below.) Needs are distinguished from wants, the latter term being reserved for desires that are not necessarily individually or socially beneficial. Needs can be usefully defined as that which "persons must achieve if they are to avoid sustained and serious harm" (Doyal and Gough 1991, p. 50). Instead of subjective utility, such needs or "instrumental values" (Samuels 1997; Tool 1995) are revealed via some instituted social process of technical or scientific inquiry. As the pioneering environmental economist K. William Kapp (1978, p. 297) proposed, "social choices are made not in terms of subjectively experienced deficiencies and wants but in terms of objective requirements or scientifically determined standards. The relative urgency of these requirements is not subjectively felt but objectively (i.e. often technically) established." This shift back to an objective and needs-based approach is tantamount to a restoration of the concept of use-value (interpreted properly in terms of social usefulness), which was central to classical economics.

But one must not deny the problematic nature of this venture, or indeed of science itself. Consigning policy choices to experts, especially when they are contrary to the wishes of a large number of people, is a major potential threat to democratic norms and procedures. This difficulty is more severe in regard to environmental needs than health problems. Many people are more willing to accept the advice of their doctor than to radically alter their lifestyle to reduce their carbon footprint.

I postpone to the next chapter a discussion of how needs-based policy approaches can be reconciled with democracy, which in turn can be used as an engine of policy and moral development. My immediate concern is to expose the limitations of utilitarian approaches and establish both needs and moral values at the center of environmental policy. To do this we need an alternative theoretical framework. But even then there is no easy solution to the policy dilemmas. One must stress the ongoing, fallible, and open-ended nature of inquiry and address the problem of designing institutions that are appropriate for the democratic evaluation and revision of need satisfiers. Crucially, approaches based on human need see the formulation of environmental policy as driven by ongoing scientific analysis and public debate rather than simply by attempts to monetize and quantify the current wishes of individuals.

The growing environmental crisis requires us to prioritize questions of sustainability; to rescue moral values from subjective, private, ephemeral, or relativist incarcerations; to undermine the culture of consumerism and self-gratification that economics has helped to sustain; and to reinstate notions of the common good.

One policy feature is already implied. Appeals to appropriate moral values and not merely perceived self-interest should become part of economic policy. As Fred Hirsch (1977, p. 12) argues, instead of reliance on "the self-interest principle," economic policy should pay much more heed to "the role played by the supporting ethos of social obligation both in the formation of the relevant public policies and in their efficient transmission to market opportunities." Hirsch points to the futility of positional, keeping-up-with-the-Joneses competition in the context of increasing scarcity. He argues that to break the circle there has to be a moral appeal, and one based on cooperation rather than self-interest. Those who stress the ecological as well as the social limits to growth come to a similar conclusion.[6] Clearly, conspicuous consumption that exists simply to enhance status relative to others—what Hirsch calls "positional goods"—can be cut equally across the board without any loss of welfare (Frank 1999, 2011). But any consumption-constraining strategy would be unlikely to work without a strong supportive moral case.

An appeal to morality is neither unrealistic nor utopian. Many people try to act morally when faced with these dilemmas. Respondents to surveys that ask people to value the outcome of a proposed environmental policy—through an approach known as contingent valuation—often exhibit moral commitments rather than unalloyed self-interest. Mark Sagoff (1988b, p. 62) reports survey evidence that indicates that "respondents believe that environmental policy—for example the degree of pollution permitted in national parks—involves ethical, cultural, and aesthetic questions over which society must deliberate on the merits, and that this has nothing to do with pricing the satisfaction of preferences at the margin." A study by David A. Schkade and John W. Payne (1994) showed that in such surveys, moral considerations dominate matters of self-interest. Another overview concluded that responses concerning contingent valuation of the environment "are dominated by citizen judgments concerning desirable social goals rather than by consumer preferences" (Blamey, Common, and Quiggin 1995, p. 285). Clive Spash (2000) points out that a large proportion of respondents in willingness-to-pay surveys refrain from giving an

---

6. See, for instance, Daly and Cobb (1990), Meadows, Meadows, and Randers (1992), and Sagoff (2004).

environmental resource a monetary value on the grounds of ethical beliefs in their intrinsic, nontradeable value. Substantial evidence suggests people can be committed to the preservation of a natural phenomenon—such as a rare species or a wilderness area—without perceiving any personal benefit. We may conclude that appeals to values such as fairness and cooperation, concern for other species, and the legacy for future human generations are superior to a reliance on self-interest alone.

Hence, to be successful, any government committed to the protection of the natural environment must campaign on the basis of moral imperatives such as duty and compassion, address concerns for animals and succeeding generations of humans, and not rely simply on self-interest and a calculus of pecuniary costs and benefits. It also means that environmental policy analysts have to consider the political context of their evaluations and tackle the difficult problem of designing institutions within which democratic impulses and scientific knowledge can fruitfully interact.

To repeat: this does not mean that policies based on monetary incentives have no place. Indeed, pecuniary proposals can be reinforced by complementary appeals to moral values. Appeals simply to moral duty, on the one hand, or reliance on perceived self-interest, on the other, are likely to be of limited effect if they are employed alone. Carefully articulated combinations of the two types of incentive are likely to be more successful. Such an approach would involve much more than "looking solemn and uttering pious sentiments concerning our moral duty."

Contrary to the suggestion that they are ephemeral, values are difficult both to build and dislodge. An appeal to values is no easy policy fix. Yet once norms such as cooperation and fairness become reinforced, their effects can span both current and future generations. Unlike the appeal to self-interest, the transmission of such reinforced values is a way of addressing the intergenerational problem that has perplexed utilitarians in general and neoclassical environmental economists in particular (Spash 1993; Howarth 1995; P. Brown 1998).

The perspective advanced earlier in this book, that some moral values have a universal and biological foundation, as well as a dependence on a concordant social culture, offers the beginnings of an alternative. We are biologically and culturally primed to be sensitive to such issues as fairness, care for the needs of others, and an undespoiled environment (Haidt and Joseph 2004, 2008). In addition, we have evolved dispositions to respect those in authority (Milgram 1974).

Of course, respect for authority can be dangerous, especially when leaders are malevolent, uncaring, or incompetent. But government has a duty to act in accordance with our interests and not merely our preferences. Governments and other opinion leaders have a responsibility to use the respect they are granted as a license for insightful leadership rather than simply seeking the satiation of declared wants. They should build on our positive impulses, concerning caring for others and for the environment. We need to develop political institutions that maximize the chances of enlightened and compassionate government, and provide mechanisms for the removal of deficient leaderships. This problem is discussed in more detail in the next chapter.

The interplay of self-interest and moral impulses can lead to changes in manifest preferences and behavior. While neoclassical economics takes the individual as given and downplays her ethical feelings, the alternative approach suggested here would attempt to raise moral awareness and thereby shift people's preferences. Neoclassical economics typically ignores the importance of educating people and persuading them to adjust their values and priorities. Yet education is vital—alongside pecuniary and other incentives—if we are to deal with such massive problems as climate change.[7]

9.2. In Search of an Overarching Analytical Framework

But we need much more than an attack on neoclassical economics and an appeal to moral values. Given that neoclassical welfare analysis is misguided, we urgently need an alternative. I offer a few suggestions for moving in that direction.[8]

A key problem in the application of welfare principles to the environment is that the economy and the ecosystem involve different dimensions of assessment, often leading to conflicting evaluations. Although the global economy depends on the ecosystem, the latter would suffer much less pollution and damage if humanity were simply to disappear. Yet the eutha-

---

7. Appreciation of the value of a policy sometimes comes after the event. Rutland Water is the largest nonnatural reservoir in England. Before its official opening in 1976, its construction was opposed by every local organization, including local authorities, political parties, local media, conservation groups, and farming associations (Ovens and Sleath 2008). Yet a few years later, it became an enormously popular and biodiverse recreational area, for bird watching, cycling, walking, fishing, canoeing and sailing, while providing massive employment and revenue for the locality. People often resist change, even when it is beneficial and subsequently welcomed. Enlightenment on the value of a change may sometimes depend on its implementation.

8. My suggestions should be compared with the interesting work of Binder (2010). We both consider the biological foundations of human capabilities and needs, but his approach is different in several respects.

nasia of civilization is hardly a worthy welfare goal. Environmental policy is unavoidably about compromise—minimizing environmental damage while addressing human welfare priorities. The vital question is how to weigh an amount of environmental damage against an amount of human welfare enhancement.

A pragmatic response by ecological economists who reject utility theory has been to insist on pluralist approaches and combinations of monetary, aesthetic and ecological evaluations to guide policy (Norgaard 1989, 1994; Sagoff 2004; Vatn 2005). But ultimately, different measures must be reconciled—implicitly or explicitly—to make a decision.

The different dimensions of evaluation are strictly incommensurable: they involve different factors that are ranked or measured in different ways using different units. If we give all environmental losses and welfare gains a money price, then we downgrade ethical values, undermine the potentially positive role of moral discourse, and fall into the pit of self-interest. Nevertheless, any policy recommendation involves an implicit preference ordering, consistent with some well-ordered utility function. The neoclassical mistake is to regard utility as the sole ex ante and ex post basis of policy evaluation. But any consistent and coherent policy recommendation is compatible with some utility function as an ex post result. Utility is not a driving motive but a summary description of an actual or hypothetical outcome. (And as argued previously, because we are concerned with causal explanations rather than ex post descriptions, utilitarianism is an impoverished theory of behavior.) Despite their incommensurability, any relevant policy stance unavoidably involves weighing up different things, each against the other, encompassing them all within a single cardinal or ordinal metric.

A key problem is to choose the viewpoint or site of overall evaluation. A number of rival and controversial alternatives are available. One is the "deep ecology" of Arne Næss (1989). Opposing anthropocentric modes of evaluation, Næss attempts to establish the whole ecosystem as the analytical viewpoint. But one of the criticisms of "deep ecology" is that it fails to do just that, and instead smuggles in an anthropocentric view under an ecocentric guise (Oksanen 1997; Keulartz 1998). That is unavoidable: it is simply impossible for us to take a different viewpoint, untainted by anthropocentric values and biases. It is also undesirable. If faced with the choice between the extinction of the white rhinoceros or the giant panda, on the one hand, and human welfare, on the other, we shall choose ourselves.

But it is beyond the scope of the present work to review the rival ethical viewpoints concerning ecological questions, including the question of the rights of other species (Singer 1975). The objectives here are more basic:

1   We need an overarching analytical framework to encompass ecological and social phenomena.
2   We need a welfare theory that prioritizes long-term sustainability rather than simply the current satisfaction of human individuals.
3   While individual incentives are important, the social sciences must appeal to moral imperatives that transcend satisfaction or perceived self-interest.

A possible approach to at least the first of these objectives would be the modified law of thermodynamics developed by the economist Nicholas Georgescu-Roegen (1971). This "entropy law" applies to both matter and energy and presumes that the universe is moving irreversibly from a relatively ordered and organized state to the chaotic outcome of maximum disorder or entropy. Human productive activity transforms raw materials and other input with low entropy into waste with higher entropic value.

According to this approach, the universal and ongoing increase of entropy can be delayed locally by the ultimately transient rigidities and barriers in ordered entities or systems. Hence biotic evolution creates islands of order, which locally resist the march of entropy for a while, to eventually succumb and degrade. Islands of higher negentropy may evolve within a universe where entropy is steadily increasing overall. The Nobel Laureate Erwin Schrödinger (1944) was among the prominent advocates of the view that life feeds on negative entropy (negentropy) from its environment. Subsequently a number of authors synthesized the entropy principle with a Darwinian view of evolution (J. Collier 1986; Brooks and Wiley 1988; Brooks et al. 1989; Weber et al. 1989).

But the entropy law approach to economic phenomena does not tell us how different entropic states are to be ordered or valued. Georgescu-Roegen (1971, pp. 4, 7, 10, 146–47) upheld that the concept of entropy had multiple meanings and could neither be readily measured nor treated as an instrumental variable. In a critique of the application of the idea to economics, Elias Khalil (1990) argued that economic valuation and entropic valuation are different and separable. This led to an unresolved debate (Khalil 1991; Lozada 1991).

In the meantime, abstract formulations of Darwinian theory have made some progress, leading to interpretations that stress that the evolutionary process is very much about the selection, retention, and development of more complex information.[9] In this approach, information is often defined in the inclusive sense of Claude E. Shannon and Warren Weaver (1949) as a signal that when received causes some action. Of course, this definition omits key features of information, ideas, and knowledge in the human domain, particularly meanings and interpretations. With human evolution, it is essential to bring these into the picture. But the more abstract Shannon-Weaver definition is appropriate for the general phenomena under discussion and applicable to the evolution of nonhuman organisms as well. Darwinian evolution involves to storage, copying, and development of more complex information—local increases in negentropy, defined in informational terms.

9.3. Using Evolutionary Thinking to Connect Economic and Ecological Values

Darwinism is compatible with the entropy approach and adds two further extensions.[10] First, by addressing all evolving systems, Darwinism offers an explanatory framework that covers populations of natural organisms, and it applies to sets of social entities including human institutions. Second, by establishing the importance of morality for the survival of human groups—as outlined in chapter 5—Darwinism provides a basis for developing universal ethical principles.

Regarding the first extension, Darwin (1859, 1871) hinted that his evolutionary principles would apply to social phenomena such as the development of language and the selection of ethical ideas. This insight was taken up episodically by a number of writers such as Walter Bagehot (1872), David Ritchie (1896), Thorstein Veblen (1899b), Albert G. Keller (1915), Adolf Berle (1950), and Donald T. Campbell (1965). Recently the idea has become prominent again in the social sciences (Aldrich et al. 2008; Blute 2010; Hodgson and Knudsen 2010).

This idea of generalizing Darwinian principles to cover the social as well as the natural domain means neither the explanatory reduction of the former to the latter, nor the presumption that the mechanisms and other relevant features in each domain are similar. As evolutionary economist Sidney G. Winter (1987) writes,

9. See, for example, Wicken (1987), N. Clark (1991), Dennett (1995), Adami, Ofria, and Collier (2000), Crutchfield and Schuster (2003), Beinhocker (2006, 2011), and Hodgson and Knudsen (2010).

10. This section develops some material from Hodgson (2010b).

natural selection and evolution should not be viewed as concepts developed for the specific purposes of biology and possibly appropriable for the specific purposes of economics, but rather as elements of the framework of a new conceptual structure that biology, economics and other social sciences can comfortably share.

Although generalized Darwinian principles apply to both social and biological systems, they offer no short-cut theoretical explanations or answers. As in biology, detailed examination of the particular mechanisms is also required. Darwinian principles are not like Newtonian laws that can predict accurately the motion of bodies through space. Instead, Darwinism is a general meta-theoretical framework within which particular auxiliary explanations must be placed. The nature of these auxiliary explanations will vary from domain to domain.

Nevertheless, the provision of this meta-theoretical framework is an important step. In particular, the idea of generalizing Darwinism to socioeconomic evolution challenges the longstanding idea among social scientists that social and biological phenomena should be completely partitioned—and that social scientists have little to learn from biology and vice versa. A generalized Darwinism is consistent with the idea that human society is embedded in the natural world and depends on it for its survival.

A generalized Darwinism systematizes the process of empirical inquiry and organizes detailed knowledge pertaining to a wide variety of evolutionary processes. Furthermore, Darwinian ideas have important implications for social scientists concerning the rationality and psyche of human agents (Richards 1987; Cosmides and Tooby 1994a, 1994b; Hodgson 2010a). Assumptions concerning human agents must be consistent with our understanding of human evolution. Darwinian evolution involves the development, retention, and selection of information concerning adaptive solutions to survival problems faced by organisms in their environment. It raises questions of causality and requires explanations of origin. This applies in particular to the dispositional programs behind human thought and behavior. Contrary to much mainstream economics, individuals and their preferences cannot simply be taken as given.

Crucially, Darwinism focuses our attention on mechanisms through which variety is preserved and created. Two of the most important mechanisms identified by Darwin (1859) and retained in modern biology involve locational considerations. First, the migration of a group to another area with a different physical environment, and second the use or creation of different niches, remain two of the most important mechanisms to explain speciation. Related ideas would seem to transfer directly to the social or economic domain. In these cases, the new environment and the (relative) isolation of a group from the majority create new opportunities for variation.

Similar arguments apply to human institutions as well as biological organisms, notwithstanding the fact that the nature and mechanisms of mutation and separation are very different. The general ideas of mutation and physical separation particularly apply to the evolution of languages and all sorts of customs. For example, relative isolation and language change leads to subdivision and often the creation of new languages. Furthermore, there is now a growing literature on how firms may perform differently in different contexts, such as under different regulatory regimes or among different types of financial institutions (Amable 2000; Aoki 2001; Hall and Soskice 2001; Boyer 2005; Kenworthy 2006; Gagliardi 2009).

The above considerations are of general importance for understanding the evolution of organizations, and they are particularly relevant for ecological economics. Much of the policy agenda for ecological economics is a matter of appropriate institutional design, to establish incentives that are consistent with environmental goals, to process flows of information to guide policy, and to deal with unforeseen disturbances and shocks.

In this vein, there is the important literature on the robustness of socioecological systems, which helps to identify social and ecological vulnerabilities to disturbances. John Anderies, Marco Janssen, and Elinor Ostrom (2004), for example, identify the link between resource users and public infrastructure providers as a key variable affecting such robustness. They develop a set of appropriate institutional design principles. In line with the Darwinian emphasis on the role of variety in the processes of adaptation and selection, C. Dustin Becker and Elinor Ostrom (1995) emphasize the importance of institutional diversity in coping with complex developments in environmental systems.[11]

Much of this middle-range literature fails to mention Darwinism. But for similar reasons, many applied biologists are not obliged to refer to general Darwinian evolutionary principles when they carry out concrete studies. Much of biology proceeds by assuming but not mentioning the core Darwinian principles of variation, inheritance, and selection. Darwinian theory is at a high level of abstraction. Middle-range theory has to be con-

---

11. Similar themes are prominent in a special issue of the *Journal of Institutional Economics* on institutions and ecosystems (Janssen 2006). Ostrom (2009) proposes a polycentric governance approach to deal with climate change.

sistent with this theory, but it does not necessarily involve applying it at every turn. Instead, Darwinian theory is a way of organizing our understanding of different evolving systems and organizing explanations that operate on different levels.

Moreover, an explicit recognition of the role of Darwinism in these contexts may stimulate useful theoretical and applied developments on interactions between organizations and ecosystems. Darwinism may provide a meta-theoretical framework wherein fragmented and diverse insights may be integrated and further developed. Furthermore, although Darwinism does not immediately provide the answers, this unifying framework may help to generate some basic principles and policy guidelines that span the social and ecological domains. It may facilitate the development of our understanding of the institutional developments that are vital to deal with pressing environmental problems, including climate change.[12]

As noted above, Darwinism can also enhance the discussion of vital moral values. Recent work on the evolution of cooperation and morality has rehabilitated Darwin's (1871) view that humans have inherited and culturally reinforced dispositions toward moral or altruistic behaviors that help to sustain the social group.[13]

But bringing Darwinism into the framing of environmental policy does not mean that one has to accept that any evolved moral dispositions are necessarily the right ones to deal with current environmental problems. An evolved *is* does not imply an *ought*. Darwinism is explanatory and indicative rather than prescriptive. It points to evolved moral dispositions, necessary for survival in structured social groups that use a sophisticated language, that underlie culturally enhanced and transmitted moral norms. This does not mean that they are sufficient, adequate, or always warranted. Instead, these underlying dispositions have to be understood in the process of development of new or enhanced moral norms and imperatives.

9.4. Summary and Conclusion: Rudiments of an Evolutionary Ecological Economics

Biological and cultural evolution have endowed us with moral dispositions that are vital in the endeavor to retain a sustainable natural environ-

12. Foxon (2011) provides an analysis of the coevolution of institutions and technologies with explicit reference to Darwinian theory.

13. See, for example, Boehm (1999, 2000, 2011), Nichols (2004), Gintis et al. (2005), Tancredi (2005), de Waal (2006), Hauser (2006), Joyce (2006), Haidt and Joseph (2008), and Bowles and Gintis (2011).

ment. Evolved values such as fairness, sympathy, and conservation are vital resources in this struggle (Douglas 1966; Haidt and Joseph 2004, 2008). They are neither ephemeral nor transient. They are prompted by biological cues and often become rooted in our habits of thought and action.[14] They should be neither ignored nor reduced to preference functions. It is vital to understand the evolutionary mechanisms involved in the generation and transmission of these values. On the basis of this understanding, governments and organizations can help to enhance the values that are conducive to ecological and environmental sustainability.

This does not mean that self-interest is unimportant or can be ignored. Appeals to moral values and individual self-interest are not always rivalrous and can be complementary. For example, fuel price increases that encourage people to switch from private motor cars to public transport may prompt travelers to rationalize their changed behavior in terms of their dedication to green values, which in turn might encourage others to make the same decision.[15]

Attempts to assess the environment in exclusively pecuniary terms— such as willingness-to-pay and contingent valuation—are not simply inadequate: they are dangerous and counterproductive. Their focus on self-interested pecuniary evaluation belittles moral values and altruistic commitments. Altruism and morality are either ignored or diminished to a cash value. In assuming this reducibility at the outset, willingness-to-pay and contingent valuation fail by elementary standards concerning the objectivity of questionnaire design. But mainstream economists give them the seal of scientific legitimacy. They become standard practice and governments use them for guidance. Both economists and politicians become accomplices in a process of moral degradation, where appropriate moral values are crowded out by endorsements of unlimited consumerism and greed. With the benefits of recent research, we know that these approaches are morally deficient and based on faulty science. Humans have inherited

14. For perspectives on the role of habits in carbon-using behavior and for improving energy and climate policies, see Verplanken, Aarts, and Van Knippenberg (1997), Aarts and Dijksterhuis (2000), Bamberg, Ajzen, and Schmidt (2003), Maréchal (2009, 2010), and Maréchal and Lazaric (2010).

15. Although he rightly focuses on morality, Sagoff (2004) makes an untenable separation between moral motivation, on the one hand, and willingness to pay to protect an environmental resource, on the other. To some degree, pecuniary transactions also depend on moral values and commitments. The market is not, and cannot be, a morality-free zone (Hirschman 1982; Brittan and Hamlin 1995; Schultz 2001; McCloskey 2006; Friedman 2008; Minkler 2008; Zak 2008; Henrich et al. 2010).

moral dispositions to care for others. The scientific credentials of willing-ness-to-pay and contingent valuation approaches are deficient.

A second major problem with the mainstream approach is its assumption that preferences and moral values are given. But although our under-standing of human evolution supports the notion that some dispositions toward morality and altruism are inherited in our genes, the contempo-rary evidence supports Darwin's (1871) view that morality proper cannot emerge without extensive deliberation and a sophisticated language. Mo-rality is a cultural phenomenon with essential biological grounding. Its evolution depends on both cultural and genetic transmission, like other manifestations of "dual inheritance" or gene-culture coevolution (Boyd and Richerson 1985; Durham 1991).

Accordingly, the development of attitudes toward the natural environ-ment depends in part on parenting, the education system, and the social culture. Hence governments and other involved agencies should not sim-ply canvass existing, partially informed opinion and ground policy on these soundings. They also have duties to educate the population, so that it becomes more aware of the issues, and to promote ethical values consis-tent with ecological sustainability. Government has a responsibility to edu-cate or persuade adults, and to promote specific educational values, and it should become much more than a mirror of public opinion.

Libertarians will point to the dangers of government power and pro-paganda. The perils should not be belittled. But the alternatives are not as simple as some libertarians suggest. The dilemma is neither between big government and small government, nor between government as solution and government as problem. When government is minimal, then other horrors can arise. Consider Somalia and the Congo in recent years. Both minimal and maximal states can menace human liberty.

No effective government is simply a conduit for popular opinion. Some people have specialist skills. The opposed claims of creationists and evolu-tionists are not of equal weight or status. If there were no ground to claim that one person knows better than another, then all education would be unwarranted, and the process of scientific advance would be completely wrecked. We would never seek an expert opinion on anything. It is pre-cisely because we believe that some people do know better that we employ experts, cultivate scientific research, and spend huge amounts of private and public money on educating adults and children. It is no insult to claim that some people know better than others. The problem is instead of plac-ing excessive power or trust in particular institutions that are difficult to monitor or call to account.

Consequently the problem is partly one of establishing suitable political institutions. A crucial advantage of political democracy is that it places the power to remove a government in the hands of the electorate. But that does not mean that all existing preferences are sacrosanct or that all scientific claims should be put to the popular vote. Viable democracy also depends on experts. And governments should use expert opinion to educate and lead the people.

A crucial problem is that experts too are fallible, and the democratic opinion poll is a highly unsuitable mechanism for the determination of scientific truth or advance. Because science and scientific education are central to the problem of dealing with such pressing environmental problems as climate change, we have to face up to the problem of reconciling the unavoidable elitism of science with the populism and democracy of government.

In the next chapter, I draw on the ideas of John Dewey in an attempt to deal with these problems (Dewey 1916, 1929, 1935, 1938, 1939; Dewey and Tufts 1932). Dewey argued for an experimental and evolutionary approach (Gouinlock 1978; Ryan 1995; K. Evans 2000; Sabel and Zeitlin 2008; Kallis and Norgaard 2010). Rather than developing static ethical goals, Dewey tried to identifying institutions and methods for refining ethical and policy judgments. Policy is a matter of evolutionary trial and error, with the emphasis on effective feedback mechanisms to learn from mistakes as well as successes. Democracy itself is more than a system of election and a source of legitimacy, but also a means of developing a considerate public spirit within a pluralistic culture, which relies increasingly on science and experiment rather than rigid dogma. The primary role of experts is to outline feasible alternatives and their likely consequences. Institutional design must be cautious and experimental, looking at the whole system as well as particular microinteractions. The development of such an evolutionary policy approach must be placed at the top of the agenda of ecological economics.

TEN

Toward an Evolutionary and Institutional Approach to Policy

Even to-day the tendency to construct rigid and absolute "ideals," and to seek to impose them upon the world of phenomena as practical reforms, is the commonest of errors.

—John A. Hobson (1901)

If . . . social cooperation plays the distinctive part it seems to do in human survival, then it may be argued that the highest value attaches to the conduct and the emotions which sustain society in the elaborate structure it has attained, and to assist it further in useful modes of coöperation. This will seem to furnish a criterion for Human Welfare in its higher reaches, by stressing the feelings, beliefs, interests, activities, and institutions . . . which enrich human personality through the largest measure of sociality.

—John A. Hobson (1929)

The evils in current social judgments of ends and policies arise . . . from importations of judgments of value from outside of inquiry. The evils spring from the fact that the values employed are not determined in and by the process of inquiry: for it is assumed that certain ends have an inherent value so unquestionable that they regulate and validate the means employed, instead of ends being determined on the basis of existing conditions as obstacles-resources.

—John Dewey (1938)

Unavoidably at the center of debate in any kind of welfare economics is the role of the state. Classic Pigovian welfare economics rests on the assumption that the state is capable of detecting externalities and of calculating social costs, and it is motivated to devise the taxes and subsidies to maximize social welfare. Critics point to problems with the concepts of externality and social cost, the difficulties of measuring them, and to the alleged self-interest of state functionaries. Since the 1970s, there has been a shift toward policies that involve an extension of private property rights and a diminished role for the state.

Political science has gone through a parallel transformation. Public choice theory emerged in the 1960s and had a major impact on political theory (Buchanan and Tullock 1962; Niskanen 1971; Mueller 1979). Its basic theoretical unit is the rational, utility-maximizing individual. While rational choice theory burst the disciplinary barriers and swept economics into other social sciences, there were significant islands of resistance. Especially within politics, rational choice theory was countered by the claim that its predictions had been empirically falsified (Green and Shapiro 1994).

As explained in chapter 3, my own position differs from both advocates and typical critics of rational choice. Payoff maximization is falsified by many experiments. But utility functions and utility maximizers can be devised, in principle, to fit any data. They are unfalsified and unfalsifiable. So when pressed by the critics, the defenders of rational choice would adjust their utility functions to deal with the empirical evidence, sometimes to move back to a more self-regarding version of political man when the critical pressure was removed.

Ultimately, the debate has to be resolved at the explanatory level, in terms of what offers the best causal explanation of the phenomena. A fundamental problem with rational choice theory is that it provides no explanation of either the origin of the utility function or the psychological mechanisms behind choice and behavior. It is a summary description of preference rankings, without providing any theory of how and what we prefer. It is uninformed by our deeper knowledge of psychology, anthropology, sociology, or human evolution.

Chapter 5 has shown that our understanding of human evolution rehabilitates the component of moral motivation. This cannot adequately be captured by, or added to, a standard utility function. If every human actor has moral feelings and the potential to act morally, then this should be taken into account in explanations of behavior and the design of policies.

This chapter is divided into five sections. The first section criticizes the public choice literature and posits a needs-based approach as an alternative. The second section considers the role of institutionalized science in understanding needs in modern democracies. The third section sketches an evolutionary approach to policy development, based on institutions that help identify needs and monitor policies to meet them. The fourth section considers institutional and moral conditions for the operation of a market economy. The final section brings the policy threads together and raises the linked questions of economic inequality and social solidarity. All this is meant to be suggestive and preliminary rather than a final answer to all the policy dilemmas that we face today. Moral communities are necessary but not easy to build.

This is not to revive the old debate between planning and markets, socialism and capitalism. Modern complex economies unavoidably involve both markets and states. Markets and private property are essential spurs to competition and innovation. But as pointed out in the first chapter, without states there cannot be law, property, money, banks, or corporations. Arguments that property or law goes back to the tribes, or even to our ape-like ancestors, confuse property with possession and law with custom. Well-established property rights, backed by a system of contract law, emerged in classical antiquity and depended on the development of complex state institutions. Property does not become fully developed until it has the capacity to be used as collateral, and such a role has yet to become global, even today (De Soto 2000; Steiger 2008). The state is also the essential backbone of a capitalist economy. Even the most die-hard of libertarians should acknowledge it as such. And the most die-hard of socialists should acknowledge the crucial role of markets. What is necessary, as with many institutions, is to learn how state powers can be channeled, countervailed, or restrained for social benefit rather than for tyranny. It is here, as noted below, that democracy comes in.

10.1. Public Service, Morality, and the State

Surely, power can corrupt, and corruption is rife in many countries. But there are reasons to enter public service other than for individual gain. Its pattern and extent varies in time and space, but moral motivation is important for many in politics and public administration (Rowthorn 1996). We have the most extensive evidence on this for the United States, where empirical research has shown that public servants, when compared with other citizens, are more concerned about moral behavior, in regard to personal honesty, integrity, social justice, and fairness (Chapman 1993; Brewer and Selden 1998; Rainey 2009).

This does not mean that public servants are paragons of moral virtue. We know that corruption and unethical behavior can be contagious or systemic. Consider the systemic political malpractice exposed in the 2009–10 expenses scandal in the Parliament of the United Kingdom. Instead of raising the salaries of Members of Parliament and risking popular disapproval, government officials colluded for years in an unaudited system of encouraging politicians to claim actual or fictitious expenses to boost their incomes. The dubious morality of this Parliament-wide practice remained unchallenged until it was exposed in a national newspaper by the public release of information detailing personal expenses claims. A few individual politicians have subsequently been convicted of malpractice (Wikipedia 2011d). But the successive governments who tolerated this ethically deficient system—and tried to withhold the information from the public—are also morally culpable. Malpractice can arise even in countries with relatively low levels of corruption. But this case shows that it was a problem of policy and rule design, and not one of irredeemably selfish motivation.

While people often act selfishly, practical politics and public administration are also infused with questions concerning the construction, observance, and promulgation of law, to an extent not found in ordinary life. Although law and morality are not the same thing, the law always carries strong ethical overtones and is often driven by moral commitments. Hence the discourse of public service is permeated with explicit ethical questions. Questions of moral responsibility are thus more salient. But on the other hand, the temptations and rewards of malpractice in the public sector are greater. The pressures to act morally and immorally have both to be taken into account.

The standard literature on public choice overlooks or belittles the moral dimension. Adopting a morally denuded model of rational choice, it captures neither the ethical facet of public service nor its vulnerability to systemic erosion. Crucially, instead of devoting attention to measures that would raise ethical standards in the public sphere, the public choice approach takes the individual as given and subsumes all government activity under a calculus of individual greed. The "small government" policy implications of much research in this genre follow readily and are contained in its premises.

At the most fundamental level, this is not primarily an argument concerning how selfish or unselfish, or moral or immoral, politicians are. I do not substitute self-regarding individuals by moral or altruistic heroes and heroines. This is not primarily a question of swapping one type of individual for another, but understanding that the structured interaction between individuals may enhance or corrupt human moral capacities. It is largely a matter of social structures and cultures, and of diverse individuals who to varying extents are molded by their circumstances.

The public choice literature builds on an amoral pleasure machine and gives us a distorted picture of the workings of political systems. As Richard Bronk (2009, p. 6) puts it, the widespread acceptance of "its cynical assumption (that those in government are not motivated by anything but their own interest) has helped corrode the social norm of 'public service' and consequently trust in government." We have to develop a more adequate view of the role of the state and government in economic affairs.

A starting point for an alternative approach to welfare economics is to reject the treatment of the individual as always the best judge of her welfare. It is replaced in part by the argument that government can—in some limited circumstances and under some conditions—be a better judge of our needs. In practice, this is already accepted in capitalist democracies. Their governments prohibit many consensual behaviors (drugs, incest, vote buying, and so on). They prioritize health and education. But generally the overall criteria for such prohibitions and promotions are unclear, ad hoc, and undertheorized.

Libertarians ask: how possibly can government know better than the individuals involved? They point to individual preferences, tacit and local knowledge, and the manifest limitations and dangers of state bureaucracy. In the preceding chapter, it was pointed out that if there were no ground to claim that one person knows better than another, then all education would be unwarranted, and the process of scientific advance would be derailed. Precisely because we believe that some people do know better, we employ experts and educate people. The problem instead is designing institutions where decisions and expert advice can be routinely monitored and scrutinized, not overlooking the problem of who monitors the monitors. In some way, our public institutions have to be called to account.

The alternative, needs-based approach outlined here depends critically on the role of both the natural and social sciences in establishing genuine individual and social needs.[1] The distinction between needs and wants, between the desirable and the desired, has already been established in chapter 8. Needs are essentially requirements for human development and for avoiding serious harm.

Morality plays an important role alongside need. Without trying to prescribe a true an invincible morality, we need to promote moral systems that

---

1. References on needs include Hobson (1929), Maslow (1954), Sen (1985a, 1999), Thomson (1987), Doyal and Gough (1991), Nussbaum and Sen (1993), Corning (2000, 2011), Gough (2000, 2004), Nussbaum (2000, 2003).

dovetail with the promotion of human need and sustain the institutional and political structures that can allow needs, and possible need satisfiers, to be revealed, scrutinized, and prioritized.

The role of science here is to show how fundamental needs can be met and what need-satisfying options are available. But science itself is not enough to establish needs-based policies. Science has to be sufficiently well understood by policymakers to inform policy. In a democracy, it also has to be adequately understood by the population for those policies to be endorsed. Furthermore, science cannot provide a resolution to many policy dilemmas or be an adequate guide to prioritization when faced with limited resources. But its central informing role is crucial, and for that reason we next consider the nature of modern science systems and how they can be sustained.

10.2. Science Systems in Modern Societies

Humans have used technology for tens of thousands of years.[2] But less than four hundred years ago, political and economic conditions emerged that allowed the institutionalization of science and technology in parts of Western Europe. This led to dramatic ongoing changes in technology and the conditions of life.

The modern scientific and technological revolution followed the establishment of science and technology within organized bodies of systematic and codified knowledge. As expressions of this process, the Royal Society of London for the Improvement of Natural Knowledge was formed in 1662 and the Académie de Science, was formed in 1666 in France. By the twentieth century, the institutions of science and technology had become extensive and complex "epistemic communities" and "machineries of knowing" (Haas 1992; Knorr-Cetina 1981), entwining professional associations, universities, corporations, and states on a global scale (Hull 1988; Mokyr 1990, 2003; Lundvall 1992; Huff 1993; Kitcher 1993; R. Nelson 1993; Bowler and Morus 2005; Lipsey, Carlaw, and Bekar 2005).

The outcomes of this revolution are manifest. Between 1800 and 2000, "life expectancy at birth rose from about 30 years to a global average of 67 years, and to more than 75 years in several developed countries (Lancaster 1990; Riley 2001; Fogel 2004). In part, this dramatic change in longevity followed the development of cures for several major diseases. It meant a huge revolution in health and well-being, albeit with very un-

---

2. Part of this section condenses material from Hodgson and Knudsen (2010, chap. 8).

evenly distributed benefits. In the same 200-year period, the time taken to cross the Atlantic was reduced from several weeks to a few hours (by airplane). Global communications became near-instantaneous. Computations previously taking several days could be accomplished in a fraction of a second by a computer. And humankind's capacity for destruction reached awesome bounds.

There is a consensus among economic and other historians that the institutionalization of science and technology depended on other specific institutional props. Property rights had to be sufficiently well established so as to provide sufficient incentives for the necessary investment of time and resources. The political system had to be polycentric to allow freedom of scientific inquiry without destructive interference by political or religious authorities. Providing incentives for research and innovation, Western countries developed patent laws. Relatively autonomous institutions such as universities and business corporations permitted independent inquiry and investment. It was the powerful combination of a capitalist economy, a relatively pluralist polity, and institutionalized science and technology that fueled the economic take-off of the West in the eighteenth century.

The institutionalization of science and technology meant that experimental results—determined by natural laws and other regularities—could be checked by the professional scientific community. It may be objected that experimental verification falls foul of the problem that all observation is theory-laden, and no theory-free empirical foundation is possible. Philip Kitcher (1993) circumvents such arguments by emphasizing that science is a process involving a trained community of diverse and interacting investigators. The institutionalization of science and technology created organizational machines of discovery and application, notwithstanding the theory-bound nature of observation. Against postmodernist fashion, Kitcher (1993) offers a powerful defense of the notion that science, in a progressive and cumulative manner, does indeed discover significant truths about nature, and that this ongoing practical process is embodied in an organized social system of skilled scientists. Scientific inquiry is not a solitary encounter with nature: it involves critical and ongoing social conversations with peers. Hence the relevant epistemology for modern science is social rather than individual. Groups of individuals, operating according to various rules for modifying their individual procedures of enquiry, succeed through their critical interactions in generating a progressive sequence of consensus practices.

Crucially, the scientific and technological community institutionalizes procedures through which new results can be established and errors can be corrected. Although science depends on much more than facts, the role of evidence and experiment is crucial.[3] An important habit of thought common to a viable scientific community is the acknowledgment of the authority of accredited evidence. The mechanisms of scrutiny and accreditation are themselves institutionalized.

Today it is impossible for any individual to have an understanding of anything more than a small part of scientific knowledge. Like law, it is impossible for an individual to know or understand everything. The system is institutionalized so that the synergetic cooperation of different specialists is possible.

Thorbjørn Knudsen and I argue that the modern institutionalization of science and technology amounts to a new level or system of information replication in the evolution of human society (Hodgson and Knudsen 2010, chap. 8). Previous major information transitions include the evolution of language, writing, and law. Each information transition amounts to a new way of storing, correcting, and replicating key information that is relevant for human survival. Here information must be understood not principally in terms of symbols or representations, but in the habits, routines, and customs of a community. A similar conceptualization of information and knowledge is found in the literature on pragmatism.[4]

Modern, institutionalized science and technology constitutes a unique system for storing, correcting, and replicating information. Knowledge is obtained through interaction and communication within a social elite of trained scientists, engineers, and technicians. Institutional mechanisms such as peer review and publication screen new contributions for quality and help to bring about episodic clusters of consensus, which in turn allow for further specialization and cumulative enquiry. Leaving aside important meta-discourses or tool kits such as mathematics and philosophy, most viable scientific disciplines involve a culture of empirical testing and inquiry. Science, as we are often reminded, is a social system (Merton 1996). It further operates through moral commitments, principally in terms of com-

---

3. Science cannot be *entirely* a matter of fact. Some ontological presuppositions are necessary to all scientific inquiry (Veblen 1919; Quine 1953; Bunge 1974, 1977; Bhaskar 1975; Chalmers 1985). The facts do not speak for themselves, but their presence is essential.

4. On this aspect of pragmatism, see James (1890), Veblen (1919), Dewey (1922), Joas (1993, 1996), Kilpinen (2000). See Hodgson and Knudsen (2010, pp. 77–79, 132–36) on why habits, routines, and customs are chosen as replicators of information rather than ideas or "memes" (Dawkins 1976). Pragmatists such as James (1890) and Dewey (1910) saw instincts and habits as underlying emergent expressions such as ideas. Philosophy and social theory can then be rendered consistent with the facts of human evolution and psychology (Hodgson 2010a).

mitments to the truth, honest reporting, and open identification of sources (Hagstrom 1965).

As Kitcher (1993) argues at length, a scientific discipline cannot evolve unless there is sufficient diversity of established opinion. If the scientific consensus is absolute and permits little dissent, then there is little chance of novel development and future advance. Some minority opinions must be able to survive within the institutions of science. Uniformity stifles evolution. But Kitcher also points out that the other extreme—where there is so much diversity that consensus is lacking—is also detrimental for the development of science. Without a sizeable cluster of consensus, there is inadequate bedrock to build and monitor any research program that is sufficiently powerful to generate a progressive dynamic of new questions and results. Diversity and pluralism within scientific disciplines must be neither too little nor too great.

From this perspective, it is possible to conceive of scientific disciplines being in a state of crisis, their development arrested by too much diversity or too little. Since the breakdown of its Parsonian consensus in the 1970s, sociology has been diagnosed as having too much internal pluralism and lacking in adequate consensus (Vaughan, Sjoberg, and Reynolds 1993). The opposite criticism has been leveled against economics: it was dominated by one core set of assumptions and methods from about 1970 to 1995 (Hodgson, Mäki, and McCloskey 1992). Economics began to exhibit more mainstream diversity in the 1990s, but an enduring accusation since the 1970s is that it prioritizes the development of mathematical technique over empirically grounded explanation (Ward 1972; Blaug 1997; Krugman 2009). A scientific discipline can get diverted onto suboptimal tracks.

Apart from potential failures within the science system itself, another vital issue is whether that system is able to get enough support and funding from society at large. In an autocracy, its survival depends on the dispositions of powerful institutions such as the state. In a democracy, as well as state and corporate donors, its development depends also on the willingness of the population to vote for politicians who promote the funding of science.

Science is unavoidably elitist. It depends on the interactions and evaluations of a selected group of highly trained experts and specialists. The validity or otherwise of a scientific theory or result is not decided by popular vote: it is established in opinion by persuading the elite that the underlying reasoning is sound and consistent with the evidence. Hence there is a tension in a democratic society between, on the one hand, the ethos of popular endorsement and, on the other hand, the requirement that an essentially elitist system of science should be funded and its advice should be heeded in the development of public policies.

A partial but vital remedy is to improve the public understanding of science. A basic and broad appreciation of the essentials of the natural and social sciences should be part of general education. Yet science itself places difficulties in the way. The rapid growth and specialization of science makes such a policy of general education difficult to implement. But in many developed countries, little attempt is made to raise the level of general scientific education for all students. Instead, the prevailing concern is to produce yet more specialists to serve in the many varied niches of employment. Education systems have evolved to serve the demands of business rather than to give people the necessary scientific background to participate in democratic debate. Critics point to the decline of broad and questioning inquiry, and the rise of narrower forms of professional training. Students are less encouraged to pursue big questions. They are urged instead to acquire qualifications that signal skills that will command a premium on the jobs market.[5]

The problem is dramatized by public opposition to some key findings of modern science. In the United States, for example, a 2005 Gallup poll found that 53 percent expressed their belief that God created human beings "exactly in the way the Bible describes it," and 65 percent of those surveyed thought that creationism was definitely or probably true (Wikipedia 2011b). The issue is so prominent that no recent candidate for the US presidency believes in the evolution of humans from ape-like ancestors or, for fear of losing votes, is able publicly to express that belief. This is a catastrophic shortfall in the public understanding of science. Religion alone cannot explain the popularity of creationism, as large numbers of Christians, Jews, Muslims, Hindus, and Buddhists accept that humans evolved from ape-like ancestors. It is largely a matter of ignorance and poor education.

As noted in the preceding chapter, less than half of respondents in some developed countries see rising global temperatures as a result of human activities (Pelham 2009). Yet the scientific community is overwhelmingly of the opinion that human activity is to blame (IPCC 2007). Arguably, this public misunderstanding is more serious than in the case of evolution because public resistance to the scientific consensus gives no encouragement

5. Veblen (1918) warned of the problems of the domination of education by business. See Bloom (1988), D. Bok (2003), Kirp (2003), Washburn (2005), and Greenberg (2007) for discussions of the commercialization of modern education systems.

to people to reduce their carbon footprint and blocks urgent government action to reduce carbon emissions and promote green energy. This is a potentially catastrophic breakdown of creative synergy between the science system and the democratic polity.

To create systems that meet human needs, we rely critically on science. Science systems in modern developed countries have never been so powerful, but the weak link is the low level of popular education in the broad nature and key achievements of natural and social science. A revised approach to economic and social welfare requires reform of the education systems in all countries. Too much emphasis is put on educating people to fit specialist slots in the world of business, and far too little on educating them as informed, active, and constructively critical citizens.

John Dewey's (1916) view of the role of education was similar. He saw educational institutions as vital instruments in the development of the individual and society as a whole, and the creation of a "social intelligence" of informed appraisal of need satisfiers. His ideas on an evolutionary framework for policy development inspire the following section.

10.3. Evolutionary Policy Development

An evolutionary and democratic approach to policy development relies critically on a healthy system of institutionalized science and an adequate level of generalist education. It is essentially dynamic, learning from mistakes. Instead of the search for the once-and-for-all (Pareto) optimum, the aim is to set up a process of ongoing inquiry with cumulative learning.

Against dogmatic goals or unquestionable ideals, Dewey sought conditions and habits of public scrutiny and debate that led to both innovation and experiment. Dewey (1929) exposed the futility of seeking absolute knowledge and certainty. For him, knowledge is an active capability rather than a fixed end or goal. In the context of uncertainty and complexity, Dewey favored an experimental, process-oriented, and participative democracy. Institutional design had to be cautious and experimental. The primary role of experts is to lay out the feasible policy alternatives and their likely consequences and to feed this information into informed public debate (Gouinlock 1978; Ryan 1995; K. Evans 2000).[6]

Dewey (1916, 1935, 1938, 1939) stressed the need for an open-ended, flexible, and experimental approach to the practical determination of hu-

---

6. For similar evolutionary approaches to policy, see Lindblom (1959, 1984), Nelson and Winter (1982, pt. 4), and Martinez Alier, Munda, and O'Neill (1998).

man need satisfiers and the enhancement of welfare. Dewey (1935, p. 92) embraced a "method of experimental and coöperative intelligence" based on science. He looked forward to the time when "the method of intelligence and experimental control is the rule in social relations and social direction." The "social intelligence" required to establish this process is not simply the sum of the intelligences of the individuals involved, but involves their enhancement through interaction and dialogue.

For Dewey, the development of these habits was through an extension of democratic values. Habits of respectful dialogue and public spiritedness had to be nurtured from the earliest years, in both the family and the school. Schooling had not simply to be a preparation for citizenship but an arena of involvement in citizenship itself, where crucial habits of tolerant, experimental, cooperative, and self-motivated inquiry were formed.

Dewey proposed that we construct an ongoing process for improving policies and value judgments. Such a process is experimental, and it must rely on collective evaluation and debate to draw conclusions from the empirical outcomes of each trial. Value judgments are treated as tools in the search for outcomes that serve human needs. In that sense, they are "instrumental," and the process is one of "instrumental valuation."[7] We test them by putting them into practice and judging collectively whether they enhance human life and lead to human flourishing. Dewey's evaluative rubric involves a meta-ethical framework of evaluation, a theory of individual development, and a foundation for policy analysis.

Science should drive the processes of meeting individual and social needs. We have basic and intermediate needs such as food, shelter, healthcare, security, a safe environment, interactions, education, and autonomy. These objective and transcultural needs are essential for human survival and self-realization. Their fulfillment requires the ability to participate in the social setting in which the individual operates (Doyal and Gough 1991; Gough 2000, 2004).

But even with this science-driven agenda, there are often dilemmas of prioritization and areas of uncertainty that cannot be resolved by science. Once need satisfiers are identified, then it is necessary to prioritize. No administrative authority can do everything at once. There are resource limitations, including bounded cognitive as well as limited material resources.

---

7. But note that "instrumentalism" is defined in a number of different ways (Samuels 1997). In particular, Dewey's "sense of 'instrumentalism' is quite different from more familiar senses" (Godfrey-Smith 2002, p. S9).

Institutional mechanisms and routines have to be built up to deliver any policy.

Further problems arise with the development of need satisfiers. For example, for personal development and psychological health, individuals need interaction with others. But as society and technology evolve, new opportunities for interaction emerge and individuals who lack access to these facilities may be at a relative disadvantage. Consider, for example, access to the Internet. Citizens outside the Internet lack access to electronic commerce, cheaper products, and major forms of social interaction. To maintain social inclusion and equality of opportunity, some emerging technologies become new priorities.

In several zones of policy, science is of less help. Questions about the design of a democratic system, electoral boundaries, the appropriate dress to allow or ban in public, and what drugs should be illegal often involve balancing different pros and cons and diverse public sensibilities. Problems of this kind are abundant in the social sciences, which deal with context-dependent phenomena of massive complexity. Scientific studies can sometimes be useful in these circumstances, but they are unlikely to be able to resolve these questions.

And there are limits to trial and experiment. Unbounded experimentation is impossible because it is costly and even potentially dysfunctional. As in nature, evolution is a powerful engine of adaptation, but it is enormously wasteful. Unavoidably, those in authority have to guide and restrict the scope for experimentation. And the second-order criteria involved in making these restrictions can be even less subject to experimental testing.

I use the term "evotopia" to describe a dynamic system that contrasts with fixed utopias, such as the socialist system of collective property or the individualized free-market system of modern libertarians (Hodgson 1999a). By contrast, an evotopia should foster learning, enhance human capacities, systematically incorporate growing knowledge, and adapt to changing circumstances. Science would be the guide for serving human needs, but many other moral and policy questions are matters for open and adaptive dialogue. An evotopia would embrace the following principles:

- Complexity, uncertainty, and incomplete knowledge make any fully rational, social, or economic policy or design impossible. All policies are fallible, and hence they must be explicitly provisional and practically adaptable.
- Much policy should be formulated by experimentation and with a variety of routines, institutions, and structures. Only on the basis of such a variety

can policies and institutions be given any comparative and pragmatic evaluation.

- Inbuilt structural variety is important for helping the system deal with and adapt to unforeseen changes: variety is essential to learning and adaptability at both the systemic and the individual levels.

- The impossibility of omniscience, in institutions or individuals, means that neither can be relied on as a final judge of what is required. A learning, adapting system enjoins a democratic and participatory dialogue, covering both scientific and normative issues, in which the prevailing policies, and principles of morality and justice, are repeatedly scrutinized.

Structural variety is a key evotopian principle. A similar postulate is found in systems theory. Some subsystemic and structural variety is to cope with a degree of unforeseen change (Ashby 1952, 1956; Beer 1972; Luhmann 1982; Hodgson 1984). We have to conceive of "a system that would continue to operate despite radical changes in its environment" (Boguslaw 1965, p. 142). As a result, it is necessary to ensure that "some degree of variability" is continuously generated. Also necessary is the capability to detect changes in the system's environment and to find solutions to the new problems that emerge. But this first principle does not inform us about the nature and range of such variety. It is a task of evotopian discourse at a middle-range level of theorizing to address this question.

The market has a necessary but qualified role in an evotopian economy. Failure to appreciate its essential role in a complex and innovative economy is a major leftist error. Devolved ownership and control provide scope for diversity and experimentation. Such private property implies the ability to trade goods and services. Markets are processors and signalers of imperfect but essential price information. But in principle the market cannot be relied on as the single and supreme regulatory institution. It is implausible to make every human interaction a legal exchange contract for goods or services. Furthermore, the evidence of numerous policy experiments in recent decades suggests that neither markets nor privatization is a universal panacea (Nelson 1981, 2003, 2005a; Kenworthy 1995; Moreau 2004; Martinez 2009).

There is some evidence that, on the average, privately owned firms are more efficient and more profitable than comparable state-owned firms (Megginson and Netter 2001).[8] But when we compare national economic

---

8. The evidence on output quality is less decisive. The survey evidence is also less comprehensive when it comes to areas of activity that are traditionally in the public domain. Further-

systems with one another, then several of the best-performing economies have relatively high levels of state intervention and regulation (Kenworthy 1995; Evans and Rauch 1999; Reinert 2007). Privatization is not a universal panacea. When they work, markets entail complementary institutions and regulatory policies. Government economic involvement and regulatory policies can provide opportunities rather than mere constraints. Carefully constructed frameworks of regulation can increase the capacity of the economy to innovate and adapt, and even improve the functioning of markets themselves (Traxler and Unger 1994; Chang and Rowthorn 1995).

Accordingly, flexibility and adaptability are not necessarily gained by giving markets full rein. A complex economy has a diversity of idiosyncratic goals and functioning principles, requiring overarching, nonmarket frameworks of communication and regulation. Dynamic growth and flexibility can be thwarted by placing all subsystems under the pecuniary and contractarian dictates of the market. This is true a fortiori with matters such as education, health, and environmental policy.

An interesting experimental form of governance structure has evolved (without much prior overall design) within the European Union (EU). Although it has many institutional problems, including a weak strategic center and severe difficulties with its flawed monetary system, the EU provides an important case study of an evolutionary policy approach. Sometimes called the "open method of coordination" (De la Porte, Pochet, and Room 2001; Room 2011), this involves the exchange of information on "best practice" exemplars between the member states, the use of benchmarks to assess performance, regular reporting, the setting of performance targets at national and regional levels, and multilateral surveillance (Zeitlin and Pochet 2005; Sabel and Zeitlin 2008).

As Charles Sabel and Jonathan Zeitlin (2008) explain, EU governance is multilevel, with law-making capacities at the EU, national, and regional tiers. Within this political structure, Member States and EU institutions establish goals concerning such matters as social inclusion, full employment, environmental quality, and much else, with criteria for gauging their achievement. National ministries, regulatory authorities, and other relevant actors are given scope to advance these ends as they see fit. But they must report regularly on their performance and participate in a peer

---

more, when it comes to high transaction-cost services such as healthcare, the largely private and comparatively expensive US healthcare system results in that country being way down the league table of healthcare indicators, while state-run systems in Britain and even Cuba perform better and are more efficient by several indicators (Evans et al. 2001; Dixon and Mossialos 2002; Retziaff-Roberts, Chang, and Rubin 2004; OECD 2010).

review in which their results are compared with those using other means to the same general ends. In turn, the framework goals, performance measures, and decision-making procedures are periodically revised in the light of outcomes. Although it was not established by a common treaty of the EU nation states, this model of policy development has diffused across a range of policy domains, including telecommunications, energy, drug authorization, occupational health and safety, employment promotion, social inclusion, pensions, healthcare, environmental protection, food safety, maritime safety, financial services, competition policy, state aid, antidiscrimination policy, and fundamental rights. This is a recursive process of policymaking and revision through interactive deliberation between EU and national actors.

10.4. Conditions for a Dynamic Market Economy

Even the most privatized or market-driven of economies require the state. This fact is recognized even by many libertarians, including Friedrich Hayek (1960). Theories of the spontaneous evolution of property and contract rely on reputation and other effects, which depend on small numbers of well-informed traders (Sened 1997). These conditions are absent in complex and larger-scale societies, and consequently rehabilitate a role for the state in the enforcement of property rights and contracts (Steiger 2008; Hodgson 2009).

Contrary to much contemporary rhetoric, it is not possible to organize every productive activity as a commodity exchange or market. As noted in chapter 1, some markets and exchanges are prohibited even in the most market-driven of modern economies. To maintain a free market for labor, workers must be employed under a contract that allows exit, subject to notice of maximum a few months. To bind employees into a longer contract would be to reintroduce a form of bondage. The prohibition of extended futures markets for labor is an important safeguard of the freedom of the employee. *Under capitalism, there can be no such futures market for labor,* and consequently nonmarket measures have to fill the gap.

The employer cannot tie the worker into the firm by contract for more than a few months, and the worker has the option to leave after a short period of notice. Consequently, if the employer spends money on employee training and skill development, then this investment may be lost. As a result, without compensatory arrangements, employers will underinvest in human learning and education. As Alfred Marshall (1920, p. 568) pointed out: "we meet the difficulty that whoever may incur the expense of invest-ing capital in developing the abilities of the workman, these abilities will be the property of the workman himself: and thus the virtue of those who have aided him must remain for the greater part its own reward." Marshall argued that the development of skills in the capitalist enterprise must de-pend "in great measure on the unselfishness of the employer."

This system shortfall, due to a missing market, has a number of rem-edies. With due credit to Marshall, relying on employer unselfishness is hardly a viable strategic solution because employers face competition from other firms and an obligation to make profits. Another possible remedy is for employers to offer wages at above the market rate. But all employ-ers face the same difficulty, and wages would rise across the board. What would happen is an "arms race" of employee compensation, each firm try-ing to improve on the wages offered by the others, in an attempt to re-tain their skilled workers. Ironically, it is the very "imperfections" of the market system that come to the rescue here. If works face high transaction costs in moving from one job to the other, or if labor markets are local and limited, or if workers are tied into a job due to family or other circum-stances, then they are less likely to exit the firm. A third mechanism would be for employers to create a corporate culture of excellence and commit-ment that engenders loyalty among the workers and to encourage "voice" rather than "exit" as a mechanism for dealing with grievances (Hirschman 1970). A fourth option would be for the state to subsidize employee train-ing, as happens (with some success) in some countries and some US states (Holzer et al. 1993; Van Horn and Fichtner 2003).

Another solution is to introduce worker cooperatives. Because the work-ers own the cooperative firm, it has a stronger incentive to give them train-ing, and workers are less likely to leave. The other pros and cons of worker cooperatives are too complex to go into here, but it should be noted that prominent "proofs" of their alleged suboptimality are based on equilib-rium models (Vanek 1970). Learning is essentially an out-of-equilibrium process, and once we consider dynamic rather than static efficiency, the prominent suboptimality proofs become irrelevant (Hodgson 1999a). There is a prime facie case for a healthy cooperative sector, alongside other forms (Bonin, Jones, and Putterman 1993).

This crucial "missing market" problem with the system of capitalist employment has been rarely discussed since Marshall, with notable excep-tions such as John Maurice Clark (1923), Kenneth Arrow (1962), and Don-ald Stabile (1996). In a major mainstream text on missing or incomplete markets, they are treated ahistorically as outcomes of the limitations of the human psyche (Magill and Quinzii 1996) rather than the consequence of historically specific social structures.

Long-term contracts for labor would be tantamount to slavery. Any capitalism that claims to be based on universal individual liberty must exclude a market for slaves. Likewise it would exclude the rearing of children to be sold for profit. (Surrogate motherhood may allow the selling of parenting rights, but by law it cannot involve the selling of children themselves.) Consequently, under liberal capitalism, the production and rearing of children is not organized like other commodities.

In principle we can conceive of alternative child-rearing possibilities, such as the Israeli *kibbutzim*. In any case, some form of family institution steps in, given this missing market for children. Despite two centuries of pronouncements on the obsolete status of the family by anarchists, feminists, utopians, and revolutionary socialists, the family endures as an adaptable institution, which is neither driven by the profit motive nor organized by the state. Nevertheless, the state provides the legal framework through which families operate. The family typically combines a degree of voluntary association by adults, with customary moral obligations, and legal rights and duties.

The family is at variance with the twin utopias of socialism and promarket individualism. Individualists who regard the market as the solution to problems of organization and allocation give inadequate explanation of why they refrain from the commercialization of all family relations. If, by contrast, they cherish "family values" and the solidity of that institution, then they have to recognize the practical and moral limits of market imperatives and pecuniary exchange.[9]

Although the family is itself a nonmarket institution, it provides an essential role for supplying new generations of labor, socialized in the values of the prevailing culture, for the capitalist system. As noted in chapter 5, the early years of child development are vital for establishing a moral sense.

---

9. In Hodgson (1999a, chap. 3), I noted an inconsistency or incompleteness in Hayek's position. In response, Steven Horwitz (2005) points out that Hayek defends the family. That is not the point. Neither Hayek nor Horwitz provides a clear reason, from his pro-market perspectives, why the family should not be replaced by a set of short-term commercial contracts between individuals, for sex, child rearing, and household services. From their standpoint, how can lifetime marriage and fidelity be defended? Hayek and Horwitz see the market as an ideal economic arrangement but do not explain adequately why the market is supposedly ideal in one context but not in another. Lacking any good argument why market relations should not invade and dissolve this institution, the arguments of both Hayek and Horwitz thus become juxtapositions of inconsistent principles and prerogatives.

Again, the family plays a crucial role. The nonmarket institution of the family is the realm of basic education and socialization. It inculcates the moral values of cooperation, loyalty, and respect for others that are vital for the capitalist system. Capitalism is necessarily impure. Overall it depends on other nonmarket institutions, from the state to the family.

So far we have mostly examined *necessary* institutional conditions for the operation of a capitalist market economy. We now give more examples of *optional* conditions that can enhance the dynamism or viability of the capitalist system.

A number of measures that generally improve human welfare are unlikely to emerge spontaneously. In employment, these include a minimum wage and limits on the length of the working week. The need for legislation over the latter was acknowledged by John Stuart Mill (1848, chap. 11), who otherwise wished to limit the size of government. It is quite possible that a system of industrial relations and remuneration can be stuck in a suboptimal equilibrium, and the state can help reconfigure institutions in a move to a superior set of arrangements. Given the lack of full information, maintenance of minimum quality standards for products such as food has also been a longstanding task of the state.

Problems of limited knowledge, asymmetric information, and bounded rationality are ubiquitous in markets where quality variation is possible—as in most markets. Historically, various measures have emerged to deal with this problem, including reputation signaling devices such as branding and trademarks, product appellations, business organizations, and state controls. Markets themselves require durable organizations to deal with the ubiquitous problem of limited information.

Other—far from universal—features are not strictly necessary for the existence of capitalism, but their implementation may be required for humanity under capitalism to reach a higher potential. A market system devolves a great deal of decision making to the individual and requires that person to enter into (often complex) contracts with others. The individual has to carry out numerous basic transactions and act responsibly. People cannot function effectively in a system of contracts and markets if they are deprived of food, shelter, basic education, or fruitful social interaction. By engagement in a social culture, people acquire the education and capabilities to deliberate effectively and serve their autonomous goals. These are conditions for social inclusion.[10]

Hence it is possible to deduce the desirability of a welfare state from

10. See Gray (1993, pp. 306–14) and O'Neill (1998, chaps. 5–7).

libertarian political principles. James Sterba (1985) establishes the need for welfare provision to ensure that the poor can exercise their (libertarian) rights to life and property. Justifying taxation, Michael Davis (1987) argues that beneficiaries of state services (such as public health programs that reduce epidemics and police services that improve personal security) have the duty to pay for them.

Proposals for a basic income guarantee, supplied by the state, are partially justified on the grounds that individuals require a minimum income to function as free and choosing agents. The idea of a basic income has a long pedigree going back to Thomas Paine. It involves paying everyone a regular sum of money, irrespective of other income or wealth, or whether working or not. The principle is that everyone has the unconditional right to the means of survival, so that they can make use of their liberty, have some autonomy, function as effective citizens, and participate in civil society. These are conditions of adequate and educated inclusion in the market world of choice and trade.

A basic income would also reward caring work, which is typically performed by family members or relatives. Caring work is of enormous scale and has huge social benefit. But it is typically underestimated and uncompensated (Folbre 1995; Folbre and Nelson 2000; Nussbaum 2000; Jochimsen 2003). A basic income would also encourage new entrepreneurs and creative artists, and reduce migration from the countryside to the cities in search of work. There would be a huge saving in administration costs of often complex social security and welfare schemes.

The most common—but not the only—way of funding an unconditional basic income scheme is out of general taxation. This burden would be relieved by abolishing tax-free allowances (that is the amount of income that can be earned without paying tax) and making all income above the basic income allowance liable to tax. Some studies show that there may be a small reduction in labor supply as a result of the introduction of a basic income (Government of Canada 1994). This demerit is less serious when there is mass unemployment and could be alleviated by raising wages in low-paid jobs.

Some form of unconditional basic income—whether partially or wholly adequate for survival—have been pledged or introduced in several nations or states, including Alaska and Brazil. Several developed countries have legal minimum income entitlements. Public support for a basic income is found across the political spectrum. In 1968, James Tobin, Paul Samuelson, John Kenneth Galbraith, and another 1,200 economists signed a document calling for the US Congress to introduce a system of income guarantees and supplements. Winners of the Nobel Prize in Economics who fully support a basic income include Milton Friedman, Friedrich Hayek, James Meade, Herbert Simon, and Robert Solow.[11]

10.5. From Inequality to Social Solidarity

Levels of inequality in the distribution of income and wealth vary hugely from country to country. Measures of inequality have also increased in many countries since the 1970s, partly because of the undermining of manufacturing occupations in developed countries by increasing competition from China and elsewhere (Wood 1994, 1995). The evidence suggests that without countervailing measures, widening national or international markets can lead to greater national or global inequality.

The case for some redistribution of income or wealth to reduce inequality can be made from a utilitarian standpoint, as long as one abandons the Pareto criterion. Arthur Pigou (1920) made such a case before that criterion was the norm in economics. With recent developments in "happiness economics" a non-Paretian utilitarianism has returned. With empirical evidence of the declining marginal happiness of wealth and income, it becomes possible to recommend some redistribution of income to increase the average level of happiness in a population. Richard Layard (2005) and others report evidence that in societies where inequality is lower, average happiness tends to be higher.

A major study of the effects of inequality is *The Spirit Level* by Richard Wilkinson and Kate Pickett (2009). Their book argues that inequality has pernicious effects on societies, including the erosion of trust, increases in anxiety and illness, and the encouragement of excessive consumption. Using data from 23 developed countries and the separate states of the United States, they observe negative correlations between inequality and physical health, mental health, education, child well-being, social mobility, trust, and community life. They also find positive correlations between inequality and drug abuse, imprisonment, obesity, violence, and teenage pregnancies. They suggest, but do not establish in detail, that inequality creates adverse health and other outcomes through the psychosocial stress that is generated through interactions in an unequal society. Their work has attracted both strong support and scholarly criticism, particularly regarding the construction of their sample, the omission of some developed countries, and their analysis of the results. But other studies corroborate some of

---

11. See Van Parijs (1992, 1995), Corning (2011), and Wikipedia (2011a).

these negative outcomes. For example, Robert D. Putnam's (2000, p. 359) empirical and theoretical work on the decline of "social capital" (by which he means involvement in social networks and community relations conducive to collective action) in the United States since the 1950s led him to conclude: "Community and equality are mutually reinforcing."

A massive literature—too extensive to review here—examines the relationship between inequality and economic performance (Galbraith and Berner 2001). While some inequality provides high-powered incentives for entrepreneurs and other high flyers, an unequal society also wastes the talent of many on middle and lower incomes who have less access to high-quality education, to a supportive subculture, and to financial backing. Robert J. Barro (2000) finds that, after introducing controls for education, fertility, and investment, there is no significant correlation between inequality and economic growth.[12]

The normative evaluation of the unequal distribution of income and wealth has been sidelined by economists and the Pareto criterion. It needs to be brought back to the center of economic research. Further investigation on the comparative performances and outcomes in different countries with different degrees of inequality is required, along with the design of redistributive fiscal measures that stifle neither ambition nor enterprise.

I am not advocating an equalization of income and wealth. Some inequality flows inevitably and justifiably from a system that relies on individual and group incentives. But extremes of inequality should be tackled. Countries with high or rapidly growing inequality such as the United States, China, India, Russia, Britain, and Brazil should seek exemplars among high-income countries that have much lower levels of inequality and exhibit greater moral solidarity. The best cases are in Scandinavia.

According to the United Nations Human Development Report for 2009, within the 22 most highly developed countries, those with the lowest in-

---

12. Analysis by the author of data from the United Nations Human Development Report for 2009 (United Nations Development Programme 2009) shows a significant negative correlation between the human development indices (HDI) and the Gini coefficients for 93 countries with an HDI above 0.5, which include India and China. (Some low HDI countries also have a low Gini coefficient because most of the population is poor.) But inequality accounts for only 28 percent of the variation in the HDI. When the sample is enlarged to include 137 countries for which there are data, there is still a negative correlation between the HDI and the Gini coefficients, but the amount of variation explained drops to 14 percent. Both these regressions suggest that increases in inequality will tend to lower the HDI. Despite their limitations, these results undermine the idea that inequality is necessary for capital accumulation and development.

come inequality were Denmark, Finland, Norway, Sweden, and Japan.[13] In the year 2000, in Denmark, Finland, Norway, and Sweden, the ratio between the income of the top decile and the income of the bottom decile ranged between 2.7 and 3.0. In the United States and the United Kingdom in the same year, it was 5.5 and 4.6 respectively (Brandolini and Smeeding 2008).

All modern developed economies face major problems of social cohesion (Fukuyama 1999). Numerous socially excluded groups and individuals have diminished access to key institutions and resources, particularly as a result of unemployment, poverty, or poor education, preventing them from full participation in the societies in which they live. There are also fissures of social class and ethnicity that cut across modern societies, diminishing social cohesion and undermining a common moral discourse of solidarity.

These deepening rifts in modern society are problems in themselves, leading to increased crime and other social ills. They also make their own repair more problematic. Redistributive tax systems and common welfare provision are all the more difficult to develop in a morally fragmented society. Policymakers should prioritize measures to reverse this decay. Politicians should sometimes appeal to our better nature and not always to our worst.

For social scientists, this is a vital area of research. Just as we now have extensive survey data on corruption, the rule of law, consumer confidence, and much else, we also need more survey evidence on the prevalence of moral norms that sustain cooperation and public spiritedness. Thanks to the dominance of "economic man," this task has been mostly ignored. It would be central to a social science that faces up to the problems of the twenty-first century.

It is beyond the scope of the present work to explore these important issues in more detail. But the case has been made for abandoning the misplaced ideology of rational, self-interested individualism that has dominated economics in the twentieth century. Humans are moral beings, and a task of social science is to understand the role of morality in social life and the possibilities for moral community. Neither social nor natural science can provide us with a system of morality, but each one can point to feasible options and help us reevaluate our commitments and priorities.

13. United Nations Development Programme (2009). "Most highly developed" is defined here as an HDI of 0.85 or above.

These arguments cut across the traditional political dichotomies of left and right. From the French revolution onwards, the so-called left appealed to morality and sometimes religion to justify egalitarian or socialist ideals. But left-leaning morality has since received a battering. The rise of Marxism dramatically marginalized leftist moral discourse. Marxists treat all morality with suspicion. Partially influenced by Marxism, a much broader strand of modern leftism prioritizes the distribution of vital goods and services to the deprived, without additional attention to the role of morality in human motivation. Theft is thus blamed on poverty rather than a crumbling social morality. Also within the modern left, a widespread amoralism masquerades as cultural or moral relativism. As a result of various leftist assaults on moral discourse, much moral thinking has been captured by the conservative right.

The left persuasively emphasizes human needs. The libertarian right champions choice and liberty. This book brings both strands together and doubly bridges the political divide. First, individual choice and democracy are important in an evolutionary process of enlightenment, especially concerning needs and the possibility of their satisfaction. Second, concern about need shortfalls is a major factor in human moral motivation, and this aspect of motivation should be enlightened and enhanced. In at least two ways, the current political spectrum is spanned.

Economics is a social science, and it cannot solely be about the attributes of individuals. We have to understand both individual psychology and the way social institutions structure, constrain, and help develop our capacities. Economies have also to be understood as engines of wealth within social systems, relying on individuals who are always in a process of learning and development rather than fixed preference functions or pleasure machines. Understanding the complexities of human motivation means appreciating our moral feelings and deliberations, as well as our selfishness. These attributes are formed and changed in interactions with others. Economics is not just about individuals; it is a social science where principles matter.

REFERENCES

Aarts, Henk, and Dijksterhuis, Ap. (2000). "The Automatic Activation of Goal-Directed Behavior: The Case of Travel Habit." *Journal of Environmental Psychology* 20:75–82.

Acemoglu, Daron, and Verdier, Thierry. (2000). "The Choice between Market Failures and Corruption." *American Economic Review* 90 (1): 194–211.

Ackerman, Robert. (1976). *The Philosophy of Karl Popper*. Amherst: University of Massachusetts Press.

Adami, Christoph, Ofria, Charles, and Collier, Travis C. (2000). "Evolution of Biological Complexity." *Proceedings of the National Academy of Sciences* 97 (9): 4463–68.

Adler, Moshe. (1992). "The Quality Guaranteeing Price with Market Anonymity." *International Journal of Game Theory* 21:313–23.

Agassi, Joseph. (1960). "Methodological Individualism." *British Journal of Sociology* 11 (3): 244–70.

———. (1975). "Institutional Individualism." *British Journal of Sociology* 26 (2): 144–55.

Aidt, Toke S. (2003). "Economic Analysis of Corruption: A Survey." *Economic Journal* 113 (8): F632–52.

Akerlof, George A. (1991). "Procrastination and Obedience." *American Economic Review (Papers and Proceedings)* 81 (2): 1–19.

Akerlof, George A., and Kranton, Rachel E. (2005). "Identity and the Economics of Organizations." *Journal of Economic Perspectives* 19 (1): 9–32.

Akerlof, George A., and Shiller, Robert J. (2009). *Animal Spirits: How Human Psychology Drives the Economy and Why It Matters for Global Capitalism*. Princeton, NJ: Princeton University Press.

Alchian, Armen A. (1991). "Development of Economic Theory and Antitrust: A View from the Theory of the Firm." *Journal of Institutional and Theoretical Economics* 147 (1): 232–34.

Alchian, Armen A., and Demsetz, Harold. (1972). "Production, Information Costs, and Economic Organization." *American Economic Review* 62 (4): 777–95.

Aldrich, Howard E., Hodgson, Geoffrey M., Hull, David L., Knudsen, Thorbjørn, Mokyr, Joel, and Vanberg, Viktor J. (2008). "In Defence of Generalized Darwinism." *Journal of Evolutionary Economics* 18 (5): 577–96.

Alexander, J. McKenzie. (2007). *The Structural Evolution of Morality*. Cambridge: Cambridge University Press.

Alexander, Richard D. (1987). *The Biology of Moral Systems*. New York: Aldine de Gruter.

Allett, John. (1981). *New Liberalism: The Political Economy of J. A. Hobson*. Toronto: University of Toronto Press.

Allingham, Michael G., and Sandmo, Agnar. (1972). "Income Tax Evasion: A Theoretical Analysis." *Journal of Public Economics* 1 (3–4): 323–38.

Alvey, James E. (2000). "An Introduction to Economics as a Moral Science." *International Journal of Social Economics* 27 (12): 1231–51.

Althusser, Louis, and Balibar, Étienne. (1970). *Reading Capital*. Translated from the French edition of 1968 by Ben Brewster. London: NLB.

Amable, Bruno. (2000). "Institutional Complementarity and Diversity of Social Systems of Innovation and Production." *Review of International Political Economy* 7 (4): 645–87.

———. (2003). *The Diversity of Modern Capitalism*. Oxford: Oxford University Press.

Anderies, John M., Janssen, Marco A., and Ostrom, Elinor. (2004) "A Framework to Analyze the Robustness of Social-Ecological Systems from an Institutional Perspective." *Ecology and Society* 9 (1): 18. http://www.ecologyandsociety.org/vol9/iss1/art18/.

Andreoni, James (1990). "Impure Altruism and Donations to Public Goods: A Theory of Warm-Glow Giving." *Economic Journal* 100 (2): 464–77.

———. (1995). "Cooperation in Public Goods Experiments: Kindness or Confusion?" *American Economic Review* 85 (4): 891–904.

Andreoni, James, Erard, B., and Feinstein, Jonathan. (1998). "Tax Compliance." *Journal of Economic Literature* 36 (2): 818–60.

Andvig, Jens Christian. (2006). "Corruption and Fast Change." *World Development* 34 (2): 328–40.

Andvig, Jens Christian, and Moene, Karl Ove. (1990). "How Corruption May Corrupt." *Journal of Economic Behavior and Organization* 13 (1): 63–76.

Aoki, Masahiko. (2001). *Toward a Comparative Institutional Analysis*. Cambridge, MA: MIT Press.

Arendt, Hannah. (1958). "What Was Authority?" In *Authority*, edited by Carl J. Friedrich, 81–112. Cambridge, MA: Harvard University Press.

Argyres, Nicholas S. (1996). "Evidence on the Role of Firm Capabilities in Vertical Integration Decisions." *Strategic Management Journal* 17 (1): 129–50.

Argyris, Chris, and Schön, Donald A. (1996). *Organizational Learning II: Theory, Method, and Practice*. Reading, MA: Addison-Wesley.

Aristotle. (1962). *The Politics*. Translated, with an introduction by T. A. Sinclair. Harmondsworth: Penguin.

Arrow, Kenneth J. (1951). *Social Choice and Individual Values*. New York: Wiley.

———. (1962). "The Economic Implications of Learning by Doing." *Review of Economic Studies* 29 (2): 155–73.

———. (1963). "Uncertainty and the Welfare Economics of Medical Care." *American Economic Review* 53 (5): 941–73.

———. (1965). "Uncertainty and the Welfare Economics of Medical Care: Reply (The Implications of Transaction Costs and Adjustment Lags)." *American Economic Review* 55:154–58.

———. (1984). *The Economics of Information*. Cambridge, MA: Belknap Press.

———. (1986). "Rationality of Self and Others in an Economic System." *Journal of Business* 59 (4.2): S385–99.

———. (1994). "Methodological Individualism and Social Knowledge." *American Economic Review (Papers and Proceedings)* 84 (2): 1–9.

Ashby, W. Ross. (1952). *Design for a Brain*. New York: Wiley.

———. (1956). *An Introduction to Cybernetics*. New York: Wiley.

Ashton, Toni. (1998). "Contracting for Health Services in New Zealand: A Transaction Cost Analysis." *Social Science and Medicine* 46 (3): 357–67.

Atkinson, Anthony B. (2009). "Economics as a Moral Science." *Economica* 76:791–804.

Aumann, Robert J., and Brandenburger, Adam. (1995). "Epistemic Conditions for Nash Equilibrium." *Econometrica* 63 (5): 1161–80.

Axelrod, Robert M. (1984). *The Evolution of Cooperation*. New York: Basic Books.

Ayres, Clarence E. (1918). *The Nature of the Relationship Between Ethics and Economics*. Chicago: University of Chicago Press.

———. (1944). *The Theory of Economic Progress*. Chapel Hill: University of North Carolina Press.

———. (1952). *The Industrial Economy: Its Technological Basis and Institutional Destiny*. Boston: Houghton Mifflin.

———. (1961). *Toward a Reasonable Society: The Values of Industrial Civilization*. Austin: University of Texas Press.

Backhaus, Ursula. (unpublished). "A History of Thought on Health Economics." University of Erfurt.

Backhouse, Roger E., and Medema, Stephen G. (2009). "Defining Economics: The Long Road to Acceptance of the Robbins Definition." *Economica* 76:805–20.

Bagehot, Walter. (1872). *Physics and Politics, or, Thoughts on the Application of the Principles of "Natural Selection" and "Inheritance" to Political Society*. London: Henry King.

Baldry, Jonathan C. (1986). "Tax Evasion Is Not a Gamble: A Report on Two Experiments." *Economics Letters* 22 (4): 333–35.

Bamberg, Sebastian, Ajzen, Icek, and Schmidt, Peter. (2003). "Choice of Travel Mode in the Theory of Planned Behavior: The Role of Past Behaviour, Habit, and Reasoned Action." *Basic and Applied Social Psychology* 25:175–87.

Bandura, Albert, and Walters, Richard H. (1963). *Social Learning and Personality Development*. New York: Holt, Rinehart and Winston.

Banfield, Edward C. (1975). "Corruption as a Feature of Governmental Organization." *Journal of Law and Economics* 18 (3): 587–605.

Bardhan, Pranab K. (1997). "Corruption and Development: A Review of the Issues." *Journal of Economic Literature* 35 (3): 1320–46.

Barbalet, Jack. (2001). *Emotion, Social Theory and Social Structure*. Cambridge: Cambridge University Press.

———. (2008). "Pragmatism and Economics: William James' Contribution." *Cambridge Journal of Economics* 32 (5): 797–810.

Barr, Nicholas. (1992). "Economic Theory and the Welfare State: A Survey and Interpretation." *Journal of Economic Literature* 30 (2): 741–80.

Barro, Robert J. (2000). "Inequality and Growth in a Panel of Countries." *Journal of Economic Growth* 7 (1): 5–32.

Baumol, William J., and Oates, Wallace E. (1988). *The Theory of Environmental Policy*. 2nd ed. Cambridge: Cambridge University Press.

BBC News. (2001). "Waiting Lists." *BBC News*, May 11. http://news.bbc.co.uk/vote2001/hi/english/main_issues/sections/facts/newsid_1134000/1134218.stm#top, http://www.bbc.co.uk/otr/intext/20010603_whole.html.

———. (2005). "Blair Promises Action on GP Row." *BBC News*, April 29. http://news.bbc.co.uk/1/hi/uk_politics/vote_2005/frontpage/4495865.stm.

Bechara, Antoine, and Damasio, Antonio R. (2005). "The Somatic Marker Hypothesis: A Neural Theory of Economic Decision." *Games and Economic Behavior* 52 (2): 336–72.

Becker, C. Dustin, and Ostrom, Elinor. (1995). "Human Ecology and Resource Sustainability: The Importance of Institutional Diversity." *Annual Review of Ecology and Systematics* 26:113–33.

Becker, Gary S. (1968). "Crime and Punishment: An Economic Approach." *Journal of Political Economy* 76 (2): 169–217.

———. (1974). "A Theory of Social Interactions." *Journal of Political Economy* 82 (6): 1063–93.

———. (1976a). "Altruism, Egoism, and Genetic Fitness: Economics and Sociobiology." *Journal of Economic Literature* 14 (2): 817–26.

———. (1976b). *The Economic Approach to Human Behavior*. Chicago: University of Chicago Press.

———. (1991). *A Treatise on the Family*. 2nd ed. Cambridge, MA: Harvard University Press.

———. (1996). *Accounting for Tastes*. Cambridge, MA: Harvard University Press.

———. (1998). "The Causes and Cures of Corruption." *Project Syndicate*, February 26. http://www.project-syndicate.org/commentary/bec6/English.

Becker, Markus C. (2004). "Organizational Routines: A Review of the Literature." *Industrial and Corporate Change* 13 (4): 643–77.

Beer, Stafford. (1964). *Cybernetics and Management*. London: Science Editions.

———. (1972). *Brain of the Firm*. London: Allen Lane.

Beinhocker, Erik D. (2006). *The Origins of Wealth: Evolution, Complexity, and the Radical Remaking of Economics*. New York: Random House.

———. (2011). "Evolution as Computation: Integrating Self-Organization with Generalized Darwinism." *Journal of Institutional Economics* 7 (3): 393–423.

Bell, Stephanie A. (2001). "The Role of the State and the Hierarchy of Money." *Cambridge Journal of Economics* 25 (2): 149–63.

Benedict, Ruth. (1934a). "Anthropology and the Abnormal." *Journal of General Psychology* 10 (1): 59–82.

———. (1934b). *Patterns of Culture*. New York: New American Library.

Ben-Ner, Avner, and Putterman, Louis. (2000). "Some Implications of Evolutionary Psychology for the Study of Preferences and Institutions." *Journal of Economic Behavior and Organization* 43 (1): 91–99.

Benson, Susanne G., and Dundis, Stephen P. (2003). "Understanding and Motivating Health Care Employees: Integrating Maslow's Hierarchy of Needs, Training and Technology." *Journal of Nursing Management* 11 (5): 315–20.

Bentham, Jeremy. (1789). *An Introduction to the Principles of Morality and Legislation*. London: Froude.

Bergström, Sören. (1993). "Value Standards in Sub-sustainable Development: On the Limits of Ecological Economics." *Ecological Economics* 7 (1): 1–18.

Berle, Adolf A. (1950). *Natural Selection of Political Forces*. Lawrence: University of Kansas Press.

Bhaskar, Roy. (1975). *A Realist Theory of Science*. Leeds: Leeds Books.

———. (1979). *The Possibility of Naturalism: A Philosophic Critique of the Contemporary Human Sciences*. Brighton: Harvester.

———. (1986). *Scientific Realism and Human Emancipation*. London: Verso.

———. (1989). *Reclaiming Reality: A Critical Introduction to Contemporary Philosophy*. London: Verso.

———. (1991). *Philosophy and the Idea of Freedom*. Oxford: Basil Blackwell.

———. (1993). *Dialectic: The Pulse of Freedom*. London: Verso.

Bhaskar, Roy, and Collier, Andrew. (1998). "Introduction: Explanatory Critiques." In *Critical Realism: Essential Readings*, edited by Margaret S. Archer, Roy Bhaskar, Andrew Collier, Tony Lawson, and Alan Norrie, 385–94. London: Routledge.

Binder, Martin. (2010). *Elements of an Evolutionary Theory of Welfare: Assessing Welfare When Preferences Change*. London: Routledge.

Binmore, Kenneth. (1994). *Playing Fair: Game Theory and the Social Contract*. Vol. 1. Cambridge, MA: MIT Press.

———. (1998a). "Evolutionary Ethics." In *Game Theory, Experience, Rationality*, edited by Werner Leinfellner and Eckehart Köhler, 277–83. Boston: Kluwer.

———. (1998b). *Just Playing: Game Theory and the Social Contract*. Vol. 2. Cambridge, MA: MIT Press.

———. (1998c). Review of *Complexity and Cooperation*, by Robert Axelrod. *Journal of Artificial Societies and Social Situations* 1 (1). http://jasss.soc.surrey.ac.uk/JASSS/1/1/review1.html.

———. (1999). "Why Experiment in Economics?" *Economic Journal* 109 (2): F16–F24.

———. (2005). *Natural Justice*. Oxford: Oxford University Press.

Binmore, Kenneth, and Shaked, Avner (2010). "Experimental Economics: Where Next?" *Journal of Economic Behavior and Organization* 73:87–100.

Blackmore, Susan. (1999). *The Meme Machine*. Oxford: Oxford University Press.

Blair, Margaret M. (1999). "Firm-Specific Human Capital and Theories of the Firm." In *Employees and Corporate Governance*, edited by Margaret M. Blair and Mark Roe, 58–89. Washington, DC: Brookings.

———. (2003). "Locking in Capital: What Corporate Law Achieved for Business Organizers in the Nineteenth Century." *UCLA Law Review* 51 (2): 387–455.

Blamey, R. K., Common, M., and Quiggin, J. (1995). "Respondents to Contingent Valuation Surveys: Consumers or Citizens?" *Australian Journal of Agricultural Economics* 39 (3): 263–88.

Blass, Thomas. (1991). "Understanding Behavior in the Milgram Obedience Experiment: The Role of Personality, Situations, and Their Interactions." *Journal of Personality and Social Psychology* 60 (3): 398–413.

Blaug, Mark. (1992). *The Methodology of Economics: Or How Economists Explain*. 2nd ed. Cambridge: Cambridge University Press.

———. (1997). "Ugly Currents in Modern Economics." *Options Politiques* 18 (17): 3–8. Reprinted in *Fact and Fiction in Economics: Models, Realism and Social Construction*, edited by Uskali Mäki. Cambridge: Cambridge University Press, 2002.

———. (1998). "Where Are We Now in British Health Economics?" *Health Economics* 7:S63–S78.

Bleichrodt, Han, and Pinto, Jose Luis. (2006). "Conceptual Foundations for Health Utility Measurement." In *The Elgar Companion to Health Economics*, edited by Andrew M. Jones, 347–58. Cheltenham: Edward Elgar.

Bliss, Christopher, and Di Tella, Rafael. (1997). "Does Competition Kill Corruption?" *Journal of Political Economy* 105 (5): 1001–23.

Blute, Marion. (2010). *Darwinian Sociocultural Evolution: Solutions to Dilemmas in Cultural and Social Theory*. Cambridge: Cambridge University Press.

Block, Walter, ed. (1989). *Economics and the Environment: A Reconciliation*. Vancouver: Fraser Institute.

Bloom, Allan. (1988). *The Closing of the American Mind*. New York: Simon and Schuster.

Boehm, Christopher. (1999). *Hierarchy in the Forest: The Evolution of Egalitarian Behavior*. Cambridge, MA: Harvard University Press.

———. (2000). "The Origin of Morality as Social Control." *Journal of Consciousness Studies* 7 (1–2): 149–83.

———. (2011). *Moral Origins: Social Selection and the Evolution of Virtue, Altruism and Shame.* New York: Basic Books.

Bogdan, Radu. (2000). *Minding Minds: Evolving a Reflexive Mind in Interpreting Others.* Cambridge, MA: MIT Press.

Boguslaw, Robert. (1965). *The New Utopians: A Study of System Design and Social Change.* Englewood Cliffs, NJ: Prentice-Hall.

Bok, Derek. (2003). *Universities and the Market Place: The Commercialization of Higher Education.* Princeton, NJ: Princeton University Press.

Bok, Sissela. (1978). *Lying: Moral Choice in Public and Private Life.* New York: Pantheon.

———. (1995). *Common Values.* Columbia, MO: University of Missouri Press.

Boland, Lawrence A. (1981). "On the Futility of Criticizing the Neoclassical Maximization Hypothesis." *American Economic Review* 71 (5): 1031–36.

Bonin, John P., Jones, Derek C., and Putterman, Louis. (1993). "Theoretical and Empirical Studies of Producer Cooperatives: Will Ever the Twain Meet?" *Journal of Economic Literature* 31 (3): 1290–320.

Boulding, Kenneth E. (1966). "The Concept of Need for Health Services." *Milbank Memorial Fund Quarterly* 44:202–23.

———. (1969). "Economics as a Moral Science?" *American Economic Review* 59 (1): 1–12.

Bourdieu, Pierre. (1977). *Outline of a Theory of Practice.* Cambridge: Cambridge University Press.

———. (1990). *The Logic of Practice.* Stanford, CA: Stanford University Press.

Bowers, Peter. (1993). "Pricing the Environment: A Critique." *International Review of Applied Economics* 7 (1): 91–107.

Bowie, Norman E. (1988). "The Paradox of Profit." In *Papers on the Ethics of Administration,* edited by N. Dale Wright. Provo, UT: Brigham Young University Press.

———. (1991). "The Firm as a Moral Community." In *Morality, Rationality and Efficiency: New Perspectives on Socio-Economics,* edited by Richard M. Coughlin, 169–83. Armonk, NY: M. E. Sharpe.

Bowler, Peter J., and Morus, Iwan Rhys. (2005). *Making Modern Science: A Historical Survey.* Chicago: University of Chicago Press.

Bowles, Samuel. (1998). "Endogenous Preferences: The Cultural Consequences of Markets and Other Economic Institutions." *Journal of Economic Literature* 36 (1): 75–111.

———. (2004). *Microeconomics: Behavior, Institutions, and Evolution.* Princeton, NJ: Princeton University Press.

———. (2006). "Group Competition, Reproductive Leveling, and the Evolution of Human Altruism." *Science* 314:1569–72.

———. (2008). "Policies Designed for Self-Interested Citizens May Undermine 'The Moral Sentiments': Evidence from Economic Experiments." *Science* 320:1605–9.

Bowles, Samuel, Choi, Jung-Kyoo, and Hopfensitz, Astrid. (2003). "The Co-Evolution of Individual Behaviors and Social Institutions." *Journal of Theoretical Biology* 223 (2): 135–47.

Bowles, Samuel, and Gintis, Herbert. (2005a). "Can Self-Interest Explain Cooperation?" *Evolutionary and Institutional Economics Review* 2 (1): 21–41.

———, eds. (2005b). *Moral Sentiments and Material Interests: The Foundations of Cooperation in Economic Life.* Cambridge, MA: MIT Press.

———. (2011). *A Cooperative Species: Human Reciprocity and Its Evolution.* Princeton, NJ: Princeton University Press.

Boyd, Robert, and Richerson, Peter J. (1980). "Sociobiology, Culture and Economic Theory." *Journal of Economic Behavior and Organization* 1 (1): 97–121.

———. (1985). *Culture and the Evolutionary Process.* Chicago: University of Chicago Press.

———. (1992). "Punishment Allows the Evolution of Cooperation (or Anything Else) in Sizable Groups." *Ethology and Sociobiology* 13:171–95.

Boyd, Robert, Gintis, Herbert, Bowles, Samuel, and Richerson, Peter J. (2003). "Evolution of Altruistic Punishment." *Proceedings of the National Academy of Sciences* 100 (6): 3531–35.

Boyer, Robert. (2005). "Coherence, Diversity, and the Evolution of Capitalisms—The Institutional Complementarity Hypothesis." *Evolutionary and Institutional Economics Review* 2 (1): 43–80.

Brandolini, Andrea, and Smeeding, Timothy M. (2008). "Inequality (International Evidence)." *The New Palgrave Dictionary of Economics.* 2nd ed. Edited by Steven N. Durlauf and Lawrence E. Blume. http://www.dictionaryofeconomics.com/article?id=pde2008_I000273.

Braybrooke, David. (1987). *Meeting Needs.* Princeton, NJ: Princeton University Press.

Brennan, Geoffrey, and Tullock, Gordon. (1982). "An Economic Theory of Military Tactics: Methodological Individualism at War." *Journal of Economic Behavior and Organization* 3 (3): 225–42.

Brewer, Gene A., and Selden, Sally C. (1998). "Whistle-blowers in the Federal Civil Service: New Evidence of the Public Service Ethic." *Journal of Public Administration Research and Theory* 8 (3): 413–39.

Brittan, Samuel, and Hamlin, Alan, eds. (1995). *Market Capitalism and Moral Values: Proceedings of Section F (Economics) of the British Association for the Advancement of Sciences Keele 1993.* Aldershot: Edward Elgar.

Bromley, Daniel W. (1991). *Environment and Economy: Property Rights and Public Policy.* Oxford: Basil Blackwell.

Bromley, Daniel W., and Paavola, Jouni, eds. (2002). *Economics, Ethics, and Environmental Policy: Contested Choices.* Oxford: Basil Blackwell.

Bronk, Richard. (2009). *The Romantic Economist: Imagination in Economics.* Cambridge: Cambridge University Press.

Brooks, Daniel R., Collier, John, Maurer, Brian A., Smith, Jonathan D. H., and Wiley, E. O. (1989). "Entropy and Information in Evolving Biological Systems." *Biology and Philosophy* 4 (4): 407–32.

Brooks, Daniel R., and Wiley, E. O. (1988). *Evolution as Entropy: Toward a Unified Theory of Biology.* 2nd ed. Chicago: University of Chicago Press.

Brown, Donald E. (1991). *Human Universal.* New York: McGraw-Hill.

Brown, James A. C. (1954). *The Social Psychology of Industry.* Harmondsworth: Penguin.

Brown, Peter G. (1998). "Toward an Economics of Stewardship: The Case of Climate." *Ecological Economics* 26 (1): 11–21.

Buchanan, James M., and Tullock, Gordon. (1962). *The Calculus of Consent: Logical Foundations of Constitutional Democracy.* Ann Arbor: University of Michigan Press.

Bukovansky, Mlada. (2006). "The Hollowness of Anti-Corruption Discourse." *Review of International Political Economy* 13 (2): 181–209.

Bunge, Mario A. (1959). *Causality: The Place of the Causal Principle in Modern Science.* Cambridge, MA: Harvard University Press.

———. (1974). *Treatise on Basic Philosophy.* Vol. 2, *Interpretation and Truth.* Dordrecht, Holland: Reidel.

———. (1977). *Treatise on Basic Philosophy*. Vol. 3, *Ontology I: The Furniture of the World*. Dordrecht, Holland: Reidel.

———. (2000). "Ten Modes of Individualism—None of Which Works—and Their Alternatives." *Philosophy of the Social Sciences* 30 (3): 384–406.

Burke, Edmund. (1757). *A Philosophical Enquiry into the Origin of Our Ideas of the Sublime and the Beautiful*. London: Dodsley.

Bush, Paul Dale. (1987). "The Theory of Institutional Change." *Journal of Economic Issues* 21 (3): 1075–116.

Caldwell, Bruce J. (2004). *Hayek's Challenge: An Intellectual Biography of F. A. Hayek*. Chicago: University of Chicago Press.

Camerer, Colin F. (2003). *Behavioral Game Theory: Experiments in Strategic Interaction*. Princeton, NJ: Princeton University Press.

Camerer, Colin F., and Fehr, Ernst. (2006). "When Does 'Economic Man' Dominate Social Behavior?" *Science*, January 6, pp. 47–52.

Camerer, Colin F., Loewenstein, George, and Prelec, Drazen. (2005). "Neuroeconomics: How Neuroscience Can Inform Economics." *Journal of Economic Literature* 43 (1): 9–64.

Camic, Charles. (1987). "The Making of a Method: A Historical Reinterpretation of the Early Parsons." *American Sociological Review* 52 (4): 421–39.

———. (1989). "*Structure* After 50 Years: The Anatomy of a Charter." *American Journal of Sociology* 95 (1): 38–107.

Campbell, Donald T. (1965). "Variation, Selection and Retention in Sociocultural Evolution." In *Social Change in Developing Areas: A Reinterpretation of Evolutionary Theory*, edited by H. R. Barringer, G. I. Blanksten, and R. W. Mack, 19–49. Cambridge, MA: Schenkman.

Campbell, William F. (1967). "Adam Smith's Theory of Justice, Prudence, and Beneficence." *American Economic Review—Papers and Proceedings* 57 (2): 571–77.

Canterbery, E. Ray, and Marvasti, A. (1994). "Two Coases or Two Theorems." *Journal of Economic Issues* 28 (1): 218–26.

Caporael, Linda, Dawes, Robyn, Orbell, John, and van de Kragt, Alphons. (1989). "Selfishness Examined: Cooperation in the Absence of Egoistic Incentives." *Behavioral and Brain Sciences* 4:683–98.

Carpenter, Jeffrey P., and Matthews, Peter Hans. (2009). "What Norms Trigger Punishment?" *Experimental Economics* 12 (3): 272–88.

Carpenter, Jeffrey P., Matthews, Peter Hans, and Ong'ong'a, Okomboli (2004). "Why Punish? Social Reciprocity and the Enforcement of Prosocial Norms." *Journal of Evolutionary Economics* 14 (4): 407–29.

Carruthers, Peter, and Chamberlain, Andrew, eds. (2000). *Evolution and the Human Mind: Modularity, Language and Meta-Cognition*. Cambridge: Cambridge University Press.

Carter, Richard, and Hodgson, Geoffrey M. (2006). "The Impact of Empirical Tests of Transaction Cost Economics on the Debate on the Nature of the Firm." *Strategic Management Journal* 27 (5): 461–76.

Cartier-Bresson, Jean. (1997). "Corruption Networks, Transaction Security and Illegal Social Exchange." *Political Studies*,45 (3): 463–76.

Casebeer, William D. (2003). *Natural Ethical Facts: Evolution, Connectionism, and Moral Cognition*. Cambridge, MA: MIT Press.

Castro Caldas, José, Narciso Costa, Ana, and Burns, Tom R. (2007). "Rethinking Economics: The Potential Contribution of the Classics."' *Cambridge Journal of Economics* 31 (1): 25–40.

Chalmers, Alan F. (1985). *What Is This Thing Called Science?* Milton Keynes: Open University Press.

Champlin, Dell P., and Knoedler, Janet T. (2008). "Universal Health Care and the Economics of Responsibility." *Journal of Economic Issues* 42 (4): 913–38.

Chang, Ha-Joon. (2002). "Breaking the Mould: An Institutionalist Political Economy Alternative to the Neo-Liberal Theory of the Market and the State." *Cambridge Journal of Economics* 26 (5): 539–59.

Chang, Ha-Joon, and Rowthorn, Robert E., eds. (1995). *The Role of the State in Economic Change.* Oxford: Clarendon Press.

Chapman, Richard A., ed. (1993). *Ethics in Public Service.* Edinburgh: Edinburgh University Press.

Charness, Gary, and Rabin, Matthew. (2002). "Understanding Social Preferences with Simple Tests." *Quarterly Journal of Economics* 117 (3): 817–69.

Cheung, Steven N. S. (1983). "The Contractual Nature of the Firm." *Journal of Law and Economics* 26 (2): 1–21.

Christensen, Paul P. (1991). "Driving Forces, Increasing Returns and Ecological Sustainability." In *Ecological Economics: The Science and Management of Sustainability,* edited by Robert Constanza, 75–87. New York: Columbia University Press.

Churchland, Paul M. (1989) *A Neurocomputational Perspective: The Nature of Mind and the Structure of Science* Cambridge, MA: MIT Press.

Clark, John Maurice. (1923). *Studies in the Economics of Overhead Costs.* Chicago: University of Chicago Press.

Clark, Norman G. (1991). "Organization and Information in the Evolution of Economic Systems." In *Evolutionary Theories of Economic and Technological Change: Present Status and Future Prospects,* edited by Pier Paolo Saviotti and J. Stanley Metcalfe, 88–107. Reading: Harwood.

Clinard, Marshall B. (1990). *Corporate Corruption: The Abuse of Power.* New York: Praeger.

Coase, Ronald H. (1937). "The Nature of the Firm." *Economica,* n.s., 4:386–405.

———. (1960). "The Problem of Social Cost." *Journal of Law and Economics* 3 (1): 1–44.

———. (1976). "Adam Smith's View of Man." *Journal of Law and Economics* 19 (3): 529–46.

———. (1984). "The New Institutional Economics." *Journal of Institutional and Theoretical Economics* 140:229–31.

———. (1988a). *The Firm, the Market, and the Law.* Chicago: University of Chicago Press.

———. (1988b). "The Nature of the Firm: Origin, Meaning, Influence." *Journal of Law, Economics, and Organization* 4 (1): 3–47.

Cohen, Jonathan D. (2005). "The Vulcanization of the Human Brain: A Neural Perspective on the Interactions Between Cognition and Emotion." *Journal of Economic Perspectives* 19 (1): 3–24.

Cohen-Charash, Yochi, and Spector, Paul E. (2001). "The Role of Justice in Organizations: A Meta-Analysis." *Organizational Behavior and Human Decision Processes* 86 (2): 278–321.

Colander, David C. (2005a). "The Future of Economics: The Appropriately Educated in Pursuit of the Knowable." *Cambridge Journal of Economics* 29 (6): 927–41.

———. (2005b). "The Making of an Economist Redux." *Journal of Economic Perspectives* 19 (1): 175–98.

Colander, David C., Holt, Richard P. F., and Rosser, J. Barkley, Jr. (2004a). "The Changing Face of Economics." *Review of Political Economy* 16 (4): 485–99.

———. (2004b). *The Changing Face of Economics: Interviews with Cutting Edge Economists.* Ann Arbor: University of Michigan Press.

Colby, Anne, and Kohlberg, Lawrence. (1987). *The Measurement of Moral Judgement.* Vol. 1. Cambridge: Cambridge University Press.

Collard, David. (1978). *Altruism and Economy: A Study in Non-Selfish Economics* Oxford: Martin Robertson.

Collier, Andrew. (1994). *Critical Realism: An Introduction to Roy Bhaskar's Philosophy.* London: Verso.

Collier, John. (1986). "Entropy and Evolution." *Biology and Philosophy* 1 (1): 5–24.

Collins, Randall, and Hickman, Neal. (1991). "Altruism and Culture as Social Products." *Voluntas* 2 (2): 1–15.

Combs, James G., and Ketchen, David J., Jr. (1999). "Explaining Interfirm Cooperation and Performance: Toward a Reconciliation of Predictions from the Resource-Based View and Organizational Economics." *Strategic Management Journal* 20 (9): 867–88.

Commons, John R. (1924). *Legal Foundations of Capitalism.* New York: Macmillan.

———. (1925). "Marx To-Day: Capitalism and Socialism." *Atlantic Monthly,* November, 682–93.

———. (1934). *Institutional Economics—Its Place in Political Economy.* New York: Macmillan.

Conner, Kathleen R., and Prahalad, C. K. (1996). "A Resource-Based Theory of the Firm: Knowledge versus Opportunism." *Organization Science* 7 (5): 477–501.

Connolly, Sheelah, Bevan, Gwyn, and Mays, Nicholas. (2010). *Funding and Performance of Healthcare Systems in the Four Countries of the UK before and after Devolution.* London: Nuffield Trust.

Cook, Scott D. N., and Yanow, Dvora. (1993). "Culture and Organizational Learning." *Journal of Management Inquiry* 2 (4): 373–90. Reprinted in *Organizational Learning,* edited by Michael D. Cohen and Lee S. Sproull. London: Sage, 1996.

Cordes, Christian, Richerson, Peter, McElreath, Richard, and Strimling, Pontus. (2008). "A Naturalistic Approach to the Theory of the Firm: The Role of Cooperation and Cultural Evolution." *Journal of Economic Behavior and Organization* 68 (1): 125–39.

———. (2011). "How Does Opportunistic Behavior Influence Firm Size? An Evolutionary Approach to Organizational Behavior." *Journal of Institutional Economics* 7 (1): 1–21.

Corning, Peter A. (2000). "Biological Adaptation in Human Societies: A 'Basic Needs' Approach." *Journal of Bioeconomics* 2:41–86.

———. (2011). *The Fair Society: The Science of Human Nature and the Pursuit of Social Justice.* Chicago: University of Chicago Press.

Cosmides, Leda. (1989). "The Logic of Social Exchange: Has Natural Selection Shaped How Humans Reason? Studies with the Wason Selection Task." *Cognition* 31: 187–276.

Cosmides, Leda, and Tooby, John. (1994a). "Better than Rational: Evolutionary Psychology and the Invisible Hand." *American Economic Review (Papers and Proceedings)* 84 (2): 327–32.

———. (1994b). "Beyond Intuition and Instinct Blindness: Towards an Evolutionary Rigorous Cognitive Science." *Cognition* 50 (1–3): 41–77.

Crawford, Sue E. S., and Ostrom, Elinor. (1995). "A Grammar of Institutions." *American Political Science Review* 89 (3): 582–600.

Cropanzano, Russell, Prehar, Cynthia A. and Chen, Peter Y. (2002). "Using Social Exchange Theory to Distinguish Procedural from Interactional Justice." *Group Organization Management* 27 (3): 324–51.

Cropper, Maureen L., and Oates, Wallace E. (1992). "Environmental Economics: A Survey." *Journal of Economic Literature* 30 (2): 675–740.

Crutchfield, James P., and Schuster, Peter. (2003). *Evolutionary Dynamics: Exploring the Interplay of Selection, Accident, Neutrality, and Function.* Oxford: Oxford University Press.

Culyer, Anthony J., ed. (1991). *The Economics of Health.* 2 vols. Aldershot: Edward Elgar.

———. (1995). "Need: The Idea Won't Do—But We Still Need It." *Social Science and Medicine* 40 (6): 727–30.

Culyer, Anthony J., Lavers, R. J., and Williams, Alan. (1971). "Social Indicators: Health." *Social Trends* 2:31–42.

Culyer, Anthony J., Maynard, Alan K., and Williams, Alan. (1981). "Alternative Systems of Health Care Provision: An Essay on Motes and Beams." In *A New Approach to the Economics of Health Care,* edited by Mancur Olson, 131–50. Washington: American Enterprise Institute.

Culyer, Anthony J., and Newhouse, Joseph P., eds. (2000). *Handbook of Health Economics.* Amsterdam: Elsevier.

Culyer, Anthony J., and Wagstaff, A. (1993). "Equity and Equality in Health and Health Care." *Journal of Health Economics* 12:431–57.

Cunynghame, Henry. (1892). "Some Improvements in Simple Geometrical Methods of Treating Exchange Value, Monopoly and Rent." *Economic Journal* 2 (1), March, pp. 35–52.

Daly, Herman E., and Cobb, John B., Jr. (1990). *For the Common Good: Redirecting the Economy Towards Community, the Environment and a Sustainable Future.* London: Green Print.

Damasio, Antonio R. (1994). *Descartes' Error: Emotion, Reason, and the Human Brain.* New York: Putnam.

Danielson, Peter A. (1992). *Artificial Morality: Virtuous Robots for Virtual Games.* London: Routledge.

———, ed. (1998). *Modeling Rationality, Morality and Evolution.* Oxford: Oxford University Press.

Darwin, Charles R. (1859). *On the Origin of Species by Means of Natural Selection, or the Preservation of Favoured Races in the Struggle for Life.* London: Murray.

———. (1871). *The Descent of Man, and Selection in Relation to Sex.* 2 vols. London: Murray.

———. (1872). *The Expression of the Emotions in Man and Animals.* London: John Murray.

Dasgupta, Partha. (1991). "The Environment as a Commodity." In *Economic Policy Towards the Environment,* edited by Dieter Helm, 25–51. Oxford: Basil Blackwell.

David, Robert J., and Han, Shin-Kap. (2004). "A Systematic Assessment of the Empirical Support for Transaction Cost Economics." *Strategic Management Journal* 25 (1): 39–58.

Davis, Douglas D., and Holt, Charles A. (1993) *Experimental Economics.* Princeton, NJ: Princeton University Press.

Davis, John B., ed. (2001). *The Social Economics of Health Care.* London: Routledge.

———. (2003). *The Theory of the Individual in Economics: Identity and Value.* London: Routledge.

———. (2006). "The Turn in Economics: Neoclassical Dominance to Mainstream Pluralism?" *Journal of Institutional Economics* 2 (1): 1–20.

———. (2007). "Akerlof and Kranton on Identity in Economics: Inverting the Analysis." *Cambridge Journal of Economics* 31 (3): 349–62.

———. (2011). *Individuals and Identity in Economics*. Cambridge: Cambridge University Press.

Davis, Michael. (1987). "Nozick's Argument *for* the Legitimacy of the Welfare State." *Ethics* 97:576–94.

Dawes, Robyn M., and Thaler, Richard H. (1988). "Anomalies: Cooperation." *Journal of Economic Perspectives* 2 (3): 187–97.

Dawkins, Richard. (1976). *The Selfish Gene*. Oxford: Oxford University Press.

———. (2003). *The Devil's Chaplain: Reflections on Hope, Lies, Science, and Love*. Boston: Houghton Mifflin.

———. (2006). *The God Delusion*. Boston: Houghton Mifflin.

Deacon, Terrence W. (1997). *The Symbolic Species: The Co-Evolution of Language and the Brain*. New York: Norton.

Deakin, Simon. (1998). "The Evolution of the Contract of Employment, 1900–1950: The Influence of the Welfare State." In *Governance, Industry and Labour Markets in Britain and France: The Modernising State in the Mid-Twentieth Century*, edited by Noel Whiteside and Robert Salais, 213–30. London: Routledge.

Deci, Edward L. (1975). *Intrinsic Motivation*. New York: Plenum Press.

Deci, Edward L., and Ryan, Richard M. (2000a). "Self-Determination Theory and the Facilitation of Intrinsic Motivation, Social Development, and Well-Being." *American Psychologist* 55 (1): 68–78.

———. (2000b). "The 'What' and 'Why' of Goal Pursuits: Human Needs and the Self-Determination of Behavior." *Psychological Inquiry* 11 (4): 227–68.

De Jong, G. (1994). "The Fitness of Fitness Concepts and the Description of Natural Selection." *Quarterly Review of Biology* 69 (1): 3–29.

De la Porte, Caroline, Pochet, Philippe, and Room, Graham. (2001). "Social Benchmarking, Policy Making and New Governance in the EU." *Journal of European Social Policy* 11 (4): 291–307.

Demsetz, Harold. (2011). "The Problem of Social Cost: What Problem? A Critique of the Reasoning of A. C. Pigou and R. H. Coase." *Review of Law and Economics* 7 (1): 1–13.

Dennett, Daniel C. (1995). *Darwin's Dangerous Idea: Evolution and the Meanings of Life*. London: Allen Lane.

De Soto, Hernando. (2000). *The Mystery of Capital: Why Capitalism Triumphs in the West and Fails Everywhere Else*. New York: Basic Books.

Devlin, Patrick. (1965). *The Enforcement of Morals*. Oxford: Oxford University Press.

de Waal, Frans B. M. (1982). *Chimpanzee Politics: Power and Sex Among Apes*. New York: Harper and Row and Jonathan Cape.

———. (1996). *Good Natured: The Origin of Right and Wrong in Humans and Other Animals*. Cambridge, MA: Harvard University Press.

———. (2006). *Primates and Philosophers: How Morality Evolved*. Princeton, NJ: Princeton University Press.

Dewey, John. (1910). *The Influence of Darwin on Philosophy and Other Essays in Contemporary Philosophy*. New York: Henry Holt.

———. (1916). *Democracy and Education*. New York: Macmillan.

———. (1922). *Human Nature and Conduct: An Introduction to Social Psychology*. New York: Henry Holt.

———. (1929). *The Quest for Certainty: A Study of the Relation of Knowledge and Action*. New York: Minton, Balch.

———. (1935). *Liberalism and Social Action*. New York: G. P. Putnam's Sons.

———. (1938). *Logic: The Theory of Enquiry*. New York: Henry Holt.

———. (1939). *Theory of Valuation*. Chicago: University of Chicago Press.

Dewey, John, and Tufts, James H. (1932). *Ethics*. Rev. ed. New York: Henry Holt.

Diamond, Jared. (1991). *The Rise and Fall of the Third Chimpanzee*. London: Vintage.

Dickenson, Henry D. (1933). "Price Formation in a Socialist Community." *Economic Journal* 43:237–50.

———. (1939). *Economics of Socialism*. Oxford: Oxford University Press.

Di Tella, Rafael, and MacCulloch, Robert. (2006). 'Some Uses of Happiness Data in Economics,' *Journal of Economic Perspectives*, 20(1), Winter, pp. 25–46.

Dixon, Anna, and Mossialos, Elias, eds. (2002). *Health Care Systems in Eight Countries: Trends and Challenges*. London: European Observatory on Health Care Systems and London School of Economics and Political Science.

Dixon, Robert. (1999). "The Origin of the Term 'Dismal Science' to Describe Economics." Working Paper No 1999/715, Department of Economics, University of Melbourne.

Doeringer, Peter B., and Piore, Michael J. (1971). *Internal Labor Markets and Manpower Analysis*. Lexington, MA: Heath.

Donato, R. (2010). "Extending Transaction Cost Economics: Towards a Synthesised Approach for Analysing Contracting in Health Care Markets with Experience from the Australian Private Sector." *Social Science and Medicine* 71 (11): 1989–96.

Dopfer, Kurt. (2004). "The Economic Agent as Rule Maker and Rule User: *Homo Sapiens Oeconomicus*." *Journal of Evolutionary Economics* 14 (2): 177–95.

Dopfer, Kurt, Foster, John, and Potts, Jason. (2004). "Micro-Meso-Macro." *Journal of Evolutionary Economics* 14 (3): 263–79.

Dore, Ronald P. (1961). "Function and Cause." *American Journal of Sociology* 26 (6): 843–53.

———. (1983). "Goodwill and the Spirit of Market Capitalism." *British Journal of Sociology* 34 (4): 459–82.

Dosi, Giovanni, and Marengo, Luigi. (1994). "Some Elements of an Evolutionary Theory of Organizational Competences." In *Evolutionary Concepts in Contemporary Economics*, edited by Richard W. England, 157–78. Ann Arbor: University of Michigan Press.

Douglas, Mary T. (1966). *Purity and Danger: An Analysis of Concepts of Pollution and Taboo*. London: Routledge and Kegan Paul.

———. (1986). *How Institutions Think*. London: Routledge and Kegan Paul.

———. (1990). "Converging on Autonomy: Anthropology and Institutional Economics." In *Organization Theory: From Chester Barnard to the Present and Beyond*, edited by Oliver E. Williamson, 98–115. Oxford: Oxford University Press.

Doyal, Leonard, and Gough, Ian. (1991). *A Theory of Human Need*. London: Macmillan.

Dunn, Stephen P. (2006). "Prolegomena to a Post Keynesian Health Economics." *Review of Social Economy* 64 (3): 273–99.

Dupré, John A., ed. (1987). *The Latest on the Best: Essays on Evolution and Optimality*. Cambridge, MA: MIT Press.

Durham, William H. (1991). *Coevolution: Genes, Culture, and Human Diversity*. Stanford, CA: Stanford University Press.

Durkheim, Émile. (1982). *The Rules of Sociological Method*. Translated from the French edition of 1901 by W. D. Halls, with an introduction by Steven Lukes. London: Macmillan.

———. (1984). *The Division of Labour in Society*. Translated from the French edition of 1893 by W. D. Halls with an introduction by Lewis Coser (London: Macmillan).

Earl, Peter E. (2010). "Economics Fit for the Queen: A Pessimistic Assessment of Its Prospects." *Prometheus* 28 (3): 209–25.

Easterlin, Richard A. (1995) 'Will Raising the Incomes of all Increase the Happiness of All?' *Journal of Economic Behavior and Organization*, 27(1), June, pp. 35–47.

Eccles, Robert G. (1981). "The Quasifirm in the Construction Industry." *Journal of Economic Behavior and Organization* 2:335–57.

Eckstein, Susan. (2001). "Community as Gift-Giving: Collective Roots of Volunteerism." *American Sociological Review* 66 (6): 829–51.

Edgeworth, Francis Y. (1881). *Mathematical Psychics: An Essay on the Application of Mathematics to the Moral Sciences*. London: Kegan Paul.

Ehrlich, Paul R. (2000). *Human Natures: Genes, Cultures and the Human Prospect*. Washington DC: Island Press.

Eibl-Eibesfeldt, Irenäus. (1989). *Human Ethology*. New York, Aldine de Gruyter.

Eisenhauer, Joseph G. (2008). "Ethical Preferences, Risk Aversion and Taxpayer Behavior." *Journal of Socio-Economics* 37 (1): 45–63.

Eisenhauer, Joseph G., Geide-Stevenson, Doris, and Ferro, David L. (2011). "Experimental Estimates of Taxpayer Ethics," *Review of Social Economy* 69 (1): 29–53.

Ekelund, Robert B., Jr., and Hébert, Robert F. (2002). "The Origins of Neoclassical Economics."*Journal of Economic Perspectives* 16 (3): 197–215.

Elder-Vass, Dave. (2010a). *The Causal Power of Social Structures*. Cambridge: Cambridge University Press.

Elder-Vass, Dave. (2010b). "Realist Critique without Ethical Naturalism and Moral Realism." *Journal of Critical Realism* 9 (1): 33–58.

Ellman, Michael. (1989). *Socialist Planning*. 2nd ed. Cambridge: Cambridge University Press.

Elster, Jon. (1982). "Marxism, Functionalism and Game Theory." *Theory and Society* 11 (4): 453–82.

———. (1985). *Making Sense of Marx*. Cambridge: Cambridge University Press.

———. (1986). *The Multiple Self*. Cambridge: Cambridge University Press.

———. (1998). "Emotions and Economic Theory." *Journal of Economic Literature* 36 (1): 47–74.

Engelman, Dirk, and Fischbacher, Urs. (2009). "Indirect Reciprocity and Strategic Reputation Building in an Experimental Helping Game." *Games and Economic Behavior* 67 (2): 399–407.

Etzioni, Amitai. (1968). "Basic Human Needs, Alienation and Inauthenticity." *American Sociological Review* 33 (6): 870–85.

———. (1988). *The Moral Dimension: Toward a New Economics*. New York: Free Press.

———. (1999). *Essays in Socio-Economics*. Berlin: Springer.

Evans, David B., Tandon, Ajay, Murray, Christopher J. L., and Lauer, Jeremy A. (2001). "Comparative Efficiency of National Health Systems: Cross National Econometric Analysis." *British Medical Journal* 323:307–10.

Evans, Karen G. (2000). "Reclaiming John Dewey: Democracy, Inquiry, Pragmatism, and Public Management." *Administration and Society* 32 (3): 308–28.

Evans, Nicholas, and Levinson, Stephen C. (2009). "The Myth of Language Universals: Language Diversity and Its Importance for Cognitive Science." *Behavioral and Brain Sciences* 32 (5): 429–92.

Evans, Peter, and Rauch, James E. (1999). "Bureaucracy and Growth: A Cross-National Analysis of the Effects of 'Weberian' State Structures on Economic Growth." *American Sociological Review* 64:748–65.

Evans, Robert G. (1974). "Supplier-Induced Demand: Some Empirical Evidence and Implications." In *The Economics of Health and Medical Care*, edited by Mark Perlman, 162–73. London: Macmillan.

Evensky, Jerry. (2005a). *Adam Smith's Moral Philosophy: A Historical and Contemporary Perspective on Markets, Laws, Ethics, and Culture.* Cambridge: Cambridge University Press.

———. (2005b) "Adam Smith's Theory of Moral Sentiments: On Morals and Why They Matter to a Liberal Society of Free People and Free Markets." *Journal of Economic Perspectives* 19 (3): 109–30.

Fama, Eugene F. (1980). "Agency Problems and the Theory of the Firm." *Journal of Political Economy* 88 (2): 288–307.

Farrar, Shelley, Yi, Deokhee, Sutton, Matt, Chalkley, Martin, Sussex, Jon, and Scott, Anthony. (2009). "Has Payment by Results Affected the Way That English Hospitals Provide Care? Difference-in-Differences Analysis." *British Medical Journal* 339:b3047.

Fehr, Ernst, and Camerer, Colin F. (2007). "Social Neuroeconomics: The Neural Circuitry of Social Preferences." *Trends in Cognitive Science* 11 (1): 419–27.

Fehr, Ernst, and Falk, Armin. (2002a). "Psychological Foundations of Incentives." *European Economic Review* 46 (4): 687–724.

———. (2002b). "Reciprocal Fairness, Cooperation and Limits to Competition." In *Intersubjectivity in Economics: Agents and Structures*, edited by Edward Fullbrook, 28–44. London: Routledge.

Fehr, Ernst, and Fischbacher, Urs. (2002). "Why Do Social Preferences Matter—The Impact of Non-Selfish Motives on Competition, Cooperation and Incentives." *Economic Journal* 112:C1–C33.

Fehr, Ernst, and Gächter, Simon. (2000a). "Cooperation and Punishment in Public Goods Experiments." *American Economic Review* 90 (4): 980–95.

———. (2000b). "Fairness and Retaliation: The Economics of Reciprocity." *Journal of Economic Perspectives* 14 (3): 159–81.

———. (2002). "Altruistic Punishment in Humans." *Nature* 415:137–40.

Fehr, Ernst, and Gintis, Herbert. (2007). "Human Motivation and Social Cooperation: Experimental and Analytical Foundations." *Annual Review of Sociology* 33:3.1–3.22.

Felin, Teppo, and Foss, Nicolai J. (2009). "Social Reality, the Boundaries of Self-Fulfilling Prophecy, and Economics."*Organization Science* 20 (3): 654–68.

Field, Alexander J. (1979). "On the Explanation of Rules Using Rational Choice Models." *Journal of Economic Issues* 13 (1): 49–72.

———. (1981). "The Problem with Neoclassical Institutional Economics: A Critique with Special Reference to the North/Thomas Model of Pre-1500 Europe." *Explorations in Economic History* 18 (2): 174–98.

———. (1984). "Microeconomics, Norms and Rationality." *Economic Development and Cultural Change* 32 (4): 683–711.

———. (1991). "Do Legal Systems Matter?" *Explorations in Economic History* 28 (1): 1–35.

———. (2001). *Altruistically Inclined? The Behavioral Sciences, Evolutionary Theory, and the Origins of Reciprocity.* Ann Arbor: University of Michigan Press.

———. (2007). "Beyond Foraging: Evolutionary Theory, Institutional Variation, and Economic Performance." *Journal of Institutional Economics* 3 (3): 265–91.

———. (2008). "Why Multilevel Selection Matters." *Journal of Bioeconomics* 10 (3): 203–28.

Fishburn, Peter C. (1970). *Utility Theory for Decision Makers.* New York: Wiley.

Fiske, Alan Page. (1991). *Structures of Social Life: The Four Elementary Forms of Human Relations: Communal Sharing, Authority Ranking, Equality Matching, Market Pricing.* New York: Free Press.

Fitzgibbons, Athol. (1995). *Adam Smith's System of Liberty, Wealth and Virtue: The Moral and Political Foundations of "The Wealth of Nations."* Oxford: Oxford University Press.

Fleischacker, Samuel (2004). *On Adam Smith's Wealth of Nations: A Philosophical Companion*. Princeton, NJ: Princeton University Press.

Fligstein, Neil. (1996). "Markets as Politics: A Political-Cultural Approach to Market Institutions." *American Sociological Review* 61 (4): 656–73.

———. (2001). *The Architecture of Markets: An Economic Sociology of Twenty-First Century Capitalist Societies*. Princeton, NJ: Princeton University Press.

Flood, Merrill M. (1958). "Some Experimental Games." *Management Science* 5 (1): 5–26.

Fodor, Jerry. (1983). *The Modularity of Mind*. Cambridge, MA: MIT Press.

Fogel, Robert William. (2004). *The Escape from Hunger and Premature Death, 1700–2100: Europe, America, and the Third World*. Cambridge: Cambridge University Press.

Folbre, Nancy (1995). "'Holding Hands at Midnight': The Paradox of Caring Labor." *Feminist Economics* 1 (1): 73–92.

———. (2009). *Greed, Lust and Gender: A History of Economic Ideas*. Oxford: Oxford University Press.

Folbre, Nancy, and Nelson, Julie A. (2000). "For Love or Money—Or Both?" *Journal of Economic Perspectives* 14 (4): 123–40.

Foley, Caroline A. (1893). "Fashion." *Economic Journal* 3 (3): 458–74.

Foot, Philippa. (1976). "The Problem of Abortion and the Doctrine of the Double Effect." In *Virtues and Vices and Other Essays in Moral Philosophy*, 19–32. Oxford: Basil Blackwell.

Foss, Nicolai Juul. (1993). "Theories of the Firm: Contractual and Competence Perspectives." *Journal of Evolutionary Economics* 3 (2): 127–44.

———. (1996). "Firms, Incomplete Contracts, and Organizational Learning." *Human Systems Management* 15 (1): 17–26.

Foss, Nicolai Juul, and Knudsen, Christian, eds. (1996). *Towards a Competence Theory of the Firm*. London: Routledge.

Foster, John Fagg. (1981). "The Relation Between the Theory of Value and Economic Analysis." *Journal of Economic Issues* 15 (4): 899–905.

Foxon, Timothy J. (2011). "A Coevolutionary Framework for Analysing a Transition to a Sustainable Low Carbon Economy." *Ecological Economics* 70 (12): 2258–67.

Franco, Lynne Miller, Bennett, Sara, and Kanfer, Ruth. (2002). "Health Sector Reform and Public Sector Health Worker Motivation: A Conceptual Framework." *Social Science and Medicine* 54 (8): 1255–66.

Frank, Robert H. (1987). "If Homo Economicus Could Choose His Own Utility Function, Would He Want One With a Conscience?" *American Economic Review* 77 (3): 593–604.

———. (1988). *Passions Within Reason: The Strategic Role of the Emotions*. New York: Norton.

———. (1993). "The Strategic Role of the Emotions: Reconciling Over- and Undersocialized Accounts of Behavior." *Rationality and Society* 5 (2): 160–84.

———. (1994). "Group Selection and 'Genuine' Altruism." *Behavioral and Brain Sciences* 17 (4): 620–21.

———. (1999). *Luxury Fever: Why Money Fails to Satisfy in an Era of Excess*. New York: Free Press.

———. (2011). *The Darwin Economy: Liberty, Competition, and the Common Good*. Princeton, NJ: Princeton University Press.

Frank, Robert H., Gilovich, Thomas, and Regan, Dennis T. (1993). "Does Studying Economics Inhibit Cooperation?" *Journal of Economic Perspectives* 7 (2): 159–71.

———. (1996). "Do Economists Make Bad Citizens?" *Journal of Economic Perspectives* 10 (1): 187–92.

Frey, Bruno S. (1992). "Tertium Datur: Pricing, Regulating and Intrinsic Motivation." *Kyklos* 45 (2): 161–84.

———. (1997a). *Not Just for Money: An Economic Theory of Personal Motivation.* Aldershot: Edward Elgar.

———. (1997b). "On the Relationship between Intrinsic and Extrinsic Work Motivation." *International Journal of Industrial Organization* 15:427–39.

Frey, Bruno S., and Bohnet, Iris. (1995). "Institutions Affect Fairness: Experimental Investigations." *Journal of Institutional and Theoretical Economics* 151 (2): 286–303.

Frey, Bruno S., and Jegen, Reto. (2001). "Motivation Crowding Theory." *Journal of Economic Surveys* 15 (5): 589–623.

Frey, Bruno S., and Stutzer, Alois (2000) 'Happiness, Economy and Institutions,' *Economic Journal*, 110(7), October, pp. 918–38.

———. (2002) *Happiness and Economics: How the Economy and Institutions Affect Well-Being* Princeton, NJ: Princeton University Press.

———. (2005) 'Happiness Research: State and Prospects,' *Review of Social Economy*, 62(2), June, pp. 206–28.

Friedman, Allen, and Schwarz, Ted. (1989). *Power and Greed: Inside the Teamsters Empire of Corruption.* New York: Franklin Watts.

Friedman, Daniel. (2008). *Morals and Markets: An Evolutionary Account of the Modern World.* London: Palgrave Macmillan.

Friedman, James W. (1971). "A Non-Cooperative Equilibrium for Supergames." *Review of Economic Studies* 38 (1): 1–12.

Friedman, Milton. (1953). "The Methodology of Positive Economics." In *Essays in Positive Economics*, 3–43. Chicago: University of Chicago Press.

Froud, Julie, Haslam, Colin, Johal, Sukhdev, and Williams, Karel. (2000). "Shareholder Value and Financialization: Consultancy Promises, Management Moves." *Economy and Society* 29 (1): 80–110.

Fukuyama, Francis. (1999). *The Great Disruption: Human Nature and the Reconstitution of Social Order.* New York: Free Press.

Fullbrook, Edward (1998). "Caroline Foley and the Theory of Intersubjective Demand." *Journal of Economic Issues* 32 (3): 709–31.

Fuller, Lon L. (1967). *Legal Fictions.* Stanford, CA: Stanford University Press.

———. (1969). *The Morality of Law.* Rev. ed. New Haven, CT: Yale University Press.

Gagliardi, Francesca. (2009). "Financial Development and the Growth of Cooperative Firms." *Small Business Economics* 32 (4): 439–64.

Galbraith, John Kenneth. (1958). *The Affluent Society.* London: Hamilton.

Galbraith, James K., and Berner, Maureen, eds. (2001). *Inequality and Industrial Change: A Global View.* Cambridge: Cambridge University Press.

Gardiner, John A. (1993). "Defining Corruption." *Corruption and Reform* 7 (2): 111–24.

Garrouste, Pierre, and Saussier, Stéphane. (2005). "Looking for a Theory of the Firm: Future Challenges." *Journal of Economic Behavior and Organization* 58 (2): 178–99.

Gefter, Amanda, and Harris, Sam. (2010). "Crusader for Science." *New Scientist* 16: 46–47.

Georgescu-Roegen, Nicholas. (1971). *The Entropy Law and the Economic Process.* Cambridge, MA: Harvard University Press.

Gerschlager, Caroline, ed. (2005). *Deception in Markets: An Economic Analysis.* Basingstoke: Palgrave Macmillan.

Ghiselin, Michael T. (1974). *The Economy of Nature and the Evolution of Sex.* Berkeley: University of California Press.

Gilbert, Margaret. (1989). *On Social Facts.* London: Routledge.

———. (2001). "Social Rules as Plural Subject Phenomena." In *On the Nature of Social and Institutional Reality,* edited by Eerik Lagerspetz, Heikki Ikäheimo, and Jussi Kotkavirta, 1–31. Jyväskylä: SoPhi Academic Press.

Gindis, David. (2007). "Some Building Blocks for a Theory of the Firm as a Real Entity." In *The Firm as an Entity: Implications for Economics, Accounting and Law,* edited by in Yuri Biondi, Arnaldo Canziani, and Thierry Kirat, 266–91. London: Routledge.

———. (2009) "From Fictions and Aggregates to Real Entities in the Theory of the Firm." *Journal of Institutional Economics* 5 (1): 25–46.

Gintis, Herbert. (1972). "A Radical Analysis of Welfare Economics and Individual Development." *Quarterly Journal of Economics* 86 (4): 572–99.

———. (1974). "Welfare Criteria with Endogenous Preferences: The Economics of Education." *International Economic Review* 15 (2): 415–30.

———. (2000). "Strong Reciprocity and Human Sociality." *Journal of Theoretical Biology* 206:169–79.

———. (2006). "Behavioral Ethics Meets Natural Justice." *Politics, Philosophy and Economics* 5 (1): 5–32.

———. (2007). "A Framework for the Integration of the Behavioral Sciences." *Behavioral and Brain Sciences* 30 (1): 1–16.

———. (2009). *The Bounds of Reason: Game Theory and the Unification of the Behavioral Sciences.* Princeton NJ: Princeton University Press.

Gintis, Herbert, Bowles, Samuel, Boyd, Robert, and Fehr, Ernst, eds. (2005). *Moral Sentiments and Material Interests: The Foundations of Cooperation in Economic Life.* Cambridge, MA: MIT Press.

Glaeser, Edward L., Johnson, Simon, and Shleifer, Andrei. (2001). "Coase versus the Coaseans." *Quarterly Journal of Economics* 116 (3): 853–99.

Glimcher, Paul W., Dorris, Michael C., and Bayer, Hannah M. (2005). "Physiologic Utility Theory and the Neuroeconomics of Choice." *Games and Economic Behavior* 52:213–56.

Gneezy, Uri, and List, John A. (2006). "Putting Behavioral Economics to Work: Testing for Gift Exchange in Labor Markets Using Field Experiments." *Econometrica* 74 (5): 1365–84.

Goddard, Maria, Hauck, Katharina, Preker, Alex, and Smith, Peter C. (2006). "Priority Setting in Health—A Political Economy Perspective." *Health Economics Policy and Law* 1 (1): 79–90.

Godfrey-Smith, Peter. (2002). "Dewey on Naturalism, Realism and Science." *Philosophy of Science* 69:S25–S35.

Goldberg, Victor P. (1980). "Relational Exchange: Economics and Complex Contracts." *American Behavioral Scientist* 23 (3): 337–52.

Goodall, Jane. (1986). *The Chimpanzees of Gombe.* Cambridge, MA: Harvard University Press.

Goode, Richard, and Griffiths, Paul E. (1995). "The Misuse of Sober's Selection for/Selection of Distinction." *Biology and Philosophy* 10 (1): 99–108.

Gordon, Barry J. (1964). "Aristotle and the Development of Value Theory." *Quarterly Journal of Economics* 78 (1): 115–28.

Gorsky, Martin. (2011). "Coalition Policy Towards the NHS: Past Contexts and Current

Trajectories." History & Policy, January. http://www.historyandpolicy.org/papers/policy-paper-111.html.

Gough, Ian. (2000). *Global Capital, Human Needs and Social Policies*. Basingstoke: Palgrave Macmillan.

———. (2004). "Human Well-Being and Social Structures: Relating the Universal and the Local." *Global Social Policy* 4:289–311.

Gouinlock, James. (1978). "Dewey's Theory of Moral Deliberation." *Ethics* 88 (3): 218–28.

Government of Canada. (1994). "Improving Social Security in Canada—Guaranteed Annual Income: A Supplementary Paper." http://www.canadiansocialresearch.net/ssrgai.htm#Disposable.

Gowdy, John M. (2004). "Altruism, Evolution, and Welfare Economics." *Journal of Economic Behavior and Organization* 53 (1): 69–73.

Gowdy, John M., and Iorgulescu Polimeni, Raluca. (2005). "The Death of Homo Economicus." *International Journal of Social Economics* 32 (11): 924–38.

Graaff, Jan de V. (1957). *Theoretical Welfare Economics*. Cambridge: Cambridge University Press.

Graham, Jesse, Haidt, Jonathan and Nosek, Brian A. (2009). "Liberals and Conservatives Use Different Sets of Moral Foundations." *Journal of Personality and Social Psychology* 96:1029–46.

Granovetter, Mark. (1985). "Economic Action and Social Structure: The Problem of Embeddedness." *American Journal of Sociology* 91 (3): 481–510.

Gray, John. (1993). *Post-Liberalism*. London: Routledge.

Green, David G., and Casper, Laura. (2000). *Delay, Denial and Dilution: The Impact of NHS Rationing on Heart Disease and Cancer*. London: Institute for Economic Affairs.

Green, Donald, and Shapiro, Ian. (1994). *Pathologies of Rational Choice Theory: A Critique of Applications in Political Science*. New Haven, CT: Yale University Press.

Greenberg, Daniel S. (2007). *Science for Sale: The Perils, Rewards, and Delusions of Campus Capitalism*. Chicago: University of Chicago Press.

Greene, J. D., and Haidt, Jonathan (2002). "How (and Where) Does Moral Judgement Work?" *Trends in Cognitive Sciences* 6 (12): 517–23.

Grossman, Sanford J., and Hart, Oliver D. (1986). "The Costs and Benefits of Ownership: A Theory of Vertical and Lateral Integration." *Journal of Political Economy* 94 (4): 691–719.

Gruber, Howard E. (1974). *Darwin on Man: A Psychological Study of Scientific Creativity, together with Darwin's Early and Unpublished Notebooks*. Transcribed and annotated by P. H. Barret. New York: Dutton.

Guardian. (2010). "US Embassy Cables: Russia Is Virtual 'Mafia State,' Says Spanish Investigator." Guardian, December 2. http://www.guardian.co.uk/world/us-embassy-cables-documents/247712.

———. (2011). "News of the World Phone Hacking." Guardian, July 6. http://www.guardian.co.uk/politics/blog/2011/jul/06/news-of-the-world-phone-hacking-live#block-26.

Gui, Benedetto, and Sugden, Robert. (2005). *Economixs and Social Interaction: Accounting for Interpersonal Relations*. Cambridge: Cambridge University Press.

Güth, Werner. (1995). "On Ultimatum Bargaining Experiments—A Personal Review." *Journal of Economic Behavior* 27:329–44.

Guzmán, Ricardo Andrés, Rodriguez-Sicken, Carlos, and Rowthorn, Robert. (2007).

"When in Rome, Do as the Romans Do: The Coevolution of Altruistic Punishment, Conformist Learning, and Cooperation." *Evolution and Human Behavior* 28:112–17.

Haas, Peter M. (1992). "Introduction: Epistemic Communities and International Policy Coordination." *International Organization* 46 (1): 1–35.

Habermas, Jürgen. (1991). "What Is Universal Pragmatics?" In *Communication and the Evolution of Society*, edited by Thomas McCarthy, 1–68. Cambridge: Polity.

———. (1993). *Justification and Application*. Cambridge: Polity.

Hagstrom, Warren O. (1965). *The Scientific Community*. New York: Basic Books.

Hahnel, Robin, and Sheeran, Kristen A. (2009). "Misinterpreting the Coase Theorem." *Journal of Economic Issues* 43 (1): 215–38.

Haidt, Jonathan. (2001). "The Emotional Dog and the Rational Tail: A Social Interactionist Approach to Moral Judgment." *Psychological Review* 108:814–34.

Haidt, Jonathan, and Joseph, Craig. (2004). "Intuitive Ethics: How Innately Prepared Intuitions Generate Culturally Variable Virtues." *Daedalus* 133 (4): 55–66.

———. (2008). "The Moral Mind: How Five Sets of Innate Intuitions Guide the Development of Many Culture-Specific Virtues, and Perhaps Even Modules." In *The Innate Mind*, edited by Peter Carruthers, S. Laurence, and S. Stich, 3:367–444.

Hall, Peter A., and Soskice, David. (2001). *Varieties of Capitalism: The Institutional Foundations of Comparative Advantage*. Oxford: Oxford University Press.

Hamilton, Walton H. (1932). "Statement by Walton H. Hamilton." In *Medical Care for the American People*, 189–200. Chicago: University of Chicago Press.

Hamilton, William D. (1964). "The Genetical Evolution of Social Behavior." *Journal of Theoretical Biology* 7 (1): 1–32.

Hamlin, J. Kiley, Wynn, Karen, and Bloom, Paul. (2007). "Social Evaluation by Preverbal Infants." *Nature* 450:557–60.

Hammermesh, Daniel S., and Soss, Neal M. (1974). "An Economic Theory of Suicide." *Journal of Political Economy* 82 (1): 83–98.

Hammersley, Martin. (2002). "Research as Emancipatory: The Case of Bhaskar's Critical Realism." *Journal of Critical Realism* 1 (1): 33–48.

Hammerstein, Peter, ed. (2003a). *Genetic and Cultural Evolution of Cooperation*. Cambridge, MA: MIT Press.

———, ed. (2003b). "Why Is Reciprocity So Rare in Social Animals?" In Hammerstein (2003a), 83–93.

Hanemann, W. Michael. (1995). "Contingent Valuation and Economics." In *Environmental Valuation: New Perspectives*, edited by K. G. Willis and J. T. Corkindale. Cheltenham: CAB International.

Hansard. (1997). "Hospital Waiting Lists." http://www.publications.parliament.uk/pa/cm199798/cmhansrd/v0980630/debtext/80630–04.htm. Retrieved 30 June 2006.

———. (1998). "National Health Service." http://www.parliament.the-stationery-office.co.uk/pa/ld199899/ldhansrd/v0981209/text/81209–05.htm. Retrieved 30 June 2006.

———. (2002). "Column 1071." http://www.publications.parliament.uk/pa/cm200102/cmhansrd/v0020124/debtext/20124–18.htm. Retrieved 30 June 2006.

Hansmann, Henry, Kraakman, Reinier, and Squire, Richard. (2006). "Law and the Rise of the Firm." *Harvard Law Review* 119 (5): 1333–1403.

Hardin, Garrett. (1968). "The Tragedy of the Commons." *Science* 162:1243–48.

Harding, Sandra G., ed. (1976). *Can Theories Be Refuted? Essays on the Duhem-Quine Thesis*. Dordrecht: Reidel.

Hare, Richard M. (1952). *The Language of Morals*. Oxford: Oxford University Press.

Harris, Sam. (2010). *The Moral Landscape: How Science Can Determine Human Values*. New York: Free Press.

Harrison, Glenn W. (1989). "Theory and Misbehavior of First-Price Auctions." *American Economic Review* 79 (4): 749–62.

Hart, Herbert L. A. (1961). *The Concept of Law*. Oxford: Oxford University Press.

Hatfield, Elaine, Cacioppo, John T. and Rapson, Richard L. (1993). "Emotional Contagion." *Current Directions in Psychological Science* 2 (3): 96–99.

Hauser, Marc D. (2006). *Moral Minds: How Nature Designed Our Universal Sense of Right and Wrong*. New York: Harper Collins.

Hausman, Daniel M. (1992). *The Inexact and Separate Science of Economics*. Cambridge: Cambridge University Press.

Hausman, Daniel M., and McPherson, Michael S. (1993). "Taking Ethics Seriously: Economics and Contemporary Moral Philosophy." *Journal of Economic Literature* 31 (2): 671–731.

———. (1996). *Economic Analysis and Moral Philosophy*. Cambridge: Cambridge University Press.

Hayek, Friedrich A. (1942). "Scientism and the Study of Society, Part I." *Economica* 9: 267–91.

———. (1945). "The Use of Knowledge in Society." *American Economic Review* 35 (4): 519–30.

———. (1948). *Individualism and Economic Order*. London: Routledge.

———. (1960). *The Constitution of Liberty*. London: Routledge and Kegan Paul.

———. (1967). "Notes on the Evolution of Systems of Rules of Conduct." In *Studies in Philosophy, Politics and Economics*, 66–81. London: Routledge and Kegan Paul.

———. (1973). *Law, Legislation and Liberty*. Vol. 1, *Rules and Order*. London: Routledge and Kegan Paul.

———. (1988). *The Fatal Conceit: The Errors of Socialism*. *The Collected Works of Friedrich August Hayek*. Vol. 1, edited by William W. Bartley III. London: Routledge.

He, Zengke. (2000). "Corruption and Anti-Corruption in Reform China." *Communist and Post-Communist Studies* 33:243–70.

Heinsohn, Gunnar, and Steiger, Otto. (2000). "The Property Theory of Interest and Money." In *What is Money?*, edited by John Smithin, 67–100. London: Routledge.

Helm, Dieter, ed. (1991). *Economic Policy Towards the Environment*. Oxford: Basil Blackwell.

Helm, Dieter, and Pearce, David. (1991). "Economic Policy Towards the Environment: An Overview." In *Economic Policy Towards the Environment*, edited by Dieter Helm, 1–24. Oxford: Basil Blackwell.

Hendry, John. (2002). "The Principal's Other Problems: Honest Incompetence and the Specification of Objectives." *Academy of Management Review* 27 (1): 98–113.

Henrich, Joseph. (2004). "Cultural Group Selection, Coevolutionary Processes and Large-Scale Cooperation." *Journal of Economic Behavior and Organization* 53 (1): 3–35.

Henrich, Joseph, and Boyd, Robert. (1998). "The Evolution of Conformist Transmission and the Emergence of Between Group Differences." *Evolution and Human Behavior* 19:215–42.

———. (2001). "Why People Punish Defectors: Why Conformist Transmission Can Stabilize Costly Enforcement of Norms in Cooperative Dilemmas." *Journal of Theoretical Biology* 208 (1): 79–89.

Henrich, Joseph, Boyd, Robert, Bowles, Samuel, Camerer, Colin, Fehr, Ernst, and Gintis,

Herbert (2004). *Foundations of Human Sociality: Economic Experiments and Ethnographic Evidence from Fifteen Small-Scale Societies*. Oxford: Oxford University Press.

Henrich, Joseph, Boyd, Robert, Bowles, Samuel, Camerer, Colin, Fehr, Ernst, Gintis, Herbert, and McElreath, Richard. (2001). "In Search of Homo Economicus: Behavioral Experiments in 15 Small-Scale Societies." *American Economic Review (Papers and Proceedings)* 91 (2): 73–84.

Henrich, Joseph, Ensminger, Jean, McElreath, Richard, Barr, Abigail, Barrett, Clark, Bolyanatz, Alexander, Cardenas, Juan Camilo, Gurven, Michael, Gwako, Edwins, Henrich, Natalie, Lesorogol, Carolyn, Marlowe, Frank, Tracer, David, and Ziker, John. (2010). "Markets, Religion, Community Size, and the Evolution of Fairness and Punishment." *Science* 327 (5972): 1480–84.

Henrich, Joseph, and Gil-White, Francisco J. (2001). "The Evolution of Prestige: Freely Conferred Deference as a Mechanism for Enhancing the Benefits of Cultural Transmission." *Evolution and Human Behavior* 22 (3): 165–96.

Henrich, Joseph, McElreath, Richard, Barr, Abigail, Ensminger, Jean, Barrett, Clark, Bolyanatz, Alexander, Cardenas, Juan Camilo, Gurven, Michael, Gwako, Edwins, Henrich, Natalie, Lesorogol, Carolyn, Marlowe, Frank, Tracer, David, and Ziker, John. (2006). "Costly Punishment Across Human Societies." *Science*, 312 (5781): 1767–70.

Herzberg, Frederick, Mausner, Bernard, and Snyderman, Barbara Bloch. (1959). *The Motivation to Work*. New York: Wiley.

Hicks, John R. (1934). "Léon Walras." *Econometrica* 2 (4): 338–48.

———. (1939). "The Foundations of Welfare Economics. *Economic Journal* 49 (4): 696–712.

Hildred, William, and Watkins, Larry. (1996). "The Nearly Good, the Bad, and the Ugly in Cost-Effectiveness Analysis of Health Care." *Journal of Economic Issues* 30 (3): 755–75.

Hill, Kim R., Walker, Robert S., Boži🯅evi🯅, Miran, Eder, James, Headland, Thomas, Hewlett, Barry, Hurtado, A. Magdalena, Marlowe, Frank, Wiessner, Polly, and Wood, Brian. (2011). "Co-Residence Patterns in Hunter-Gatherer Societies Show Unique Human Social Structure." *Science* 331 (6022): 1286–89.

Hindess, Barry. (1977). *Philosophy and Methodology in the Social Sciences*. Brighton: Harvester.

Hirsch, Fred. (1977). *Social Limits to Growth*. London: Routledge.

Hirschman, Albert O. (1970). *Exit, Voice, and Loyalty: Responses to Decline in Firms, Organizations, and States*. Cambridge, MA: Harvard University Press.

———. (1982). "Rival Interpretations of Market Society: Civilizing, Destructive, or Feeble?" *Journal of Economic Literature* 20 (4): 1463–84.

Hirshleifer, Jack. (1977). "Economics from a Biological Viewpoint." *Journal of Law and Economics* 20 (1): 1–52.

———. (1978). "Natural Economy versus Political Economy." *Journal of Social and Biological Structures* 1:319–37.

Hirst, Paul Q. (1975). *Durkheim, Bernard and Epistemology*. London: Routledge and Kegan Paul.

Hobson, John A. (1901). *The Social Problem: Life and Work*. London: James Nisbet.

———. (1921). *Problems of a New World*. London: George Allen.

———. (1929). *Wealth and Life: A Study in Values*. London: Macmillan.

Hodgson, Geoffrey M. (1984). *The Democratic Economy: A New Look at Planning, Markets and Power*. Harmondsworth: Penguin.

———. (1988). *Economics and Institutions: A Manifesto for a Modern Institutional Economics*. Cambridge: Polity Press.

———. (1993). *Economics and Evolution: Bringing Life Back into Economics*. Cambridge: Polity Press.

———. (1994). "Optimisation and Evolution: Winter's Critique of Friedman Revisited." *Cambridge Journal of Economics* 18 (4): 413–30.

———. (1997a). "Economics, Environmental Policy and the Transcendence of Utilitarianism." In *Valuing Nature? Ethics, Economics and the Environment*, edited by John Foster, 48–63. London: Routledge.

———. (1997b). "The Ubiquity of Habits and Rules." *Cambridge Journal of Economics* 21 (6): 663–84.

———. (1998a). "The Approach of Institutional Economics." *Journal of Economic Literature* 36 (1): 166–92.

———. (1998b). "Evolutionary and Competence-Based Theories of the Firm." *Journal of Economic Studies* 25 (1): 25–56.

———. (1999a). *Economics and Utopia: Why the Learning Economy Is Not the End of History*. London: Routledge.

———. (1999b). *Evolution and Institutions: On Evolutionary Economics and the Evolution of Economics*. Cheltenham: Edward Elgar.

———. (2001). *How Economics Forgot History: The Problem of Historical Specificity in Social Science*. London: Routledge.

———. (2002). "The Legal Nature of the Firm and the Myth of the Firm-Market Hybrid." *International Journal of the Economics of Business* 9 (1): 37–60.

———. (2003). "The Enforcement of Contracts and Property Rights: Constitutive versus Epiphenomenal Conceptions of Law." *International Review of Sociology* 13 (2): 373–89.

———. (2004a). "Darwinism, Causality and the Social Sciences." *Journal of Economic Methodology* 11 (2): 175–94.

———. (2004b). *The Evolution of Institutional Economics: Agency, Structure and Darwinism in American Institutionalism*. London: Routledge.

———. (2004c). "Opportunism Is Not the Only Reason Why Firms Exist: Why an Explanatory Emphasis on Opportunism Can Mislead Management Strategy." *Industrial and Corporate Change* 13 (2): 403–20.

———. (2005). "Alfred Marshall versus the Historical School?" *Journal of Economic Studies* 32 (4): 331–48.

———. (2006a) *Economics in the Shadows of Darwin and Marx: Essays on Institutional and Evolutionary Themes* (Cheltenham: Edward Elgar).

———. (2006b). "What Are Institutions?" *Journal of Economic Issues* 40 (1): 1–25.

———. (2007a). "Institutions and Individuals: Interaction and Evolution." *Organization Studies* 28 (1): 95–116.

———. (2007b). "Meanings of Methodological Individualism." *Journal of Economic Methodology* 14 (2): 211–26.

———. (2008a). "An Institutional and Evolutionary Perspective on Health Economics." *Cambridge Journal of Economics* 32 (2): 235–56.

———. (2008b). "Markets." In *The Elgar Companion to Social Economics*, edited by John B. Davis and Wilfred Dolfsma, 251–66. Cheltenham: Edward Elgar.

———. (2008c). "Markets." *The New Palgrave Dictionary of Economics*. 2nd ed. Basingstoke: Macmillan.

———. (2008d). "Prospects for Economic Sociology." *Philosophy of the Social Sciences* 38 (1): 133–49.

———. (2009). "On the Institutional Foundations of Law: The Insufficiency of Custom and Private Ordering." *Journal of Economic Issues* 43 (1): 143–66.

———. (2010a). "Choice, Habit and Evolution." *Journal of Evolutionary Economics* 20 (1): 1–18.

———. (2010b). "Darwinian Coevolution of Organizations and the Environment." *Ecological Economics* 69 (4): 700–706.

———. (2011). "The Eclipse of the Uncertainty Concept in Mainstream Economics." *Journal of Economic Issues* 45 (1): 159–75.

Hodgson, Geoffrey M., and Huang, Kainan (2012). "Evolutionary Game Theory and Evolutionary Economics: Are they Different Species?" *Journal of Evolutionary Economics* 22:345–66.

Hodgson, Geoffrey M., and Jiang, Shuxia (2007). "The Economics of Corruption and the Corruption of Economics: An Institutionalist Perspective." *Journal of Economic Issues* 41 (4): 1043–61.

Hodgson, Geoffrey M., and Knudsen, Thorbjørn. (2004). "The Complex Evolution of a Simple Traffic Convention: The Functions and Implications of Habit." *Journal of Economic Behavior and Organization* 54 (1): 19–47.

———. (2007). "Firm-Specific Learning and the Nature of the Firm: Why Transaction Costs May Provide an Incomplete Explanation." *Revue Économique* 58 (2): 331–50.

———. (2010). *Darwin's Conjecture: The Search for General Principles of Social and Economic Evolution.* Chicago: University of Chicago Press.

Hodgson, Geoffrey M., Mäki, Uskali, and McCloskey, Donald. (1992). "A Plea for a Pluralistic and Rigorous Economics [Signed by 44 Leading Economists]." *American Economic Review* 82 (2): xxv.

Hoffman, Elizabeth, McCabe, Kevin A., and Smith, Vernon L. (1998). "Behavioral Foundations of Reciprocity: Experimental Economics and Evolutionary Psychology." *Economic Inquiry* 36 (3): 335–52.

Holzer, Harry J., Block, Richard N., Cheatham, Markus, and Knott, Jack H. (1993). "Are Training Subsidies for Firms Effective? The Michigan Experience." *Industrial and Labor Relations Review* 46 (4): 625–36.

Honderich, Ted. (1985). *Morality and Objectivity: A Tribute to J. L. Mackie.* London: Routledge and Kegan Paul.

Hopkins, Jonathan. (2002). "States, Markets and Corruption: A Review of Some Recent Literature." *Review of International Political Economy* 9 (3): 574–90.

Horwitz, Steven. (2005). "The Functions of the Family in the Great Society." *Cambridge Journal of Economics* 29 (5): 669–84.

Howarth, Richard B. (1995). "Sustainability under Uncertainty: A Deontological Approach." *Land Economics* 71 (4): 417–27.

Hsiao, William C. (1995). "Abnormal Economics in the Health Sector." *Health Policy* 32:125–39.

Huang, Yasheng. (2008). *Capitalism with Chinese Characteristics: Entrepreneurship and the State.* Cambridge: Cambridge University Press.

Huff, Toby. (1993). *The Rise of Early Modern Science: Islam, China and the West.* Cambridge: Cambridge University Press.

Hughes, David, Griffiths, Lesley, and McHale, Jenny V. (1997). "Do Quasi-Markets Evolve? Institutional Analysis and the NHS." *Cambridge Journal of Economics* 21 (2): 259–76.

Hull, David L. (1988). *Science as a Process: An Evolutionary Account of the Social and Conceptual Development of Science*. Chicago: University of Chicago Press.

Huntington, Samuel P. (1968). *Political Order in Changing Societies*. New Haven, CT: Yale University Press.

Hurley, Jeremiah. (2000). "An Overview of the Normative Economics of the Health Sector." In *Handbook of Health Economics*, edited by Anthony J. Cuyler and Joseph P. Newhouse, 55–118. Amsterdam: Elsevier.

Huxley, Thomas Henry, and Huxley, Julian. (1947). *Evolution and Ethics, 1893–1943*. London: Pilot Press.

Ichniowski, Casey, and Shaw, Kathryn. (2003). "Beyond Incentive Pay: Insiders' Estimates of the Value of Complementary Human Resource Management Practices." *Journal of Economic Perspectives* 17 (1): 155–80.

Ingham, Geoffrey. (2004). *The Nature of Money*. Cambridge: Polity Press.

IPCC. (2007). *Climate Change 2007: The Physical Science Basis (Summary for Policy Makers)*. Geneva: Intergovernmental Panel on Climate Change.

Ireland, Paddy W. (2010). "Limited Liability, Shareholder Rights and the Problem of Corporate Irresponsibility." *Cambridge Journal of Economics* 34 (5): 837–56.

Iwai, Katsuhito. (1999). "Persons, Things and Corporations: The Corporate Personality Controversy and Comparative Corporate Governance." *American Journal of Comparative Law* 47 (4): 583–632.

Jacobides, Michael G., and Hitt, Lorin M. (2005). "Losing Sight of the Forest for the Trees? Productive Capabilities and Gains from Trade as Drivers of Vertical Scope." *Strategic Management Journal* 26 (13): 1209–27.

Jacobs, Michael. (1991). *The Green Economy: Environment, Sustainable Development and the Politics of the Future*. London: Pluto Press.

———. (1994). "The Limits of Neoclassicism: Towards an Institutional Environmental Economics." In *Social Theory and the Global Environment*, edited by Michael Redclift and Ted Benton, 67–91. London: Routledge.

Jaenisch, Rudolf, and Bird, Adrian. (2003). "Epigenetic Regulation of Gene Expression: How the Genome Integrates Intrinsic and Environmental Signals." *Nature Genetics*, supplement, 33:245–54.

Jain, Arvind K. (2001). "Corruption: A Review." *Journal of Economic Surveys* 15 (1): 71–120.

James, William. (1890). *The Principles of Psychology*. 2 vols. New York: Henry Holt.

Jan, Stephen. (2000). "Institutional Considerations in Priority Setting: Transactions Cost Perspective on PBMA." *Health Economics* 9:631–41.

Janssen, Marco A. (2006). "Historical Institutional Analysis of Social-Ecological Systems." *Journal of Institutional Economics* 2 (2): 127–31.

Janssen, Peter P. M., de Jonge, Jan, and Bakker, Arnold B. (1999). "Specific Determinants of Intrinsic Work Motivation, Burn-Out and Turn-Over Intentions: A Study Among Nurses." *Journal of Advanced Nursing* 29 (6): 1360–69.

Jensen, Keith, Call, Joseph, and Tomasello, Michael. (2007). "Chimpanzees Are Rational Maximizers in an Ultimatum Game." *Science* 318 (5847): 107–9.

Jensen, Michael C., and Meckling, William H. (1976). "Theory of the Firm: Managerial Behavior, Agency Costs and Ownership Structure." *Journal of Financial Economics* 3 (4): 305–60.

Jevons, William Stanley. (1871). *The Theory of Political Economy*. London: Macmillan.

Joas, Hans. (1993). *Pragmatism and Social Theory*. Chicago: University of Chicago Press.

———. (1996). *The Creativity of Action*. Chicago: University of Chicago Press.

Jochimsen, Maren A. (2003). *Careful Economics: Integrating Caring Activities and Economic Science*. Boston: Kluwer Academic.

Jones, Andrew M., ed. (2006). *The Elgar Companion to Health Economics* Cheltenham: Edward Elgar.

Joyce, Richard. (2006). *The Evolution of Morality*. Cambridge, MA: MIT Press.

Kagan, Jerome. (1984). *The Nature of the Child*. New York: Basic Books.

Kagel, John H., Battalio, Raymond C., and Green, Leonard. (1995). *Economic Choice Theory: An Experimental Analysis of Animal Behaviour*. Cambridge: Cambridge University Press.

Kagel, John H., Battalio, Raymond C., Rachlin, Howard, and Green, Leonard. (1981). "Demand Curves for Animal Consumers." *Quarterly Journal of Economics* 96 (1): 1–16.

Kahneman, Daniel. (1994). "New Challenges to the Rationality Assumption." *Journal of Institutional and Theoretical Economics* 150 (1): 18–36.

———. (2003a). "Maps of Bounded Rationality." *American Economic Review* 93 (5): 1449–75.

———. (2003b). "A Psychological Perspective on Economics." *American Economic Review (Papers and Proceedings)* 93 (2): 162–68.

Kahneman, Daniel, Knetsch, J. L., and Thaler, Richard H. (1986a). "Fairness and the Assumptions of Economics." *Journal of Business* 59:285–300.

Kahneman, Daniel, Knetsch, J. L., and Thaler, Richard H. (1986b). "Fairness as a Constraint on Profit Seeking: Entitlements in the Market." *American Economic Review* 76 (4): 728–41.

Kahneman, Daniel, Slovic, Paul, and Tversky, Amos, eds. (1982). *Judgment Under Uncertainty: Heuristics and Biases*. Cambridge: Cambridge University Press.

Kaldor, Nicholas. (1939). "Welfare Propositions in Economics and Interpersonal Comparisons of Utility." *Economic Journal* 49 (3): 549–52.

Kallis, Giorgos, and Norgaard, Richard B. (2010). "Coevolutionary Ecological Economics." *Ecological Economics* 69 (4): 690–99.

Kapp, K. William. (1976). "The Nature and Significance of Institutional Economics." *Kyklos* 29 (2): 209–32.

———. (1978). *The Social Costs of Business Enterprise*. 3rd ed. Nottingham: Spokesman.

Kaufmann, Daniel. (1997). "Corruption: The Facts." *Foreign Policy* 107 (1): 114–31.

Keller, Albert Galloway. (1915). *Societal Evolution: A Study of the Evolutionary Basis of the Science of Society*. New York: Macmillan.

Kenworthy, Lane. (1995). *In Search of National Economic Success: Balancing Competition and Cooperation*. Thousand Oaks, CA: Sage.

———. (2006). "Institutional Coherence and Macroeconomic Performance." *Socio-Economic Review* 4 (1): 69–91.

Keulartz, Jozef. (1998). *Struggle for Nature: A Critique of Radical Ecology*. London: Routledge.

Keynes, John Maynard. (1933). *Essays in Biography*. London: Macmillan.

———. (1936). *The General Theory of Employment, Interest and Money*. London: Macmillan.

———. (1973). *The Collected Writings of John Maynard Keynes*. Vol. 14, *The General Theory and After, Part II: Defence and Development*. London: Macmillan.

Khalil, Elias L. (1990). "Entropy Law and Exhaustion of Natural Resources: Is Nicholas Georgescu-Roegen's Paradigm Defensible?" *Ecological Economic* 2 (2): 163–78.

———. (1991). "Entropy and Nicholas Georgescu-Roegen's Paradigm: A Reply." *Ecological Economics* 3 (1): 161–63.

Khan, Mushtaq. (2006). "Corruption and Governance." In *The New Development Economics: After the Washington Consensus*, edited by S. Kwame Jomo and Ben Fine, 200–221. London: Zed Press.

Khurana, Rakesh. (2007). *From Higher Aims to Hired Hands: The Social Transformation of American Business Schools and the Unfilfilled Promises of Management as a Profession.* Princeton, NJ: Princeton University Press.

Kilpinen, Erkki. (2000). *The Enormous Fly-Wheel of Society: Pragmatism's Habitual Conception of Action and Social Theory.* Helsinki: University of Helsinki.

Kincaid, Harold. (1997). *Individualism and the Unity of Science: Essays on Reduction, Explanation, and the Social Sciences.* Lanham, MD: Rowman and Littlefield.

Kirp, David L. (2003). *Shakespeare, Einstein, and the Bottom Line: The Marketing of Higher Education.* Cambridge, MA: Harvard University Press.

Kitcher, Philip. (1987). "Why Not the Best? In *The Latest on the Best: Essays on Evolution and Optimality*, edited by John A. Dupré, 77–102. Cambridge, MA: MIT Press.

———. (1993). *The Advancement of Science: Science without Legend, Objectivity without Illusions.* Oxford: Oxford University Press.

Klamer, Arjo. (1989). "A Conversation with Amartya Sen." *Journal of Economic Perspectives* 3 (1): 135–50.

Knight, Frank H. (1921). *Risk, Uncertainty and Profit.* Boston: Houghton Mifflin.

Knight, Jack. (1992). *Institutions and Social Conflict.* Cambridge: Cambridge University Press.

Knorr-Cetina, Karin D. (1981). *The Manufacture of Knowledge: An Essay on the Constructivist and Contextual Nature of Science.* Oxford: Pergamon.

Kogut, Bruce, and Zander, Udo. (1996). "What Firms Do? Coordination, Identity, and Learning." *Organization Science* 7 (5): 502–18.

Kohlberg, Lawrence. (1969). "Stage and Sequence—the Cognitive-Developmental Approach to Socialization." In *Handbook of Socialization Theory and Research*, edited by D. A. Goslin. Chicago: Rand McNally.

Kontopoulos, Kyriakos M. (1993). *The Logics of Social Structure.* Cambridge: Cambridge University Press.

Koslowski, Peter, ed. (1995). *The Theory of Ethical Economy in the Historical School: Wilhelm Roscher, Lorenz von Stein, Gustav Schmoller, Wilhelm Dilthey and Contemporary Theory.* Berlin: Springer.

———, ed. (1997). *Methodology of the Social Sciences, Ethics, and Economics in the Newer Historical School: From Max Weber and Rickert to Sombart and Rothacker.* Berlin: Springer.

Kropotkin, Petr A. (1902). *Mutual Aid: A Factor of Evolution.* London: Heinemann.

Krugman, Paul R. (2009). "How Did Economists Get It So Wrong?" *New York Times*, September 2. http://www.nytimes.com/2009/09/06/magazine/06Economic-t.html.

Kwong, Julia. (1997). *The Political Economy of Corruption in China.* Armonk NY: M. E. Sharpe.

Labelle, R., Stoddart, G., and Ruffles, T. (1994). "An Examination of the Meaning and Importance of Supplier-Induced Demand." *Journal of Health Economics* 13:347–68.

Lacey, Hugh. (1997). "Neutrality in the Social Sciences: On Bhaskar's Argument for an Essential Emancipatory Impulse in Social Science." *Journal for the Theory of Social Behaviour* 27 (2–3): 213–41.

Lachmann, Ludwig M. (1969). "Methodological Individualism and the Market Economy." In *Roads to Freedom: Essays in Honour of Friedrich A. von Hayek*, edited by Erich W. Streissler, 89–103. London: Routledge and Kegan Paul.

Lambsdorff, Johann Graf. (2007). *The Institutional Economics of Corruption and Reform.* Cambridge: Cambridge University Press.

Lambsdorff, Johann Graf, Taube, Markus, and Schramm, Matthias, eds. (2004). *The New Institutional Economics of Corruption.* London: Routledge.

Lancaster, Henry Oliver. (1990). *Expectations of Life: A Study in the Demography, Statistics, and History of World Mortality.* Berlin: Springer-Verlag.

Lancaster, Kelvin. (1966). "A New Approach to Consumer Theory." *Journal of Political Economy* 74 (2): 132–57.

Landa, Janet. (1994). *Trust, Ethnicity, and Identity: Beyond the New Institutional Economics of Ethnic Trading Networks, Contract Law, and Gift Exchange.* Ann Arbor: University of Michigan Press.

Lane, Robert E. (1992). "Work as 'Disutility' and Money as 'Happiness': Cultural Origins of a Basic Market Error." *Journal of Socio-Economics* 21 (1): 43–64.

Lange, Oskar R., and Taylor, Frederick M. (1938). *On the Economic Theory of Socialism*, ed. Benjamin E. Lippincott (Minneapolis: University of Minnesota Press).

Langlois, Richard N. (1992). "Transaction Cost Economics in Real Time." *Industrial and Corporate Change* 1 (1): 99–127.

———. (1995a). "Capabilities and Coherence in Firms and Markets." In *Resource-Based and Evolutionary Theories of the Firm: Towards a Synthesis*, edited by Cynthia A. Montgomery, 71–100. Boston: Kluwer Academic.

———. (1995b). "Do Firms Plan?" *Constitutional Political Economy* 6:247–61.

Langlois, Richard N., and Savage, Deborah A. (2001). "Standards, Modularity, and Innovation: The Case of Medical Practice." In *Path Dependence and Path Creation*, edited by Raghu Garud and Peter Karnøe, 149–68. Mahwah, NJ: Lawrence Erlbaum.

Lascaux, Alex. (2008). "Trust and Uncertainty: A Critical Re-assessment." *International Review of Sociology* 18 (1): 1–18.

Lave, Jean, and Wenger, Etienne. (1991). *Situated Learning: Legitimate Peripheral Participation.* Cambridge: Cambridge University Press.

Lavoie, Donald. (1985). *Rivalry and Central Planning: The Socialist Calculation Debate Reconsidered.* Cambridge: Cambridge University Press.

Lawson, Tony. (2003). *Reorienting Economics.* London: Routledge.

Layard, Richard. (2005). *Happiness: Lessons from a New Science.* London: Allen Lane.

Le Grand, Julian. (1993). *Quasi-Markets and Social Policy.* London: Macmillan.

Ledyard, John O. (1995). "Public Goods: A Survey of Experimental Research." In *The Handbook of Experimental Economics*, edited by John H. Kagel and Alvin E. Roth, 111–94. Princeton, NJ: Princeton University Press.

Lemieux, Thomas, Fortin, Bernard, and Frechette, Pierre. (1994). "The Effect of Taxes on Labor Supply in the Underground Economy." *American Economic Review* 84 (1): 231–54.

Lewontin, Richard C. (1974). *The Genetic Basis of Evolutionary Change.* New York: Columbia University Press.

Leff, Nathaniel. (1964). "Economic Development through Bureaucratic Corruption." *American Behavioral Scientist* 8 (3): 8–14.

Leibenstein, Harvey. (1982). "The Prisoner's Dilemma in the Invisible Hand: An Analysis of Intrafirm Productivity." *American Economic Review (Papers and Proceedings)* 72 (2): 92–97.

Lerner, Abba P. (1934). "Economic Theory and Socialist Economy." *Review of Economic Studies* 2:157–75.

Levin, Mark, and Satarov, Georgy. (2000). "Corruption and Institutions in Russia." *European Journal of Political Economy* 16 (1): 113–32.

Leys, Colin. (1965). "What Is the Problem about Corruption?" *Journal of Modern African Studies* 3 (2): 215–30.

Lindbladh, Eva, and Lyttkens, Carl Hampus. (2002). "Habit versus Choice: The Process of Decision-Making in Health-Related Behavior." *Social Science and Medicine* 55:451–65.

Lindblom, Charles E. (1959). "The Science of 'Muddling Through." *Public Administration Review* 19 (1): 79–88.

———. (1984). *The Policy-Making Process*. Englewood Cliffs, NJ: Prentice-Hall.

Lindgren, Kristian. (1992). "Evolutionary Phenomena in Simple Dynamics." In *Artificial Life II*, edited by Christopher G. Langton, Charles Taylor, J. Doyne Farmer, and Steen Rasmussen, 295–312. Redwood City, CA: Addison-Wesley.

Lipsey, Richard G., Carlaw, Kenneth I., and Bekar, Clifford T. (2005). *Economic Transformations: General Purpose Technologies and Long Term Economic Growth*. Oxford: Oxford University Press.

Lipsey, Richard G., and Lancaster, Kelvin (1956). "The General Theory of Second Best." *Review of Economic Studies* 24 (1): 11–32.

List, John A. (2006). "Field Experiments: A Bridge between Lab and Naturally Occurring Data." *Advances in Economic Analysis and Policy* 6 (2), art. 8. http://www.field experiments.com/uploads/97-full.pdf.

Little, Ian M. D. (1950). *A Critique of Welfare Economics*. Oxford: Oxford University Press.

Locke, Edwin A., and Latham, Gary P. (2004). "What Should We Do about Motivation Theory? Six Recommendations for the Twenty-First Century." *Academy of Management Review* 29 (3): 389–403.

Loewenstein, George. (2000). "Emotions and Economic Theory and Economic Behavior." *American Economic Review (Papers and Proceedings)* 90 (2): 426–32.

Lopes, Helena, Santos, Ana C., and Teles, Nuno. (2009). "The Motives for Cooperation in Work Organisations." *Journal of Institutional Economics* 5 (3): 259–88.

Lorenz, Edward H. (1999). "Trust, Contract and Economic Cooperation." *Cambridge Journal of Economics* 23 (3): 301–15.

Lowry, S. Todd. (1976). "Bargain and Contract Theory in Law and Economics." *Journal of Economic Issues* 10 (1): 1–22.

Lozada, G. A. (1991). "A Defense of Nicholas Georgescu-Roegen's Paradigm." *Ecological Economics* 3 (1): 157–60.

Lu, Xiaobu. (2000). "Booty Socialism, Bureau-preneurs, and the State in Transition: Organizational Corruption in China." *Comparative Politics* 32 (3): 273–94.

Luhmann, Niklas. (1982). *The Differentiation of Society*. New York: Columbia University Press.

Lui, Francis T. (1985). "An Equilibrium Queuing Model of Bribery." *Journal of Political Economy* 93 (4): 760–81.

Lukes, Steven. (1969). "Methodological Individualism Reconsidered." *British Journal of Sociology* 19:119–29.

———. (1973). *Individualism*. Oxford: Basil Blackwell.

———. (1985). *Marxism and Morality*. Oxford: Oxford University Press.

Lundvall, Bengt-Åke, ed. (1992). *National Systems of Innovation: Towards a Theory of Innovation and Interactive Learning*. London: Pinter.

Lutz, Mark A. (1990). *Social Economics: Retrospect and Prospect*. Boston: Kluwer Academic.

———. (1999). *Economics for the Common Good: Two Centuries of Social Economic Thought in the Humanistic Tradition.* London: Routledge.———.

———. (2000). "On the Connecting of Socio-Economics with Communitarianism." *Journal of Socio-Economics* 29 (4): 314–47.

Lutz, Mark A., and Lux, Kenneth. (1979). *The Challenge of Humanistic Economics* Menlo Park, CA: Benjamin/Cummings.

———. (1988). *Humanistic Economics: The New Challenge.* New York: Bootstrap Press.

Lux, Kenneth. (1990). *Adam Smith's Mistake: How a Moral Philosopher Invented Economics and Ended Morality.* Boston: Shambhala.

Machlup, Fritz. (1937). "Monopoly and Competition: A Classification of Market Positions." *American Economic Review* 27 (3): 445–51.

———. (1972). "The Universal Bogey: Economic Man." In *Essays in Honour of Lord Robbins,* edited by Maurice Peston and Bernard Corry, 99–117. London: Weidenfeld and Nicolson.

MacIntyre, Alasdair. (1981). *After Virtue: A Study in Moral Theory.* London: Duckworth.

Mackie, John Leslie. (1977). *Ethics: Inventing Right and Wrong.* Harmondsworth: Penguin.

MacLeod, Bently, and Parent, Daniel. (1999). "Job Characteristics and the Form of Compensation." *Research in Labor Economics* 18:177–242.

Magill, Michael, and Quinzii, Martine. (1996). *Theory of Incomplete Markets.* 2 vols. Cambridge, MA: MIT Press.

Malthus, Thomas Robert. (1820). *Principles of Political Economy.* London: John Murray.

Manion, Melanie. (1996). "Corruption by Design: Bribery in Chinese Enterprise Licensing." *Journal of Law, Economics, and Organization* 12 (1): 167–95.

Mansbridge, Jane J., ed. (1990). *Beyond Self-Interest.* Chicago: University of Chicago Press.

Mantzavinos, Chris. (2001). *Individuals, Institutions and Markets.* Cambridge: Cambridge University Press.

Marcus, Gary. (2004). *The Birth of the Mind: How a Tiny Number of Genes Creates the Complexity of the Human Mind.* New York: Basic Books.

Maréchal, Kevin. (2009). "An Evolutionary Perspective on the Economics of Energy Consumption: The Crucial Role of Habits." *Journal of Economic Issues* 43 (1): 69–88.

———. (2010). "Not Irrational but Habitual: The Importance of Behavioral Lock-in in Energy Consumption." *Ecological Economics* 69 (5): 1104–14.

Maréchal, Kevin, and Lazaric, Nathalie. (2010). "Overcoming Inertia: Insights from Evolutionary Economics into Improved Energy and Climate Policies." *Climate Policy* 10 (1): 103–19.

Marengo, Luigi. (1992). "Coordination and Organizational Learning in the Firm." *Journal of Evolutionary Economics* 2 (4): 313–26.

Marglin, Stephen A. (1974). "What Do Bosses Do? The Origins and Functions of Hierarchy in Capitalist Production." *Review of Radical Political Economics* 6 (2): 60–112.

———. (2010). *The Dismal Science: How Thinking Like an Economist Undermines Community.* Cambridge, MA: Harvard University Press.

Margolis, Howard. (1982). *Selfishness, Altruism, and Rationality: A Theory of Social Choice.* Chicago: University of Chicago Press.

Marshall, Alfred. (1885). "The Present Position of Economics." In *Memorials of Alfred Marshall,* edited by Arthur C. Pigou, 152–74. London: Macmillan.

———. (1920). *The Principles of Economics.* 8th ed. London: Macmillan.

Marshall, S. J., and Biddle, S. J. H. (2001). "The Transtheoretical Model of Behavior

Change: A Meta-Analysis to Physical Activity and Exercise." *Annals of Behavioral Medicine* 23:229–46.

Martinez, Mark A. (2009). *The Myth of the Free Market: The Role of the State in a Capitalist Economy.* Sterling, VA: Kumarian Press.

Martinez Alier, Joan. (1991). "Ecological Perception, Environmental Policy and Distributional Conflicts: Some Lessons from History." In *Ecological Economics: The Science and Management of Sustainability,* edited by Robert Constanza, 118–36. New York: Columbia University Press.

Martinez Alier, Joan, Munda, Giuseppi, and O'Neill, John. (1998). "Weak Comparability of Values as a Foundation for Ecological Economics." *Ecological Economics* 26 (3): 277–86.

Marwell, Gerald, and Ames, Ruth. (1981). "Economists Free Ride, Does Anyone Else? Experiments on the Provision of Public Goods IV." *Journal of Public Economics* 15 (3): 295–310.

Marx, Karl. (1867). *Das Kapital: Kritik der politischen Ökonomie.* Vol. 1. Hamburg: Meissner.

Marx, Karl, and Engels, Frederick. (1976). *Karl Marx and Frederick Engels, Collected Works.* Vol. 6, *Marx and Engels: 1845–1848.* London: Lawrence and Wishart.

Maslow, Abraham H. (1954). *Motivation and Personality.* New York: Harper and Row.

Mason, Roger S. (1995). "Interpersonal Effects on Consumer Demand in Economic Theory and Marketing Thought, 1890–1950." *Journal of Economic Issues* 29 (3): 871–81.

Matthew, G. K. (1971). "Measuring Need and Evaluating Services." In *Portfolio for Health,* edited by Gordon McLachlan, 27–46. London: Oxford University Press.

Mauro, Paolo. (1995). "Corruption and Growth." *Quarterly Journal of Economics* 110 (3): 681–712.

Maynard, Alan. (1991). "Developing the Health Care Market." *Economic Journal* 101: 1277–86.

Mayr, Ernst. (1988). *Toward a New Philosophy of Biology: Observations of an Evolutionist.* Cambridge, MA: Harvard University Press.

McCloskey, Deirdre N. (2006). *The Bourgeois Virtues: Ethics for an Age of Commerce.* Chicago: University of Chicago Press.

McCrink, Koleen, Bloom, Paul, and Santos, Laurie R. 2010. "Children's and Adult's Judgments of Equitable Resource Distrinutions." *Developmental Science* 13 (1): 37–45.

McMaster, Robert. (1995). "Competitive Tendering in UK Health and Local Authorities: What Happens to the Quality of Services?" *Scottish Journal of Political Economy* 42 (4): 409–27.

———. (2002). "The Analysis of Welfare State Reform: Why the 'Quasi-Markets' Narrative Is Descriptively Inadequate and Misleading." *Journal of Economic Issues* 36 (3): 769–94.

———. (2003a). "The Process of Market Orientation in the UK's National Health Service." In *Globalisation, Social Capital, and Inequality,* edited by Wilfred Dolfsma and Charlie Dannreuther, 144–75. Cheltenham: Edward Elgar.

———. (2003b). "A Socio-Institutionalist Critique of the 1990s' Reforms of the United Kingdom's National Health Service." *Review of Social Economy* 60 (3): 403–33.

———. (2004). "A Utilitarian Twist? Performance Measurement in the English National Health Service." *Journal of Economic Issues* 38 (2): 429–37.

———. (2008). "Beware of Those Offering 'Gold Standards': Evidence-Based Medicine and the Potential for Institutional Change in Clinical-Medical Provision." *Journal of Economic Issues* 42 (4): 885–912.

McMaster, Robert, and Sawkins, John W. (1996). "The Contract State: Trust, Distortion, and Efficiency." *Review of Social Economy* 54 (2): 145–67.

McMillan, John. (2002). *Reinventing the Bazaar: A Natural History of Markets*. New York: Norton.

McPake, Barbara, Kumaranayake, Lilani, and Normand, Charles. (2002). *Health Economics: An International Perspective*. London: Routledge.

Meadows, Donella H., Meadows, Dennis L., and Randers, Jorgen. (1992). *Beyond the Limits: Global Collapse or a Sustainable Future*. London: Earthscan Publications.

Medema, Steven G. (1994). *Ronald H. Coase*. Basingstoke: Macmillan.

Megginson, William L., and Netter, Jeffry M. (2001). "From State to Market: A Survey of Empirical Studies on Privatization." *Journal of Economic Literature* 39 (2): 321–89.

Meikle, Scott. (1995). *Aristotle's Economic Thought*. Oxford: Oxford University Press.

Ménard, Claude. (1995). "Markets as Institutions versus Organizations as Markets? Disentangling Some Fundamental Concepts." *Journal of Economic Behavior and Organization* 28 (2): 161–82.

———. (1996). "On Clusters, Hybrids, and Other Strange Forms: The Case of the French Poultry Industry." *Journal of Institutional and Theoretical Economics* 152 (1): 154–83.

Menger, Carl. (1871). *Grundsätze der Volkwirtschaftslehre*. Tübingen: J. C. B. Mohr. Translated and published in English as Menger (1981).

———. (1883). *Untersuchungen über die Methode der Sozialwissenschaften und der politischen Ökonomie insbesondere*. Tübingen: J. C. B. Mohr. Published in English as Menger (1985).

———. (1981). *Principles of Economics*. Translated by James Dingwall and Bert F. Hoselitz from Menger (1871). New York: New York University Press.

———. (1985). *Investigations into the Method of the Social Sciences with Special Reference to Economics*. Edited by Louis Schneider. Translated by Francis J. Nock from Menger (1883). New York: New York University Press.

Merton, Robert K. (1996). *On Social Structure and Science*. Chicago: University of Chicago Press.

Mesquita, Bruce Bueno de. (2009).*The Predictioneer's Game*. New York: Random House.

Metcalfe, J. Stanley. (1998). *Evolutionary Economics and Creative Destruction*. London: Routledge.

Meyer, John P., Becker, Thomas E., and Vandenberghe, Christian. (2004). "Employee Commitment and Motivation: A Conceptual Analysis and Integrative Model." *Journal of Applied Psychology* 89 (6): 991–1007.

Meyer, John P., Becker, Thomas E., and Van Dick, Rolf. (2006). "Social Identities and Commitments at Work: Toward an Integrative Model." *Journal of Organizational Behavior* 27 (5): 665–83.

Midgley, Mary. (2003). *Myths We Live By*. London: Routledge.

Milgram, Stanley. (1974). *Obedience to Authority: An Experimental View*. New York: Harper and Row.

Milgrom, Paul R., and Roberts, John. (1992). *Economics, Organisation, and Management*. Englewood Cliffs, NJ: Prentice-Hall.

Milinski, Manfred, Semmann, Dirk, and Krambeck, Hans-Jürgen. (2002). "Reputation Helps Solve the 'Tragedy of the Commons.'" *Nature* 415:224–26.

Mill, John Stuart. (1844). *Essays on Some Unsettled Questions of Political Economy*. London: Longman, Green, Reader and Dyer.

———. (1848). *Principles of Political Economy with Some of Their Applications to Social Philosophy*. London: Parker.

————. (1863). *Utilitarianism, Liberty and Representative Government*. London: Parker, Son, and Bourn.

Miller, Seumas. (2011). "Corruption." *The Stanford Encyclopedia of Philosophy*. February 2. http://plato.stanford.edu/entries/corruption/.

Miller, Seumas, Roberts, Peter, and Spence, Edward. (2005). *Corruption and Anti-Corruption: An Applied Philosophical Approach*. Englewood Cliffs, NJ: Prentice-Hall.

Minkler, Lanse P. (1999). "The Problem with Utility: Towards a Non-consequentialist/ Utility Theory Synthesis." *Review of Social Economy* 57 (1): 4–24.

————. (2004a). "Lying, Integrity, and Cooperation." *Review of Social Economy* 62 (1): 27–50.

————. (2004b). "Shirking and Motivations in Firms: Survey Evidence on Worker Attitudes." *International Journal of Industrial Organization* 22 (6): 863–84.

————. (2008). *Integrity and Agreement: Economics When Principles Also Matter*. Ann Arbor: University of Michigan Press.

Mises, Ludwig von. (1949). *Human Action: A Treatise on Economics*. London: William Hodge.

Mishan, Ezra J. (1960). "A Survey of Welfare Economics, 1939–59." *Economic Journal* 70 (2): 197–265.

Mishra, Ajit. (2006). "The Persistence of Corruption: Some Theoretical Perspectives." *World Development* 34 (2): 349–58.

Mo, Pak Hung. (2001). "Corruption and Economic Growth." *Journal of Comparative Economcs* 29 (1): 66–79.

Mokyr, Joel. (1990). *The Lever of Riches: Technological Creativity and Economic Progress*. Oxford: Oxford University Press.

Mokyr, Joel. (2003). *The Gifts of Athena: Historical Origins of the Knowledge Economy*. Princeton, NJ: Princeton University Press.

Montes, Leonidas. (2003). "*Das Adam Smith Problem*: Its Origins, the Stages of the Current Debate, and One Implication for Our Understanding of Sympathy." *Journal of the History of Economic Thought* 25 (1): 63–90.

Montgomery, Cynthia A., ed. (1995). *Resource-Based and Evolutionary Theories of the Firm: Towards a Synthesis*. Boston: Kluwer Academic.

Mooney, Gavin. (1994). *Key Issues in Health Economics*. Hemel Hempstead: Harvester Wheatsheaf.

Moore, G. E. (1903). *Principia Ethica*. Cambridge: Cambridge University Press.

Moreau, François. (2004). "The Role of the State in Evolutionary Microeconomics." *Cambridge Journal of Economics* 28 (6): 847–74.

Moss, Lyndsay. (2005). "Complaints over GP Appointments Still Await a Cure." *Independent*, September 7.

Muchlinski, Peter. (2010). "Limited Liability and Multinational Enterprises: A Case for Reform." *Cambridge Journal of Economics* 34 (5): 915–28.

Mueller, Dennis C. (1979.) *Public Choice*. Cambridge: Cambridge University Press.

Murrell, Peter. (1991). "Can Neoclassical Economics Underpin the Reform of Centrally Planned Economies?" *Journal of Economic Perspectives* 5 (4): 59–76.

Myint, Hla (1946). "The Classical View of the Economic Problem." *Economica*, n.s., 13 (50): 119–30.

Myrdal, Gunnar. (1968). *Asian Drama: An Inquiry into the Poverty of Nations*. Harmondsworth: Penguin.

National Health Service for England. (2010). *The NHS Constitution*. London: Department of Health.

Næss, Arne. (1989). *Ecology, Community and Lifestyle: Outline of an Ecosophy.* Cambridge: Cambridge University Press.

Nelson, Julie A. (1995). "Feminism and Economics." *Journal of Economic Perspectives* 9 (2): 131–48.

Nelson, Richard R. (1981). "Assessing Private Enterprise: An Exegesis of Tangled Doctrine." *Bell Journal of Economics* 12 (1): 93–111.

——, ed. (1993). *National Innovation Systems: A Comparative Analysis.* Oxford: Oxford University Press.

——. (2003). "On the Complexities and Limits of Market Organization." *Review of International Political Economy* 10 (4): 697–710.

——. (2005a). *The Limits of Market Organization.* New York: Russell Sage Foundation.

——, ed. (2005b). *Technology, Institutions and Economic Growth.* Cambridge, MA: Harvard University Press.

Nelson, Richard R., and Winter, Sidney G. (1982). *An Evolutionary Theory of Economic Change.* Cambridge, MA: Harvard University Press.

——. (2002). "Evolutionary Theorizing in Economics." *Journal of Economic Perspectives* 16 (2): 23–46.

Neumann, John von, and Morgenstern, Oskar. (1944). *The Theory of Games and Economic Behavior.* Princeton, NJ: Princeton University Press.

Newhouse, Joseph P. (1996). "Reimbursing Health Plans and Health Providers: Selection Versus Efficiency in Production." *Journfl of Economic Literature* 34 (3): 1236–63.

Nichols, Shaun. (2004). *Sentimental Rules: On the Natural Foundations of Moral Judgment.* Oxford: Oxford University Press.

Niskanen, William A. (1971). *Bureaucracy and Representative Government.* Chicago: Aldine-Atherton.

Nooteboom, Bart. (2000). *Learning and Innovation in Organizations and Economies.* Oxford: Oxford University Press.

——. (2002). *Trust: Forms, Foundations, Failures and Figures.* Cheltenham: Edward Elgar.

——. (2004a). "Governance and Competence: How Can They Be Combined?" *Cambridge Journal of Economics* 28 (4): 505–25.

——. (2004b). *Inter-Firm Collaboration, Learning and Networks: An Integrated Approach.* London: Routledge.

Norgaard, Richard B. (1989). "The Case for Methodological Pluralism." *Ecological Economics* 1 (1): 37–57.

——. (1990). "Economic Indicators of Resource Scarcity: A Critical Essay." *Journal of Environmental Economics and Management* 18:19–25.

——. (1994). *Development Betrayed: The End of Progress and a Coevolutionary Revisioning of the Future.* London: Routledge.

North, Douglass C. (1990). *Institutions, Institutional Change and Economic Performance.* Cambridge: Cambridge University Press.

Nove, Alexander. (1979). *Political Economy and Soviet Socialism.* London: George Allen and Unwin.

——. (1983). *The Economics of Feasible Socialism.* London: George Allen and Unwin.

Nowak, Martin A. (2006). "Five Rules for the Evolution of Cooperation." *Science* 314 (5805): 1560–63.

Nowak, Martin A., and Sigmund, Karl. (2005). "Evolution of Indirect Reprocity." *Nature* 437: 1291–98.

Nozick, Robert. (1977). "On Austrian Methodology." *Synthese* 36:353–92.

Nussbaum, Martha C. (2000). *Women and Economic Development: The Capabilities Approach*. Cambridge: Cambridge University Press.

———. (2001). *Upheavals of Thought: The Intelligence of Emotions*. Cambridge: Cambridge University Press.

———. (2003). "Capabilities as Fundamental Entitlements: Sen and Social Justice." *Feminist Economics* 9 (2–3): 33–59.

Nussbaum, Martha C., and Sen, Amartya, eds. (1993). *The Quality of Life*. Oxford: Clarendon Press.

Nye, Joseph S. (1967). "Corruption and Political Development: A Cost-Benefit Analysis." *American Political Science Review* 61 (2): 417–27.

Oksanen, Markku. (1997). "The Moral Value of Biodiversity." *Ambio* 26 (8): 541–45.

O'Neill, John. (1973). *Modes of Individualism and Collectivism*. London: Heinemann.

———. (1993). *Ecology, Policy and Politics*. London: Routledge.

———. (1998). *The Market: Ethics, Knowledge and Politics*. London: Routledge.

Oppenheimer, Stephen. (2004). *The Real Eve*. New York: Carroll and Graf. Published in the United Kingdom as *Out of Eden* (London: Constable and Robinson).

Organisation for Economic Co-operation and Development. (2010). *OECD Health Data 2010*. OECD Internet subscription database. Paris: OECD.

Orlitzky, Marc, Schmidt, Frank L., and Rynes, Sara L. (2003). "Corporate Social and Financial Performance: A Meta-Analysis." *Organization Studies* 24 (3): 403–41.

Osteen, Mark, ed. (2002). *The Question of the Gift: Essays Across Disciplines*. London: Routledge.

Osterloh, Margit, Frost, Jetta, and Frey, Bruno S. (2002). "The Dynamics of Motivation in New Organizational Forms." *International Journal of the Economics of Business* 9 (1): 61–77.

Ostrom, Elinor. (1986). "An Agenda for the Study of Institutions." *Public Choice* 48: 3–25.

———. (1990). *Governing the Commons: The Evolution of Institutions for Collective Action*. Cambridge: Cambridge University Press.

———. (1998). "A Behavioral Approach to the Rational Choice Theory of Collective Action." *American Political Science Review* 92 (1): 1–21.

———. (2000). "Crowding Out Citizenship." *Scandinavian Political Studies* 23 (1): 3–16.

———. (2009). "A Polycentric Approach for Coping with Climate Change." World Bank Research Working Paper No. 5095, October.

Ostrom, Elinor, Gardner, Roy, and Walker, James. (1992). "Covenants with and without a Sword: Self-Governance Is Possible." *American Political Science Review* 86 (2): 404–17.

———. (1994). *Rules, Games, and Common-Pool Resources*. Ann Arbor: University of Michigan Press.

Oswald, Andrew J. (1997). "Happiness and Economic Performance." *Economic Journal* 107 (6): 1815–31.

Ouellette, Judith A., and Wood, Wendy. (1998). "Habit and Intention in Everyday Life: The Multiple Processes by Which Past Behavior Predicts Future Behavior." *Psychological Bulletin* 124:54–74.

Ovens, Robert, and Sleath, Sheila, eds. (2008). *The Heritage of Rutland Water*. Oakham: Rutland Local History Society.

Paavola, Jouni. (2007). "Institutions and Environmental Governance: A Reconceptualization." *Ecological Economics* 63 (1): 93–103.

Paavola, Jouni, and Adger, Neil. (2005). "Institutional Ecological Economics." *Ecological Economics* 53 (3): 353–68.

Pack, Spencer J. (1991). *Capitalism as a Moral System: Adam Smith's Critique of the Free Market Economy*. Aldershot: Edward Elgar.

Page, Talbot. (1991). "Sustainability and the Problem of Valuation." In *Ecological Economics: The Science and Management of Sustainability*, edited by Robert Constanza, 58–74. New York: Columbia University Press.

Palmer, Craig T., and Steadman, Lyle B. (1997). "Human Kinship as a Descendant-Leaving Strategy: A Solution to an Evolutionary Puzzle." *Journal of Social and Evolutionary Systems* 20 (1): 39–51.

Panchanathan, Karthik, and Boyd, Robert. (2003). "A Tale of Two Defectors: The Importance of Standing for Evolution of Indirect Reciprocity." *Journal of Theoretical Biology* 224 (1): 115–26.

———. (2004). "Indirect Reciprocity Can Stabilize Cooperation Without the Second-Order Free Rider Problem." *Nature*, November 25, pp. 499–502.

Pareto, Vilfredo. (1935). *The Mind and Society*. 4 vols. Translated from the Italian edition of 1923 by A. Bongiorno and A. Livingston. Edited by A. Livingston. London: Jonathan Cape.

———. (1971). *Manual of Political Economy*. Translated from the French edition of 1927 by A. S. Schwier. Edited by A. S. Schwier and A. N. Page. New York: Augustus Kelley.

Parra, Carlos M. (2005). "Rules and Knowledge." *Evolutionary and Institutional Economics Review* 2 (1): 81–111.

Parsons, Talcott. (1937). *The Structure of Social Action*. 2 vols. New York: McGraw-Hill.

Pauer-Studer, Herlinde. (2006). "Indentity, Commitment and Morality." *Journal of Economic Methodology* 13 (3): 349–69.

Pearce, David W., and Turner, R. Kerry. (1990). *Economics of Natural Resources and the Environment*. New York: Harvester Wheatsheaf.

Peirce, Charles Sanders. (1878). "How to Make Our Ideas Clear." *Popular Science Monthly* 12:286–302.

———. (1893) 'Evolutionary Love,' *The Monist*, 3, pp. 176–200. Reprinted in Peirce, Charles Sanders (1923) *Chance, Love, and Logic*, ed. M. R. Cohen (New York: Harcourt, Brace), pp. 272–5.

Pelham, Brett W. (2009). "Awareness, Opinions about Global Warming Vary Worldwide." Gallup World, April 22. http://www.gallup.com/poll/117772/Awareness-Opinions-Global-Warming-Vary-Worldwide.aspx#2.

Pellegrini, Lorenzo. (2011). *Corruption, Development and the Environment*. Berlin: Springer.

Pellegrini, Lorenzo, and Gerlagh, Reyer. (2004). "Corruption's Effect on Growth and Is Transmission Channels." *Kyklos* 57 (3): 429–56.

Penn, Anna A., and Shatz, Carla J. (1999). "Brain Waves and Brain Wiring: The Role of Endogenous and Sensory-Driven Neural Activity in Development." *Pediatric Research* 45 (4): 447–58.

Penrose, Edith T. (1959). *The Theory of the Growth of the Firm*. Oxford: Basil Blackwell. Reprinted 1995 (Oxford: Oxford University Press).

Pettit, Philip. (2005). "Construing Sen on Commitment." *Economics and Philosophy* 21 (1): 15–32.

Phelps, C. E. (1986). "Induced Demand—Can We Ever Know Its Extent?' *Journal of Health Economics* 5:355–65.

Phillips, Michael J. (1994). "Reappraising the Real Entity Theory of the Corporation." *Florida State University Law Review* 21:1061–1123.

Piaget, Jean. (1965). *The Moral Judgment of the Child*. Translated from the French edition of 1932 (New York: Free Press).

Pickhardt, Michael. (2005). "Some Remarks on Self-Interest, the Historical Schools and the Evolution of the Theory of Public Goods." *Journal of Economic Studies* 32 (3): 275–93.

Pieters, Rik, and Baumgartner, Hans. (2002). "Who Talks to Whom? Intra- and Interdisciplinary Communication of Economics Journals." *Journal of Economic Literature* 40 (2): 483–509.

Pigou, Arthur C. (1903). "Some Remarks on Utility." *Economic Journal* 13 (1): 58–68.

———. (1913). "The Interdependence of Different Sources of Demand and Supply in a Market." *Economic Journal* 23 (1): 19–24.

———. (1920) *The Economics of Welfare* London: Macmillan.

———. (1937). *Socialism versus Capitalism*. London: Macmillan.

Pinker, Steven. (1994). *The Language Instinct: The New Science of Language and Mind*. London: Allen Lane.

Piore, Michael J. (2003). "Society as a Pre-Condition for Individuality: Critical Comments." *Socio-Economic Review* 1 (1): 119–22.

Pipes, Richard. (1999). *Property and Freedom*. New York: Alfred A. Knopf.

Platt, Michael L., and Glimcher, Paul W. (1999). "Neural Correlates of Decision Variables in Parietal Cortex." *Nature* 400 (6741): 233–38.

Plsek, Paul E., and Greenhalgh, Trisha. (2001). "The Challenge of Complexity in Health Care." *British Medical Journal* 323:625–28.

Polanyi, Karl. (1947). "Our Obsolete Market Mentality: Civilization Must Find a New Thought Pattern." *Commentary* 3:109–17.

Polanyi, Karl, Arensberg, Conrad M., and Pearson, Harry W., eds. (1957). *Trade and Market in the Early Empires*. Chicago: Henry Regnery.

Polinsky, A. Mitchell, and Shavell, Steven. (2001). "Corruption and Optimal Law Enforcement." *Journal of Public Economics* 81 (1): 1–24.

Popper, Karl R. (1945a). *The Open Society and Its Enemies*. 2 vols London: Routledge and Kegan Paul.

———. (1945b). "The Poverty of Historicism III." *Economica* 11 (1): 69–89.

———. (1960). *The Poverty of Historicism*. London: Routledge and Kegan Paul.

Poppo, Laura, and Zenger, Todd. (1998). "Testing Alternative Theories of the Firm: Transaction Cost, Knowledge-Based, and Measurement Explanations for Make-or-Buy Decisions in Information Services." *Strategic Management Journal* 19 (2): 853–77.

Posner, Richard A. (1980). "A Theory of Primitive Society, with Special Reference to Law." *Journal of Law and Economics* 23 (1): 1–53.

Potts, Jason. (2000). *The New Evolutionary Microeconomics: Complexity, Competence, and Adaptive Behaviour*. Cheltenham: Edward Elgar.

Poundstone, William. (1992). *Prisoner's Dilemma*. New York: Doubleday.

Prendergast, Canice. (1999). "The Provision of Incentives in Firms." *Journal of Economic Literature* 37 (1): 7–63.

Price, Michael E., Cosmides, Leda, and Tooby, John. (2002). "Punitive Sentiment as an Anti-Free-Rider Device." *Evolution and Human Behavior* 23:203–31.

Putnam, Robert D. (2000). *Bowling Alone: The Collapse and Revival of American Community*. New York: Simon and Schuster.

Quine, Willard van Orman. (1953). *From a Logical Point of View*. Cambridge, MA: Harvard University Press.

———. (1960). *Word and Object*. Cambridge, MA: Harvard University Press.

Rainey, Hal G. (2009). *Understanding and Managing Public Organizations*. 3rd ed. San Francisco, CA: Jossey-Bass.

Raphael, D. D. (1985). *Adam Smith*. Oxford: Oxford University Press.

Rawls, John. (1971). *A Theory of Justice*. Cambridge, MA: Harvard University Press.

Redfield, Robert. (1950). "Maine's *Ancient Law* in the Light of Primitive Societies." *Western Political Quarterly* 3 (4): 574–89.

———. (1957). *The Primitive World and Its Transformations*. Ithaca, NY: Cornell University Press.

Rees, Ray. (1985). "The Theory of Principal and Agent." *Bulletin of Economic Research* 37 (1): 3–26 and 37 (2): 75–97.

Regan, Milton C. (2007). "Moral Intutitions and Organizational Culture." *Saint Louis University Law Journal* 51: 941–87.

Reinert, Erik S. (2007). *How Rich Countries Got Rich . . . and Why Poor Countries Stay Poor*. London: Constable.

Reinhardt, Uwe E. (1985). "The Theory of Physician-Induced Demand: Reflections After a Decade." *Journal of Health Economics* 14:187–93.

Reisman, David. (1993). *The Political Economy of Health Care*. London: Macmillan.

Retziaff-Roberts, Donna, Chang, Cyril F., and Rubin, Rose M. (2004). "Technical Efficiency in the Use of Health Care Resources: A Comparison of OECD Countries." *Health Policy* 69 (1): 55–72.

Ricardo, David. (1951–1973). *The Works and Correspondence of David Ricardo*. 11 vols. Edited by Piero Sraffa and Maurice H. Dobb. Cambridge: Cambridge University Press.

Rice, Thomas. (2001). "Should Consumer Choice Be Encouraged in Health Care?" In *The Social Economics of Health Care*, edited by John B. Davis, 9–39. London: Routledge.

Richards, Robert J. (1987). *Darwin and the Emergence of Evolutionary Theories of Mind and Behavior*. Chicago: University of Chicago Press.

Richardson, George B. (1972). "The Organisation of Industry." *Economic Journal* 82: 883–96.

Richerson, Peter J., Boyd, Robert, and Henrich, Joseph. (2011). "Gene-culture Coevolution in the Age of Genomics." *Proceedings of the National Association of Science* 107 (supp. 2): 8985–92.

Ridley, Matt. (1996). *The Origins of Virtue: Human Instincts and the Origins of Cooperation*. Harmondsworth: Penguin.

Riley, James C. (2001). *Rising Life Expectancy: A Global History*. Cambridge: Cambridge University Press.

Ritchie, David G. (1896). "Social Evolution." *International Journal of Ethics* 6 (2): 165–81.

Rizzolatti, Giacomo, Sinigaglia, Corrado, and Anderson, Frances. (2007). *Mirrors in the Brain: How Our Minds Share Actions, Emotions, and Experience*. Oxford: Oxford University Press.

Robbins, Lionel. (1932). *An Essay on the Nature and Significance of Economic Science*. London: Macmillan.

Roberts, Simon. (1979). *Order and Discipline: An Introduction to Legal Anthropology*. New York: St. Martin's Press.

Robinson, J., and Casalino, L. (1996). "Vertical Integration and Organizational Networks in Califormia Medical Care." *Health Affairs* 15 (1): 7–22.

Robinson, Paul H., Kurzban, Robert, and Jones, Owen D. (2007). "The Origins of Shared Intuitions of Justice." *Vanderbilt Law Review* 60 (6): 1633–88.

Robson, Arthur J. (2001). "Why Would Nature Give Individuals Utility Functions?" *Journal of Political Economy* 109 (4): 900–14.

Rodseth, Lars, Wrangham, Richard W., Harrigan, Alisa M., and Smuts, Barbara B. (1991). "The Human Community as a Primate Society." *Current Anthropology* 32 (3): 221–41.

Roemer, John E. (1982). *A General Theory of Exploitation and Class*. Cambridge, MA: Harvard University Press.

Room, Graham. (2011). *Complexity, Institutions and Public Policy: Agile Decision-Making in a Turbulent World*. Cheltenham: Edward Elgar.

Root, Hilton. (1996). "Corruption in China: Has It Become Systemic?" *Asian Survey* 36 (8): 741–57.

Rose-Ackerman, Susan. (1999). *Corruption and Government: Causes, Consequences and Reform*. Cambridge: Cambridge University Press.

Rotemberg, Julio J. (2006). "Altruism, Reciprocity and Cooperation in the Workplace." In *Handbook of the Economics of Giving, Altruism and Reciprocity*, edited by Serge-Christophe S. Kolm and Jean Mercier Ythier, 1:1371–1407. North-Holland: Elsevier.

Rothschild, Emma. (2001). *Economic Sentiments: Adam Smith, Condorcet, and the Enlightenment*. Cambridge, MA: Harvard University Press.

Rowthorn, Robert E. (1996). "Ethics and Economics: An Economist's View." In *Economics and Ethics?*, edited by Peter D. Groenewegen, 15–33. London: Routledge.

Rumelt, Richard P. (1984). "Towards a Strategic Theory of the Firm." In *Competitive Strategic Management*, edited by R. B. Lamb, 56–70. Englewood Cliffs, NJ: Prentice-Hall.

Runciman, Walter Garry. (2001). "From Nature to Culture, from Culture to Society." In *The Origin of Human Social Institutions*, edited by Walter Garry Runciman, 235–54. Oxford: Oxford University Press.

———. (2002). "Heritable Variation and Competitive Selection as the Mechanism of Sociocultural Evolution." In *The Evolution of Cultural Entities*, edited by Michael Wheeler, John Ziman, and Margaret A. Boden, 9–25. Oxford: Oxford University Press.

Ruskin, John. (1866). *Unto This Last: Four Essays on the First Principles of Political Economy*. London: John Wiley.

Rutherford, Malcolm H. (2011). *The Institutionalist Movement in American Economics, 1918–1947: Science and Social Control*. Cambridge: Cambridge University Press.

Ryan, Alan. (1995). *John Dewey and the High Tide of American Liberalism*. New York: Norton.

Sabel, Charles F., and Zeitlin, Jonathan. (2008). "Learning from Difference: The New Architecture of Experimentalist Governance in the EU." *European Law Journal* 14 (3): 271–327.

Sagoff, Mark. (1988a). *The Economy of the Earth: Philosophy, Law, and the Environment*. Cambridge: Cambridge University Press.

———. (1988b). "Some Problems with Environmental Economics." *Environmental Ethics* 3 (1): 55–74.

———. (2004). *Price, Principle and the Environment*. Cambridge: Cambridge University Press.

Sah, Raaj. (1991). "Social Osmosis and Patterns of Crime." *Journal of Political Economy* 99 (6): 1272–95.

Sally, David. (1995). "Conversation and Cooperation in Social Dilemmas: A Meta-Analysis of Experiments from 1958–1992." *Rationality and Society* 7 (1): 58–92.

Sampson, Geoffrey. (2005). *The Language Instinct Debate*. London: Continuum.

Samuels, Warren J. (1989). "The Legal-Economic Nexus." *George Washington Law Review* 57 (6): 1556–78.

———. (1997). "Instrumental Valuation." In *The Economy as a Process of Valuation*, edited by Warren J. Samuels, Steven G. Medema, and A. Allan Schmid, 1–71. Cheltenham: Edward Elgar.

Samuelson, Paul A. (1937). "A Note on the Measurement of Utility." *Review of Economic Studies* 4 (2): 155–61.

———. (1947). *Foundations of Economic Analysis*. Cambridge, MA: Harvard University Press.

———. (1948). *Economics*. New York: McGraw-Hill.

Samuelson, Paul A., and Nordhaus, William D. (2001). *Economics*. 17th ed. New York: McGraw-Hill.

Sandholtz, Wayne, and Koetzle, William. (2000). "Accounting for Corruption: Economic Structure, Democracy, and Trade." *International Studies Quarterly* 44:31–50.

Sappington, David E. M. (1991). "Incentives in Principal-Agent Relationships." *Journal of Economic Perspectives* 5 (2): 45–66.

Sarnecki, John. (2007). "Developmental Objections to Evolutionary Modularity." *Biology and Philosophy* 22 (4): 529–46.

Sawyer, R. Keith. (2005). *Social Emergence—Societies as Complex Systems*. Cambridge: Cambridge University Press.

Sayer, Andrew. (1997). "Critical Realism and the Limits to Critical Social Science." *Journal for the Theory of Social Behaviour* 27 (4): 473–88.

Sayre-McCord, Geoffrey. (1988). *Essays on Moral Realism*. Ithaca, NY: Cornell University Press.

Schaffer, Mark E. (1989). "Are Profit-Maximisers the Best Survivors? A Darwinian Model of Economic Natural Selection." *Journal of Economic Behavior and Organization* 12 (1): 29–45.

Schkade, David A., and Payne, John W. (1994). "How People Respond to Contingent Valuation Questions: A Verbal Protocol Analysis of Willingness to Pay for an Environmental Regulation." *Journal of Environmental Economics and Management* 26 (1): 88–109.

Schmoller, Gustav. (1900). *Grundriss der allgemeinen Volkswirtschaftslehre, Erster Teil*. München und Leipzig: Duncker und Humblot.

Schneider, Friedrich, and Pommerehne, Werner W. (1981). "Free-Riding and Collective Action: An Experiment in Public Microeconomics." *Quarterly Journal of Economics* 96 (4): 689–704.

Schneider, Michael P. (1996). *J. A. Hobson*. London: Macmillan.

Schotter, Andrew R. (1981). *The Economic Theory of Social Institutions*. Cambridge: Cambridge University Press.

Schrödinger, Erwin. (1944). *What Is Life?* Cambridge: Cambridge University Press.

Schultz, Walter J. (2001). *The Moral Conditions of Economic Efficiency*. Cambridge: Cambridge University Press.

Schumpeter, Joseph A. (1908). *Das Wesen und der Hauptinhalt der theoretischen Nationalökonomie*. Munich: Duncker und Humblot. English edition published as *The Nature and Essence of Economic Theory*. (2010). Translated by Bruce A. McDaniel. New Brunswick, NJ: Transaction.

———. (1909). "On the Concept of Social Value." *Quarterly Journal of Economics* 23 (2): 213–32.

———. (1934). *The Theory of Economic Development: An Inquiry into Profits, Capital, Credit, Interest, and the Business Cycle*. Translated by Redvers Opie from the second German edition 1926. Cambridge, MA: Harvard University Press.

———. (1942). *Capitalism, Socialism and Democracy*. London: George Allen and Unwin.

———. (1954). *History of Economic Analysis*. New York: Oxford University Press.

Schwartz, Shalom H. (1994). "Are There Universal Aspects in the Structure and Contents of Human Values?" *Journal of Social Issues* 50 (4): 19–45.

Scott, Anthony, Maynard, Alan, and Elliott, Robert, eds. (2003). *Advances in Health Economics*. Chichester: John Wiley.

Screpanti, Ernesto. (2007). *Libertarian Communism: Marx, Engels and the Political Economy of Freedom*. London: Palgrave Macmillan.

Seagle, William. (1941). *The Quest for Law*. New York: Alfred A. Knopf.

Searle, John R. (1995). *The Construction of Social Reality*. London: Allen Lane.

Seligson, Mitchell A. (2002). "The Impact of Corruption on Regime Legitimacy." *Journal of Politics* 64 (2): 408–33.

Sen, Amartya K. (1970). *Collective Choice and Social Welfare*. San Francisco: Holden Day, Oliver and Boyd.

———. (1973). *On Economic Inequality*. Oxford: Clarendon Press.

———. (1977). "Rational Fools: A Critique of the Behavioral Foundations of Economic Theory." *Philosophy and Public Affairs* 6 (4): 317–44.

———. (1979). "Personal Utilities and Public Judgements: Or What's Wrong with Welfare Economics." *Economic Journal* 89 (3): 537–58.

———. (1982). *Choice, Welfare and Measurement*. Oxford: Basil Blackwell.

———. (1985a). *Commodities and Capabilities*. Amsterdam: North-Holland.

———. (1985b). "Goals, Commitment, and Identity." *Journal of Law and Economic Organization* 1 (2): 341–55.

———. (1987a). *On Ethics and Economics*. Oxford Basil Blackwell.

———. (1987b). "Rational Behaviour." *The New Palgrave Dictionary of Economics*. Edited by John Eatwell, Murray Milgate, and Peter Newman. London: Macmillan.

———. (1999). *Development as Freedom*. New York: Alfred A. Knopf.

———, ed. (2002). *Rationality and Freedom*. Cambridge MA: Harvard University Press.

———. (2004). "Social Identity. " *Revue de Philosophie Economique* 9 (1) : 2–26.

Sen, Amartya K., and Williams, Bernard, eds. (1982). *Utilitarianism and Beyond*. Cambridge: Cambridge University Press.

Sened, Itai. (1997). *The Political Institution of Private Property*. Cambridge: Cambridge University Press.

Shafer-Landau, Russ. (2003). *Moral Realism: A Defense*. Oxford: Oxford University Press.

Shannon, Claude E., and Warren Weaver (1949). *The Mathematical Theory of Communication*. Chicago: University of Illinois Press.

Shleifer, Andrei, and Vishny, Robert W. (1993). "Corruption." *Quarterly Journal of Economics* 108 (3): 599–617.

Siakantaris, Nikos. (2000). "Experimental Economics Under the Microscope." *Cambridge Journal of Economics* 24 (3): 267–81.

Simon, Herbert A. (1957). *Models of Man: Social and Rational. Mathematical Essays on Rational Human Behavior in a Social Setting*. New York: Wiley.

———. (1986). "Rationality in Psychology and Economics." *Journal of Business* 59 (4), pt. 2: S209–24.

———. (1990). "A Mechanism for Social Selection and Successful Altruism." *Science* 250: 1665–68.

———. (1991). "Organizations and Markets." *Journal of Economic Perspectives* 5 (2): 25–44.

Singer, Peter. (1975). *Animal Liberation: A New Ethics for Our Treatment of Animals*. New York: Random House.

Skarlicki, Daniel P., and Folger, Robert. (1997). "Retaliation in the Workplace: The Roles of Distributive, Procedural, and Interactional Justice." *Journal of Applied Psychology* 82 (3): 434–43.

Skyrms, Brian. (1996). *Evolution of the Social Contract*. Cambridge: Cambridge University Press.

———. (2004). *The Stag Hunt and the Evolution of Social Structure*. Cambridge: Cambridge University Press.

Slemrod, Joel. (2003). "Tax from any Angle: Reflections on Multi-Disciplinary Tax Research." *National Tax Journal* 56 (1), pt. 2: 145–51.

Slovic, Paul, and Lichtenstein, Sarah. (1983). "Preference Reversals: A Broader Perspective." *American Economic Review* 73 (4): 596–605.

Smart, J. J. C., and Williams, Bernard. (1973). *Utilitarianism: For and Against*. Cambridge: Cambridge University Press.

Smith, Adam. (1759). *The Theory of Moral Sentiments; or, An Essay Towards an Analysis of the Principles by which Men Naturally Judge Concerning the Conduct and Character, First of their Neighbours, and Afterwards of Themselves*. London: Millar.

———. (1776). *An Inquiry into the Nature and Causes of the Wealth of Nations*. 2 vols. London: Strahan and Cadell.

———. (1976). *The Theory of Moral Sentiments*. Edited by D. D. Raphael and A. L. MacFie. Oxford: Clarendon. Originally published 1759.

Smith, Peter B., and Bond, Michael Harris. (1993). *Social Psychology Across Cultures: Analysis and Perspectives*. Needham Heights, MA: Allyn and Bacon.

Smith, Vernon L. (1982). "Microeconomic Systems as an Experimental Science." *American Economic Review* 72 (5): 923–55.

Smithin, John, ed. (2000). *What Is Money?* London: Routledge.

Sober, Elliott. (1980). "Evolution, Population Thinking and Essentialism." *Philosophy of Science* 47:350–83.

———. (1981). "Holism, Individualism, and the Units of Selection." In *Philosophy of Science Association 1980*, edited by P. D. Asquith and R. N. Giere, 2:93–121. East Lansing, MI: Philosophy of Science Association.

———. (1984). *The Nature of Selection: Evolutionary Theory in Philosophical Focus*. Cambridge, MA: MIT Press.

Sober, Elliott, and Wilson, David Sloan. (1998). *Unto Others: The Evolution and Psychology of Unselfish Behavior*. Cambridge, MA: Harvard University Press.

Söderbaum, Peter. (1992). "Neoclassical and Institutional Approaches to Development and the Environment." *Ecological Economics* 5 (2): 127–44.

Soderquist, Larry D. (2000). "Theory of the Firm: What a Corporation Is." *Journal of Corporation Law* 25 (2): 375–81.

Soros, George. (2008). *The New Paradigm for Financial Markets: The Credit Crisis of 2008 and What It Means*. New York: Public Affairs.

Soudek, Josef. (1952). "Aristotle's Theory of Exchange: An Enquiry into the Origins of Economic Analysis." *Proceedings of the American Philosophical Society* 96 (1): 45–75.

Spash, Clive L. (1993). "Economics, Ethics, and Long-Term Environmental Damages." *Environmental Ethic* 15 (2): 117–32.

———. (2000). "Multiple Value Expression in Contingent Valuation: Economics and Ethics." *Environmental Science Technology* 34 (8): 1433–38.

———. (2002). *Greenhouse Economics: Values and Ethics*. London: Routledge.

Spencer, David A. (2003). "Love Labour's Lost? The Disutility of Work and Work Avoidance in the Economic Analysis of Labor Supply." *Review of Social Economy* 61 (2): 235–50.

Sperber, Dan. (2005). "Modularity and Relevance: How Can a Massively Modular Mind Be Flexible and Context-Sensitive?" In *The Innate Mind: Structure and Contents*, edited by Peter Carruthers, S. Laurence, and S. Stich, 53–68. Oxford: Oxford University Press.

Spithoven, Antoon. (2011). "It's the Institutions, Stupid! Why U.S. Health Care Expenditure Is So Different from Canada's." *Journal of Economic Issues* 45 (1): 75–95.

Stabile, Donald R. (1996). *Work and Welfare: The Social Cost of Labor in the History of Economic Thought*. Westport, CT: Greenwood Press.

Staveren, Irene van. (2007). "Beyond Utilitarianism and Deontology: Ethics in Economics." *Review of Political Economy* 19 (1): 21–35.

———. (2009). "Communitarianism and the Market." *Review of Social Economy* 67 (1): 25–47.

Steele, David Ramsay. (1992). *From Marx to Mises: Post-Capitalist Society and the Challenge of Economic Calculation*. La Salle, IL: Open Court.

Steers, Richard M., and Porter, Lyman W., eds. (1991). *Motivation and Work Behavior*. New York: McGraw-Hill.

Steiger, Otto, ed. (2008). *Property Economics: Property Rights, Creditor's Money and the Foundations of the Economy*. Marburg: Metropolis.

Steinfeld, Robert J. (2001). *Coercion, Contract, and Free Labor in the Nineteenth Century*. Cambridge: Cambridge University Press.

Stephens, David W., McLinn, C. M., and Stevens, J. R. (2002). "Discounting and Reciprocity in an Iterated Prisoner's Dilemma." *Science* 298 (5610): 2216–18.

Sterba, James P. (1985). "A Libertarian Justification for the Welfare State." *Social Theory and Practice* 11 (3): 285–306.

Stiglitz, Joseph E. (1987). "Principal and Agent." *The New Palgrave Dictionary of Economics*. Edited by John Eatwell, Murray Milgate, and Peter Newman. London: Macmillan.

———. (1994). *Whither Socialism?* Cambridge, MA: MIT Press.

———. (2008). "The Fall of Wall Street Is to Market Fundamentalism What the Fall of the Berlin Wall Was to Communism.'" Interview with Nathan Gardels. *Huffington Post*, September 16. http://www.huffingtonpost.com/nathan-gardels/stiglitz-the-fall-of-wall_b_126911.html.

Stonier, Alfred, and Bode, Karl. (1937). "A New Approach to the Methodology of the Social Sciences." *Economica*, n.s., 4 (2): 406–24.

Stout, Lynne A. (2008). "Taking Conscience Seriously." In *Moral Markets: The Critical Role of Values in the Economy*, edited by Paul J. Zak, 157–72. Princeton, NJ: Princeton University Press.

Stroup, Timothy. (1984). "Edward Westermarck: A Reappraisal." *Man* 19 (4): 575–92.

Sugden, Robert. (1986). *The Economics of Rights, Co-operation and Welfare*. Oxford: Basil Blackwell.

———. (1991). "Rational Choice: A Survey of Contributions from Economics and Philosophy." *Economic Journal* 101 (4): 751–85.

———. (2001). "Ken Binmore's Evolutionary Social Theory." *Economic Journal* 111 (2): F213–43.

Svensson, Jakob. (2005). "Eight Questions about Corruption." *Journal of Economic Perspectives* 19 (3): 19–42.

Tancredi, Laurence. (2005). *Hardwired Behavior: What Neuroscience Reveals about Morality*. Cambridge: Cambridge University Press.

Tanzi, Vito. (2000). *Politics, Institutions and the Dark Side of Economics*. Cheltenham: Edward Elgar.

Taylor, Michael J. (1996). "Good Government: On Hierarchy, Social Capital and the Limitations of Rational Choice Theory." *Journal of Political Philosophy* 4 (1): 1–28.

Teece, David J., and Pisano, Gary. (1994). "The Dynamic Capabilities of Firms: An Introduction." *Industrial and Corporate Change* 3 (3): 537–56.

Thaler, Richard H., and Sunstein, Cass R. (2008). *Nudge: Improving Decisions About Health, Wealth, and Happiness*. New Haven, CT: Yale University Press.

Thomson, Garrett. (1987). *Needs*. London: Routledge and Kegan Paul.

Thomson, Judith Jarvis. (1976). "Killing, Letting Die, and the Trolley Problem." *Monist* 59:204–17.

Tirole, Jean. (1996). "A Theory of Collective Reputations." *Review of Economic Studies* 63 (1): 1–22.

Tisak, Marie S., and Turiel, Elliot. (1984). "Children's Conceptions of Moral and Prudential Rules." *Child Development* 55:1030–39.

Titmuss, Richard M. (1970). *The Gift Relationship: From Human Blood to Social Policy*. London: George Allen and Unwin.

Tomasello, Michael, with Dweck, Carol, Silk, Joan, Skyrms, Brian, and Spelke, Elizabeth. 2009. *Why We Cooperate*. Cambridge, MA: MIT Press.

Tool, Marc R. (1995). *Pricing, Valuation and Systems: Essays in Neoinstitutional Economics*. Aldershot: Edward Elgar.

Towle, Angela. (1998). "Changes in Health Care and Continuing Medical Education for the 21st Century." *British Medical Journal* 316 (7127). doi: 10.1136/bmj.316.7127.301.

Townshend, Jules. (1990). *J. A. Hobson*. Manchester: Manchester University Press.

Toporowski, Jan. (2010). "Corporate Limited Liability and the Financial Liabilities of Firms." *Cambridge Journal of Economics* 34 (5): 885–93.

Transparency International. (2007). "Frequently Asked Facts about Corruption." Accessed January 29, 2012. http://www.transparency.org/news_room/faq/corruption_faq.

———. (2010). "Corruption Perceptions Index 2010 Results." Accessed January 29, 2012. http://www.transparency.org/policy_research/surveys_indices/cpi/2010/results.

Traxler, Franz, and Unger, Brigitte. (1994). "Governance, Economic Restructuring, and International Competitiveness." *Journal of Economic Issues* 28 (1): 1–23.

Treisman, Daniel. (2000). "The Causes of Corruption: A Cross-National Study." *Journal of Public Economics* 76 (3): 399–457.

Trevino, Linda Klebe. (1992). "Moral Reasoning and Business Ethics: Implications for Research, Education, and Management." *Journal of Business Ethics* 11 (5–6): 445–59.

Trivers, Robert L. (1971). "The Evolution of Reciprocal Altruism." *Quarterly Review of Biology* 46 (1): 35–57.

Tullock, Gordon. (1994). *The Economics of Non-Human Societies*. Tuscon: Pallas Press.

Tyler, Tom R., and Blader, Steven L. (2000). *Cooperation in Groups: Procedural Justice, Social Identity, and Behavioral Engagement*. Philadelphia: Psychology Press.

Uchida, Satoshi, and Sigmund, Karl. (2009). "The Competition of Assessment Rules for Indirect Reciprocity." *Journal of Theoretical Biology*. doi:10.1016/j.jtbi.2009.11.013.

Udéhn, Lars. (2001). *Methodological Individualism: Background, History and Meaning*. London: Routledge.

———. (2002). "The Changing Face of Methodological Individualism." *Annual Review of Sociology* 28:479–507.

United Nations Development Programme. (2009). "Human Development Report 2009.

Overcoming Barriers: Human Mobility and Development." Accessed January 29, 2012. http://hdr.undp.org/en/reports/global/hdr2009/.

United Nations Office on Drugs and Crime. (2011). "UNODC's Action against Corruption and Economic Crime." Accessed January 29, 2012. http://www.unodc.org/unodc/en/corruption/index.html?ref=menuside.

Van Horn, Carl E., and Fichtner, Aaron R. (2003). "An Evaluation of State-Subsidized, Firm-Based Training: The Workforce Development Partnership Program." *International Journal of Manpower* 24 (1): 97–111.

Van Parijs, Philippe, ed. (1992). *Arguing for Basic Income: Ethical Foundations for a Radical Reform*. London: Verso.

———. (1995). *Real Freedom for All: What (If Anything) Can Justify Capitalism?* Oxford: Clarendon Press.

Vanberg, Viktor J. (1994). *Rules and Choice in Economics*. London: Routledge.

———. (2000). "Rational Choice and Rule-Based Behavior: Alternative Heuristics." In *Normen und Instituzionem: Entstehung und Virkungen*, edited by R. Metze, K. Mühler, and Karl-Dieter Opp. Leipzig: Leipziger Universitätvarlag.

———. (2001). "Markets and the Law." In *International Encyclopedia of the Social and Behavioral Sciences*, edited by Neil J. Smelser and Paul B. Baltes, 9221–27. Amsterdam: Elsevier.

———. (2002). "Rational Choice versus Program-Based Behavior: Alternative Theoretical Approaches and Their Relevance for the Study of Institutions." *Rationality and Society* 14 (1): 7–53.

———. (2004). "The Rationality Postulate in Economics: Its Ambiguity, Its Deficiency and Its Evolutionary Alternative." *Journal of Economic Methodology* 11 (1): 1–29.

———. (2008). "On the Economics of Moral Preferences." *American Journal of Economics and Sociology* 67 (4): 605–28.

Vanek, Jaroslav. (1970). *The General Theory of Labor-Managed Market Economies*. Ithaca, NY: Cornell University Press.

Vatn, Arild. (2005). *Institutions and the Environment*. Cheltenham: Edward Elgar.

Vaughan, Ted R., Sjoberg, Gideon, and Reynolds, Larry T., eds. (1993). *A Critique of Contemporary American Sociology*. New York: Ge-neral Hall.

Veblen, Thorstein B. (1898). "Why Is Economics Not an Evolutionary Science?" *Quarterly Journal of Economics* 12 (3): 373–97.

———. (1899a). "The Preconceptions of Economic Science: II." *Quarterly Journal of Economics* 13 (4): 396–426.

———. (1899b). *The Theory of the Leisure Class: An Economic Study in the Evolution of Institutions*. New York: Macmillan.

———. (1901). "Gustav Schmoller's Economics." *Quarterly Journal of Economics* 16 (1): 69–93.

———. (1904). *The Theory of Business Enterprise*. New York: Charles Scribner's Sons.

———. (1909). "The Limitations of Marginal Utility." *Journal of Political Economy* 17 (9): 620–36.

———. (1914). *The Instinct of Workmanship, and the State of the Industrial Arts*. New York: Macmillan.

———. (1918). *The Higher Learning in America: A Memorandum on the Conduct of Universities by Business Men*. New York: Huebsch.

———. (1919). *The Place of Science in Modern Civilization and Other Essays*. New York: Huebsch.

Vercoe, Moanna, and Zak, Paul J. (2010). "Inductive Modeling Using Causal Studies in Neuroeconomics: Brains on Drugs." *Journal of Economic Methodology* 17 (2): 133–46.

Verplanken, Bas, Aarts, Henk, and Van Knippenberg, Ad. (1997). "Habit, Information Acquisition, and the Process of Making Travel Mode Choices." *European Journal of Social Psychology* 27:539–60.

Vidaver-Cohen, Deborah. (1998). "Moral Climate in Business Firms: A Conceptual Framework for Analysis and Change." *Journal of Business Ethics* 17 (11): 1211–26.

Viner, Jacob. (1927). "Adam Smith and Laissez Faire." *Journal of Political Economy* 35 (2): 198–232.

———. (1960). "The Intellectual History of Laissez Faire."' *Journal of Law and Economics* 3 (1): 45–69.

Vollan, Bjørn. (2008). "Socio-ecological Explanations for Crowding-Out Effects from Economic Field Experiments in Southern Africa." *Ecological Economics* 67 (4): 560–73.

Vorzimmer, Peter J. (1977). *Charles Darwin: The Years of Controversy; The Origin of Species and Its Critics, 1859–1882.* Philadelphia: Temple University Press.

Vromen, Jack J. (2001). "The Human Agent in Evolutionary Economics." In *Darwinism and Evolutionary Economics,* edited by John Laurent and John Nightingale, 184–208. Cheltenham: Edward Elgar.

———. (2010). "On the Surprising Finding that Expected Utility Is Literally Computed in the Brain." *Journal of Economic Methodology* 17 (1): 17–36.

Vroom, Victor H. (1964). *Work and Motivation.* New York: Wiley.

Wade, Michael J. (1976). "Group Selection Among Laboratory Populations of *Tribolium.*" *Proceedings of the National Academy of Sciences USA* 73: 4604–7.

———. (1978). "A Critical Review of the Models of Group Selection." *Quarterly Review of Biology* 53:101–14.

Walras, Léon. (1874). *Éléments d'économie politique pure, ou théorie de la richesse sociale.* Lausanne: Rouge.

Walshe, Kieran. (2010). "Reorganisation of the NHS in England." *British Medical Journal* 341:c3843. doi: 10.1136/bmj.c3843.

Walzer, Michael. (1994). *Thick and Thin: Moral Argument at Home and Abroad.* Notre Dame, IN: University of Notre Dame Press.

Ward, Benjamin. (1972). *What's Wrong with Economics?* London: Macmillan.

Warren, Mark E. (2004). "What Does Corruption Mean in a Democracy?" *American Journal of Political Science* 48 (2): 328–43.

Washburn, Jennifer. (2005). *University Inc. The Corporate Corruption of American Higher Education.* New York: Basic Books.

Wason, Peter C. (1983). "Realism and Rationality in the Selection Task." In *Thinking and Reasoning: Psychological Approaches,* edited by Jonathan St. B. T. Evans. London: Routledge and Kegan Paul.

Watkins, John W. N. (1952a). "Ideal Types and Historical Explanation." *British Journal for the Philosophy of Science* 3 (1): 22–43.

———. (1952b). "The Principle of Methodological Individualism." *British Journal for the Philosophy of Science* 3 (2): 186–89.

———. (1957). "Historical Explanation in the Social Sciences." *British Journal for the Philosophy of Science* 8 (2): 104–17.

Webb, James L. (2002). "Dewey: Back to the Future." *Journal of Economic Issues* 36 (4): 981–1003.

Weber, Bruce H., Depew, David J., Dyke, Charles, Salthe, Stanley N., Schneider, E. D.,

Ulanowicz, R. E., and Wicken, Jeffrey S. (1989). "Evolution in Thermodynamic Perspective: An Ecological Approach." *Biology and Philosophy* 4 (4): 373–405.

Weber, Max. (1927). *General Economic History*. Translated by Frank H. Knight from the German edition 1923. London: Allen and Unwin

———. (1968). *Economy and Society: An Outline of Interpretative Sociology*. 2 vols. Translated from the German edition of 1921–1922 by G. Roth and C. Wittich. Berkeley: University of California Press.

Weingast, Barry R. (2005). "The Constitutional Dilemma of Economic Liberty." *Journal of Economic Perspectives* 19 (3): 89–108.

Weissman, David. (2000). *A Social Ontology*. New Haven, CT: Yale University Press.

Westermarck, Edward. (1891). *The History of Human Marriage*. London: Macmillan.

———. (1932). *Ethical Relativism*. London: Kegan Paul, Trench, Trubner.

Whinston, Michael D. (2003). "On the Transaction Cost Determinants of Vertical Integration." *Journal of Law, Economics and Organization* 19 (1): 1–23.

Whitaker, John K., ed. (1996). *The Correspondence of Alfred Marshall*. 3 vols. Cambridge: Cambridge University Press.

White, Gordon. (1996). "Corruption and the Transition from Socialism in China." *Journal of Law and Society* 23 (1): 149–69.

White, Michael V. (2002). "Doctoring Adam Smith: The Fable of the Diamonds and Water Paradox." *History of Political Economy* 34 (4): 659–83.

Wicken, Jeffrey S. (1987). *Evolution, Thermodynamics, and Information: Extending the Darwinian Paradigm*. Oxford: Oxford University Press.

Wicksteed, Philip H. (1910). *The Commonsense of Political Economy, including a Study of the Human Basis of Economic Law*. London: Macmillan.

Wiessner, Polly. (2005). "Norm Enforcement among the Ju/'hoansi Bushmen: A Case of Strong Reciprocity?" *Human Nature* 16 (2): 115–45.

Wight, Jonathan B. (2009). "Adam Smith on Instincts, Affection, and Informal Learning: Proximate Mechnisms in Multilevel Selection." *Review of Social Economy* 67 (1): 95–113.

Wikipedia. (2011a). "Basic Income Guarantee." Accessed February 28, 2012. http://en.wikipedia.org/wiki/Basic_income_guarantee#cite_note-5.

———. (2011b). "Level of Support for Evolution." Accessed February 28, 2012. http://en.wikipedia.org/wiki/Level_of_support_for_evolution.

———. (2011c). "News International Phone Hacking Scandal." Accessed February 28, 2012. http://en.wikipedia.org/wiki/News_International_phone_hacking_scandal.

———. (2011d). "United Kingdom Parliamentary Expemses Scandal." Accessed February 28, 2012. http://en.wikipedia.org/wiki/United_Kingdom_Parliamentary_expenses_scandal.

Wilkinson, Richard, and Pickett, Kate. (2009). *The Spirit Level: Why More Equal Societies Almost Always Do Better*. London: Allen Lane.

Williams, George C. (1966). *Adaptation and Natural Selection*. Princeton, NJ; Princeton University Press.

Williamson, Oliver E. (1975). *Markets and Hierarchies: Analysis and Anti-Trust Implications: A Study in the Economics of Internal Organization*. New York: Free Press.

———. (1985). *The Economic Institutions of Capitalism: Firms, Markets, Relational Contracting*. London: Macmillan.

———. (1991). "Comparative Economic Organization: The Analysis of Discrete Structural Alternatives." *Administrative Science Quarterly* 36 (2): 269–96.

———. (1993). "Opportunism and Its Critics." Special issue, *Managerial and Decision Economics* 14 (2): 97–107.

———. (2002). "The Lens of Contract: Private Ordering." *American Economic Review (Papers and Proceedings)* 92 (2): 438–43.

Wilson, David Sloan. (1980). *The Natural Selection of Populations and Communities*. Menlo Park, CA: Benjamin/Cummings.

———. (1983). "The Group Selection Controversy: History and Current Status." *Annual Review of Ecology and Systematics* 14:159–88.

———. (1999). "A Critique of R. D. Alexander's Views on Group Selection." *Biology and Philosophy* 14:431–49.

———. (2002). *Darwin's Cathedral: Evolution, Religion, and the Nature of Society*. Chicago: University of Chicago Press.

Wilson, David Sloan, and Sober, Elliott. (1994). "Reintroducing Group Selection to the Human Behavioral Sciences." *Behavioral and Brain Sciences* 17 (4): 585–608.

Wilson, David Sloan, and Wilson, Edward O. (2007). "Rethinking the Theoretical Foundations of Sociobiology." *Quarterly Review of Biology* 82 (4): 327–48.

Winch, Donald. (1978). *Adam Smith's Politics: An Essay in Historiographic Revision*. Cambridge Studies in the History and Theory of Politics. Cambridge: Cambridge University Press.

Winter, Sidney G., Jr. (1964). "Economic 'Natural Selection' and the Theory of the Firm." *Yale Economic Essays* 4 (1): 225–72.

———. (1987). "Natural Selection and Evolution." *The New Palgrave Dictionary of Economics*. Edited by John Eatwell, Murray Milgate, and Peter Newman. London: Macmillan.

Witt, Ulrich. (2003). "Economic Policy Making in Evolutionary Perspective." *Journal of Evolutionary Economics* 13 (2): 77–94.

Wood, Adrian. (1994). *North-South Trade, Employment and Inequality: Changing Fortunes in a Skill-Driven World*. Oxford: Clarendon Press.

———. (1995). "How Trade Hurt Unskilled Workers." *Journal of Economic Perspectives* 9 (3): 57–80.

Wood, Wendy, and Neal, David T. (2007). "A New Look at Habits and the Habit-Goal Interface." *Psychological Review* 114 (4): 843–63.

Wood, Wendy, Quinn, Jeffrey M., and Kashy, D. (2002). "Habits in Everyday Life: Thought, Emotion, and Action." *Journal of Personality and Social Psychology* 83:1281–97.

Woodward, Jane. (2003). *Making Things Happen: A Theory of Causal Explanation*. Oxford: Oxford University Press.

World Bank. (1997). *Helping Countries Combat Corruption: The Role of the World Bank*. Washington, DC: World Bank.

Wright, Robert. (1994). *The Moral Animal: Why We Are the Way We Are: The New Science of Evolutionary Psychology*. New York: Vintage.

Yezer, Anthony M., Goldfarb, Robert S., and Poppen, Paul J. (1996). "Does Studying Economics Discourage Cooperation? Watch What We Do, Not What We Say or How We Play." *Journal of Economic Perspectives* 10 (1): 177–86.

Young, Jeffrey T. (1997). *Economics as a Moral Science: The Political Economy of Adam Smith*. Cheltenham: Edward Elgar.

Zak, Paul J. (2004). "Neuroeconomics." *Philosophical Transactions of the Royal Society of London B (Biology)*, 359:1737–48.

———, ed. (2008). *Moral Markets: The Critical Role of Values in the Economy*. Princeton, NJ: Princeton University Press.

Zeitlin, Jonathan, and Pochet, Philippe, eds. (2005). *The Open Method of Co-Ordination in ActiINon: The European Employment and Social Inclusion Strategies.* Brussels: Presses Interuniversitaires Européannes—Peter Lang.

Zerbe, Richard O. (2007). "The Legal Foundation of Cost-Benefit Analysis." *Charleston Law Review* 2 (1): 93–184.

Zizzo, Daniel John. (2008). "Anger and Economic Rationality." *Journal of Economic Methodology* 15 (2): 147–67.

Zwirn, Gregor. (2007). "Methodological Individualism or Methodological Atomism: The Case of Friedrich Hayek." *History of Political Economy* 39 (1): 47–80.

INDEX